DATE DUE

DEMCO 38-296

THE FOREIGN POLICY OF
RUSSIA

THE FOREIGN POLICY OF
RUSSIA
Changing Systems, Enduring Interests

Robert H. Donaldson
Joseph L. Nogee

M.E. Sharpe

Armonk, New York
London, England

Copyright © 1998 by M. E. Sharpe, Inc.

Library of Congress Cataloging-in-Publication Data

Donaldson, Robert H.
The foreign policy of Russia : changing systems, enduring interests
/ by Robert H. Donaldson and Joseph L. Nogee.
p. cm.
Includes bibliographical references and index.
ISBN 0–7656–0046–3 (alk. paper). — ISBN 0–7656–0047–1 (ppk. :
alk. paper)
1. Soviet Union—Foreign relations. 2. Russia (Federation)—
Foreign relations. I. Nogee, Joseph L. II. Title.
DK266.45.D66 1998
327.47—DC21
98–14390
CIP

Printed in the United States of America

BM (c) 10 9 8 7 6 5 4 3 2 1
BM (p) 10 9 8 7 6 5 4 3 2 1

Contents

Maps		vii
Acknowledgments		ix
1.	The Tsarist Roots of Russia's Foreign Policy	3
2.	Soviet Foreign Policy: From Revolution to Cold War	23
3.	Soviet Foreign Policy: The Cold War	62
4.	Domestic Factors in the Making of Russian Foreign Policy	108
5.	Russia and the Near Abroad	155
6.	Russia and the West	189
7.	Russia and the "Non-West"	233
8.	Conclusion	283
Notes		293
Index		311

Maps

Europe   98

Commonwealth of Independent States   158

Acknowledgments

We thank the following individuals who read all or part of the manuscript and made helpful suggestions: Daniel S. Papp, April Jones, Deborah Melikian, Brian Surratt, and Eric Wigginton. We alone are responsible for errors of fact or interpretation.

We also thank our respective institutions, the University of Tulsa and the University of Houston, for their support of our work.

Finally, we are grateful to our families for their encouragement and support, and for their tolerance of the many distractions from family life that writing a book entails.

THE FOREIGN POLICY OF
RUSSIA

1

The Tsarist Roots of
Russia's Foreign Policy

Territory and Climate

The foreign policy of Russia—whether in its tsarist, Soviet, or democratic form—is an expression in some measure of certain relatively fixed geopolitical realities. As it began to escape the confines of Muscovy—the principality with Moscow at its center—the expanding state soon encompassed vast and often forbidding territories. At its peak size, after more than four centuries of expansion, the Russian Empire (including Poland and Finland) covered just under nine million square miles—over one-sixth of the earth's land surface. After World War II, the Soviet Union, including portions of prewar Poland, Finland, and other East European states, as well as fragments of prewar Germany and Japan, had an area of about 8.6 million square miles. Today's Russia, the successor to the largest of the USSR's fifteen republics, has an area of 6,592,850 square miles—still the largest of any country in the world and almost twice the size of second-ranked Canada. From east to west, it spans more than 6,000 miles and eleven time zones; from north to south, it extends about 2,800 miles.

However, much of this vast land is inhospitable. Located in the high northern latitudes, with no mountain ranges in the north to shield it from frigid Arctic blasts, Russia experiences climatic extremes of bitter cold during the long winters and intense heat during the brief summers. Compared to North America, Russia extends considerably farther northward, with most of its land area north of 50° latitude. St. Petersburg, at 59.5° north, lies more northerly than Juneau, Alaska. Moscow, at 55.5° north, is situated somewhat more northerly than Edmonton, Alberta. Even the southernmost part of Russia, in the Caucasus, is just at 41° north—the same latitude as Cheyenne, Wyoming; Cleveland, Ohio; or New Haven, Connecticut. About one-half of the country is in the permafrost zone, where the subsoil is permanently frozen; most of Russia's major ports and rivers are frozen for part of the year.

Although Russia is a country rich in natural resources, this harsh climate limits the ability to exploit them. Vast reserves of petroleum, natural gas, coal, gold, bauxite, and iron ore lie far from the most populated areas, and some are virtually inaccessible. Apart from its brutal effects on workers, the extreme cold hinders the operation of equipment, and the summer marshiness and omnipresent mud make transportation extremely difficult.

The largely unfavorable combinations of soil conditions, temperature ranges, and precipitation produce a situation in which less than 15 percent of the land is sown in crops. The northernmost soil and vegetation zone, known as the tundra, is a treeless plain, with poorly developed soils and little precipitation. The zone to the south of the tundra is the taiga, comprising well over half the country's land. Its winters are cold and summers are hot; the soils are leached and not very fertile. Much of this rolling land is covered with coniferous forests. South of the taiga in European Russia is an area of mixed forests, with milder winters and more fertile soils. In the southern part of European Russia and Western Siberia are the steppes—grassy plains, with hot summers and cold winters. The soil is black and fertile (*chernozem*), and crops include wheat and sugar beets. The rest of the land is either semidesert or mountainous.

From west to east, the five geological regions are Russia are: the European Plain, the Ural Mountains, the West Siberian Plain, the Central Siberian Plateau, and the Eastern Siberian Uplands. On the European side of Russia are the Caucasus Mountains, located between the Black and Caspian Seas, and reaching heights up to 18,510 feet (Mount Elbrus, the highest point in Europe). The Ural Mountains, the dividing line between Europe and Asia, are low and rounded, averaging 2,000 feet in height; they are rich in deposits of iron, copper, and other metals. The major Siberian mountain ranges are the Altai, in the southern part of Western Siberia; the Sayan, in Eastern Siberia; and the Verkhoiansk, in Northeast Siberia.

In European Russia, the major rivers flow north to south. In their northern reaches, they are frozen for six months a year; in the south, for about two months. From west to east, the largest river systems cutting across the European Plain are the Dniester, the Dnieper, the Don, the Volga, and the Ural. The first two, largely in Ukraine but with Russian tributaries, empty into the Black Sea; the third flows into the Sea of Azov (which connects to the Black Sea). The latter two empty into the Caspian Sea, which is really a vast inland saltwater lake. The three major river systems in Siberia—the Ob, the Yenisei, and the Lena—flow south to north, to the Arctic Ocean. The Amur River flows easterly along the border with China and empties into the Pacific Ocean.

For over two centuries, Russia has been the most populated among the countries of Europe. (Although the European part of Russia constitutes a relatively small part of Russian territory, the largest proportion of the population lives there.) A combination of territorial expansion and rapid population growth propelled the population of the Russian Empire from 17.5 million in 1700 (second to France among the European states) to 37 million in 1800 (one-third larger than France). By 1914, with 171 million people, Russia was two-and-one-half times larger than Germany, which ranked second in Europe. A combination of territorial loss, war, famine, and political persecution slowed the growth considerably, and in 1940 the Soviet Union had 194 million people. With more than 20 million lost in World War II, the USSR's population had grown to 209 million by 1959. High birth rates among the non-Slavic peoples of the Soviet Union helped drive the population to about 290 million at the time of the dissolution of the USSR. Russia, which had 147.4 million in 1989, the time of the last official census, was estimated to have declined to about 146.5 million by October 1997—a population smaller than that of the Russian Empire on the eve of World War I. Of this total, ethnic Russians—who were barely one-half the population of the USSR at the time of its dissolution—make up 83 percent, and the rest is distributed among nearly 100 minority nationalities. About three-fourths of Russia's people now live in urban areas.

The natural decrease in population—attributed to an aging population, a low birth rate, and poor public health—was partially offset by migration into Russia from other areas of the former Soviet Union. Nevertheless, the decline in the country's population was expected by the State Statistical Commission to continue until at least 2010, dropping by an additional six million. The mortality rate, which had been increasing (especially for men) in the 1980s and early 1990s, was said by the Commission in 1997 to have dropped again to 14.5 deaths per thousand, and the birth rate to be holding steady at 9.1 per thousand.

The Legacy of the Tsars

The origins of Russian foreign policy can be traced to the period (1462–1505) when Ivan III (Ivan the Great) reigned over the Muscovite state. The year 1480 saw the formal collapse of the two-and-one-half-century-long "Tatar yoke," as the dominion of the Mongol warrior Genghis Khan and his successors over Russia is popularly known. Ivan had already begun to undermine Tatar power through his policy of "collecting of the Russian lands." The thriving trade center of Novgorod was subjected to Moscow's rule in the 1470s, and the regions around Perm and Tver were incorporated in the following decade. Ivan's westward conquests embroiled him in wars with Poland, which continued under his son Vasily III (ruled 1505–1533), who brought Smolensk into Moscow's orbit in 1514.

Ivan the Great was the first ruler of Moscow to use the title "tsar." His wife Sophia, niece of the last Byzantine emperor, encouraged him to claim the title, which was derived from "Caesar" and was meant—in the wake of the fall of Constantinople to the infidel Turks—to convey supremacy over both the spiritual and the earthly realms. Tsar Ivan was determined to build a strong central state based on his hegemony over other princely families— a policy that drove him to acquire additional lands with which to reward his followers. This linkage of strong rule at the center and expansionism continued under Ivan IV, who ruled from 1533 to 1584. The reign of "Ivan the Terrible" saw the further strengthening of autocracy, symbolized in the institution of the *Oprichnina,* which had features of a secret police force as well as a parallel administrative structure subordinate personally to the tsar.

Externally, Ivan IV began the expansion of Muscovite power into non-Russian territories through the conquest in the 1550s of the southern Khanates of Kazan and Astrakhan. Gaining access thereby to the Caspian Sea, Ivan also sought, unsuccessfully, to defeat the last remnant of the Tatar empire, on the Black Sea peninsula of Crimea. Even more bitter failure was experienced on Muscovy's western frontier when the Peace of Yam Zapolie with Poland in 1582, and a treaty with Sweden a year later, confirmed the loss of prior territorial gains in Livonia (much of present-day Latvia and Estonia), on the Baltic seacoast. Perhaps the most significant of Ivan IV's expansions, however, was the first stage of the conquest of Siberia, which began in 1581. Experiencing only spotty resistance from nomadic tribes, Moscow's forces reached the Ob and Irtysh rivers by the end of the decade. Moving in a northeasterly direction, the entire Siberian conquest, from the Urals to the Pacific Ocean, was accomplished before the midpoint of the 1600s.

The three decades following Ivan the Terrible's death were turbulent times for the young Muscovite state. Ivan's weak son, Fyodor I, left no heir, and was succeeded by the ruthless boyar Boris Godunov. Boris's demise, in the midst of terrible famine, ushered in the "Time of Troubles," climaxed by the occupation of Moscow by Polish forces. With the expulsion of the Poles, a new tsar, Michael I, was elected in 1613, and the dynasty of the Romanovs began its lengthy occupancy of the Russian throne. Michael and his son Alexis (ruled 1645–1676) fought eight more wars with Poland, the fruit of which was the incorporation into the Muscovite state of the eastern part of Ukraine, including its capital, the seat of "old Rus," Kiev.

The full flowering of Russian foreign policy took place under the strong leadership of Alexis's son, Peter I (Peter the Great), who reigned from 1689 to 1725. Not only did Peter transform his country into one of the great powers of Europe, but in 1721 he renamed it the Russian Empire and himself Emperor of Russia. Fascinated by the sea from an early age, Peter dreamed of acquiring ports and building a great navy. Frustrated in his efforts to wrest the fortress of Azov on the Black Sea from the Turks, Peter enjoyed his greatest military successes in the Great Northern War against Sweden (1700–1721), fought in the interests of acquiring a coast and ports on the Baltic Sea, for both military and commercial purposes. As early as 1703, Peter began building a new city on the marshlands near the Baltic Sea, which he named St. Petersburg; in 1713, he made it his capital. Although the ultimately decisive battle against Charles XII of Sweden was fought in 1709 at Poltava, the war was ended only in 1721 by the Treaty of Nystad, which effectively confirmed Sweden's decline and its replacement by Russia as a great European power. The treaty formalized Russia's incorporation of Livonia, Ingria (the area southwest of St. Petersburg), and parts of Finland.

Moving Russia's capital westward was only one way in which Peter the Great brought Russia into a European orbit. He himself made two lengthy journeys to Europe, and he brought back many ideas on how to "westernize" his country. These changes had a far-reaching impact on the administrative structure, educational system, and economy of Russia.

Peter's forays southward were less enduring. He first acquired and then lost access to the Black Sea in wars with Turkey. A war against Persia in 1722–23 resulted in the acquisition of the western shores of the Caspian Sea, including the town of Baku, but these gains were relinquished by his successors. Nor was there territorial expansion in the Far East during Peter's time. The Treaty of Nerchinsk, concluded with China in the same year Peter assumed power, kept Mongolia in the Chinese sphere of influence and confined Russia's colonization to the area north of the Amur River. Supplemented just after Peter's death by the Treaty of Kyakhta, which established certain trade and diplomatic regulations, the agreement at Nerchinsk effectively delimited Russian and Chinese spheres for the next century and a half.

Six monarchs (three women and three men) ruled the Russian Empire in the thirty-seven years between the death of Peter the Great and the beginning of the next significant period in Russian foreign policy: the reign of Catherine the Great. During this interim, Russia participated in three wars: it fought another war with Turkey (1738–39), at last gaining a Black Sea coast through the Treaty of Belgrade; it fought again with Sweden, gaining the Finnish city of Vyborg in the Peace of Abo (1743); and it participated, from 1757 to 1762, in the Seven Years War in Europe, first on the side of Austria and then as an ally of Prussia.

With the accession of Catherine II in 1762, Russia withdrew into neutrality as the war reached its conclusion. But the empress was soon pursuing an active foreign policy, which resulted in adding significant territories to the Russian Empire. Catherine was a full partner in European continental politics, demonstrating Russia's dominance in its immediate neighborhood through its victory in yet another war with Sweden (1787–90) and through three partitions of Poland (1772, 1793, and 1795). The partitions gave Catherine White Russia (Belorussia, or Belarus), Lithuania, and western Ukraine; in all, about two-thirds of former Poland was transferred to the Russian Empire.

Equally impressive expansion in the south was produced by two wars with Turkey (1768–74 and 1787–92). The Treaty of Kuchuk Kainardji (1774) and the Treaty of Jassy (1792) gave Russia much of the northern Black Sea coastline, including Azov and Crimea, and extending as far eastward as the mouth of the Dniester River. As one of the fruits of these victories, the great Black Sea port of Odessa was founded in 1796, the year of Catherine's death. By that time she had added another 200,000 square miles to her realm.

Thanks in part to the relative stability of European military organization and technique, Russia had been able to catch up with its western neighbors by borrowing expertise from them. Indeed, it now had an advantage by virtue of the sheer size of its population and by its willingness to spend about three-fourths of the state's finances on the military. This was clearly demonstrated during the course of the Napoleonic Wars, at the end of which Russia's army—with a force of 800,000—was superior to any other on the continent. Not until the Industrial Revolution changed the scale of European warfare during the nineteenth century would Russia fall behind again.[1]

Russia's power gave Alexander I (1801–1825) a major role to play at the Congress of Vienna (1815), which constructed post-Napoleonic Europe. By this time, yet another European land (Finland) had been added to the Empire, and wars with Turkey and Persia had led to the incorporation of Bessarabia, Baku, and Georgia. Although his tutors had filled his head with Enlightenment ideas, Alexander's multinational empire gave him a vested interest in suppressing nationalism and preserving the status quo. The Holy Alliance, largely his creation, emerged from Vienna as the embodiment of the principle of legitimism, and Russia began to play its role as the "gendarme of Europe." This policy was even more evident under Alexander's successor, his brother Nicholas I, who ruled with an iron hand from 1825 to 1855. "Autocracy, Orthodoxy, and Nationalism" were the guiding ideas of his regime. In 1849, Nicholas sent 200,000 Russian troops to suppress a revolution in Hungary, thus ensuring that one of the last vestiges of the great revolutionary wave of 1848 in Europe would not spread to the Russian Empire.

The conservatism of Nicholas I did not translate into a purely defensive foreign policy. He and his ministers were devoted to the objective of expanding Russia's realms southward—to capture Constantinople and seize control of the Dardanelles and Bosporus Straits, thereby controlling passage from the Black Sea to the Mediterranean. Russia's growing naval base at Sevastopol would have greater strategic significance if the tsar, rather than the Turkish Sultan, controlled the passage of warships in and out of Russia's back door. The Ottoman Empire, in Russia's eyes, was the "sick man of Europe," and Russia was eager to make arrangements to inherit his territory before he died.

In the cause of protecting the sultan's Orthodox Christian subjects in Greece, who had been struggling for independence since 1821, the Russians went to war against Turkey in 1828, concluding it the following year in the Peace of Adrianople. Its terms not only declared Greek independence but transferred Turkish possessions in the Caucasus to the tsar, brought Russia's frontier to the southern mouth of the Danube, and gave her a protectorate over the Orthodox Christians inhabiting the Danubian provinces of Moldavia and Walachia.

Apparently, for Nicholas, not only were the principles of legitimism and defense of the status quo to be subordinated when Russian strategic interests dictated, but struggles for national liberation of Christians under Muslim rule were to be treated differently from nationalist revolts within the Muslim family. In 1833 he responded affirmatively to the Ottoman Sultan's call for assistance in putting down a revolt by Mohammed Ali, his vassal in Egypt. The tsar's reward was the Treaty of Unkiar Skelessi, which gave Russia the right to use the straits for passage of its warships but denied the right to other nations. Britain and France were disturbed by the strategic import of the concessions thus handed to the tsar. Together with the Austrians and Prussians, they insisted upon a multilateral arrangement (the London Convention of 1841), which reversed the terms of Unkiar Skelessi and closed the straits to all foreign warships in time of peace.

Conflicting ambitions of the Russians, British, and French in the Near East reopened the struggle for strategic advantage in the Ottoman lands. When French President (soon to be Emperor) Louis Napoleon won a concession from the Sultan for protection of Catholics and Christian holy places in Palestine, Tsar Nicholas demanded similar privileges in defense of Orthodox Christians. Having failed to persuade the British to join in an outright partition of the Ottoman Empire, Nicholas proceeded to demand a Russian protectorate in Turkey. Encouraged by Britain, the Turks declared war on Russia in October 1853, and the British and French joined them six months later.

Neither side distinguished itself militarily in the Crimean War, but the Russian performance was especially dismal. Despite its growth in population (from 51 million in 1816 to 76 million in 1860) and in textile and iron production, Russia was falling far behind in economic strength. While Russian iron production doubled in the first part of the nineteenth century, that of Britain increased thirty-fold. A lack of capital or consumer demand and the absence of a sufficiently large middle class seriously impeded Russia's industrial takeoff. While Russia had little more than 500 miles of railroads in 1850, the United States had 8,500 miles. And none of Russia's railroads extended south of Moscow. The tsar had to rely on horse transport to move his army to the Crimea, taking as much as three months to move troops to the front, whereas the British and French could reach it by sea in three weeks. The army thought to be the strongest in Europe at the time of the Hungarian revolution of 1849 was soon exposed as shockingly backward, with inadequate weaponry and poor leadership, and with many of its large contingents tied down in internal policing duties.[2]

Following the death of Nicholas I, his son Alexander II (1855–1881) agreed to the terms of the Treaty of Paris (1856), which ended the Crimean War and stripped Russia of many of its recent territorial gains. The tsar ceded the mouths of the Danube and part of Bessarabia, and he forfeited some of his conquests in the Caucasus. The Danubian principalities were placed under the joint guarantee of the powers, and the Black Sea was neutralized. Turkey was admitted to the Concert of Europe, and the powers promised to respect its integrity and independence. Russia, thus frustrated in its ambitions toward the south, turned its attention inward, toward reform, and confined its external expansion to Asia, where resistance was weaker.

The need for internal political, economic, and social reform in Russia had long been debated by the intelligentsia, who were roughly divided into two camps: Westernizers and Slavophiles. The former group, ashamed of Russia's past and present and attracted by the ideas of the French Revolution, believed that Russia's great mission could be fulfilled only by advancing further on the road Peter the Great had pioneered—imitation of the West. A tragic fate had been suffered in December 1825, at the time of the accession of Nicholas I, by a group of young officers, students, professionals, and nobles (the Decembrists), who had sought to force Westernization on Russia through revolution. In their wake, writers as diverse as the liberal Granovskii, the romantic Herzen, and the radical realist Belinskii continued to insist that Russia must follow the West.

The Slavophiles did not dispute that Russia was backward and needed change, but they saw its salvation not in servile imitation of the West, with its materialism and its ideas of rationalism and individualism. Rather, they sought a return to what they regarded as Russia's true traditions—the faith of its people and the people's sense of belonging to a community. Russia's faults, the Slavophiles believed, were traceable to Peter's introduction of foreign models and his subordination of the Orthodox Church to the state. According to thinkers such as Karamzin, Kirevskii, and Aksakov, a reformed Russia could fulfill its mission by helping to civilize the West. The most influential book to insist on the uniqueness of Russia and its mission was Nicholas Danilevskii's *Russia and Europe* (1871).

Both sides idealized their models. As the Slavophiles readily pointed out, the real West was a grimmer place than Westernizers claimed; but it was just as true that Russia's traditions were not as happy as the Slavophiles imagined.[3] The debate over the extent of Russia's "special mission," and whether the Western experience was something to imitate or avoid, lasted for much of the nineteenth century. In the twentieth century, it resurfaced in arguments among Russian Marxists as the century opened, and in debates among post-Soviet Russian writers and politicians as it closed.

With Russia's weaknesses so sharply exposed in the Crimean War, Alexander II introduced a series of significant reforms, many of which seem designed to avoid the more radical changes urged by both Westernizers and Slavophiles. The most important of these was the emancipation of the serfs, proclaimed in February 1861. This was followed in the next few years by financial, educational, judicial, and administrative reforms, and by an edict to reduce censorship. The change in the legal status of the peasantry was slow to produce benefits in increased agricultural production, but the reforms did have a more noticeable impact in spurring railway construction and industrialization of the economy under state sponsorship. Although the reforms allowed Russia to close some of the distance between itself and the rest of Europe, in its class structure and in the total absence of constitutional or popular rule, Russia remained a rigid and centralized autocracy.

In the wake of its humiliating defeat in the Crimean War, Russia pursued an especially active policy in Asia and the Far East. Russian incursions into Chinese territory in the Amur River region, in violation of the provisions of the Treaty of Nerchinsk, actually began just prior to the war and were intensified during the conflict, in anticipation of an Anglo-French naval attack. After the war, the annexation of the Amur region was legalized in 1858, but the Russians pressed further into Chinese territory, founding Vladivostok in 1860. The same year, the Treaty of Peking established a new border along the Ussuri River. China thus formally ceded to Russia the territory south to Vladivostok. The Russo-Chinese border in the Central Asian region of Turkestan was also revised, allowing the Russians to shift their attention there.

Over the course of two decades, from the time of the capture of Tashkent in 1865 until the conquest of Merv in 1884, Russia penetrated further into Central Asia and subdued and incorporated Transcaspia and Turkestan. The initial conquests were justified by Russia to the other powers by citing the need to defend its subjects and settlements against raids and robbery by subjects of the ruling khans, with each new expansion of the boundary bringing Russia into contact with new raiders. While securing the frontier may indeed have been the initial aim, these territories possessed mineral wealth and were a source of raw cotton. In light of the simultaneous Anglo-Russian conflicts of interest in the Balkans, Russia's policy of expansion in Central Asia also served to bring useful pressures to bear on the British, who feared that Russia would press all the way into India. These concerns were at least temporarily alleviated in 1885, when the two countries signed an agreement delineating the northern boundary of Afghanistan, effectively making it the terminus of the Russian advance.

In contrast to the steadiness of Russia's expansion on the Eurasian land-mass, this period also witnessed an important withdrawal from an area to which Tsar Alexander II apparently felt Russia had overextended itself. Russian fur traders had begun to work in the Aleutian Islands and the southern coast of Alaska as early as the 1760s. The Russian American Company in 1799 was given a monopoly over hunting and commerce southward to the fifty-fifth parallel (the southern tip of present-day Alaska). In 1812 the company established a new base for hunting and food supply at Fort Ross, just seventy miles north of San Francisco. Although pressured by both Spain and Mexico, the Russians did not abandon Fort Ross until 1841. The vulnerability of these North American possessions became evident to Russia during the Crimean War, just as the economic benefits began to disappear. Hostility toward Britain influenced the decision to sell Alaska to the United States instead; this was accomplished in 1867, for a price of $7.2 million.

The hiatus in Russian activity in Turkey and the Balkans came to an end in the 1870s. At the beginning of the decade, Russia seized an opportunity (in the wake of the Franco-Prussian War) unilaterally to abrogate the Black Sea clauses of the Treaty of Paris. This action was supported the following year by a convention recognizing the right of both Russia and Turkey to maintain naval forces in the Black Sea. Russian territorial ambitions stirred again at mid-decade, with the occurrence of uprisings against Turkey in Bulgaria and in Bosnia-Herzegovina, and with the outbreak of war between Turkey and Serbia.

These events further fanned the flames of the burgeoning Pan-Slavist movement, which transformed the Slavophile ideology into a foreign policy. Since the fifteenth century, Russian churchmen had regarded Moscow as the "Third Rome," but the nineteenth century brought the notion that the tsar, as head of the Russian Orthodox Church, had a special mission to protect Orthodox Christians against the excesses of Ottoman rule. Pan-Slavists disagreed on whether "Slavdom" included only those who were Orthodox, or all who spoke a Slavic tongue. They also were divided between the Greater Slav idea (with all Slav nations treated as equals) and the Lesser Slav idea (emphasizing the dominant role of the Russian state and the Orthodox religion). The 1863 revolt of the Poles against Russian rule, suppressed with great fury by the tsar, diminished the appeal of the Greater Slav idea. The foreign policy consequences of the Lesser Slav idea—although it was imperialistic—were distinctly less risky in that the object of Russia's liberating zeal would be the Slavic subjects of the sultan, rather than those who lived under Austro-Hungarian or German rule.[4]

With the eruption of the Balkan conflict, amid great popular excitement, the Russian government allowed the public collection of funds for the anti-Turkish cause and permitted Russian army officers to enlist as volunteers against the Turks. The defeat of the Serbs provoked a rare public speech by the tsar, in which he referred to the sufferings of Christians in the Balkans and the "cause of Slavdom," ending with the prayer: "May God help us to fulfill our sacred mission."[5] A few months later, Russia declared war on Turkey, and in March 1878 it was able to dictate peace terms in the Treaty of San Stefano. By its terms, the independence of Serbia and Montenegro was recognized and both received territory; Romania was declared independent; Bulgaria was granted autonomy under an elected prince and Russian military occupation; and Bulgaria was to be substantially enlarged to include most of Macedonia and an Aegean seacoast. Russia received Ardahan, Kars, Batum, and Bayazid from Turkey.

Like the Treaty of Unkiar Skelessi forty-five years before, the Treaty of San Stefano was distinctly not to the liking of most of the other great powers, and they proceeded to call an international meeting to force Russia to modify its terms. With German Chancellor Bismarck as the "honest broker," the Congress of Berlin (June 1878) left Russian Pan-Slavists furious (especially at Germany and Austria) and left the nationalist aspirations of Serbia and Bulgaria unfulfilled. The size of Bulgaria was significantly reduced, and Serbia and Montenegro also lost territory. Austria was given a mandate to occupy Bosnia and Herzegovina. Russia kept Batum, Kars, and Ardahan and gained southern Bessarabia from Romania (thereby ensuring Romanian hostility).

Aware that a frustrated and isolated Russia could go shopping for allies among Germany's enemies, in the wake of the Congress of Berlin Bismarck devised a plan whereby Russia could achieve some of its security objectives in the Black Sea in return for alignment with the German powers. Germany and Austria had formed an alliance in 1879, and Bismarck proceeded to revive the idea of a Three Emperors' League (*Dreikaiserbund*). Temporarily delayed by the assassination of Tsar Alexander II, the three-way alliance was finally implemented by his son and heir, Alexander III (1881–1894). The highly secret treaty, signed in June 1881, effectively protected Russia against attack in the Black Sea by stating that if Turkey violated the principle of closure of the straits, the three powers would warn the sultan that he had put himself in a state of war with the aggrieved power (Russia). The three powers also agreed that modifications in the territorial status quo in Turkey should take place only after agreement among them, though Austria reserved the right to annex Bosnia and Herzegovina whenever it saw fit. The treaty was renewed once, in 1884, but was allowed to lapse in 1887 because of the tsar's growing dissatisfaction with Austrian policy.

Determined to keep Russia away from France, Bismarck devised a secret Russo-German Treaty (the "Reinsurance Treaty") in which the two empires promised each other neutrality if either became involved in a war with a third power, with the exception of an aggressive war of Germany against France or of Russia against Austria. In Russia's interests, the treaty once more reaffirmed the principle of closure of the straits, but it also went farther, promising German moral and diplomatic support "to the measures which His Majesty may deem it necessary to take to control the key of his empire" (i.e., the entrance to the Black Sea). The Germans also recognized Russia's predominant influence in Bulgaria and promised to aid in re-establishing a pro-Russian government there.

The Reinsurance Treaty came up for renewal in 1890, in the wake of Bismarck's dismissal as chancellor, and the young Kaiser Wilhelm II was persuaded by his new advisors to allow it to lapse. This proved a fatal mistake, as it virtually drove the Russians into the arms of the French, setting the stage for the transformation of the European system into a rigid bipolarity of opposing coalitions. The initial Franco-Russian convention of August 1891 was only a vague agreement that the two states would discuss measures to be taken if the peace were endangered or if either were menaced. The following year the Russians agreed in principle to a draft military convention. But the actual formalization occurred only at the end of 1893—and not as a treaty, which would have required legislative ratification in France, but as a highly secret military convention. It provided that if France were attacked by Germany, or by Italy supported by Germany, Russia would employ all available forces against Germany; if Russia were attacked by Germany, or by Austria supported by Germany, France would employ all available forces against Germany. Specific levels of troop commitments were specified in the agreement. Additionally, if the forces of the Triple Alliance (Germany, Austria, Italy) or any one member of it mobilized, France and Russia committed to mobilize without delay.

With the maintenance of the status quo in the Balkans seemingly ensured for the time being, Russia again turned its attention eastward, with the powerful Finance Minister Count Sergei Witte as lead strategist. In 1891, Russia decided to build a 5,000-mile railroad from Moscow to Vladivostok, for both strategic and commercial reasons. But since Vladivostok is not ice-free, Russia also renewed its interest in obtaining such a port, either in Korea (Pusan) or on the Liaotung Peninsula. These ambitions directly conflicted with those of Japan, which feared being cut off from the vast Chinese market. Taking matters into its own hands, Japan launched a war against China in 1894, as a result of which it took from China the offshore islands of Formosa and the Pescadores as well as the Liaotung Peninsula. Determined to drive Japan back off the mainland and prevent the premature partition of China, Count Witte enlisted German and French assistance in pressuring Japan to yield the peninsula.

At the coronation of Tsar Nicholas II in 1896, the Chinese ambassador was induced by a bribe to accept a fifteen-year defensive alliance whereby Russia undertook to defend China from attack and China agreed that a Russian railway could be built across Manchuria to Vladivostok (the Chinese Eastern Railway). Two years later, to the great consternation of the Japanese, China granted Russia a twenty-five-year lease of the Liaotung Peninsula, including Dairen and Port Arthur. Japan sought a conciliatory solution, proposing a division of spoils, in true imperialist fashion, with Japan to be granted predominant influence in Korea in return for recognizing Russia's primacy in Manchuria. Confident of its superior position (though unprepared for war), Russia refused the offer.

Seeking a European partner in its quest to block Russian expansion in the Far East, Japan concluded an alliance with Britain in 1902. The following year, as the first trains passed over his Trans-Siberian Railway, Count Witte was dismissed. In the face of growing internal political unrest, Witte's rival in the tsar's court, V.K. Pleve, counseled an even more aggressive policy, arguing that Russia needed "a little victorious war to stop the revolutionary tide."[6] In February 1904 the Japanese launched a surprise attack on the Russian fleet at Port Arthur. Besieged for most of the year, the city fell to the Japanese in December. Further military reversals followed, as the Russians lost a major land battle at Mukden and suffered the loss of a naval fleet of thirty-two vessels in the Tsushima Straits in May 1905. By this time, fueled by humiliation in the Far East, a revolution had erupted in

Russia, and the government was impelled to seek an end to the war with Japan. With U.S. President Theodore Roosevelt serving as mediator, a settlement was reached at Portsmouth, New Hampshire, in September 1905. By its terms, the Russians retained their influence in northern Manchuria and escaped the payment of indemnity, but were forced to recognize Japanese preponderance in Korea and to cede to Japan the southern half of Sakhalin Island as well as their rights in the Liaotung Peninsula and Port Arthur. Two years later Russia signed a convention with Japan explicitly renouncing interest in Korea and southern Manchuria, in return for Japanese recognition of Russia's special interests in northern Manchuria and Outer Mongolia.

Ironically, the forcible limitation placed on St. Petersburg's expansionist ambitions in the Far East removed a point of contention between Russia and Britain and helped open the way to the Anglo-Russian Entente, concluded in August 1907. The two powers settled their remaining imperial differences, with Britain recognizing a Russian sphere of interest in northern Persia, Russia recognizing preponderant British influence in Afghanistan, and both sides recognizing Chinese suzerainty in Tibet. Britain also assured the tsar that it would not obstruct Russia's long-standing desire to open up the Bosporus and Dardanelles Straits to Russian warships in the Black Sea, thus facilitating a revival of Russian interests in the Balkans.

More sensitive than ever to public opinion in the wake of the 1905 Revolution, the Russian government again took up the banner of Pan-Slavism. The fervor for liberation of the Southern Slavs ultimately halted a possible agreement between Russia and Austria, negotiated secretly between their foreign ministers, Izvolskii and Aehrenthal, in which Austria would have supported a change in the rules governing passage through the straits in return for Russian approval of Austria's annexation of Bosnia and Herzegovina. When Austria rushed to proclaim the annexation in October 1908, the Pan-Slavist outcry in Russia led Prime Minister Stolypin to direct Izvolskii to condemn the Austrian action and instead champion Serbia's claims on these Slavic lands. The ensuing diplomatic crisis hardened the lines between the Triple Alliance and the Triple Entente in Europe, ruined the prospects for a peaceful accommodation of Russian ambitions in the straits, and strengthened Russia's determination to create a barrier against further Austrian influence in the Balkans.

When war finally broke out in the Balkans in August 1914, sparked by the assassination in Sarajevo of Archduke Franz Ferdinand, heir to the Austro-Hungarian throne, by a Bosnian Serb nationalist, it quickly escalated into a European and then a World War that none of the great powers truly wanted. By many indicators, Russia was in a much stronger position for such a war than it had been earlier. Its population was three times that of Germany and four times that of Britain, and Russia's standing army was the largest in Europe, with 1.3 million front-line troops and up to 5 million reserves. Russia's industrial output was growing at an average annual rate of 5 percent between 1860 and 1913, and ranked fourth in the world. Railway construction was proceeding at great speed, and Russia was the world's second largest producer of oil.

But, as Paul Kennedy has noted, Russia was "simultaneously powerful and weak."[7] Much of its industry was devoted to food and textiles, and output per capita amounted to only one-quarter of Germany's and one-sixth of Britain's. Given the population growth, annual real national product was expanding by only 1 percent per capita. Eighty percent of the population worked in the inefficient agricultural sector. The average Russian's income was about one-quarter of the average Englishman's, but the average Russian was forced to part with over half of his income for defense. Industrialization had been carried out with forced savings from the population as well as substantial foreign borrowing; Russia's foreign debt was the largest in the world. Most decisively, Russian strength was further undermined by the weakness and ineptitude of its government, starting with Tsar Nicholas II, "a Potemkin village in person."[8]

His great-grandfather's (and namesake's) war in the Crimea had exposed Russia's weaknesses, as had his own war against the upstart Japanese, and yet the tsar and his advisors missed every opportunity to turn away from the path that ultimately not only devastated the country but destroyed the regime itself, in the process opening the way to communist revolution and to the imposition of the Soviet state on the Russian empire.

Expansionism in Tsarist Foreign Policy

Having sketched the broad outlines of Russian foreign policy under the tsars, we can now turn to a search for patterns in tsarist diplomacy, and for explanations of how these were shaped by peculiarities of Russia's geography, of the organization of the tsarist state, of ideology, and of the prevailing norms and characteristics of the international system.

Not surprisingly, the dominant theme most analysts find in the foreign policy of Russia under the tsars is that of expansionism. This is sometimes expressed in a tendency to fill internal vacuums, and sometimes in a push toward the open sea. There are variations in the explanations given for this four-centuries-long pattern of expanding the boundaries of the Russian state. Some analysts stress factors that portray Russia as an unprovoked aggressor fulfilling some messianic or autocratic urge, and others depict a regime haunted by its vulnerability to invasion and obsessed with the search for security.

Russia's geopolitical situation partially explains several facets of Russian expansionism. The vastness and openness of the Russian landmass, and the absence of natural barriers within or around it, help to account for the obsessive concern by Russia's rulers for its security, as these factors permitted easy invasion by neighboring powers and, alternatively, relatively easy outward expansion of Russian power. On those occasions when invasion has occurred—most notably, with Napoleon in 1812 and Hitler in 1941–43—Russian military commanders have had the luxury of being able to trade space for time, while enlisting the harsh climate as their ally in defeating the invader. Conversely, long distances have sometimes turned into logistical nightmares for Russian generals seeking to move forces or supplies to the front. This was especially so prior to the development of a network of railways in the country (as in the Crimean War), but it remains true in the absence of an all-weather network of highways, on terrain where mud can be a greater impediment than snow or ice.

Finally, from the time of Peter the Great, when Russia's aspirations for naval power were born, the absence of ice-free ports has often been cited as a motive for Russian expansion toward the Baltic and Black Seas and toward the warmer waters of the Pacific Ocean. Of equal importance for enhanced naval maneuverability is Russia's need for ports that provide access to open waters leading to the major oceans. Ships leaving the Baltic Sea ports must pass through narrow straits between Denmark and Sweden to reach the North Sea and the Atlantic Ocean. Naval forces leaving the Black Sea for the Mediterranean must pass through the Bosporus and Dardanelles Straits, where the rights of passage were subject to treaty restrictions for long periods. In the Far East, Vladivostok is ice-bound for part of the year, and ships departing southward toward the Pacific Ocean must pass through the Tsushima Straits. Had Russia fulfilled its ambition of acquiring Pusan in Korea, it would have controlled these straits. Only during the period when Port Arthur and Dairen were under Russian control was ice-free passage to the Yellow Sea and the Pacific possible.

Another familiar theory is that Russian expansionism was a product of the particular type of regime—that internal despotism found its outward expression in relentless expansion, and that incorporation of numerous subject nationalities required unusually heavy militarization to maintain central control. No checks and balances existed to question or block the tsars' decisions to devote enormous sums of state revenues to the armed forces. In Henry Kissinger's words:

The absolute nature of the Tsar's powers enabled Russia's rulers to conduct foreign policy both arbitrarily and idiosyncratically. . . .

To sustain their rule and to surmount tensions among the empire's various populations, all of Russia's rulers invoked the myth of some vast, foreign threat, which, in time, turned into another of the self-fulfilling prophecies that doomed the stability of Europe.[9]

Certainly, both Ivan III and Ivan IV found that the necessities of state-building were well served by expansion, as they sought to acquire new lands with which to reward their nobles. The process by which the Muscovite state was transformed into the Russian Empire by Peter I also reveals linkages between perceived internal requirements and external policies. But during the reigns of Catherine II and Alexander I, the Russian regime was not noticeably different in type from others in Europe, and it is difficult to argue that Russian foreign policies departed from the balance-of-power policies that were being pursued elsewhere.

By the time Nicholas I ascended the throne, Russia was already lagging behind the other major European powers in permitting constitutional change and expanding democracy, and this gap grew considerably over the ensuing decades. Henry Kissinger argues that "even when Russia was pursuing legitimacy, its attitudes were more messianic—and therefore imperialistic—than those of the other conservative courts."[10] An alternative view, however, would argue that policies of conservatism and preservation of dynastic legitimacy were better served by a stance of preserving the status quo than by upsetting it through expansion.[11]

Analysts who perceive a connection between regime type and expansionist policy also argue that the strong state bureaucracy and central control in Russia produced a diplomatic style that was at considerable variance with European great power norms. They describe Russian diplomacy as more secretive and suspicious, untrustworthy, and displaying unusual hostility toward the Western powers—characteristics that are said to have carried over to the Soviet period. Lord Palmerston, Britain's Russophobic foreign secretary and prime minister in the mid-nineteenth century, stated the case for Russian untrustworthiness in 1860:

The Russian government perpetually declares that Russia wants no increases of territory, that the Russian dominions are already too large. But while making these declarations in the most solemn manner, every year [it] adds large tracts of territory to the Russian dominions . . . not for the purpose of adding territory but carefully directed to occupation of certain strategical points, as starting points for further encroachments or as posts from whence some neighboring states may be kept under control or may be threatened with invasion.[12]

Denigrating tsarist diplomacy, Henry Kissinger describes Russia's foreign ministers as "little more than servants of a volatile and easily distracted autocrat, for whose favor they had to compete amidst many overriding domestic concerns."[13] Even when the tsar was a dominant personality, Kissinger observes, the autocratic system of policy-making weighed against coherence in policy, while the tsar's "princely lifestyle" made it difficult for him to concentrate attention on foreign issues over a sustained period.

Russia's greatest fault, in Kissinger's view, lay in the unwillingness of the tsars to abide by the maxims of the prevailing international system— balance-of-power politics—which resulted in a Russian expansionism that proceeded without self-imposed limits.

> But Russia seemed impelled to expand by a rhythm all its own, containable only by the deployment of a superior force, and usually by war. Throughout numerous crises, a reasonable settlement often seemed well within Russia's reach, much better in fact than what ultimately emerged. Yet Russia always preferred the risk of defeat to compromise. . . .
> Russia on the march rarely exhibited a sense of limits.[14]

In similar fashion, Kissinger and other analysts have commented on Russia's tendency when confronted with superior force or war in Europe to turn toward expansion in Asia, and to return to European objectives when more favorable circumstances prevailed.

Instances in Russian history suggest the existence of a greater sense of prudence—and a greater devotion to pragmatic, balance-of-power politics—than this analysis allows. It is true that Russia's wars were not solely defensive—undertaken out of a search for security alone—and that Russia would attack or take territory from neighboring states which were not currently threatening it. However, Russia's targets were invariably states or tribal entities that its rulers perceived to be weaker than itself, and possibly exposed to the ambitions of other states, if preemptive moves were not taken. Examples are the partitions of Poland in the late eighteenth century, Peter I's war against Persia, various wars against Turkey, and acquisition of territory from a weakened Chinese empire by means of what Beijing has long seen as "unequal treaties."

Prior to the disastrous slide into World War I, when confronted with the possibility of going to war with a stronger state, Russia would pull back. Nicholas I found himself at war with Britain and France in the Crimea only because they came to the defense of the "sick man" on the Ottoman throne. Both Alexander II and Nicholas II had occasion to back away from possible wars with Austria in the Balkans. And Nicholas II, having suffered humiliating defeat at the hands of a Japanese state which had been widely perceived as inferior in strength, sought entente with Britain soon after that war, rather than undertake another costly conflict.

Unlike the successor Soviet regime, Imperial Russia's expansionist ambitions were not global; even the expansion into North America was soon regarded as too costly to sustain. As Martin Malia argues, a "pragmatic geopolitical motivation accounts for most of Russia's constant westward expansion from the mid-17th century to Alexander I. . . . the Russian Imperial regime . . . saw no further than the Vistula, the Straits, Iran, or the Yalau."[15]

If tsarist Russia was not following the maxims of the balance of power system, how did it formulate and justify its expansionist policies? The answer, Kissinger and others believe, is that Russian expansion was largely motivated by ideology—alternatively viewed either as the triad of autocracy/orthodoxy/nationalism or as a messianic Pan-Slavism. Russia's distinctive approach to foreign policy, it is argued, arises not from a sense of insecurity, but from ideology. In Kissinger's words, Russia for most of its history "has been a cause looking for opportunity."[16] Again stressing the continuity between the tsarist and Soviet periods, Kissinger describes Russian exceptionalism as a paradox:

> Unlike the states of Western Europe, which Russia simultaneously admired, despised, and envied, Russia perceived itself not as a nation but as a cause, beyond geopolitics, impelled by faith, and held together by arms. . . . After the Revolution, the passionate sense of mission was transferred to the Communist International.
>
> The paradox of Russian history lies in the continuing ambivalence between messianic drive and a pervasive sense of insecurity. In its ultimate aberration, this ambivalence generated a fear that, unless the empire expanded, it would implode.[17]

As Kissinger notes, tsarist Russia's attitudes toward the West were ambivalent—a complex mix of hostility and admiration. At least in part, this ambivalence reflects a duality in what "the West" represents. As Bruce Porter has written, there was not only the liberal West of the Enlightenment, so beloved by many Russian "Westernizers," but also the other West—"the militarized, regimented, technological juggernaut" embodied by the armies of Charles XII, Frederick the Great, Napoleon Bonaparte, and Kaiser Wilhelm. Whereas Russia's internal cohesion and the power of the state were threatened whenever it emulated the reforming, democratizing West, the frequent interaction with the military might of the West helped ensure that "this was the West that Russia actually emulated."[18]

However accurate are Kissinger's insights on this point, he nevertheless overstates the extent to which the "passionate sense of mission" was a characteristic of official attitudes, as opposed to an undercurrent in society. As Hugh Seton-Watson demonstrates in his study of the foreign policy of Imperial Russia, occasionally the tsar would permit manifestations of Pan-Slavism to be expressed, when it suited his policy. But he could also turn it off again, if it threatened to get out of hand.[19] And much of Russia's expansion had nothing at all to do with Slavic brotherhood, but resulted from a quite pragmatic quest for gold and other valuable minerals, furs, or trading pathways to the storied markets of the Orient.

Martin Malia, a scholar who argues that Russian exceptionalism was largely confined to the Soviet period, makes the case against ascribing Russian expansionism largely to ideological motives:

> In fact, however, Russian foreign policy under the old regime was no more ideological than that of any other European powers. Like all other powers, Russia was expansionist, but essentially for geopolitical reasons. . . .
>
> Indeed, there was probably more ideology in the Western overseas expression of this expansionism than in its Russian, continental, and Eurasian forms . . .
>
> Russian foreign policy under the old regime did have an ideological component, but only toward the end. . . . Until the early 20th century, pan-Slav ideology was much more the property of society than of the government, which succumbed to it only in the immediate buildup to 1914. . . .
>
> It was with the October Revolution that Russia's international role changed fundamentally . . . to a messianic ideology.[20]

Clearly, no single motive force can be found to explain tsarist Russian expansionism; rather, the influences of geography, regime type, the international system, and ideology all weigh in, though in different proportions at different times. As we will see in the next section, there are features of tsarist diplomacy that did carry over to the Soviet period, but there are also characteristics that did not. In evaluating the legacy of the tsars, one can, however, surmise that certain lessons could be drawn from the history of the Russian Empire to help guide the foreign policy of both communist and democratic successors. From the Time of Troubles in the seventeenth century through the Crimean and Russo-Japanese Wars until World War I, Russian history teaches the dangers that overextension and war pose for internal stability. Sometimes undertaken to divert popular attention from internal problems, war more often than not exacerbates these problems—ultimately, for the tsars, causing the collapse of an empire once regarded as the mightiest in Europe.

2

Soviet Foreign Policy:
From Revolution to Cold War

The Russian Revolutionary Tradition

Emerging in the nineteenth century, movements for revolution in Russia produced political values, beliefs, and symbols that formed part of the political landscape in which the foreign policy of the late tsarist period was devised. The distinctive features of this revolutionary tradition not only helped to shape the foreign policy of the Soviet period of Russian history, but they also live on today by virtue of their importance in the political socialization of the current leadership of democratic Russia. This inheritance includes not only the ideas of Karl Marx, Vladimir Lenin, and others who shaped the Marxist-Leninist ideology, but also the political experiences and traditions of the Russian intelligentsia in the nineteenth century, which formed the distinctive environment from which Lenin's Bolsheviks emerged.

The main feature of this environment was autocracy: unrestrained political power in the hands of the tsar, wielded through a strong centralized bureaucracy and augmented by a secret police, and an economy and social order controlled by the state. The Russian Orthodox Church and strong manifestations of Russian chauvinism were the other pillars of tsarist authority over the vast multi-national empire. The nineteenth century witnessed a widening gulf between the regime and Russia's intelligentsia—the educated professionals who sometimes were termed "superfluous people" because they were divorced from practical social activity as well as from any opportunity for political participation. In short, it was an environment that sponsored utopianism rather than pragmatism, impulses toward revolution rather than gradual reform, and the eventual replacement of one autocracy and orthodoxy by another.

The mid-century debates between Westernizers and Slavophiles pointed up a tradition, visible on both sides, of *narodnichestvo*—faith in the simple laboring people, especially the peasantry, as uncorrupted by political power and bourgeois values and capable of delivering Russia onto the path of social justice. In the wake of the disillusion in the circles of the intelligentsia over the incomplete reforms of the 1860s, a populist movement grew up, known as *V narod* (going to the people). It envisioned an exodus of intelligentsia from the cities to the villages, where they would provide the peasantry with the education and insights that would lift the scales from their eyes and allow them to see the shortcomings of the regime. The movement was an utter failure. Peasants, not yet devoid of their faith in the tsar, distrusted the citified intellectuals—in some cases, going so far as to turn them over to the police.

Arising from the ashes of the utopian hopes of agrarian socialists like Alexander Herzen and Peter Lavrov was the phoenix of violent revolution. But as in the earlier division between Westernizers and Slavophiles, the intelligentsia was again divided—this time, between those who were essentially anarchists ("nihilists") and those who adhered to the more deterministic, rationalistic, and Western-oriented Marxian socialism. Lenin's genius was in synthesizing these two streams.

In the former tradition were Mikhail Bakunin, the anarchist, whose hatred for political authority was so great that he engaged in a long battle with Karl Marx, whom he considered too rational and conservative; and P.N. Tkachev, who stated that a revolutionary minority, utilizing terrorism, must seize power to forestall a middle-class revolution and the development of Russia along capitalist lines. Unlike the utopians, these men demonstrated a will to power and a contempt for the spontaneous development of the masses, in whose name they sought to achieve a "preventive revolution."

The tightly organized, highly disciplined revolutionary party advocated by Tkachev, after a campaign of terrorism in the 1870s, succeeded in 1881 in realizing its fondest wish—the assassination of Tsar Alexander II, liberator of the serfs. The consequence of this terrorism was that the new ruler, Alexander III, guided by his reactionary tutor Konstantin Pobedonostsev, opened up a period of political and social reaction, intensified chauvinism, and suppression of the revolutionaries.

Opposed to the anarchists in Russia were the first of that country's Marxists. The first Russian Marxist organization, the Emancipation of Labor, was formed by G.V. Plekhanov and others in 1883, and by 1887 Marx's *Das Kapital* was the most widely read book among Russian students. Unlike its attitude toward the populist parties, the government did not at first seek to suppress Marxist ideas or study groups, viewing Marxism as an abstruse and harmless doctrine, which in fact performed a useful service by downgrading terrorism and preaching the inevitability of capitalist development. One reason for the growth of Marxism in Russia was that industrialization was indeed proceeding rapidly at the end of the nineteenth century—even if it was proceeding under state auspices rather than through the efforts of native capitalists, and the urban proletariat was still a tiny drop in a sea of peasantry. In Marx's terms, this development was only the transition from feudalism to capitalism, and the revolutionary agenda at this stage was not the proletarian revolution and establishment of socialism but the bourgeois-democratic revolution and further development of capitalism. The dilemma for Russian Marxists was that the "progressive" course for their country seemed to require the very development of bourgeois greed and exploitation that so many Russian intelligentsia had long decried in the West. As Engels confirmed in a letter to Russian Marxists in 1892, historical materialism dictated that only after the completion of the bourgeois-democratic revolution could Russian revolutionaries pass on to the promotion of socialist revolution.

There was little formal disagreement with this principle, but much argument about what the tactics of Russian Marxists should be. The viewpoint known as "Economism" focused on improving the material condition of the Russian proletariat through trade union organization and peaceful strike movements—a position that gained force when the regime made it clear at the end of the century that it would not tolerate political agitation among the workers. Indeed, the First Conference of the Russian Social-Democratic Labor Party (RSDLP), held in Minsk in 1898, was disrupted by the arrest of some of the delegates by the tsarist police.

For those who were determined that the proletariat should have a political party, and not merely bide its time, the question of tactics arose most sharply at the Second Congress of the RSDLP, held in Brussels and London in 1903. The classical Marxist view of a two-stage revolution, obligating the proletariat at present to support the bourgeoisie in Russia in achieving the bourgeois-democratic revolution, was argued by Plekhanov and Julius Martov. (Although the majority of delegates supported this viewpoint, the loss of a vote on a relatively minor issue led to their being labeled "Mensheviks"—minority men—by Lenin and his "Bolsheviks"—majority men.) A second viewpoint, articulated by Leon Trotsky, insisted that the Russian proletariat could itself seize leadership of the bourgeois-democratic revolution, making it into a "permanent revolution" that would grow into a socialist revolution with the critical assistance of a victorious European proletariat.

Lenin agreed with Trotsky that the Russian bourgeoisie was not worthy or capable of leadership, and that the proletariat must substitute. The first-stage objective, however, was overthrow of the tsarist autocracy and establishment of a "revolutionary-democratic dictatorship of the proletariat and peasantry," which would build the material base for a socialist revolution and dictatorship of the proletariat. By 1917, Lenin had taken over Trotsky's view that this process could be more or less continuous, given outside assistance. Lenin and Trotsky and their followers, impatient with Marxist determinism, were unwilling to see the bourgeoisie seize political power. Strictly speaking, they adhered to Marx's doctrine that the bourgeois revolution must come first, but they now spoke of a revolution which was bourgeois by virtue of the tasks it would perform rather than by virtue of its leadership. Temperamentally, Lenin, more than the Mensheviks, was in keeping with the mood of the intelligentsia and with Tkachev's idea of a preventive revolution. And like Tkachev, he doubted the ability of the masses to make their own revolution. The element of political will would be supplied by the party—a centrally directed core of professional revolutionaries which would act as vanguard of the proletariat.

In effect, this Leninist conception of party as elite vanguard, showing the way to the masses, negates the Marxist notion of the proletariat itself as the revolutionary instrument. But this did not mean that the masses were not important to the revolution. Indeed, the "revolutionary situation"—the moment at which the party could seize power—would be characterized by a wave of spontaneous mass uprisings, on the back of which the party could rise to power. At such moments, it was acceptable to utilize slogans inconsistent with the party platform, if they would help to ensure a mass following. Indeed, in 1917 the Bolsheviks came to power not on the basis of their Marxist promises and programs—of which few of the workers and peasants had ever heard—but on the basis of three slogans: immediate peace, all land to the peasants, and all power to the soviets (the councils of workers' and peasants' deputies which had become half of the dual government that succeeded the tsarist regime). None of these were Marxist demands—the latter two were in fact contrary to Marx's program—but they were slogans that enabled the party to utilize the mass unrest and come to power.

The official principle of organization of the Bolshevik wing of the RSDLP—later the Communist Party of the Soviet Union (CPSU)—was what Lenin called "democratic centralism." All issues were to be fully discussed by all before a decision was reached; but once the majority had decided on a course of action, debate would cease and the party would function as a factionless monolith. The democratic element also extended in theory to the choosing of leaders—each party body was to be elected by the body below. But party practice very quickly metamorphosed into the co-optation of new members of the elite by those already in the leadership. Furthermore, in practice, no policy matter could even be opened for debate unless the leadership declared it a debatable question. And the failure of a policy line was not allowed to cast doubt on the prerogative of the leadership to continue to operate in this fashion. Rather, mistakes were blamed on scapegoats; the party itself never erred.

What Lenin did was to synthesize the Marxist dialectic method, theory of economics, and doctrine of proletarian revolution with the temperament and organizational principles of the Russian intelligentsia. However suitable it was to the Russian culture, this Bolshevik principle of democratic centralism became (in 1920, at the Second Congress of the Communist International) a precondition for any party that wished to affiliate with the Leninist movement. In this context, it caused great difficulty for parties operating in cultures where democratic theory and the practice of centralized direction by a self-chosen elite were regarded as incompatible.

Marx and Lenin on Foreign Policy

The writings of Marx and Engels contain very little that pertains to foreign policy—indeed, as little as they contain on the operation of a socialist economy. For Marx, the motivating force in the development of industrial society was internal, and the main conflict was among classes rather than nations. Nevertheless, two themes can be extricated from his writings that have relevance to foreign affairs.

The first of these, internationalism, is expressed in the closing words of the *Communist Manifesto:* "Working men of all countries, unite!"[1] The cosmopolitan character of production and the imposition on the whole world of bourgeois values meant that the distinctiveness of nations was fading. The bourgeoisie of the world was already united; likewise, the working man had no country. National sentiments, in Marx's scheme, belong to the superstructure, and will entirely pass away with the demise of capitalism. The second theme relates to the nature and function of the state and the uses of state power. Since the state is the instrument of the ruling class for exploiting other classes, it will wither away with the end of the class struggle. During the transition period of the dictatorship of the proletariat, the role of the state is the repression of the bourgeoisie and the creation of conditions for its own withering away. In Marx's view, nation-states and foreign policies would have no place in the communist era of history, when all peoples would live in harmony.

In Western Europe, Marxism evolved in a different direction than it did in Russia. After the outbreak of World War I, Lenin was prompted to formulate a doctrine on international affairs by developments in international socialist circles—and especially in the Social Democratic Party of Germany (SPD), the largest and best organized Marxist party in the world.

Legalized since 1890 and consistently gaining votes in national elections, the SPD had developed a considerable vested interest in the German state. When Lenin heard that SPD delegates in the German parliament had voted in favor of war credits to the imperial government, he was incredulous. The SPD's leadership had reasoned that since the imperial German state was on the verge of being inherited by the SPD and was under attack by reactionary tsardom, defense of the German state was an act in favor of socialism.

Disappointment with the SPD's stand, and with the attitudes of other parties of the Socialist International that had also supported the war effort, impelled Lenin to publish *Imperialism: The Highest Stage of Capitalism.*[2] A new attempt to justify Marxist internationalism, while at the same time recognizing the revolutionary potential of nationalism in less developed areas, the pamphlet depicted a positive role for international conflict in achieving the new world order. In Lenin's view, war would be the agency to defeat world capitalism, even in countries not yet ripe for socialist revolution. Lenin's theory was based on ideas borrowed from John Hobson and Rudolf Hilferding, to which Lenin added certain practical political conclusions of his own. The theory performed the dual function of explaining why Marx's predictions of the imminent fall of European capitalism had not come to pass, and of justifying the attempt to create the first socialist revolution in Russia, the most backward of major European countries.

Marx had been concerned with the capitalist as an individual entrepreneur, but Lenin sought to show how the system had developed to the point where industrial capital and finance capital had merged—the banks had stepped in as sources of finance for industry. Moreover, capital had been increasingly concentrated through the formation of huge international monopolies, which used their financial power to direct the policies of the bourgeois states. And the policy which they had imposed was imperialism—which Lenin described not merely as a policy but as a stage of capitalist development. In order to stave off the ruin of capitalism, which Marx foresaw as the result of the shrinking of the domestic market, the imperialists had turned to investment in less developed countries, using them not only as a source of raw materials, but more importantly as a market for the investment of surplus finance capital.

Thus whole nations had come to be exploited by the capitalists. Moreover, the system had been further propped up by the device of bribing the proletariat in the imperialist countries—creating a labor aristocracy which acted as partner in the plunder of the colonies, and promoting opportunism and jingoism in the socialist movement. This explained the rise of wages and reduction in class conflict within the major capitalist countries; the class struggle had been transferred to the international arena. The international proletariat now included the oppressed peoples of backward countries, both those that were actually colonies, such as India, and those that were formally independent but economically subservient, such as China.

But this stabilization of the capitalist system was inevitably impermanent, for the major imperialist powers had by the beginning of the twentieth century appropriated to themselves the major non-European areas of the world, and they were struggling among themselves for a redivision of these markets. This struggle would inevitably result in a great imperialist war; in fact, the first world war was such a war, Lenin wrote. The result of this struggle would be the overthrow of capitalism not only in a few advanced countries, but in the whole imperialist system, which was now interconnected. The revolutionary proletariat in Europe—that part which had not sold out to the capitalists—would form an alliance with the peoples of the oppressed countries. Indeed, given the interconnectedness of the system, Lenin argued that it was now likely that the first spark of the revolution would be touched off at the weakest link of the imperialist chain—in Russia—and would quickly spread to the advanced countries. Overthrow of the capitalist system in a country like Russia—a market for investment of French and other European capital—or in a colony like India would inevitably deprive the home country of major and vital markets and provide the economic spark for the downfall of the imperialist system.

This formulation by Lenin assigned importance to elements Marx did not stress; the principle of national liberation became as valid a revolutionary slogan as class struggle. Lenin shifted weight to what Marx saw as a secondary issue—the national issue. The idea that socialists should strive for independence of the colonies would have horrified Marx, who saw the force of, for example, British capital in India as progressive, because it brought industrialization. Likewise, the idea that revolution in backward countries could precede that in more advanced countries was inconceivable to Marx, because it elevated those countries to a higher plane than that to which their stage of historical development entitled them.

Lenin argued that the national problem was the Achilles heel of Britain and France, as well as of the Russian Empire. But he maintained that the problem of national exploitation was essentially economic. Once socialism resolved the problem of economic exploitation, the national problem could be resolved by arrangements such as federalism. Thus nationalism was not a completely independent force in world politics, but it was conditioned by the stage of economic development.

After Lenin, Soviet theorists continued to stress the uneven development of capitalism in the international arena, and the ongoing struggle for redivision of the world. The seeds of capitalist destruction were said to be sown primarily in the international field. The class struggle continued to be fought in the international arena, and peaceful coexistence between the world proletariat and the capitalist world could only be temporary. As a lasting legacy of Lenin's theory of imperialism, Soviet policy-makers continued to demonstrate sensitivity to the common ground between socialist states and underdeveloped countries said to be suffering from imperialist exploitation.

The "Operational Code" and Foreign Policy

In addition to the explicit beliefs and values of Marxism-Leninism, which formed part of the belief system of Soviet (and some post-Soviet) decision-makers, certain characteristic patterns of thought and action exhibited by Lenin and other Bolshevik leaders continued as an "operational code" for their successors. This term is defined by Alexander George as a set of general beliefs about issues of history and questions of politics as these bear on the problem of action—a prism influencing an actor's perceptions and diagnoses of political events, shaping estimates and definitions, and providing norms and guidelines. While not determining the decisions of its adherents, the operational code bounds the alternative ways they perceive and assess the external world.[3]

As originally set forth by Nathan Leites, the operational code sensitizes its followers to certain approaches to establishing control over people and institutions, orienting them toward the objective of mastering any situation. These precepts are based on the assumption that the party is working in a hostile environment, surrounded by internal class enemies or encircled by capitalist states, and that difficulty, danger, and conflict are the norms of political life—as opposed to the Western view that harmony is the natural political state.[4]

Given these assumptions, and the resulting unrelenting hostility to the status quo with its attendant threats from omnipresent enemies, the code dictates that its followers strive to dominate their environment. Lenin stressed organization as the means by which this control is achieved. But he also displayed great willingness to employ whatever means are necessary, while at the same time retaining tactical flexibility. Given the goal of re-making a corrupt and evil society, the code prescribes the use of whatever means will most speedily ensure attainment of the goal. In an immoral world, no means is more immoral than another; the goal is betrayed if political actors restrict their choice of means on moral grounds. In Lenin's words, "Bolshevism stands on the point of view of expediency: We shall support [any other group] depending exclusively on whether or not we should then be able better to strike a blow against our enemy."[5] The Leninist must not be obsessed with morality, for the end justifies any means. As

Trotsky expressed it: "We know that if there are obstacles on the way, they have to be swept away. If this sweeping away of obstacles increases the ruin [of Russia] for a while, then all of this must be rewarded a hundredfold by the policy of economic creativity which the working class must develop after its seizure of power."[6]

The Leninist faces a constant struggle against the tendency to fall into either of two deviations: opportunism—a readiness to adapt too much to the ephemeral conditions of the moment—and sectarianism or dogmatism—becoming so preoccupied with the final goal that one disregards the material obstacles. Official histories of Soviet foreign policy aver that throughout its history the party has steered the correct middle course. But they also reveal another feature of the Bolshevik belief system: there can be at any one moment only one correct policy. The "scientific" element of Marxism-Leninism demands certitude, and intolerance of the suggestion that more than one way might be correct.

Given the assumption of a hostile environment, in which all groups are potential enemies and all means are potentially justifiable, the principle emerges that the only good neighbor is the absolutely controlled neighbor. In establishing that control and in destroying its enemies, the party traditionally seeks to manipulate individuals into conflict with one another, exploiting the contradictions in the enemy camp. Or the party may form temporary alliances with those who share a common enemy. But these alliances are consciously impermanent, based on wariness and distrust, for ultimately the alliance must be broken. Working on the assumption that the other party is operating by the same principles of expediency, Leninists must be sure to destroy their ally before their ally turns on them.

The party must be ready to make temporary retreats in the name of survival, in order to preserve its forces from total destruction. But it must never let up its pressure, even when the enemy appears to be growing weaker. Above all, the Leninist must realize that there can be no permanent balance of power, no lasting compromises. All situations tend toward total victory or total annihilation; one must overtake the adversary or be wiped out. Appeals to conscience or interests cannot reduce hostility; constant pressure rather than reasoned negotiation is the only way to modify the enemy's conduct. In short, as Leites summarizes the operational code, it demands a constant awareness of the question, "*kto-kavo*—who will destroy whom?"[7]

The Role of Ideology in Soviet Foreign Policy

Just as the tsarist foreign policy tradition is one source of the perceptions and behavior of foreign policy decision-makers during the Soviet and post-

Soviet periods, so also the set of influences just discussed—the Russian revolutionary traditions, the writings of Marx and Lenin, and the "operational code"—have had a significant effect on Soviet and post-Soviet policy. Taken together, these influences constitute the ideology known as Marxism-Leninism.

An ideology is a comprehensive and consistent set of beliefs and values which usually begins with a critique of existing reality and a statement of goals, and contains a program for the radical transformation of society and attainment of these goals. As such, ideology consists not merely of an assessment of the situation, but an impulse toward action, toward bringing about the desired change in the situation. An adherent of the Marxist-Leninist ideology is provided both with a set of goals and with a distinctive way of looking at events which, in this case, emphasize the clash of economic classes as the motive force of historical development.

Analysts of Soviet foreign policy have long debated just how large a role ideology played in decision-making.[8] At one extreme are those who argued that on issues of foreign policy the doctrine played no active role in shaping Soviet decisions; it was retained as a rationalization and justification for the rule of the party, but doctrinal pronouncements merely masked calculations based on power considerations or national interest. At the other extreme are those—more often found in the world of statecraft than scholarship—who saw Marxism-Leninism as a blueprint providing explicit guidance to Soviet policy, and who argued that Soviet policy was thereby rendered quite distinctive. Some stressed that as ideology became less operative and relevant on the domestic level, its salience increased on the foreign-policy level.[9] In fact, this debate is highly artificial, since there was no contradiction in the Soviet mind between the demands of ideology and those of national interest. Rather, doctrinal tenets were so long-term and flexible that they could usually be made to conform to the policies which also promoted the national strength of the USSR.

Vernon Aspaturian has identified six functions of ideology: it provides (1) transcendent objectives; (2) an image of the world; (3) an action program; (4) a system of communication; (5) a means of rationalization; and (6) a symbol of continuity and legitimacy for its adherents.[10] The latter three are passive or "after-the-fact" functions, and there would be little disagreement that Marxism-Leninism played these roles in the Soviet period, providing language and symbols pervasively used in the analysis of events, a way of rationalizing actions taken in the international arena, and a symbol for the regime of the legitimacy of the continued rule of the CPSU. With respect to the former three, the more active functions, the extent to which Marxism-Leninism has performed them varies with time, with the actor, and with the circumstances. That is, the degree to which the doctrine functioned as an operative element in the belief system of Soviet leaders varied from individual to individual—often assuming a larger role in the belief systems of older members of the elite and of those who were not specialists in foreign policy—and from regime to regime, as well as with the external situation which was being faced at any given time.

With respect to the objectives of world revolution and establishment of a new type of international relations, the fact that Marxism-Leninism prescribed no strict timetable for their achievement and the conviction that history was on their side made it easier for its adherents to lengthen the time-frame without feeling that they had thereby abandoned the objectives themselves. With respect to the second function, Marxism-Leninism provides an image of the world which heightens the observer's sensitivity to change and conflict and increases attention to economic and class factors in the analysis of events. By affecting the way certain events are perceived or understood, it does not necessarily alter behavior in any particular way. As a guide to action—the third of Aspaturian's "active" functions—it follows from the very imprecision of Marx's and Lenin's pronouncements on the subject of international relations that nothing very concrete can be expected here. Indeed, it is better to think of this function as less of an "action program" and more of a push toward activism.

Content analysis of Soviet policy pronouncements has shown a stronger ideological component in the longer-range and more general statements, and far less influence on the day-to-day decisions.[11] Still, there was enough continuity in the programmatic statements of the Soviet elite to suggest that the ideology consisted of an unchanging doctrinal core together with an action program which was subject to revision and sensitive to change. Thus ideology can be seen as being at the same time both "principled" and "expedient," and the "creative interpretation" of Marxism-Leninism by Soviet leaders in the light of changed circumstances need not be viewed as either cynical manipulation or as abandonment, but rather as a mark of the importance of the doctrine, impelling the leaders to take great care in revising it.

It is entirely in the Leninist tradition to modify the action program or to discard tactics or instruments which are felt to have outlived their usefulness; flexibility is an inherent component of Leninism. But the Soviet party's leadership reserved to itself the right to restate and reinterpret doctrine, not only for itself, but for the entire world communist movement. The party leader who sought to establish his authority attempted to be seen as a learned ideologist, since a challenge to a leader cloaked in priestly robes was seen as a challenge to the sacred mission of the party itself.

The Establishment of Soviet Power

The previous chapter has already noted the debilitating effects that World War I and its attendant economic and social dislocations had upon the tsarist regime. The revolution that forced the abdication of Tsar Nicholas II occurred unexpectedly and spontaneously in March 1917 (February by the Julian calendar then used in Russia). Bread riots and strikes broke out in Petrograd (a more Russianized version of the capital's name, used during the war), and these escalated into a full-scale general strike and mutiny of soldiers in the capital garrison. After the fall of the tsar, institutions reflecting the bifurcation between the middle classes and the masses—the so-called "dual power" of the Duma (parliament) and a Provisional Government on the one hand and the Soviets of Workers' and Soldiers' Deputies on the other—coexisted uneasily for the next seven months.

Lenin was in exile in Switzerland at the time of the March revolution, and did not manage to get back to Petrograd until April 16, arriving—as documents long suppressed now establish—in a sealed railway car traveling with German assistance. Before his arrival, Bolshevik leaders were cooperating with the new dual power, and not seeking to seize power on their own. Thus they were shocked when he informed them that the first stage of the revolution had already been completed, and that the time was ripe for the establishment of the dictatorship of the proletariat. This entailed repudiation of the Provisional Government ("all power to the soviets"), seizure of power by the proletariat and poor peasants, and abolition of the institutions of police, army, and bureaucracy. Lenin's plan, initially rejected by the party's Petrograd Committee, was adopted in May.

A July demonstration against the government, now headed by Alexander Kerensky, started spontaneously but was subsequently directed by the Bolsheviks. However, it soon passed out of their control, and Lenin fled the capital to escape arrest. The threat of a Bolshevik takeover contributed to the attempt of the conservative aristocracy and military forces, under the leadership of General Lavr Kornilov, to stage a coup—the failure of which only strengthened Bolshevik popularity and helped them to win majorities in the Petrograd and Moscow soviets.

This gain in strength, together with rising peasant unrest precipitated by Kerensky's refusal to allow the peasantry to seize land from its owners, produced what Lenin perceived as a "revolutionary situation." By late September, he began to urge the Bolsheviks to seize power without waiting for scheduled elections to a Constituent Assembly. Again, there was resistance in the party, and only on October 23 did Lenin's plan command a majority. The Bolsheviks' military muscle was centered in the Military Revolutionary

Committee of the Petrograd Soviet, under Trotsky's command, together with several strategically placed units of sailors and soldiers loyal to the Bolsheviks. On November 6–7 these forces managed to capture Petrograd, meeting with surprisingly little resistance.

Having gained a majority in the Second All-Russian Congress of Soviets (after their conduct provoked a walkout of more moderate delegates), the Bolsheviks proceeded to establish as the new governing body of Russia a Council of People's Commissars (known by the acronym Sovnarkom), which was nominally responsible to the Congress of Soviets. Lenin was appointed chairman of the council (equivalent to prime minister); Trotsky, commissar of foreign affairs; and Joseph Stalin, commissar of nationalities.

The true extent of Bolshevik popularity outside of the largest cities was revealed in December, when elections to the Constituent Assembly were held. The Bolsheviks obtained only 25 percent of the votes, and when the assembly convened in January, it was dissolved after only one session. The soviets were turned into organs controlled by the Bolshevik party and withered into insignificance, and by 1922 all competing political parties had been formally proscribed.

As one of their "campaign promises," which had proved especially effective in hastening the demoralization of the armed forces, the Bolsheviks had promised to end Russia's involvement in World War I. Accordingly, the first act of the Soviet state—taken on November 8, just one day after the Bolsheviks' seizure of power—was the issuance of a Decree on Peace, approved by the Second All-Russian Congress of Soviets. Addressed to "all warring peoples and governments," it proposed the conclusion of a just and democratic peace, without annexations or indemnities. The intended targets of the document were the mass publics of the "imperialist powers"; one section appealed particularly to the "class-conscious workers" of England, France, and Germany to liberate humanity from the horrors of war and to liberate the masses from all exploitation.

But the decree failed to produce either peace or revolution. Having received no reply from other governments, Trotsky appealed to Germany for a cease-fire. Negotiations began November 27 in the eastern front headquarters of the German army in Brest-Litovsk.[12] The Germans offered a cease-fire of twenty-eight days, to be automatically renewed unless either side gave a week's notice, with an agreement that both armies would stand in position. (In fact, many German troops had already been transferred to the western front.) They acceded to a Bolshevik request for fraternization of troops and mutual dissemination of newspapers.

The armistice was signed on December 15, and five days later a conference was assembled to draft a treaty of peace. The initial German position agreed to the principles of no annexations and no indemnities as the basis for a general peace, if Russia's allies would agree. The Russians were elated, thinking that this meant that Poland and Lithuania would be returned to them, and they were crushed when a German draft revealed Berlin's position that the people of these territories had already expressed their will to withdraw voluntarily from the Russian Empire and accept a protected status within the German empire. While brandishing the threat of a separate peace with the Central Powers, Lenin and Trotsky were trying to persuade the Entente to accept a general peace, urging the workers to take the initiative if their governments failed to do so. At the same time, secret discussions with unofficial emissaries of Britain, France, and the United States considered the possibility that Russia would get allied support to break off its talks and renew war with the Germans—who had now made it clear that the price of peace, cloaked as "self-determination" rather than annexation, included Poland and much of the Baltic states.

The dissolution of the Constituent Assembly and Lenin's proclamation of the "public liquidation of formal democracy in the name of revolutionary dictatorship" had done further damage to the Bolsheviks' image in Western Europe, where they were already suspected of being German agents. Trotsky devised a plan to demonstrate to the proletariat of Europe the fundamental enmity between Germany and the Bolsheviks. His proposed formula—"we shall stop the war, but we shall not sign the peace treaty"—would put to the test Germany's willingness to resume the war. If they failed to do so, it would be a victory for Russia; if they did, the Bolsheviks would demonstrably capitulate at the point of a bayonet rather than willingly. Lenin argued for accepting the German terms in order to buy time for the Bolsheviks to consolidate their position in Russia, while allowing the two imperialist blocs to destroy each other in continued war. The majority of his colleagues, led by Bukharin, were persuaded by their own propaganda into believing that Europe's workers were ripe for revolution, and they pressed for the Russians to take up arms in the name of revolutionary war. Believing that the dangers in such a war exceeded the risk of harsher peace terms that Trotsky's plan entailed, Lenin agreed to give Trotsky's formula a try, in return for his promise not to later argue for revolutionary war.

On February 10 Trotsky, conducting the peace talks for the Russian side as a public prosecution of German imperialism, unveiled to his unbelieving audience his "no war, no peace" position and withdrew the Bolshevik delegation from the talks. Eight days later, portraying themselves as the saviors of civilization from Bolshevism, the Germans resumed their offensive. Meeting no resistance, their armies crossed 150 miles in five days. Lenin's acceptance of Germany's original peace terms was ignored; new and harsher terms were demanded on February 23. By these terms, the line of Russian non-control was shifted eastward, to include Poland, Lithuania, Latvia, Estonia, Finland, and Ukraine. Russia was to renounce interference in these territories, whose future would be determined by Germany and Austria in agreement with their populations. Additional territories in the Caucasus were to be ceded to Turkey. Together, the lost territories included 34 percent of the population of the Russian Empire, 32 percent of its agricultural land, and 54 percent of its industry. In addition to these losses, Russia was to pay a large indemnity to Germany for the costs of caring for its prisoners of war.

Outraged, most of the Bolshevik leaders again called for revolutionary war against Germany. Threatening resignation, Lenin argued that either the regime must sign the German terms, or it would be signing its own death warrant. The only way to save the world revolution was to hold onto its only foothold, Soviet Russia, even under such shameful conditions. The Russian proletariat had triumphed with relative ease, because it had confronted a rotten regime. The victory of the European proletariat would be harder to achieve, because its internal enemies were stronger, but that victory would come—and must come, if the Russian revolution was to be saved. In the meantime, Lenin told the Congress of Soviets, survival of the revolution required signing the peace: "No matter how brief, harsh and humiliating the peace may be, it is better than war, because it gives the masses a breathing space. . . . Everybody who looks reality in the face and does not deceive himself with a revolutionary phrase will agree with this."[13]

To the consternation of the diplomats of the Central Powers, who preferred not to appear to be dictating terms, a Russian delegate returned to Brest-Litovsk on March 3 and signed the treaty without discussion. Although the Congress of Soviets gave its approval, Lenin and his colleagues were denounced as traitors. The German ambassador was assassinated by members of the Left Socialist Revolutionary party, who later tried to shoot Lenin himself—an incident that led to the unleashing of the Red Terror.

Although Lenin had agreed that the Soviet government would desist from propaganda among the German troops, he later declared that he could not be held responsible for what the Bolshevik party chose to do. Indeed, propaganda was so widespread that the German eastern front commander complained that his army had become "rotten with Bolshevism." This factor, together with the need to utilize large numbers of troops to keep control of areas taken from Russia, prevented the Germans from transferring troops that might have turned the tide on the western front. On the home front, the new Soviet Embassy in Berlin became the headquarters for German revolutionary forces—not the last time that Soviet diplomats were plotting to overthrow the government to which they were accredited. On November 5 the "accidental" opening in the Berlin railway station of a Soviet trunk containing insurrectionary documents led to the expulsion of the Russian ambassador and his staff. Four days later, the Bolsheviks annulled the Treaty of Brest-Litovsk, which the Germans were also required to renounce in their surrender at Compiegne on November 11.

This episode in early Soviet foreign policy tells a great deal about what was to come. It marked an end to the age of innocence for the Bolsheviks in the international arena, and it constituted the first step in the establishment of the "socialism in one country" doctrine—the belief that Soviet socialism could be constructed even without the assistance of the European proletariat. For Lenin, signing the Treaty of Brest-Litovsk was not a betrayal of world revolution in favor of the Russian state, nor was it a choice between ideology and national interest. In his mind, these two were so interlinked that they could not be viewed as mutually exclusive. The flexibility of Leninism was revealed in Lenin's belief that power relations would change and losses could be undone; a temporary capitulation, buying time to exploit contradictions in the enemy's camp, could have the result that the Soviets would later be in a stronger position to promote their objectives. The case also illustrates the Bolshevik diplomatic style, which has been termed "demonstrative diplomacy"—using negotiations as a propaganda forum, to appeal over the heads of diplomats and directly to their peoples.

The collapse of the Brest-Litovsk arrangement and of the German threat did not, however, ensure the survival of the Bolshevik regime. A new threat of civil war, complicated by the intervention of Allied forces, continued to call it into question. The initial Allied intervention, designed to keep eastern front pressure on the Germans and safeguard Allied military supplies, received the tacit assent of the Bolsheviks. But in the summer of 1918 the intervention assumed an anti-Bolshevik tinge, as the larger Allied forces began to support rival parties who pledged to bring Russia back into the war. By the spring of 1919 British, French, U.S., and Japanese troops were openly cooperating with the White armies in the civil war, in hopes of putting an end to Bolshevism altogether. To make matters worse, an attempted proletarian revolution in Germany was crushed and its communist leaders were murdered, while short-lived Soviet-style regimes in Bavaria and Hungary were put down.

In the midst of these events, Lenin reported to the Eighth Party Congress on the prospects facing the new Soviet state. Consistent with the operational code's certainty that one side or the other must triumph, Lenin made a statement on the inevitability of war between Soviet Russia and the imperialists that was to be often quoted by his successors:

We are living not merely in a state but *in a system of states* and the existence of the Soviet Republic side by side with imperialist states for a long time is unthinkable. One or the other must triumph in the end. And before that end supervenes, a series of frightful collisions between the Soviet Republic and the bourgeois states will be inevitable. That means that if the ruling class, the proletariat, wants to hold sway it must prove its capacity to do so by its military organization.[14]

In 1920 Polish efforts to intervene in Ukraine in quest of territory led to war between Poland and Russia. Early successes of the Red Army brought it to the gates of Warsaw, again raising hopes that European revolution would result. But military disaster befell the Russians, and they were forced, in the Treaty of Riga in March 1921, to cede parts of Ukraine and Belorussia to Poland. The same month witnessed the March Action in Germany—another failed attempt at revolution. Nevertheless, by the end of 1921—despite the absence of outside assistance and due in part to the disunity of their opponents—the Civil War had ended, the Allied intervention had been liquidated, and the Bolsheviks had managed to establish their control over most of the tsarist patrimony. While their survival in isolation was a result they could never have imagined in 1917, the continuous experience of threats, both from internal "counter-revolutionaries" and from outside "imperialist" powers, amply confirmed pre-existing expectations on the part of the Bolsheviks regarding the need for vigilance and caution in dealing with the omnipresent enemy.

Russia and the West in the 1920s

Although the Russian communist regime had survived, the situation in which it found itself in 1921 was by no means comforting. In March sailors at the Kronstadt naval base had demonstrated in favor of democratization. The rebellion was crushed, and the dictatorship was further tightened, as all organized factions within the communist party were banned. Political and social unrest were exacerbated by severe economic dislocation. Large parts of the country were experiencing famine, resulting from civil war policies of forced requisition of grain from the peasantry. Industry was disorganized and badly in need of capital equipment.

Lenin's answer to this crisis was the New Economic Policy, which represented a retreat from socialist economics. The peasants were given greater freedom, and private trade and private ownership of small business were again legalized. But economic recovery could not be accomplished without obtaining capital and trade from the outside world, i.e., the capitalists. This, in turn, required that the Soviet regime overcome its virtually complete diplomatic isolation. In response to the logical question, "Why should the capitalists help the recovery of the Russian economy?" Lenin argued that, while the capitalists had not changed their stripes and could resume hostile intervention at any time, they were so economically bound up with Russia that they could not properly calculate their own interests. As Bolshevik leader Lev Kamenev so graphically expressed it, "We are convinced that the foreign capitalists, who will be obliged to work on the terms we offer them, will dig their own grave."[15]

The search for peaceful businesslike relations with the outside world— the assigned priority of the People's Commissariat of Foreign Affairs (Narkomindel)—was made more difficult by the parallel existence of the Communist International (Comintern), which was appealing to the revolutionary masses to overthrow the very governments with which Soviet diplomats were attempting to deal. Although the Soviets tried to maintain the fiction that the Comintern was simply housed in Moscow and operated independently of the Soviet government, in fact from its beginning in 1919 it was tightly controlled by the Soviet communist party. Trotsky (who had resigned as foreign minister just prior to the signing of the Treaty of Brest-Litovsk) had been succeeded by Georgii Chicherin, who was handicapped by the fact that his rank in the party was much lower than that of Grigorii Zinoviev, the head of the Comintern and one of Lenin's closest associates. Indicators of the lowly stature of the Narkomindel in the 1920s could be found not only in its constant conflict with the Comintern over control of Soviet embassies, but also in the fact that on occasion the party Politburo would deal directly with foreign affairs, bypassing Chicherin's foreign office altogether.

Foreign policy during this period was further complicated by the internal political struggle over the succession to Lenin, who suffered a stroke in 1922 and died in 1924. Of special significance was the dispute between Stalin and Trotsky on the possibility of building "socialism in one country"—a debate often misunderstood as posing an extreme choice between concentration of all resources on promoting the world revolution, or abandonment of world revolution in favor of the narrow pursuit of national interests. In fact, both agreed that the building of socialism could begin in Russia alone. But Stalin was insisting that the process could be completed in one country, whereas Trotsky argued that it could not be completed without the aid of the world revolution. In effect, there were two differing meanings of "socialism," with Stalin using Lenin's definition ("Soviet state power plus electrification"), and Trotsky adding qualities of refinement and civilization. Trotsky's followers tended to be more cosmopolitan and to have greater international experience, whereas Stalin was making a calculated appeal to the party and state bureaucracy, which had a vested interest in consolidating domestic power.

Stalin's formula did not amount to casting out world revolution altogether; he averred that the construction of socialism could not be "final" as long as the Soviet Union remained encircled by capitalism. The building of Soviet state power, he argued, was in the ultimate interest of world revolution. As Stalin expressed it in his report to the Fourteenth Party Congress in December 1925: "our struggle in our country, the struggle for the victory of the socialist elements in our country over the capitalist elements, our struggle in the work of construction, is also of international significance, for our country is the base of the international revolution, for our country is the principal lever for expanding the international revolutionary movement."[16] By 1929 Stalin was able to carry this perspective to its inevitable conclusion: that the world revolutionary movement in fact now existed primarily as an aid to the achievement of Soviet foreign policy requirements: "An internationalist is one who unreservedly, unhesitatingly, and unconditionally is prepared to defend the USSR, because the USSR is the base of the world revolutionary movement, and it is impossible to defend or advance the world revolutionary movement without defending the USSR."[17]

The strains in Soviet policy were fully evidenced in the regime's relations with the West in the 1920s. The first country to accept Lenin's offer of trade was Britain, and the Anglo-Soviet Trade Agreement of 1921 included Britain's *de facto* recognition of the Soviet regime. But the major impediment in expansion of Soviet economic relations with Western Europe was the issue of tsarist debts, which the Soviets were willing to honor only in part and only in return for credits. The Genoa Economic Conference in 1922 constituted an effort on the part of the major powers to present a united front to the Soviets on the issue of debts and to the Germans on the issue of reparations. At the conference, Chicherin brilliantly played the Germans against the British and French. The resulting Treaty of Rapallo, between Soviet Russia and Germany, as a combination of the two outcasts on the European stage, included a mutual renunciation of claims and *de jure* recognition of the Soviet regime. In fact, the treaty only strengthened a relationship which had begun in 1920, with a secret pact by which the Germans were allowed to circumvent Versailles treaty restrictions by testing weapons on Soviet soil, in return for assisting in Soviet military development.

The Narkomindel's efforts to develop relationships with Germany and Britain were seriously threatened by Comintern activities, including its support of an armed uprising instigated by German communists in 1923 and its conduct of anti-imperialist propaganda in the British colonies. The atmosphere was such that the discovery of an alleged (and probably forged) letter from Zinoviev to the British communists calling for revolutionary actions led to the defeat of a new Anglo-Russian trade treaty and to the fall of the Labour government. A raid by British authorities in 1927 on the Soviet trade delegation led to a total break in diplomatic relations between the two states. In the meantime, Soviet efforts to forestall a united capitalist front against them were frustrated by the Dawes Plan for easing Germany's reparations burden and the Locarno Treaty, which guaranteed Germany's western borders and allowed her entry into the League of Nations. Consequently, by 1927 the Soviet Union was again experiencing general isolation in Europe.

The Soviets Turn to the East

Unlike its policies in Europe, the Soviet regime's diplomatic and revolutionary activities in Asia in the 1920s were coordinated, as it allied itself with nationalist forces in the struggle against imperialism. In part, this was a continuation of the old Anglo-Russian rivalry in Asia, though it had been restated by Lenin in ideological terms. But the Soviets faced a practical problem in attempting to formulate an operational strategy based on Lenin's sensitivity to the community of interests between the peoples of the oppressed countries and the international proletariat. The difficulty arose in part because of the intractability of Asian social forces to the Marxist categories of analysis, and in part because of the intrusion of the succession struggle into Soviet policy-making.

The Soviets briefly flirted in 1919–20 with the notion of an assault on British-held India, through Afghanistan, reminiscent of three abortive plans during the tsarist period. In the fall of 1920, Lenin approved the plan of Indian communist M.N. Roy to train an army of Indian revolutionaries at Tashkent, where they would form a joint force with Soviet troops, passing through Afghanistan to the Indian frontier, and declaring a revolutionary government. Two trainloads of arms and bullion were supplied, and a number of Indians were trained, but the plan was torpedoed by British pressure, both on the Afghan king and on the Soviets, who were threatened with a rupture of trade relations unless the Tashkent school was disbanded.

This same M.N. Roy had been a major participant in a discussion, at the Second Comintern Congress in July 1920, about communist strategy in the East. He had argued against Lenin that the first priority of the Comintern should be liberation of the colonies and semi-colonies, since these were the mainstay of the imperialist system. And he had challenged Lenin's thesis that a class-based revolutionary struggle would fail, and that Asian communists needed to subordinate the struggle for socialism and instead cooperate in a united front with "bourgeois nationalists," such as Mohandas Gandhi and Sun Yat-sen, who were leading the independence movements in their countries. Lenin and Roy had agreed that once they had achieved their independence, and given the support of the proletariat of more advanced countries, Asian, African, and Latin American countries could bypass the capitalist stage of development and move rapidly toward socialism.[18]

The Soviets were active in the early 1920s in supporting nationalist and anti-British tendencies among three Muslim states on their southern border: Turkey, Iran, and Afghanistan. Under a treaty of friendship signed with Ataturk's Turkey in 1921, they extended military aid to the nationalist regime, even though it was persecuting Turkish communists. Treaties of friendship were also concluded in 1921 with Iran and Afghanistan, as those countries were able to subordinate their longstanding border rivalries and their irritation with activities of the Comintern to the need for Soviet support against the British. In 1925 a neutrality pact with Turkey was the first instance in which the Soviet Union extended technical and economic assistance to a less developed country. Relations with Turkey continued to be reasonably good until 1939, when the Soviets rekindled the traditional Russian ambitions toward the straits.

The most extensive Soviet anti-imperialist investment in Asia in the 1920s was in China, whose internal political weakness made it a tempting target for European and Japanese designs, thereby posing a threat to the Soviet Far East. This traditional Russian interest in excluding hostile powers from a weak China converged with the Marxist-Leninist impulse to strike a blow at imperialism by liberating China from its control. The dilemma for Moscow again lay in the potential contradiction between the dual objectives of national liberation and internal socialist revolution, for it was precisely the feudal and bourgeois "oppressing classes" who headed the anti-imperialist movement in China. The strategy by which the Soviets proposed to overcome the dilemma called for supporting the nationalist movement (Kuomintang) against the imperialists and their puppet government in Beijing, while assisting the Chinese communists in penetrating and assuming control over the Kuomintang. The strategy was further complicated by the fact that the Soviets were also dealing with the Beijing government, signing a treaty in 1924 that established diplomatic relations, joint management of the Chinese Eastern Railway, and Soviet withdrawal from Outer Mongolia (where they were quickly replaced by pro-Soviet Mongolian forces).

The Chinese Communist Party (CCP), founded in 1921, was regarded by the Comintern leadership as too weak to lead the anti-imperialist and anti-feudal revolution in China. Its members were instructed to join the

Kuomintang but to preserve their freedom of action, exposing the compromises of its leadership, even while the Soviet government and the Comintern supported the Kuomintang in its struggle against imperialism. Once it had served its purpose, Stalin reasoned, the Kuomintang "would be squeezed out like a lemon and then thrown away."[19]

In accord with an agreement in 1923 between the Soviet diplomat Adolph Joffe and Sun Yat-sen, the Kuomintang leadership was trained by the Soviets in political organization and military tactics. After Sun's death in 1925, one of the products of Soviet training, General Chiang Kai-shek, took over the Kuomintang leadership, and by the following year was ousting communists from key positions they had won in the organization. Despite the Chinese communists' pleas that they be allowed to withdraw, Stalin ordered them to stay in the Kuomintang, while seeking to achieve control over it. Chiang Kai-shek's northern expedition in 1926–27 brought his forces to the gates of Shanghai, a communist stronghold. The communists rose up and defeated the anti-Kuomintang forces controlling the city. Chiang waited until this was completed and then marched into the city and slaughtered the communists.

Stalin's strategy in China was under heavy fire from Trotsky, who had advocated that the CCP abandon the Kuomintang and form revolutionary soviets. Loath to admit that his policy was mistaken, Stalin still did not allow a total break, ordering the CCP to seek hegemony over the left wing of the Kuomintang, centered in Wuhan. When these forces also turned on the communists, Stalin refused to allow the CCP to concentrate on building up its support among the peasantry, arguing that they must instead prepare for an uprising of the industrial proletariat. In December 1927, needing a victory to display to the crucial Fifteenth Party Congress, Stalin ordered an uprising in Canton. It lasted long enough for Stalin to be able to claim success for his strategy, but then it collapsed, and with it, the urban base of the Chinese communists.

This experience not only destroyed the prospect of friendly relations between the USSR and the government of Chiang Kai-shek, but it also left a residue of bitterness between Stalin and Chinese communist leader Mao Zedong. No less important was the effect of Stalin's failure in China on his future perception of Asian revolutions. Having so focused his energies on the Chinese revolution, to the exclusion of other national-liberation movements, Stalin reacted to his defeat by refusing to reinvest Soviet energies and resources in another Asian revolution. For him, the "lessons of China" precluded cooperation with unreliable Asian nationalists, leaving the Soviets relatively inactive just at the time when anti-imperialist movements were heating up in India and Southeast Asia.

Changing Soviet Policy, 1928–38

The relative isolation of the Soviet regime in the late 1920s and early 1930s was a result not only of diplomatic rebuffs in Europe and revolutionary failures in China, but of internal developments as well—the decision to embark upon the "third revolution," featuring rapid industrialization and collectivization of the peasantry. Concentration on development of the economy, perceived in part as necessary for building military power, required a period of relative peace in Soviet foreign relations. For one thing, the Soviets needed to expand foreign trade and short-term credits. They sought to increase exports sharply, selling anything for which there was a foreign market, without regard to internal demand, in order to get the currency necessary to import heavy machinery. For another, they needed to avoid external adventures at a time of severe internal strain and weakness, when the regime was conducting a virtual war on the peasant majority of its population.

The militant tone of Soviet policy during this period, and the assessment of the international situation which lay behind it, bore the distinctive imprint of Joseph Stalin. In 1928 he announced that the "temporary stabilization of capitalism," which Lenin had declared in 1921, had come to an end, to be replaced by a period of revolutionary upheaval in the capitalist countries and their colonies. Moreover, the capitalists were said to be preparing a new offensive against the USSR. To help ward off this attack, the proletariat of the world must strike a blow against imperialism by concentrating its fire on the social democrats and on the national bourgeoisie in the colonies, and by taking the place of these elements in the leadership of mass movements. This militant isolationism was understandable only in terms of Stalin's perceptions of his domestic political needs. Having defeated Trotsky and his allies, he was now seeking to discredit Nikolai Bukharin, who had become identified with the policy of cooperating with European socialist parties. The Sixth Congress of the Comintern in 1928 issued the directive to foreign communists to switch from a "united front from above" strategy, in which the communist party was organizationally allied with socialist and nationalist parties, to a "united front from below," in which cooperation ended, and efforts were made to win over the followers of these parties. In this strategy, the "main enemy" was said to be the erstwhile allies on the left.

The most dramatic illustration of the effect of this policy is in the equanimity with which the Comintern and the German Communist Party (KPD) viewed the paralysis of the Weimar Republic and the rise of Hitler. They saw no immediate dangers, but rather thought the Nazis would be useful in helping to destroy the parliamentary illusions of the German masses. Initiated with the collapse of the empire and cursed with the stigma of national shame in defeat, Weimar never acquired legitimacy with the German public. With six million unemployed by 1931, Germany's lower middle class was dispossessed by the Great Depression, creating an anti-regime majority of rightists and leftists. As a member of the governing coalition, the German Social Democratic Party (SPD) was appealing to the communists for common action against the Nazis. But the KPD tactics, set by the Sixth Comintern Congress, portrayed the SPD as the *real* fascist beast. The communists celebrated every Nazi gain, believing that Hitler's victory would close the chapter on capitalism and social democracy and would open the way to communist rule.

The Nazi victory in March 1933 led to Hitler's appointment as German chancellor. Even after the Reichstag fire resulted in the banning of the KPD and arrest of its leaders, the Comintern continued to declare that the proletarian revolution was drawing nearer. Soviet foreign policy called for a continuation of military and political cooperation, in the spirit of Rapallo. In December 1933 the new Soviet foreign minister, Maksim Litvinov, said that Hitler's anti-Soviet speeches and his attacks on German communists would not deter the USSR: "We are, of course, sensitive to the sufferings of our German comrades, but we Marxists are the last who can be reproached for permitting our feelings to dictate our policy."[20] In his remarks to the Seventeenth Party Congress the following month, Stalin criticized the attitude of the German regime, but he was no friendlier to the Western capitalists, declaring, "Our orientation in the past and our orientation at the present time is toward the USSR, and toward the USSR alone."[21]

Despite the militant isolationism of 1928–33, the USSR had not been totally inactive on the diplomatic front. In 1928 it had signed the Kellogg-Briand Pact outlawing war as an instrument of policy, and the following year it had formulated with its neighbors the Litvinov Protocol—a reaffirmation of the treaty's terms within the specific region of Eastern Europe. In 1932 the Soviets signed nonaggression pacts with Poland, Finland, Latvia, Estonia, and France, and subsequently advertised their search (ultimately unsuccessful) for an "Eastern Locarno"—a guarantee of Germany's eastern borders.

But at this point the seemingly greater threat to Soviet security was in the Far East, where Japan had invaded Manchuria in 1931. Trying to keep the Japanese pointed away from Soviet territory, the Soviets offered Tokyo a nonaggression treaty and hinted at their willingness to sell the Chinese Eastern Railway (for the control of which they had fought a war with China in 1929) to the Japanese puppet regime of Manchukuo. The Japanese declaration of war on China in 1932 came as a huge relief to the Soviet Union.

Far from being pleased that their predictions of imminent imperialist collapse and proletarian victory were being borne out as international instability increased and war clouds approached, the Soviets instead perceived danger to their own security. Their greatest fear was that the capitalist powers would encourage rising German and Japanese militarism to turn toward the Soviet Union. To ensure that this would not happen, Litvinov became the most vocal advocate of disarmament and collective security. In May 1935 the Soviet Union signed treaties with both France and Czechoslovakia. The former lacked specific military provisions, such as had been contained in the Franco-Russian entente of 1891, and was intended by Moscow primarily to deny to Hitler French support or neutrality for a move against the Soviets. Likewise, the latter treaty obligated the Soviets to assist Prague only if the French also gave assistance.

This collective security policy was supplemented by a reversal in Comintern policy. The Seventh Comintern Congress in August 1935 prescribed a Popular Front policy, calling for containment of fascism through electoral alliances between communists and bourgeois and socialist parties. It also sanctioned renewed collaboration between the CCP and the Kuomintang in the struggle against Japan.

But the failure of the League of Nations to punish aggression in Manchuria or Ethiopia or to prevent Hitler's reoccupation and remilitarization of the Rhineland reawakened Soviet fears of the softness of the Western powers and their suspicions that they would try to turn Nazi aggression in Moscow's direction. When Austria was invaded in March 1938 and incorporated into the Third Reich, the West failed to act. Litvinov warned that Czechoslovakia was next, and he called for an international conference. But the USSR was not even invited to the Munich Conference in September. Although the Soviets claimed that they were willing to help the Czechs, the Poles and Romanians refused passage to Soviet troops, and the French declined to take military action. With appeasement a popular slogan, collective security was effectively dead, and the Soviets became obsessed with the need to stay out of impending conflict. For, in fact, the Soviet Union could not have been more unprepared for war. Bloody purges in 1934–38 had decimated both the party leadership and the top ranks of the military, as Stalin sought to remove all possible internal opposition to his rule. Their unintended effect was to convince both Hitler and the Western powers of the USSR's internal weakness.

Nazi–Soviet Cooperation, 1939–41

This period provides one of the best studies of Stalin's diplomatic style and of his ability to reconcile doctrinal perceptions with the interests of safeguarding the Soviet state. In 1939 he turned a desperate situation into an apparent diplomatic coup, only to have the situation reverse itself two years later.

The negotiations that produced the Nazi-Soviet Pact proceeded in two phases: a protracted period between the Munich Conference and late July 1939, during which the USSR, Britain, France, and Germany were continuously feeling one another out, followed by a dramatic month in which agreement between Hitler and Stalin was rapidly hammered out. At the opening of the first phase, the Soviets sent signals that they were determined not to have to face Hitler alone, and that they were seeking incentives to make a deal with whichever side would offer the greater assurance to their security. In the fall of 1938, the Soviet press dropped its earlier distinctions between the fascists and the Western democracies. The Soviets began referring to the coming conflict as the "second imperialist war"—a clear sign that they had no intention of being a party to it.

Stalin's report to the Eighteenth Party Congress in March 1939 opened the door to the possibility of improved relations with Germany. He characterized the British and French as "egging on and encouraging the aggressor" and warned that he would "not allow our country to be drawn into conflict by warmongers who are accustomed to have others pull the chestnuts out of the fire for them."[22] At the end of that month, the situation changed fundamentally when British Prime Minister Neville Chamberlain followed Hitler's violation of the Munich accords with a unilateral British guarantee of Polish security. This seemed to remove the risk that Poland would be attacked by Hitler with impunity—a possibility that posed the greatest danger to Moscow, since it could bring an aggressive and unopposed Nazi army to the very borders of the USSR.

Now, after the British action, Stalin was the arbiter of the situation. The British needed his support so that Hitler would be dissuaded from attacking Poland, or to gain an ally if he attacked anyway. But Hitler could now use an agreement with Russia in order to dissuade Britain from honoring its guarantee to Poland, or at least—if the British honored their guarantee—to avoid a two-front war. Stalin's greatest objective was to stay out of war, preferably while Hitler and the West were locked in a protracted battle; but at the least he needed not to have to fight Hitler alone. The British guarantee to Poland indirectly provided a guarantee to the USSR as well, since any German attack on the Soviets would have to pass through Poland. And Stalin suspected that if he were to cast his lot in a formal agreement with the British, they would leave Poland in the lurch with another Munich, leaving only the Soviets in danger. Nevertheless, talks proceeded between the Soviets and the British and French, in part to allow Stalin an opportunity to assess the likelihood that the West would indeed fight for Poland.

Stalin's other alternative—a deal with Hitler—would allow the Germans to buy Russia's neutrality at the price of giving Stalin a free hand in eastern Europe. Stalin's hints of availability included the dismissal of Litvinov, who was not only identified as an advocate of collective security against fascism, but was also a Jew. His replacement was V.M. Molotov, a member of the Politburo, who was known for his absolute subservience to Stalin. This signal, Hitler later told his generals, was decisive—"it came to me like a cannon shot as a sign of change in Moscow."[23]

On July 26 three lower-level officials met in a Berlin restaurant to discuss the specifics of a Nazi-Soviet agreement. The German assured the Russians that "there was no problem between these two countries from the Baltic to the Black Sea or in the Far East that could not be solved."[24] Over the next month, as Hitler's deadline for the attack on Poland neared, Molotov teased the German diplomats, insisting on caution. Finally, on August 20 Hitler telegraphed Stalin urging that Foreign Minister Joachim von Ribbentrop be allowed to proceed to Moscow to complete negotiations. When the German arrived, he found himself negotiating directly with Stalin.

The resulting treaty provided that if either Germany or the Soviet Union were to become involved in a war with a third country, the other would remain neutral. Although it was termed a "pact of nonaggression," the treaty omitted the usual stipulation that if one of the parties should commit an act of aggression against a third party, the other would be entitled to renounce the pact. It also omitted the standard procedures for ratification. These were clear signs that it was in fact intended to be a pact facilitating aggression. A secret protocol delimited the boundary of the two parties' spheres of influence in Eastern Europe "in the event of a territorial and political rearrangement." The northern border of Lithuania was to be the boundary in the Baltic area; Poland was to be partitioned; in southeastern Europe "attention is called by the Soviet side to its interest in Bessarabia. The German side declares its complete political disinterestedness in these areas."[25]

Stalin was evidently pleased with what seemed to be a perfect situation for the USSR: the capitalists would exhaust themselves in a long and bloody war, while the Soviets remained aloof, with a free hand in territories long separated from the Russian Empire. Moreover, the pact with Hitler allowed an easing of tensions in the Soviet Far East, where Soviet and Japanese troops had been fighting an undeclared war all summer. Hitler was eager for Japan to concentrate its energies on British and U.S. possessions in Asia and the Pacific, and evidently encouraged an armistice between the USSR and Japan, which was signed in mid-September.

Hitler's armies crushed Poland in a matter of days. Stalin, not wanting to share the blame for the aggression, delayed occupying the assigned Soviet sphere. When Russian troops finally moved into Poland, the Soviet communiqué, devoid of Marxist pretexts, could have been issued by Catherine the Great. It spoke of the disintegration of the Polish state, "now a suitable field for all manner of hazards," creating a "need to aid kindred Ukrainian and Belorussian peoples who are left defenseless."[26] Von Ribbentrop returned to Moscow at the end of September to sign a Treaty of Friendship and to revise the secret protocol, transferring Lithuania to the Soviet sphere and moving the German line of control eastward in Poland. In a significant demonstration of Stalin's willingness to be a useful partner to Hitler, trade agreements were also concluded. They helped Germany to break the British blockade by providing for critical raw materials to be sent from the USSR in return for German manufactured goods and weapons plans. By June 1940, 22 percent of German imports—many of them critical to the war effort—were coming from or through the Soviet Union.

Although the British and French had declared war on Germany, they had launched no offensive, and the German and Soviet diplomats (the latter, with reluctance) issued an appeal for peace. Western communist parties, so recently engaged in vitriolic propaganda against fascism, were directed—at enormous cost to their reputations—to join in praise for the new German "dove of peace." Additional damage was done to the international image of communism and of the Soviet Union by Moscow's bullying behavior toward Finland. In October 1939 Stalin had demanded that Finland trade strategic territories in the area of Leningrad and the Gulf of Finland in return for other Soviet territory. Finnish refusal led to an invasion by the Red Army on November 29 without a declaration of war, disguised as a response to an appeal from the revolutionary "Finnish People's Government." The Soviets were expelled from the League of Nations, and the British made preparations to assist the Finns. Hitler, seeing a potential Allied intervention in Scandinavia as a menace to Germany, rendered diplomatic assistance that resulted in a peace settlement on March 12, with Finland acceding to the original Soviet demands. But the cost of this territory to Soviet prestige was enormous, given the startling demonstration during the Winter War of Soviet military weakness and inability to crush a much smaller army.

The Russians found some consolation later in the spring of 1940, when the "phony war" in the West finally ended in a German blitzkrieg, which also ended persisting Soviet fears that the Germans would eventually team up with the British and French against the USSR. Soviet relief was short-lived, however, as French armies behind the vaunted Maginot Line surrendered in a matter of weeks. Almost immediately, the Soviets moved to consolidate the fruits of the secret protocol, annexing the three Baltic states "at the request of" new governments there, and demanding the cession by Romania of Bessarabia and northern Bukovina (the latter not mentioned in the secret protocol).

In the following month, July 1940, Hitler began planning for an attack on the USSR. Convinced that Britain was refusing to surrender because of encouragement from the Russians, and giddy with success, he took the risk of a two-front war out of a conviction that he could defeat the Soviets in five months. No more concessions were made to Stalin in the Balkans. The Germans guaranteed Romania's frontiers, moved troops into Finland, and forced the adherence of Romania, Hungary, and Bulgaria to the Axis. In an effort to cover up his intentions and possibly intimidate the British, Hitler invited Molotov to Berlin in November 1940 to discuss a possible Quadripartite Pact among Germany, Italy, Japan, and the USSR. The Russians drastically overplayed their hand, demanding, as a price of their adhering to the pact, recognition of the area south of Batum and Baku in the general area of the Persian Gulf as the center of Soviet aspirations; German troop withdrawal from Finland; a mutual assistance pact with Bulgaria; and a base within range of the straits.[27] Hitler never replied, describing Stalin as a "cold-blooded blackmailer" and telling his generals that "Russia must be brought to her knees as soon as possible."[28]

On December 18 Hitler issued the directive for Operation Barbarossa, setting the invasion date for mid-May. But two major blunders doomed his possibility of success. He allowed the Japanese to sign a neutrality pact with the Soviets in April, thereby allowing Stalin to avoid a two-front war. And he postponed the beginning of the invasion so that he could "destroy Yugoslavia militarily and as a nation" in punishment for its new government's refusal to join the Axis. Meanwhile Stalin was receiving numerous warnings of Hitler's intentions, which he treated as provocations. Convinced that Hitler wanted to strike a deal, Stalin signaled his readiness for talks by various acts of appeasement, as well as by assuming the premiership himself. The Soviets were caught in a complete tactical surprise. As he listened to the German ambassador read the declaration of war on June 22, 1941, a pale Molotov could only say, "Surely we have not deserved that."[29]

Although Stalin later claimed to have used the twenty-two months of Nazi-Soviet partnership to prepare for the German attack, his successor declared, "this is completely untrue." In his secret speech to the Twentieth Party Congress, Nikita Khrushchev said that "the necessary steps were not taken to prepare the country properly for defense and to prevent it from being caught unawares."[30] Not only had the military been seriously wounded by the purges, but Soviet war-fighting doctrine was based on the assumption that the initial attack would be immediately repelled and the bulk of the war fought on enemy territory; Soviet territory contained few tank traps or other fortifications.

Indeed, in the time Stalin had "gained," Germany had acquired all the resources of Western Europe plus vital economic assistance from the Soviet Union itself to strengthen its war machine, while Stalin had not even prepared border defenses. The "buffer zone" acquired by the Nazi–Soviet Pact was crossed by German armies in a matter of days. The result of Stalin's gamble that a long war would destroy the capitalist West was that the second front that might have been available to him against Germany in 1939 was gone in 1941 and would not be reopened for three years. The European communist parties, which had never been so popular as in the days of the Popular Front against fascism, had become demoralized and weakened by the pro-German defeatist line dictated from Moscow, in the most obvious demonstration in Comintern history of the extent to which the goals for international communism were manipulated to fit the Kremlin's interpretation of Soviet security needs. In sum, while Stalin's decision to sign the Nazi–Soviet Pact might have seemed reasonable at the time, the Soviet gains appeared much less impressive two years later.

Soviet Diplomacy During World War II

From the time of the Nazi invasion until the January 1943 victory at Stalingrad, the very survival of the USSR was in grave doubt. Hitler's initial thrust captured lands that were home to more than 40 percent of the population. Soviet losses—by their own estimate, totaling at least twenty million dead—were most severe during this period. The country's industrial production dropped by half. That the Soviet Union not only survived but emerged from the war as Europe's strongest power was a tribute to Soviet military valor and diplomatic skill.

When Stalin finally emerged from an initial gloomy silence to address the nation on July 3, he made several references to Nazi "treachery." In tacit recognition of how little reason the people had to fight for his regime, the speech was full of patriotic and nationalistic imagery; Marxist-Leninist appeals for the defense of socialism were absent.[31] The German drive stalled at the gates of Moscow in November, through a combination of circumstances: the onset of severe winter, Hitler's decision to bog his army down in attacks on Leningrad and Moscow, his failure to force Japan into the war, and the Germans' unwillingness to use humane treatment in order to tap the anti-Soviet sentiment of non-Russian nationalities.

The following month Stalin demonstrated that he was already calculating Russia's postwar political gains. Unsuccessfully pressing British foreign secretary Anthony Eden for a secret protocol to be included in a British-Soviet treaty of alliance, he sought British recognition of the Russian annexations of 1939–40, Soviet bases in Finland and Romania, and agreement on the dismemberment of Germany. In the spring, Molotov made trips to London and Washington to talk about Allied cooperation and press for opening a second front. In the United States, he found Roosevelt focusing on preservation of friendship among the Allies, preferring to postpone decisions on specific political issues.

Although they were always keenly attuned to postwar power configurations, the Soviets did not appear to have a rigid blueprint but preferred to keep their options open. Issues relating to the future of Poland were particularly sensitive, and neither the Polish government-in-exile in London nor their British patrons were willing to agree to the recognition of the boundaries established in the Nazi-Soviet pact. To create an alternative, Stalin set up a communist-dominated Union of Polish Patriots in Moscow, but he held off recognizing it as the legitimate government. However, the Soviets severed relations with the Polish government in London following their demands for an international investigation into the massacre in the Katyn Forest of thousands of Polish military officers. The Soviets had denied German charges (later proven accurate) that the atrocity had occurred during the Soviet occupation of that section of Poland. The Russians' feigned indignation was a convenient pretext to free their hand and keep open future political options.[32]

Embarrassed at the behavior of the London Poles, the British and Americans had even greater feelings of guilt when they announced to Stalin in mid-1943 that the opening of the second front would have to be postponed for yet another year. Roosevelt eagerly sought a face-to-face meeting to "win over" Stalin and calm his anger, and it was in this context that the Big Three met in Teheran in November 1943. There Stalin was able to take advantage of divisions between Churchill and Roosevelt to achieve important Soviet objectives.

Roosevelt failed to support Churchill's argument that the invasion of France should be postponed in favor of an invasion of southeastern Europe—an operation that would have altered the political fate of Eastern Europe. Roosevelt also declined, for domestic political reasons, to enter into discussions on Poland. Its fate was essentially decided in bilateral conversations where the British suggested moving Poland westward, compensating for Soviet gains to the Nazi-Soviet line by ceding German lands to Poland. The plan was illustrated by Churchill with the aid of three matches; he and Eden observed that it "pleased Stalin."[33] Well it might, for it guaranteed that no independent Polish government could accept this plan, and thus that a puppet government would have to be installed. Churchill also suggested that Russia deserved warm-water ports, and Stalin replied that "it might be well" to relax the restrictions on the movement of Soviet warships through the Turkish straits. Stalin followed with an inquiry about what might be done for the Soviets in the Far East, and Roosevelt—grateful for Stalin's expressed willingness to enter the war against Japan after the defeat of Germany—suggested the possible availability of the port of Dairen.

Stalin's apparent willingness to cooperate at Teheran so impressed his U.S. and British allies that they were offering up the very prizes he coveted. No display of this attitude was more striking than a discourse by Churchill that appeared to invite Russian imperialism:

> It was important that the nations who would govern the world after the war should be satisfied and have no territorial or other ambitions. If that question could be settled in a manner agreeable to the great powers, he felt then that the world might indeed remain at peace. He said that hungry and ambitious nations are dangerous, and he would like to see the leading nations of the world in the position of rich, happy men. The President and Marshal Stalin agreed.[34]

Churchill's and Roosevelt's focus on preserving friendship with Stalin suggests that they were staking Europe's future on their belief that the Soviet regime had changed fundamentally. Their willingness at Teheran to satisfy Stalin's "security needs" by altering the boundaries of Poland and Germany not only ensured Poland's future dependence on the USSR but also made it impossible for Germany to conclude a separate peace with the West.

In the last summer of the war in Europe, following the Allied invasion of Normandy, Stalin showed how his armies could be deployed to advance his political objectives. In Romania, for example, the Red Army was sent to occupy the entire country even after it had renounced its alliance with the Axis powers. Bulgaria, too, had abandoned Germany and was in the midst of suing for peace when the Soviet Union declared war and invaded. And in Poland, in late summer 1944, Stalin cynically employed a tactic he learned from Chiang Kai-shek. He halted the advance of the Red Army outside Warsaw while the Polish underground, rising up on command of the London Poles, was slaughtered in battle with the Nazis. Afterward, the Soviets captured the city and turned it over to their communist-dominated puppet regime.

The following month Churchill was in Moscow for a last attempt at forging a compromise between the London Poles and the Soviets. Despite pressure from both the British and the Russians, Polish premier Stanislas Mikolajczyk refused to comply with Soviet demands for territorial adjustments. An exasperated Churchill, showing again how he valued Soviet friendship, declared: "Because of quarrels between Poles we are not going to wreck the peace of Europe."[35] At this same meeting, Churchill cynically proposed a division of the other countries of Eastern Europe into Western and Soviet spheres of influence, stated in percentage terms, and Stalin quickly acquiesced to the proposal.

The fate of Poland was settled by Soviet and Allied military strategy in 1944, though it was discussed again at the last conference among Roosevelt, Churchill, and Stalin, held at the Crimean resort of Yalta in February 1945. After much discussion, Stalin gave his Western partners a small victory by agreeing to take a few London Poles into the communist-dominated "Lublin provisional government," and by promising to hold free elections in Poland "as soon as possible." However, he reserved the right to limit participation to "democratic" parties—a designation that would be made by Soviet authorities alone. A similar unacknowledged difference in interpretation lay behind Stalin's willingness to agree to sign the Declaration on Liberated Europe, which called for democratic elections to be held in all the liberated and former Axis satellite states. Roosevelt put great stock in this document, which was the focus of later Western charges of Soviet bad faith. Similarly, securing agreement on the basic structure of the United Nations was high on the agenda of the Americans, who were haunted by the memory of President Wilson's mistake of failing to build the international organization before making the final political settlement of the war.

Roosevelt was also eager to secure a reaffirmation of Stalin's willingness to bring the Soviet Union into the war against Japan three months after the German surrender. This Stalin was happy to do, in return for a share of the dismantled Japanese empire—in particular, the territories and privileges lost by the Russians in 1905. The Soviets wanted southern Sakhalin and the Kuriles from Japan, and from China they sought recognition of the independence of Outer Mongolia, access to Dairen, a naval base in Port Arthur, and joint ownership of the Chinese Eastern Railway. Roosevelt persuaded Chiang Kai-shek to accede to this territorial rearrangement in a Treaty of Alliance and Friendship, signed between China and the USSR on August 14, 1945.

In the remaining weeks of the war in Europe, the movement of Soviet troops was followed by the imposition of "friendly governments" in Eastern Europe. The role of noncommunist elements in Poland was seriously constricted; a communist government was forced on Romania, and communists assumed leading positions in Bulgaria, Hungary, and Czechoslovakia. In Yugoslavia, where Tito's communist army was the main force fighting the Germans, the coalition with noncommunist elements was abandoned. The

Soviets turned a deaf ear to Western complaints about these actions. But following Roosevelt's death in April, the successor administration of Harry Truman appeared to adopt a harder attitude toward Moscow's behavior, and in May it suspended Lend-Lease assistance to the Soviet Union.

President Truman was able to assess the Soviet leader directly at the final wartime conference, which was held in Potsdam, in occupied Germany. (The other participant, Prime Minister Churchill, suffered electoral defeat during the meetings, and was replaced by his successor, Clement Atlee.) The opening day of the conference, July 16, was also the birthday of the nuclear age in international politics. Shortly before his first meeting with Stalin, Truman was informed of the first successful test of the atomic bomb. When Stalin was "casually" informed by Truman "that we had a new weapon of unusual destructive force," he apparently "showed no special interest."[36] In fact, the Soviet Union had been actively conducting its own atomic research program, assisted by intelligence agents who were well informed about U.S. progress.

The main focus of discussion at Potsdam was the reorganization and governance of defeated Germany. There was no disagreement about the need to disarm and de-Nazify the country, but the Soviets and their Western allies adopted sharply differing positions on how to demarcate Germany's borders and dispose of its industrial capabilities. Amidst heated disagreements about political developments in their respective spheres of influence, Great Britain and the United States showed no receptivity when Stalin restated his claim to a Soviet base in the Turkish Straits.

The United States used the atomic bomb on Japan on August 6 and 9, and on the latter day—exactly three months after Germany's surrender—the Soviet Union declared war on Japan. In the week that passed between that date and the Japanese surrender, Soviet armed forces managed to occupy the northern part of Korea and moved rapidly through northern Manchuria to join up with the army of the Chinese communists. Again using his own armies to acquire his postwar political objectives, Stalin quickly occupied the territories that had been conceded to him at the Yalta Conference. However, he was rebuffed when he sought to extend Soviet influence even further by sending troops to share in the occupation of Japan.

As a result of World War II, communism had expanded from its base in the Soviet Union to extend its domain over an additional 100 million people in eleven more states of Europe: Latvia, Estonia, Lithuania (all soon reannexed into the USSR), Poland, the eastern zone of Germany, Czechoslovakia, Hungary, Romania, Bulgaria, Yugoslavia, and Albania. These states were extremely diverse nationally, religiously, and culturally, while they shared a low level of economic development as well as relative inexperience in self-rule. They also varied in the strength of their communist parties, though all were to some extent under Soviet control. As the Western leaders were slow to understand, for Stalin, the control of these governments by communist politicians loyal to him was not simply ideologically desirable, but was essential to the security needs of the Soviet Union. The gradual tightening of political and economic control over the states of the region was a logical consequence of Stalin's conviction, expressed to Yugoslav communist leader Milovan Djilas, that "everyone imposes his own system as far as his army can reach. It cannot be otherwise."[37]

The Beginning of the Cold War

The cause of the breakup of the cooperative alliance between the Soviet Union and its wartime partners has been the subject of considerable debate among American historians of the period. The "revisionists" write of the betrayal of the idealism of Roosevelt by the Truman administration, while the "orthodox" portray an abandonment of naive illusions by politicians more realistic about Soviet intentions. In fact, as the preceding pages have spelled out, the alliance was never more than a marriage of convenience, marked by misperceptions, misunderstandings, and frequent outbursts of suspicion. Despite their efforts to maintain a spirit of friendship and cooperation, Britain and the United States found themselves able to do so only by papering over their divisions with the Soviet Union, and they never succeeded in drawing Stalin into a genuine shared vision of the postwar political order.

Stalin's certainty about the inevitability of conflict after the war was expressed in a speech on February 9, 1946. In it he set forth his interpretation of the nature and meaning of the war, justified his prewar and wartime policies, and voiced his prescriptions for the future. The persistence of his Marxist-Leninist worldview is evident in his analysis of the causes of the war, which he described as an inevitable consequence of capitalism. The Soviet Union found itself in alliance with Britain and the United States for the very limited purpose of defeating fascism—a cause that would not have been achieved without Soviet participation. Far from being unprepared, he asserted, the communist party had long ago begun to provide the resources needed for victory through its policies of industrialization and collectivization and through purging its ranks of traitors and saboteurs.

As for the future, Stalin made it clear that there was to be no easing of the forced-pace drive to "organize a new mighty upsurge in the national economy." The reason for continued sacrifice, he implied, was the external threat: "Only under such conditions can we consider that our homeland will be guaranteed against all possible accidents. That will take three more Five-Year Plans, I should think, if not more. But it can be done and we will do it."[38] There would be no near-term Western effort to pry away the fruits of Soviet victory by force of arms, and this allowed a substantial reduction in Soviet armed forces. But it was clear from a remark Stalin made to Djilas in 1945 that he did indeed expect that a few years of respite would be followed by another war: "The war shall soon be over. We shall recover in fifteen or twenty years [three more Five-Year Plans!] and then we'll have another go at it."[39]

Stalin's speech was indicative of a revival of ideological militancy that had taken place in the Soviet Union following the victory at Stalingrad. After Hitler's invasion, the regime's communications with the Soviet people had been laden with patriotic symbols and evoked prerevolutionary Russian traditions. The reappearance of Marxist-Leninist orthodoxy appeared to be a ritual of purification coinciding with the liberation of Soviet territories from Nazi occupation and with the Red Army's penetration into the capitalist world beyond Soviet borders. Stalin's suspicions about ideological contamination and even betrayal fell most heavily on some of the minority nationalities; during and immediately after the war, whole nations—most notably, the Volga Germans and Crimean Tatars—were subjected to mass deportation.

This sense of threat clearly went beyond ideology; it was an expression of Stalin's deep-seated insecurity. This was amply confirmed in his later years not only by the wide-ranging purge of the Leningrad party apparatus but also in the demented "doctors' plot," through which Stalin in his last days was apparently planning to eliminate many of his closest associates. That this paranoia had a profound impact on Soviet foreign policy was documented in Khrushchev's "secret speech" to the Twentieth Party Congress in 1956. As he described it:

> Stalin was a very distrustful man, sickly suspicious. . . . Everywhere and in everything he saw 'enemies,' 'two-facers,' and 'spies.'. . . He had completely lost consciousness of reality; he demonstrated his suspiciousness and haughtiness not only in relation to individuals in the USSR, but in relation to whole parties and nations.[40]

No account of Soviet foreign policy in the postwar years, and no explanation of the origins of the Cold War, can be complete without an awareness of the extent to which Stalin's policies and personality *required* isolationism, an atmosphere of hostility, and an omnipresent enemy.

Continuity and Change in Soviet Policy
Before the Cold War

During the three decades from the Bolshevik Revolution to the beginning of the Cold War, the Soviet regime functioned in an international system that, in certain fundamental respects, more closely resembled the one faced by the tsars in the eighteenth and nineteenth centuries than the one that emerged after World War II. World War I had not changed the multipolar and Eurocentric nature of international politics, nor had it altered the basic "rules" of balance-of-power diplomacy. Although the Soviet regime differed from its tsarist predecessor in some very fundamental respects, these systemic constants—together with the enduring geopolitical realities—helped produce more continuity in Moscow's policy than might have been expected.

In the wake of the diplomatic thunderbolt that was the Nazi-Soviet pact, Winston Churchill, one of the closest and most astute observers of the diplomacy of Lenin and Stalin, characterized Moscow's policy with an enduring phrase: "It is a riddle wrapped in a mystery inside an enigma." Unfortunately, the balance of Churchill's observation has been less well remembered: "But perhaps there is a key. That key is Russian national interest."[41]

As we pointed out at the beginning of this chapter, Soviet leaders did not act as though the demands of ideology and those of the Russian national interest were in conflict. Lenin, in negotiating the Treaty of Brest-Litovsk, and Stalin, in negotiating the Nazi-Soviet Pact and in the wartime summit conferences, were constantly aware that their first priority was to ensure the survival of the Russian state and to seek ways to enhance its security, whether through acquiring "buffer" territories or through seeking respites in which to build up its economy and defense capabilities. When they had opportunities to expand, the territories that interested them were identical to those that the tsars had sought, for identical strategic reasons. As we have seen, neither Lenin nor Stalin hesitated to equate policies that pursued Russian national interests with the long-term interests of world socialist revolution. Both were adept at employing communist rhetoric to explain and justify strategic moves that served the interests of Russia.

Indeed, especially for Stalin, the primary purpose of the international communist movement was to serve the interests of Soviet foreign policy, as defined in the Kremlin, no matter how it twisted and turned to meet internal economic or political needs. Revolutionary parties or leaders who were not under Stalin's control were not to be trusted, and—as German, Iranian,

Turkish, and Chinese communists could testify—even those who were loyal were expendable if Soviet national interests demanded that they be sacrificed.

The Russia inherited by the Bolsheviks in 1917 was considerably weakened and faced powerful adversaries. In such circumstances, it was not surprising that Soviet leaders sought to enhance their security by aligning with other states to promote their interests—that is, to seek to establish a balance of power, so that they were not faced by an overwhelming hostile coalition. This required that they be capable of assessing changes in distributions of power and willing to align with other states—regardless of ideological orientation—that could help preserve the balance, often playing these states off against each other. Lenin's and Stalin's policies toward Germany, from Brest-Litovsk to Rapallo to the Nazi-Soviet Pact, amply illustrate that communist leaders were no less adept than the tsars at playing the balance-of-power "game."

At the same time, we have noted characteristics in Soviet foreign policy during this period that represented significant changes from the tsarist period. One change was in the practice of diplomacy itself—the use of techniques that have been termed "demonstrative diplomacy." These treat the negotiation as an opportunity to gain an international platform from which to proclaim revolutionary principles that will turn the peoples of other states against the very leaders with whom talks are being held. Sometimes agreements are sought and gained, but sometimes the negotiations are conducted primarily for the propaganda opportunities they present. Trotsky's behavior during the Brest-Litovsk negotiations, Chicherin's at the Genoa Conference, and Litvinov's in the League of Nations all provide evidence of the skill with which Soviet foreign ministers have conducted "demonstrative diplomacy." We also have observed numerous instances in which this dual policy—promoting revolution while conducting diplomacy—created difficulties for Soviet foreign policy, or even led, as in Soviet-British relations in 1927, to a total break in diplomatic relations.

Another element in Soviet foreign policy during this period that differentiates it from the balance of power diplomacy practiced during tsarist times was the assumption, voiced by Lenin in his famous statement of 1919 and often repeated by Stalin, of the inevitability of war between the Soviet Union and its capitalist adversaries. While the tsars fought many wars, they also showed themselves adept at avoiding conflicts with powerful rivals. Tsarist diplomacy, unlike that of the Soviets, was not conducted against a backdrop of implacable hostility toward the outside world. Whereas both Lenin and Stalin argued at particular times that peaceful coexistence with the capitalist world was possible, it was not thought to be a permanent prospect. For Stalin, the very existence of the two hostile "camps," though they could coexist with one another under certain conditions, meant that one or the other must triumph. The Soviet Union could proceed with the construction of "socialism in one country," but as long as "capitalist encirclement" prevailed, the people would have to make sacrifices in order to ensure the country's preparedness for the inevitable day of reckoning. As we have seen, this theme—far from disappearing during the years of the Allied coalition of World War II—was voiced again by Stalin in February 1946 as the prevailing prospect for the coming years of what would be termed "Cold War."

3

Soviet Foreign Policy: The Cold War

The Stalinist Approach to Cold War

The Cold War began as a struggle between two major powers, each at the head of an ideologically defined coalition. And yet this initial bipolarity was not a struggle of equals. The United States emerged from World War II with far greater economic and military strength. Even after U.S. troops (other than occupation forces) were withdrawn from Europe and the Pacific and demobilized, the United States retained unchallenged air and naval superiority, and its monopoly of the new atomic weapon gave it a formidable lead in military capability.

While Stalin expected a respite from armed conflict that would enable him to rebuild the Soviet Union's shattered economy, he nevertheless sought to deter the United States from utilizing its military strength. He did this by capitalizing on the Soviet lead in conventional arms and exploiting the perception that Western Europe was vulnerable to an attack by the Red Army. Although both sides had demobilized, U.S. reductions had left ground forces at about one-half the size of the Soviet Union's. About thirty Soviet divisions were deployed in Germany and Eastern Europe in the late 1940s, compared to about ten maintained by the West. And while an active program of atomic research was under way in the USSR, Soviet military doctrine played down the significance of nuclear weapons and stressed the importance of conventional forces and superior morale.

Stalin's political strategy combined opportunistic probing with caution about provoking a military reaction. This was demonstrated in the first postwar crisis, which occurred in Iran—a border area that had tempted Russia's rulers for centuries. When the Soviet Union broke its wartime promise to withdraw occupation troops from northern Iran and instead demanded autonomy for two communist-dominated provincial regimes it had set up there, Iran brought the dispute to the newly established United Nations Security Council. Under strong U.S.-British pressure, including an implicit threat of force, Soviet troops were withdrawn.[1]

Some voices in the West were already warning early in 1946 that a long struggle was in the offing—most notably, Winston Churchill's declaration that an "Iron Curtain" had descended across Europe, and U.S. diplomat George Kennan's pessimistic "long telegram" from Moscow. But not until the first half of 1947 did the words "Cold War" and "containment" enter the American vocabulary, as the bipolar nature of the postwar conflict became clearer. In February, Britain notified U.S. officials that it was no longer able to act as protector of the existing order in the eastern Mediterranean, where the Greek government was under serious pressure from a communist guerrilla movement and the Turkish government was facing an ominous Soviet demand for frontier adjustments and a naval base in the Turkish straits. After an intensive strategic review, President Harry Truman proposed to Congress that the United States assume the burden of leadership, not only through specific (and ultimately successful) assistance to Greece and Turkey, but through a broader commitment "to support free peoples who are resisting attempted subjugation by armed minorities or by outside pressure."[2] The Truman Doctrine was followed by a proposal from Secretary of State George Marshall—responding to a severe economic and political crisis throughout Western Europe—for massive U.S. assistance in the rebuilding of the continent.

Although the Marshall Plan was deliberately posed in nonideological terms, allowing for Soviet and East European participation, it was denounced by the Soviets as an imperialist plot to undermine the independence of the states of Europe while staving off economic collapse in the United States. In retrospect, the decision by Stalin that the USSR and its East European allies would not participate in the European Recovery Program appears seriously mistaken. As it happened, the Marshall Plan produced an economic miracle that helped to restore stability and reduce the appeal of communism in Western Europe. Had the Soviets participated, they might have shared in the economic benefits. But it is more likely that the U.S. Congress would never have appropriated large sums to a program with communist participation, in which case communist prospects in France and Italy might have mounted. At any rate, Stalin's decision served to confirm the political and economic division of Europe.

In the summer of 1947, an anonymously published article by George Kennan publicly articulated the U.S. strategy of responding to Soviet behavior with a policy aimed at "long-term, patient but firm and vigilant containment of Russian expansive tendencies" and featuring "adroit and vigilant application of counterforce at a series of constantly shifting geographical and political points, corresponding to the shifts and maneuvers of Soviet policy."[3] Almost simultaneously, at the founding conference of the Communist Information Bureau (Cominform), Stalin's lieutenant Andrei Zhdanov described a titanic conflict between two camps—the "imperialist" camp, led by a predatory and expansionist United States, and the "democratic" camp under Soviet leadership, which sought to "resist the threat of new wars and imperialist expansion, to strengthen democracy and to extirpate the vestiges of fascism."[4]

Clearly, both the USSR and the United States perceived themselves as heading coalitions struggling for peace and justice against an evil and determined rival. Thus, they saw the world in terms of "tight bipolarity," where all states would be forced to choose one side or the other, and where the struggle of ideologies left no room for compromise. But while they seemed prepared for protracted conflict, neither side appeared willing to risk provoking the other into actual warfare.

The chief purpose of the Cominform was to aid in tightening the Soviet coalition by solidifying Moscow's hold over the states of Eastern Europe and shielding them from the temptations that might be posed by U.S. aid and propaganda. The increasing similarity of these regimes was reinforced in February 1948, when the communist coup in Czechoslovakia removed from the East European political scene the last trace of accountable government. At the same time, Stalin sought to assert his authority over Yugoslavia, where Tito and his followers had created a fiercely pro-Soviet but independent communist regime. When they refused Stalin's demands, the Yugoslavs were expelled from the Cominform. Moscow and its allies mounted a campaign of unrelenting pressure, which Tito was able to resist thanks to solid internal support and timely assistance from the West. Though unwilling to risk war to remove Tito, Stalin proceeded to purge potential imitators in the states of the region and to end any deviations of policy from the orthodox Soviet pattern.

One opening remained in the Iron Curtain, because British, French, and U.S. forces continued to occupy the western sectors of Berlin—one hundred miles within the Soviet zone of Germany. In February 1948, the Western allies decided to proceed, without Soviet participation, toward economic reform in their zones of occupation in Germany, including West Berlin. They announced a currency reform as a first step toward the creation of a federal republic in Germany. The new state would be included in the European Recovery Program and possibly even in a future anti-Soviet military coalition. Seeking to force a Western retreat from this plan, the Soviets mounted a pressure campaign, which climaxed in June with the blockade of all land routes into Berlin.

The United States responded with an airlift of supplies—a continuous shuttle over the next twelve months of more than a quarter million flights. The dramatic Berlin airlift inspired the American, Canadian, and West European people and their governments to support the creation, in spring 1949, of the Federal Republic of Germany and of the North Atlantic Treaty Organization (NATO). Acknowledging defeat, the Soviet Union ended the blockade of Berlin and sponsored the creation in its own zone of occupation of the communist-ruled German Democratic Republic (GDR). Although the continuing presence of the West in Berlin was a constant irritant that Moscow would again seek to remove, the political and economic division of Europe appeared complete.

As in tsarist times, diplomatic stalemate in Europe was followed by renewed Russian attention to opportunities for expansion in Asia. There indigenous communist forces were on the verge of establishing control over the world's most populous country, and the European colonial empires in South and Southeast Asia were in the process of being toppled by nationalist revolutions. These revolutions had proceeded without Soviet leadership, in part because of preoccupations in Europe, but also because of Stalin's earlier unhappy experience in China in the 1920s. The Soviet media virtually ignored the military successes of the Chinese communists, and—unlike the resurgent communist parties of France and Italy—the CCP received no invitation to the founding congress of the Cominform. Mao Zedong's military victory was essentially complete before he obtained Soviet diplomatic recognition in October 1949. And only shortly before that did the Soviets give public endorsement to the armed struggles being conducted by the communist parties in Indochina, Indonesia, India, Burma, Malaya, and the Philippines. In so doing, they claimed that the true inspiration for the "Chinese path to revolution" was to be found in the teachings of Lenin and Stalin.

Even the conclusion in February 1950 of a Sino-Soviet treaty of alliance—after nine weeks of hard bargaining—gave signs of the ambivalence with which the Soviets regarded the Chinese communist victory. Their experiences with Tito had revealed the potential difficulties with a communist neighbor who had won victory without Soviet military assistance or political counsel. Moreover, Moscow had already established a treaty relationship with Chiang Kai-shek's regime that had produced territorial and economic benefits—control of the Chinese Eastern Railway and the base at Port Arthur—which disappeared in the new treaty. Under its terms, the Soviets were to return control of these assets no later than the end of 1952; they also undertook to render economic assistance to China in its (sure to be costly) efforts to build socialism.

That same year, however, a miscalculation on Stalin's part caused China to be diverted from its major objectives and plunged into an undeclared war with the United States in Korea. That country had been divided into U.S. and Soviet zones of occupation following the surrender of Japan. In ending the occupation in 1949, each side had turned over its zone to like-minded political forces. The North Korean regime, run by Soviet-trained communists, was militarily and politically stronger than South Korea, which seemed vulnerable to attack. The United States, which had taken no military action to prevent a communist triumph in China, had failed to include its Korean client within its announced "defense perimeter" in Asia. For Moscow, the situation presented an opportunity to unify the peninsula under a single communist regime, while demonstrating to Japan that it would be unwise to form closer security ties with the United States, which was of uncertain will.

When North Korea invaded the South on June 25, 1950, the Truman administration responded swiftly and boldly. With the United States leading, the United Nations Security Council—boycotted since January by the Soviet delegate, in protest of the continuing representation of China by Chiang's government—condemned the aggression and appealed to member states to come to the aid of South Korea. U.S. forces stationed in Japan were ordered to Korea by President Truman. He reassured Stalin that the United States sought no direct conflict with the USSR—which in 1949 had broken the U.S. monopoly and become an atomic power. Disavowing responsibility for the conflict and denying that they intended to intervene, the Russians were content to watch the spectacular initial military success of their client.

When the tide of battle in Korea turned in October, however, and United Nations forces were driving the North Koreans all the way back toward the Yalu River border with Manchuria, both the Soviets and the Chinese faced unacceptable prospects. For the Soviets, the defeat of a communist government by U.S. arms was a dangerous precedent; for China, the establishment of a hostile state on its border—or even a possible invasion of Manchuria—had to be prevented. After several fruitless warnings to the United States, and after having received assurances of Soviet aid, China sent "volunteer" forces into the fighting at the side of the North Koreans. Several months of fierce combat were followed by a bloody stalemate at the original boundary of the two occupation zones. Armistice talks commenced in July 1951, but Stalin found it advantageous to prolong a situation in which U.S. forces were tied down in endless conflict with Moscow's proxy. Moreover, China, fighting with arms purchased from the USSR, found itself diplomatically isolated and increasingly dependent on the Soviet Union.

Although Stalin was willing to experiment with new tactics in his latter years, a major reorientation of Soviet policy would have to await new leadership, which came with Stalin's death in March 1953.[5] While the Soviet Union had achieved major successes in the postwar years and had become one of the world's two nuclear superpowers, it confronted equally large challenges. The Iron Curtain dividing East from West seemed higher and more impenetrable than ever, and behind it, in Moscow's sphere, nationalist tensions and popular dissatisfaction simmered beneath the facade of socialist unity. Stalin's record in foreign policy was decidedly mixed; gains achieved through shrewd bargaining existed alongside opportunities missed because of stubborn inflexibility. Attacked by his successors as a ruthless paranoid whose policies were often divorced from reality, he was again praised by his lieutenants' heirs for his strong and single-minded leadership in building an industrial power capable of awesome military successes. Nearly a half-century after his death, the "genius leader of all mankind" continued to be a dominant, controversial, and unsettling figure both for his own people and for the entire communist world.

The Khrushchev Strategy

Although Stalin's policy had built the Soviet Union into an industrial and military superpower, it had exacted an enormous price in loss of life, human suffering, unmet needs, and personal insecurity for the elite and masses alike. It was evident to the country's new leaders that a continuation of this approach would be counterproductive. The legitimacy of their own rule depended upon restoring the authority of the CPSU, without surrendering its monopoly of political power. Further strengthening the country's economic and military capabilities required motivating the population through material incentives rather than terror. But if they were to achieve domestic stability and improve living standards, the new leaders would need to avoid confrontation with external enemies. They also would need to lessen tensions within the socialist camp—a point that was brought home only three months after Stalin's death, when demonstrations erupted in East Germany and had to be quelled with Soviet tanks.

While persuading the other members of the socialist camp to adopt a "new course" that relaxed the harsher features of the Stalinist system, the new Soviet leaders sought to improve relations in other areas of conflict as well. They resumed diplomatic relations with Greece and Israel, withdrew their territorial claims against Turkey, and—most significantly—took steps to break the stalemate and allow the conclusion of an armistice in Korea. Prime Minister Georgii Malenkov, in a speech to the Supreme Soviet on

August 8, 1953, declared that "there are no disputed or outstanding issues which cannot be settled peacefully by mutual agreement." At the same time, he warned those who perceived the new Soviet policy as a sign of weakness that the United States now had "no monopoly on the hydrogen weapon."[6]

The following year Malenkov voiced the previously heretical view that the existence of nuclear weapons meant that war between imperialism and communism would destroy world civilization. He evidently meant to use this doctrine as the basis for cutting the Soviet defense budget, but within a month he was forced by a majority of his colleagues in the collective leadership to modify his thesis to state that only capitalism would be annihilated by nuclear war.

Basking in its new status as a thermonuclear power, the Soviet Union called for a conference of foreign ministers to be held in Geneva in the spring of 1954 to consider Korean reunification and a solution to the conflict in Indochina. The Korean phase of the conference ended in deadlock, but the Indochina phase produced an agreement for a truce between France and the Vietminh National Liberation Committee, led by Ho Chi Minh and a nucleus of communists, which had been fighting French colonial forces since 1946. The Geneva agreement called for France to withdraw its troops, recognize the independence of Laos and Cambodia, and partition Vietnam pending national elections in 1956. Although both sides regarded it not as a final solution but as a springboard to further struggle, the agreement represented a victory for Asian communism.

The adroit diplomacy of Zhou Enlai at the Geneva conference signaled the re-emergence of China on the world stage, and its elevated status was confirmed later in 1954 by a renegotiation of its partnership with the USSR. A delegation of Soviet leaders traveled to Beijing to conclude a new treaty that freed China from some of the more humiliating terms imposed by Stalin. The Soviets agreed to withdraw from Port Arthur, to eliminate the joint stock companies set up in 1950, and to increase the level of credits and technical assistance to Chinese industry.

An area of conflict on which no progress was made was Germany. Soviet hopes that disunity in the West would prevent German rearmament were dashed in 1954, when the NATO allies agreed to admit the Federal Republic of Germany, bringing an army of half of million under integrated NATO command. In response, the Soviet Union assembled its East European allies in Warsaw and adopted a Pact of Mutual Assistance and Unified Command (the Warsaw Pact) that gave a symbolic symmetry to European defense arrangements.

Despite this setback, the Soviets continued to focus attention on security arrangements in central Europe. In May 1955 the Austrian State Treaty provided for withdrawal of Soviet and Western troops from their respective zones of occupation and for the permanent neutralization of the Austrian state. The cost for the Soviets was relatively low, since no communist state had been set up in the Soviet zone, and they may have hoped to provide neighboring West Germany with another lesson on the advantages of neutrality.

The Austrian treaty helped clear the way for the first big-power summit meeting since Potsdam—the Geneva Summit of 1955. The major Soviet proposal was for the mutual disbandment of NATO and the Warsaw Pact, the withdrawal of non-European (i.e., American) forces from the continent, and conclusion of a European security treaty. Neither this nor the major Western initiative—President Eisenhower's proposal to open the defense installations of each side to aerial surveillance by the other ("open skies")—produced any agreement. But the conference did bring a marked reduction in international tension ("the spirit of Geneva"), fostering the impression that the Soviet leaders (First Secretary of the CPSU Nikita Khrushchev and new Prime Minister Nikolai Bulganin) were reasonable men, with whom it was possible to negotiate.

Later in 1955, the Soviets made another attempt to "exploit the contradictions" in the Western camp by enticing its West European allies away from the United States. Their target was the West German chancellor, Konrad Adenauer, who visited Moscow in September for talks on establishing diplomatic relations and commercial ties. Using the time-honored technique of appealing to capitalist greed, the Soviets hoped to use the bait of renewed commercial relations to gain Adenauer's formal renunciation of the goal of German reunification. But Adenauer had his own initiative to pursue—offering German financial assistance in return for reunification or, as the Soviets saw it, buying the German Democratic Republic from Moscow in return for West German credits and reparations. Although the temptation must have been great, the Soviets were unwilling to deal away "their" part of Germany. Khrushchev later wrote about it in terms similar to the Western "domino theory"—the abandonment of socialism in the GDR would only have encouraged more Western pressure and set off a chain reaction: "Once you start retreating, it's difficult to stop."[7] (As we shall see, Chancellor Helmut Kohl had much better luck making the same proposal to President Gorbachev thirty-five years later, when other dominoes around the GDR had already fallen.)

When the Twentieth Congress of the CPSU convened in February 1956, the new direction in Soviet foreign policy was already evident, but the congress played a significant role by articulating and approving the changes in interpretation of Marxist-Leninist doctrine that supported a relaxation of tensions. This necessitated a turn away from Stalin's rigid two-camp worldview, which left no room for Soviet cooperation with movements and states that were noncommunist but anti-imperialist. The task was not to invent an entirely new approach but to return to Lenin's concept of a temporary strategic alliance between the USSR and various "neutralist" or "nationalist" forces against the imperialist powers.

Khrushchev justified his approach by declaring that the balance of forces in the international arena had shifted as a result of the transition from "socialism in one country" to a powerful socialist world system. This made it possible for Marxism-Leninism to triumph both in individual states and worldwide without war or violence, but through peaceful competition. In his major public address to the Twentieth Congress, Khrushchev proclaimed the major tasks of Soviet foreign policy: (1) pursuing a policy of peaceful coexistence; (2) building stronger relations among the socialist states, including Yugoslavia; (3) strengthening friendship and cooperation with neutralist and peace-loving states in Europe and the Third World; (4) pursuing closer relations with the United States and its allies; and (5) strengthening the USSR's defense potential and exposing the activities of the enemies of peace.[8]

Although these pronouncements at the Twentieth Party Congress represented a significant departure for Soviet foreign policy, Khrushchev's lengthy and controversial secret speech attacking Stalin had an even greater effect, particularly within the socialist camp. Khrushchev's explicit comments in the realm of foreign policy included criticism of Stalin's failure to prepare Soviet defenses for the German attack in 1941; Stalin's "lack of faith in the Chinese comrades," which delayed the establishment of the communist regime in Beijing; his "shameful role" in relating to Tito; his misunderstanding of the nature of the national-liberation movement in India; and his "unrealistic" assessment of the situation in Korea, leading to the creation of a "risky situation" there.[9]

Apart from its enormous impact on political, social, and cultural life in the USSR, Khrushchev's de-Stalinization campaign had dramatic consequences for Eastern Europe as well. Khrushchev's denunciation of Stalin, together with his public acknowledgment that "many roads to socialism" were permissible, was intended to help the USSR mend fences with Tito and bring him back into the Soviet camp. The Yugoslav leader traveled to Moscow in June for a "fraternal visit," during which relations between his party and the CPSU were re-established. But pleasing as they were to Tito, Khrushchev's revelations about Stalin had a shattering effect elsewhere in the socialist bloc, where Soviet authority was linked closely to Stalin's personality and policies. On Soviet initiative, the "little Stalins" ruling in Poland, Hungary, and Bulgaria had been replaced in the first half of 1956 by more reform-minded leaders, and—in another concession to Tito—the

Cominform had been abolished. Khrushchev evidently thought that the bonds of Marxism-Leninism and the institutional ties to the Warsaw Treaty Organization and the Council for Mutual Economic Assistance (CMEA) were strong enough to substitute for the late dictator's fearsome iron grip. Clearly, he overestimated how solid these ties were, particularly in the face of revelations that the "genius leader of all mankind" who had presided over the establishment of socialist regimes in Eastern Europe had in fact been a criminal and a madman for most of his career. The "posthumous rehabilitation" of the victims of blood purges in the USSR and Eastern Europe had the effect of stimulating even more searching questions about the nature of a political system that could allow such suffering and injustice.

The most profound reverberations were felt in Poland and Hungary. Strikes and demonstrations began in Poznan, Poland, in June, setting off a chain of events that culminated in October with the election of a new party leader, Wladyslaw Gomulka. Gomulka, who previously had been suspected of "Titoist" sympathies, immediately declared Poland's intention of following its own national path toward communism. A Soviet delegation headed by Khrushchev rushed to Warsaw, and there were strong hints of possible action by the Red Army. But the Poles were able to reassure the Soviets that the communist party remained in firm control and that it was committed to maintain Poland's alliance with the USSR.

This challenge was followed the same month with an even more serious rebellion on the part of the Hungarian population. This led to an attempt by the new premier, Imre Nagy, to restore multi-party politics and free elections and to withdraw Hungary from the Warsaw Pact. In the first few days of November, Soviet tanks were sent to crush the Hungarian revolution. In a coincidence that was fortunate for the Soviets, the potential negative reaction in some parts of the world to their bloody invasion of Hungary was reduced by the simultaneous invasion by Western forces of a prominent Third World neutralist state. In the eyes of many African, Asian, and Latin American nationalists, Moscow's action to prevent a defection from its East European security zone was less offensive than the British-French-Israeli invasion of Egypt in response to President Nasser's nationalization of the Suez Canal and to attacks on Israel by fedayeen terrorists in the Sinai peninsula.

While taking care not to become militarily involved, the Soviet Union championed Nasser's cause and claimed that its noisy threats had forced the retreat of imperialism. The outcome of the Suez crisis seemed to further the USSR's two chief objectives in the Middle East: hastening the decline of British and French influence in the area and combating the Western-sponsored anticommunist alliance—the Baghdad Pact of Britain, Turkey, Iran, Iraq, and Pakistan. The fact that the United States was not a party to the Suez intervention, and in fact harshly condemned it, gained little credit in the region for Washington. In fact, it produced an additional benefit of the crisis for Moscow—the weakening of Western unity.

While the Suez crisis helped to mitigate the international impact of Soviet intervention in Hungary, it did not forestall the weakening of Khrushchev's domestic political position. His rivals claimed that he had undermined Soviet authority in Eastern Europe with his unwise revelations about Stalin and his concessions to Tito. In June 1957 Khrushchev was faced with a "so-called arithmetical majority" in the Party Presidium that demanded that he step down as first secretary. The resourceful Khrushchev, with the help of Defense Minister Georgii Zhukov, turned the tables on his adversaries by summoning the Central Committee to Moscow to override the Presidium's action and remove his chief opponents (the "anti-Party group") from their positions.

As he set about repairing the damage to his own position, Khrushchev was also engaged in an effort to reconstruct the socialist bloc. This culminated in November 1957 in a meeting in Moscow of the leaders of twelve ruling communist parties. Tito was not present, since the Hungarian events had produced another rupture in Soviet-Yugoslav relations. The Moscow meeting widened the reopened breach by condemning "revisionism" in the communist movement. Mao Zedong, on the other hand, played a prominent role at the meeting, freely giving advice to the Soviets even as he acknowledged (in return for Khrushchev's promise to aid China in developing nuclear weapons) that the CPSU was at the "head" of the socialist camp. But China was clearly beginning to question the validity of Khrushchev's doctrinal interpretations and his ability to lead the socialist bloc to further successes. Under growing pressure, he needed a dramatic breakthrough.

The successful launch by the USSR of an artificial space satellite ("Sputnik") in October 1957 provided the key ingredient in Khrushchev's plan—parlaying the Soviet lead in the "space race" with the United States into an assertion of Soviet strategic superiority. In fact, the strategic military balance was quite unfavorable to the USSR, given the U.S. lead in bombers and the fact that the Soviets were not investing in missile production. But Khrushchev sought to create the opposite impression by making a series of exaggerated claims regarding Soviet rocket development. Using a combination of threats and proposals for disengagement, he sought to pressure European members of NATO into refusing an expansion of American nuclear capability on the continent and in Germany in particular.

The purpose of this elaborate missile deception was to extract political concessions from the West, particularly regarding Berlin, which had been divided into zones of occupation since 1945.[10] The three Western zones had *de facto* linkages to the Federal Republic and shared in its economic prosperity. East Berlin, occupied by Soviet forces, was a depressing study in contrast. Located one hundred miles inside the GDR, Berlin was an easily accessible escape route for East Germans, about three million of whom by 1961 had traveled from East to West Berlin and then on to West Germany. This outpouring of refugees was a dramatic and embarrassing manifestation of the side-by-side comparison of the achievements of the two economic systems. Together with the GDR's virtual diplomatic isolation, the refugee flow clearly threatened the long-term viability of the German communist regime. Khrushchev hoped to use the missile deception and a carefully deployed combination of enticements and threats to force a change in the status of Berlin. He calculated that this would shake the confidence of West Germans in their NATO partners, while producing formal recognition of Germany's division, neutralization of the two states, and a permanent ban on West German access to nuclear weapons.

Khrushchev sought to achieve a diplomatic triumph in Europe "on the cheap." His ambitious seven-year plan for the Soviet economy, unveiled at the Twenty-first Congress of the CPSU in January 1959, was designed to propel the Soviet economy to a level past that of the United States. Its fulfillment required a further diversion of resources "from guns to butter," and in January 1960 Khrushchev announced a reduction of about one-third in the size of the Soviet armed forces. Adopting ideas expounded by Malenkov in 1954, he acknowledged that nuclear war would destroy both capitalism and communism, and concluded that it was thus no longer necessary for Soviet forces to be of a size and diversity that would allow them to survive an initial nuclear attack and then to win a conventional war with the West.

Khrushchev's strategy was posited on the achievement of favorable results in negotiations on Berlin and a concomitant relaxation of international tensions. He was encouraged by a meeting of the Big Four foreign ministers (of the United States, the USSR, Great Britain, and France) in the spring of 1959, a summit meeting with President Eisenhower in the United States that autumn, and Western agreement to a Big Four summit on European security issues to be held in Paris in May 1960. As it turned out, however, the Paris summit ended in disaster. A few days before it was to open, the Soviets shot down a piloted U-2 high-altitude plane belonging to the United States, part of an ongoing series of photographic espionage flights over Soviet territory in search of the allegedly numerous (but actually fictitious) Soviet missile emplacements. When President Eisenhower, whom Khrushchev had recently hailed as a peace-loving statesman, took personal responsibility for the spy mission, the Soviets decided that the summit conference could not begin without a personal apology. To be sure, the Soviets were aware that their missile deception had probably been exposed and realized that the Paris negotiations were indeed not likely to produce Western concessions on Germany. But an opposition faction in the Soviet leadership, composed of heavy-industry and defense lobbyists and hard-line ideologists, dissatisfied with Khrushchev's defense cuts, apparently took advantage of the situation to force a harder line in Soviet policy. After the break-up of the Paris summit, the remainder of 1960 saw a lingering chill in East-West relations, climaxed by Khrushchev's belligerent performance at the United Nations, in which he banged his shoe on a desk in protest of a speech he found offensive.

The Kennedy Administration, which came to power in 1961, pledged an activist response to the Soviet challenge in Europe and the Third World. However, its first foreign policy crisis—an ill-fated U.S.-supported invasion of Cuba by anti-Castro forces at the Bay of Pigs—aroused doubts about Kennedy's resoluteness. A meeting between Kennedy and Khrushchev in Vienna in June, held in a somber atmosphere, was followed by Khrushchev's reinstatement of a deadline for a settlement on Berlin, an announced increase in the Soviet defense budget, and a suspension of the planned reduction in the size of the Soviet armed forces. Kennedy parried with increases in the U.S. defense budget and troop strength.

Khrushchev's next move caught the West by surprise. The Soviets succeeded in August 1961 in solving their immediate problem in Berlin, closing off the escape route by building a wall between the western and eastern sectors of the city. This was followed two months later by an ominous confrontation between Soviet and U.S. tanks at the border of their respective sectors, but Khrushchev again defused the crisis by withdrawing his deadline.

Khrushchev grew increasingly frustrated with the lack of movement toward his longer-range goal of changing the status of Berlin and stabilizing the situation in Germany. The long-standing Soviet fear that West Germany would gain access to nuclear weapons was now multiplied by visions of an aggressive and nuclear China. Not only was the Soviet Union's prestige at stake, but its relative strategic position was worsening. The United States had discovered that the presumed missile gap in favor of the Soviets had never existed—but only after their own strategic build-up had resulted in an actual gap favoring the United States. Khrushchev lacked the economic resources to satisfy both civilian and military needs, and he was under increasing pressure from a hard-line faction to produce a foreign policy victory. At the beginning of 1962, he was desperately seeking a way to demonstrate Soviet military might, thereby impressing the United States and China and impelling them to the negotiating table to resolve pressing political issues. His thoughts led him to a solution that was both unorthodox and bold, as he later recounted in his memoirs:

> I had the idea of installing missiles with nuclear warheads in Cuba without letting the United States find out they were there until it was too late to do anything about them. . . . In addition to protecting Cuba, our missiles would have equalized what the West likes to call the "balance of power." . . . Now they would learn just what it feels like to have enemy missiles pointing at you; we'd be doing nothing more than giving them a little of their own medicine.[11]

In addition to their military uses, the missiles probably also represented a bargaining chip that Khrushchev could employ to force the West to abandon its positions on key issues. In either context, their effectiveness depended on their being deployed without the knowledge of the United States. On October 14 a U-2 overflight of Cuba produced photographic evidence of the construction of missile installations. Eight days later President Kennedy shared it with the American public and the world. He declared that the United States would consider an attack from Cuba the equivalent of an attack by the USSR, and he announced the imposition of a naval blockade to halt further Soviet shipments. Thus seizing the strategic initiative, in full knowledge of superior U.S. conventional and nuclear power, Kennedy forced Khrushchev to dismantle and remove the Cuban missiles under United Nations supervision, in return for a face-saving pledge that the United States would not invade Cuba.[12]

In the months following the Cuban missile crisis, Khrushchev's efforts seem to have been focused on restoring an atmosphere of peaceful coexistence, with an eye to negotiating the best solutions he could reach. A treaty banning nuclear tests in the atmosphere was agreed upon in 1963; although the Chinese and the French refused to sign, the Federal Republic of Germany was among the signatories. The following year, there were signs that Khrushchev was planning a trip to Bonn for direct negotiations with the West Germans. But domestic opposition to his policies was growing, and he was forced to backtrack on de-Stalinization and to scrap plans for economic liberalization. Just two years after his humiliation in Cuba, and with the split with China moving to the point of open break, Khrushchev was forced to resign on October 14, 1964.

The Cold War in the Third World

One of Khrushchev's most important foreign policy legacies was the Soviet rediscovery of the Third World as the "vital strategic reserve of imperialism." He saw it as an arena in which the Soviets could compete with the West with high likelihood of success, but with less risk than would result from a direct challenge in the "main arena" of the bipolar struggle. Several significant events in 1955 signaled Soviet priorities and the techniques they were willing to employ in this new arena: the sale of arms (ostensibly from Czechoslovakia) to Egypt, gaining a foothold for Soviet influence in the Middle East; high-level diplomacy in South Asia, starting with a June visit to Moscow by Prime Minister Nehru of India and a return trip at the end of the year by Khrushchev and Bulganin to India, Afghanistan, and Burma; and economic assistance to the state sector of developing countries, inaugurated during the Soviet leaders' trip to India with the announcement that the Soviets would finance and construct the giant Bhilai steel mill. Although some were nominally "socialist," most of these countries were not leaning toward communism; rather, they interested Moscow for strategic and geopolitical reasons.

Adopting Lenin's perspective, Khrushchev perceived that Soviet interests were advanced by joining with nationalist and neutralist Third World states in the struggle against imperialism—a temporary alliance he called the "zone of peace." He confidently asserted that Soviet aid to state-owned industries in these countries would help to liberate them from their economic dependence on the West, while simultaneously stimulating the growth of a communist-oriented industrial proletariat.

However, it did not take long for the Soviets to lose their optimistic outlook on the prospects for socialist development in Asia and Africa. In only a few countries were communist parties even allowed to function; rarer still was one with healthy political prospects. The call for the application of "creative Marxism" in further research by Soviet scholars led to a great deal of doctrinal experimentation—a search for alternative paths by which the new states could make the transition to noncapitalist development, and thus be deemed worthy of Soviet support. This produced concepts so pliable that even the most backward economies were said to be capable of socialist development. Indeed, Soviet analysts argued, given a mutually supportive relationship with the Soviet Union, the transition to socialism could occur even without the leadership of the proletariat or of a communist party.

Certain Third World leaders found satisfaction in having their countries proclaimed as candidates for rapid development toward socialism. And Khrushchev surely was eager to seize on the new concepts to justify his claims that Soviet policies could produce victories for socialism. The Chinese, on the other hand, objected sharply to the ideological sleight-of-hand, as did Third World communists whose historical role was thereby eliminated. The most fundamental problem with Khrushchev's approach, however, was that it largely ignored the realities—that Third World countries confronted tremendous obstacles to economic development.

A wide variety of techniques were employed by Moscow in its opportunistic search for influence in the Third World. In addition to diplomatic contacts, the Soviets developed ties with a variety of political parties; promoted exchanges with labor, student, and cultural groups; disseminated massive quantities of print and radio propaganda; and employed tens of thousands of civilian and military technicians and advisors. The Soviet program of foreign aid (totaling just over $47 billion through 1988), though dwarfed in absolute terms by that of the United States, was highly selective, with four countries (India, Iraq, Afghanistan, and Turkey) receiving just under half of the total amount. Disbursed in the form of long-term credits strictly tied to the purchase of Soviet goods, economic aid was closely linked with Soviet foreign trade.

Far greater in volume was the military aid program of the Soviet Union; indeed, weapons were the chief export of the USSR to the Third World. Its military aid relationships presented Moscow with opportunities not only to extend its own political influence in strategic areas while strengthening its clients against local and regional challengers, but more concretely, to extend its military reach in ways that could alter the international balance of power. However, the program was not without its costs; Moscow did not always find itself on the prevailing side in regional conflicts, and even when it did, it did not always experience gratitude from its allies.

Soviet achievements in the Third World under Khrushchev's leadership may have been far less impressive than he had promised, but he did lay the ideological and operational foundations for long-range Soviet involvement. Although his ambition greatly exceeded Moscow's reach, Khrushchev plunged the USSR into global involvement; he extended the bipolar struggle into the "imperialist reserve" and left the United States unchallenged in no area of the world. He forged active ties with the more radical states of the Third World, for which Moscow represented an alternative source of economic and military capabilities. But lavish Soviet aid and the encouragement of radical socioeconomic change often left economic and political chaos in its wake. Khrushchev's most promising clients—Indonesia's Sukarno, Algeria's Ben Bella, and Ghana's Nkrumah—were toppled shortly after Khrushchev himself.

Despite the failures, Khrushchev's lasting accomplishment was to expand the horizons of Soviet foreign policy beyond the narrow parameters to which Stalin had confined it and to renew the appeal of Soviet doctrine beyond the rigid formulations of his predecessor. In so doing, Khrushchev won for the Soviets some valuable footholds in strategically prized and previously uncharted territories.

As in other spheres, the successor leadership continued the basic objectives of this strategy, while shifting tactics and adopting a more cautious and pragmatic style. In the face of an explicit recognition of the complex and extended nature of social change in the Third World, the emphasis in Soviet pronouncements was soon on the lengthy timetable that would be required for the new states to build socialism. As a leading Soviet analyst phrased his criticism of leaders who pushed social change too quickly, "Proclaiming socialism is not the same thing as building it."[13] The new Soviet approach to economic assistance placed greater stress on the economic feasibility of aid projects, and motivations for Soviet aid and trade were increasingly expressed in terms of mutual economic benefit. More than ever, Moscow's targets in the Third World were chosen according to the degree of Chinese or Western interest in the country, its importance to Soviet security, or its ability to provide support facilities—including airports, harbors, or sites for communications stations—for Soviet military activities.

These factors grew in significance during the years of Leonid Brezhnev's rule, as the Soviet Union deployed its sizable and growing navy in the waters surrounding the Third World. The Soviets sought to use this new capability not merely for military defense but for the political purpose of "protecting state interests in time of peace" or "showing the flag." In the Indian Ocean, for example, by the mid-1980s the Soviets were maintaining a permanent squadron of at least twenty vessels, with occasional "surges" in times of crisis to more than thirty. By expanding its navy in this fashion, Moscow showed its determination to achieve the status of a global superpower—not confined to the Eurasian land mass but capable of projecting its power far beyond its own borders.[14]

As the Soviet Union's investment in strategic Third World resources and facilities grew, its involvement in "national-liberation struggles" and regional conflicts became an issue of greater contentiousness in its relationship with the United States. At times when the Soviets were seeking "detente" or relaxation of tensions with the West in order to widen access to trade and technology or pursue negotiated settlements, their Third World involvements worked at cross purposes, despite Soviet efforts to keep the two arenas separate. Moreover, the strong forces of nationalism and the volatility of regional conflicts in Asia, Africa, and Latin America made it difficult for the USSR to establish reliable patron-client relationships. Among the high-profile reversals were some that resulted when "clients" switched sides in search of a better deal (most notably, Somalia and Egypt), and some that resulted when pro-Soviet regimes were overthrown (such as Chile's Allende and Ethiopia's Mengistu).[15] In fact, Soviet influence seemed to peak in the mid-1970s, with the coming to power of pro-Soviet regimes in Angola, Ethiopia, Nicaragua, and Afghanistan, and the spread of communism to Laos and Cambodia. Afterward, there were no new Third World successes. In the Gorbachev era, the costs of the USSR's investments in the Third World were reassessed, and class struggle and the two-camps thesis were explicitly abandoned in favor of more cooperative relationships with the West, which facilitated a scaling back of Soviet commitments and negotiated solutions to some of the more dangerous regional conflicts in the Third World.

The Sino-Soviet Conflict

In the Third World, as in all other arenas of the Cold War, no development so profoundly affected the foreign policy of the Soviet Union in the 1960s, 1970s, and 1980s as its conflict with China. The challenge to the notion that Moscow was the single center of the international communist movement, initiated by Tito, was raised to shattering heights by Mao Zedong. Yugoslavia in 1948 demonstrated that a communist regime could remain independent of the USSR, and Poland in 1956 showed the possibilities of pursuing home-grown domestic policies within the context of Soviet military control. China in the 1960s became the USSR's chief enemy and thereby forever destroyed the Marxist myth that proletarian forces engage in "international relations of a new type."

At least in part, the schism between the Soviet Union and China was a consequence of a larger change in the international system—the decline of rigid bipolarity and rise of multipolarity, as new power centers emerged in global politics. But China's challenge was not simply that of an emergent great power. Its significance and intensity were magnified by other factors, including a conflict in ideology, a personality clash between Khrushchev and Mao Zedong, long-standing national rivalries, differing levels of economic development, and a rivalry for leadership of the socialist camp. Differences that were expressed confidentially in the late 1950s were more openly communicated in the early 1960s, and by 1964 the split in the socialist system was an acknowledged reality.

Although they had no reason for devotion to Stalin, the Chinese voiced dissatisfaction with Soviet policy only with the accession of Khrushchev to the leadership of the USSR. They were disturbed by the events of the Twentieth Congress of the CPSU in 1956—not only the doctrinal revisions unilaterally announced by Khrushchev, but also his secret speech attacking Stalin. Having been persuaded (in part by the promise of assistance in their nuclear development) to refrain from an open challenge to Soviet leadership at the conference of eastern bloc states in 1957, the Chinese found Soviet behavior in the next two years intolerable. Specifically, they objected during the Middle East crisis of 1958 when Khrushchev proposed a summit conference of the traditional Big Four plus India; later that year, when the Soviet Union was thought to be insufficiently forthcoming on behalf of Chinese claims to the offshore islands of Quemoy and Matsu; and in the following year, when Moscow adopted a stance of neutrality in the border clashes between communist China and "bourgeois" India. Why, in the wake of the launch of Sputnik, the Soviets appeared more interested in peaceful coexistence with the United States and in friendship with India than in aggressively pressing the demands of their socialist ally was a point of bitter frustration with the leaders in Beijing.

For their part, the Soviets were alarmed by the bold policies adopted by China both domestically and externally. In 1958 the Chinese adopted a radical industrialization policy (the "Great Leap Forward") and a system of agrarian communes as methods of moving quickly toward the stage of full communism. Implied in their claims was a challenge to Soviet ideological preeminence. Khrushchev's response was the hastily summoned Twenty-first Party Congress in January 1959—the "Congress of the Builders of Communism"—which adopted an ambitious seven-year plan. In the foreign policy realm, China's quest for control of Taiwan and the offshore islands, its brutal repression in Tibet, and its campaign to force adjustments on the Sino-Indian border escalated global tensions at a time when Khrushchev was emphasizing peaceful coexistence and the potential fruitfulness of negotiations. In an unmistakable sign of their distrust, the Soviets in June 1959 abrogated the 1957 military aid agreement in which they had promised to give China technical data for the manufacture of the atomic bomb. At about the same time, Khrushchev was evidently supporting an unsuccessful challenge to Mao's leadership by the Chinese defense minister.[16] When these moves failed to change China's course, the Soviets curtailed their economic assistance, withdrawing between two and three thousand specialists and removing or destroying the blueprints of their projects.

In 1960 Sino-Soviet differences resurfaced, with the publication by the Chinese of a lengthy critique of the Russians under the title "Long Live Leninism."[17] In November of the same year, a conference of eighty-one communist parties in Moscow saw a dozen parties—with Albania foremost among them—support the Chinese positions. Although the overwhelming majority supported the Soviets, and a statement maintaining a facade of unity was published, the Soviets were undoubtedly humiliated by the need to lobby for support in the international communist movement. The Moscow conference proved to be the last meeting of its kind.

The Sino-Soviet conflict escalated further in the early 1960s as a result of incidents along their long border. The Chinese cited nine "unequal treaties" that had been forced on China by the tsars, and they laid claim to some 580,000 square miles of Soviet territory in the Far East. Tension also arose periodically along the Central Asian frontier, which divided the Chinese province of Xinjiang from the Soviet republics of Tajikistan, Kyrgyzstan, and Kazakhstan. Border incidents worsened in the latter half of the decade, during China's Cultural Revolution, and the two countries seemed close to open warfare in the spring of 1969, when armed clashes, involving large troop concentrations and artillery, occurred at their Far Eastern frontier along the Ussuri River. With both sides maintaining massive forces at the border, rumors circulated during the summer of 1969 that the Soviet Union might be considering a preemptive nuclear strike against China.[18] By then, each party clearly regarded the other—and no longer the United States—as its primary security threat. From the perspective of balance-of-power politics, the logic of the situation called for both sides to turn to the United States for assistance against the other. Triangular politics was to become a distinctive feature of the Cold War in the 1970s.

Brezhnev and the Policies of Detente

As a result of the massive build-up of Soviet strategic forces following the Cuban missile crisis, by 1970 the military strength of the two superpowers was approximately equal. While the United States continued to lead in many categories, the USSR pulled ahead in numbers of intercontinental ballistic missiles (ICBMs). However, the military expansion had put tremendous strain on the economy of the Soviet Union, whose rate of growth was rapidly dropping. Hesitant efforts at structural reform, led by Aleksei Kosygin, Khrushchev's successor as premier, challenged too many vested interests and were abandoned. Curtailment of military budgets was apparently not even seriously considered, given the considerable political power of military commanders and the defense industry lobbyists. Facing increasing pressures to improve the quantity and quality of consumer goods available to the Soviet population, Kosygin and Leonid Brezhnev, who had succeeded Khrushchev as head of the CPSU Secretariat, agreed that importing Western technology was their best available means of increasing economic productivity.

The new political landscape of the 1970s—emerging global tripolarity, Soviet-American military parity, and stagnation of the Soviet economy—necessitated a rethinking of Soviet foreign policy. The policy adopted by Brezhnev and his colleagues went beyond earlier practices of "peaceful

coexistence"—avoidance of war and relaxation of tensions with the West—
to include active collaboration in such areas as arms control, trade, crisis
management, and science and technology. In the West, the resulting relationship was labeled "detente" (French for "relaxation"), but in the USSR
there was never a connotation that all forms of struggle between opposing
social systems had come to an end or that genuine partnership had been
established. As Georgii Arbatov, a leading foreign policy advisor to Brezhnev, put it, "these relations will never become relations of an alliance between 'two superpowers who have divided up the world.' " Rather, "no
matter how successful the process of normalization and detente is, in the
historical sense [they] will remain relations of struggle."[19] Nevertheless, on
both sides of the ideological divide, influential politicians voiced skepticism
about the adversary's intentions and about the wisdom of cooperative
agreements.

During its first quarter century, the main battlefield of the Cold War had
been Europe, and especially divided Germany, and so it was predictable
that the first tests of the new policy took place there. The Soviet Union's
chief objective was to gain the West's acceptance of the division of Germany and its recognition of the legitimacy of the postwar territorial and
political changes in Eastern Europe. The election of Social Democratic
leader Willy Brandt as West German chancellor late in 1969 set change in
motion. Brandt's *Ostpolitik* abandoned the long-held Christian Democratic
goal of German reunification, substituting for it the more conciliatory formula of two German states within one German nation. A Soviet–West
German treaty, signed in August 1970, provided for mutual renunciation of
force and recognized the frontiers "of all states in Europe" as inviolable,
including the East German border with Poland. Thus, West Germany confirmed the division of that nation into two states and the loss of prewar
German lands in the east to Poland. These commitments were confirmed in
a separate treaty between the Federal Republic and Poland later in the year.

Chancellor Brandt's price for ratification of these treaties was a satisfactory four-power agreement on West Berlin. The West deemed it to be part
of the Federal Republic, while the Soviets still wanted West Berlin to be an
independent political entity, access to which would be controlled by East
Germany. Long and difficult negotiations produced a compromise agreement only after the replacement of hard-liner Walter Ulbricht as East German leader. The Final Quadripartite Protocol, signed by the Big Four in
June 1972, effectively removed Berlin as a source of East-West tension. It
stated that West Berlin was not a constituent part of the Federal Republic,
but it acknowledged Soviet responsibility to ensure unimpeded access to the
city. This was followed at the end of the year by a treaty between the two

German states that allowed them to establish mutual diplomatic representation and to gain admission to the United Nations, without definitively settling their permanent status.[20]

The USSR had long proposed an all-European conference on collective security as a means of gaining recognition of the postwar territorial and political status quo while reducing U.S. influence on the continent. During the late 1960s, the campaign for a European security conference took maximum advantage of the growing strains between the United States and its European allies, many of whom felt anxious about the escalating dimensions of Washington's involvement in Vietnam—an area thought by the NATO allies to be of distinctly secondary importance. The strong antiwar movement in the United States was paralleled by violent student unrest in Western Europe, the sharply anti-American tone of which was exploited by the Soviet Union and its various front organizations.

With the conclusion of the agreements on Germany and the Soviet consent to U.S. and Canadian participation, the Conference on Security and Cooperation in Europe opened in Helsinki in July 1973. The Final Act, known as the Helsinki Declaration, was signed on August 1, 1975, in a summit meeting of thirty-five states that approximated a peace conference for the war that had ended thirty years before. Brezhnev achieved his objective of gaining acknowledgment of the inviolability of the frontiers of all the states of Europe; but during the long negotiations the Soviets had to accede to the Western demand to include provisions ("Basket Three") recognizing and pledging the signatories to respect such human rights as freedom of thought, conscience, and religion; freer movement, contact among individuals, and travel; and free and wider dissemination of information. Brezhnev, who had put an end to the limited experimentation with freer expression that had been allowed in the Soviet Union during the Khrushchev period, and who had presided over a partial rehabilitation of Stalin's record, stated clearly that no such "interference in internal affairs" of the USSR would be accepted.

For U.S. President Richard Nixon and his national security advisor (later, Secretary of State) Henry Kissinger, the chief benefit of detente with the USSR was to be found in securing Soviet assistance in extricating the United States from the war in Vietnam under conditions that would not constitute a defeat. Concessions on Soviet priorities would be linked to this. As the major source of aid to North Vietnam, insuring against Hanoi's defeat, the Soviet Union had been content since the mid-1960s to see Washington tied down in an unpopular war it could not win, so long as the conflict did not escalate to the point that it threatened to draw in Moscow. To put additional pressure on Moscow, Nixon and Kissinger forged a new relationship with China, hoping to enlist Beijing's assistance toward the same objective.

Vietnam was a major topic of discussion in the summit meeting between Nixon and Brezhnev in May 1972. The United States apparently succeeded in gaining the help that it sought; a Vietnam truce agreement was signed in Paris the following January. Equally important at the summit were discussions on the limitation of strategic arms, aimed at countering developments in the arms race that threatened the strategic balance. The talks resulted in the signing of a treaty that would prohibit both sides from building a nationwide defense against ballistic missiles, by limiting the number of anti-ballistic missile (ABM) sites each side could have. The summit also produced an interim strategic arms limitation agreement (SALT I) establishing a five-year freeze on the number of offensive ballistic missiles possessed by each side, though allowing some replacements for older missiles.

A new, cooperative sphere in the Soviet-U.S. relationship was addressed in agreements on medicine, public health, the environment, space, and the prevention of naval incidents. In the commercial sphere, the two sides established a commission to discuss extension by the United States of most-favored-nation (MFN) trading status to the Soviet Union. This action was necessary to make it possible for the Soviets to pay for the technology and grain they sought to import from the United States, by giving their exports competitive access to the American market. A trade agreement in October 1972 opened the way for granting MFN status and credits in return for partial Soviet payment of the Lend-Lease debt from World War II. A separate agreement arranged for the Soviets to purchase $750 million worth of American grain over a three-year period on extremely favorable terms.

A second Nixon-Brezhnev summit was held in the United States in June 1973. With Vietnam no longer an irritant in the relationship, the two powers seemed closer than at any time since their wartime alliance. In the joint communiqué, they pledged "to turn the development of friendship and co-operation between their peoples into a permanent factor for worldwide peace."[21] Eleven agreements were signed during the summit, including a framework for the next stage in strategic arms limitations (SALT II) and an agreement on cooperation on the peaceful uses of atomic energy. The most important of the measures signed at the summit was the "Agreement on the Prevention of Nuclear War," which contained the following language:

> If at any time relations between the Parties or between either Party and other countries appear to involve the risk of a nuclear conflict, or if relations between countries not parties to this Agreement appear to involve the risk of nuclear war between the United States of America and the Union of Soviet

Socialist Republics or between either Party and other countries, the United States and the Soviet Union, acting in accordance with the provisions of this Agreement, shall immediately enter into urgent consultations with each other and make every effort to avert this risk.[22]

Throughout the Cold War, the superpowers had faced the risk that they could be dragged into conflict by allies they could not control. Such crises had occurred numerous times in the conflict in Indochina, as well as in the 1971 Bangladesh war, in which the United States had supported Pakistan and the USSR had backed India. In this accord the superpowers agreed that the need to cooperate with each other would override the interests of their allies, if necessary. Within a few months, the agreement was put to its first test—in the 1973 Yom Kippur war in the Middle East—and it proved wanting.

The war between Egypt and Syria on one side and Israel on the other began with an attack by Sadat's forces across the Suez Canal on October 6. Although the attack was a surprise to Israel and the United States, the Soviets had advance warning, but they did not act to prevent it or to consult the United States. The United States sought an immediate cease-fire, but the Soviets—having launched a massive resupply of arms to the Arabs—urged restraint only after the tide of battle had turned against their clients. Before a United Nations peacekeeping force could be organized, the Soviets had threatened unilateral intervention on behalf of the Arabs, and both super-powers had put their own military forces on high alert. Not only did the crisis raise even stronger doubts about the depth of detente, but it led to the virtual bankruptcy of Moscow's policy in the region, thanks to Henry Kissinger's brilliant "shuttle diplomacy." Realizing that whereas Moscow could supply the arms for war, apparently only the United States could achieve the peaceful return of Arab territories, Sadat broke with Moscow and agreed to a separate peace treaty with Israel, brokered by the United States.

From the high point of the Washington summit, Soviet-U.S. relations rapidly worsened. The Soviet Union's suppression of dissenters and its harassment of Jews who sought to emigrate weighed heavily with American public opinion, and led to Congressional action making MFN or trade credits dependent upon changes in Soviet policy. Angry at such interference, the Soviets eventually canceled the 1972 trade agreement. Likewise, negotiations for SALT II were stalled by U.S. concerns over the growing numbers of heavy Soviet missiles and by disagreements over how to deal with the new technology allowing for multiple independently targetable reentry vehicles (MIRVs). Weakened by the Watergate scandal, President Nixon nonetheless journeyed to Moscow in June 1974 for his final summit with Brezhnev, which produced no breakthroughs on the growing list of issues between the two superpowers. Nixon's successor, Gerald Ford, did manage to work out an agreement on further guidelines for a more far-reaching strategic arms limitation treaty during a meeting with Brezhnev in Vladivostok in November 1974. But mounting political discord in the ensuing months again put SALT II on the back burner.

While detente produced a marked change in the security environment of Europe, it was in the Third World that Brezhnev's policy ran aground. The Soviets had never understood detente as obligating them to pass up opportunities to reduce Western influence in the Third World; indeed, in their view, one of the benefits of the relaxation of tensions was that it created more favorable conditions for the pursuit of national liberation and revolutionary struggles. In addition to continuing tensions over Cuba and the crises in the Middle East, developments in Indochina presented an even greater challenge to detente. Not long after the signing of the Paris peace treaty, the United States began to complain to the Soviets about infiltration of North Vietnamese troops into the south. But the Soviets chose not to restrain their ally, and the United States was unable to strengthen the resistance of the noncommunist government in Saigon. In the spring of 1975 Vietnam was forcibly reunified under communist rule.

The fall of the right-wing dictatorship in Portugal in 1974 and the dissolution of Lisbon's empire in Africa further illustrated the differing understandings of detente. Whereas U.S. warnings to Moscow to refrain from direct support of pro-communist forces in the new government in Portugal—a NATO ally—were apparently heeded, no such caution was demonstrated by the Soviet Union in Portugal's former colonies in Africa. Soviet military aid to the Marxist faction (MPLA) in Angola's civil war was sharply increased in 1975, and Moscow introduced a new—and to Washington, even more disturbing—element when it tipped the military balance decisively by airlifting some 17,000 Cuban troops to fight on the side of the MPLA. Prevented from intervening by the action of a U.S. Congress still reeling from the Vietnam defeat, the Ford administration could only denounce the Soviet action, with the president even declaring that "detente" was no longer in his political vocabulary. But the Soviets continued to insist that they had never promised to abandon the ideological and revolutionary struggles. As one Russian remarked to his U.S. counterpart, "You Americans tried to sell detente like detergent and claimed it would do everything a detergent could do."[23]

The Soviet-Cuban victory in Angola coincided with the conclusion of the Twenty-fifth Party Congress in March 1976. General Secretary Brezhnev used this Congress to tighten his grip on party leadership and to proclaim the success of Soviet foreign policy. Citing the victory in Vietnam, treaties of friendship with Iraq and India, and normalization of relations with Germany, among other successes, Brezhnev declared that "the international position of the Soviet Union has never been more stable."[24] As we have already noted, however, this proved to be the high-water mark for Soviet influence in the Third World. The CPSU Congress had barely adjourned when Anwar Sadat unilaterally terminated the Soviet-Egyptian treaty. A year later Sudan, a long-time recipient of Soviet aid, also reversed its position and expelled all Soviet technicians and military advisors. Also in 1977, Somalia, angered at Moscow's aid to its antagonist, Ethiopia, followed suit by abrogating its treaty with Moscow, expelling Soviet advisors, and denying its naval facilities at Berbera to the Soviet navy. Even a seemingly contrary example of triumphant Soviet diplomacy and influence in 1978—a twenty-five-year security treaty with Vietnam—soon proved embarrassing. When Vietnam invaded neighboring Cambodia in support of a rebellion against its pro-Chinese government, China responded by invading Vietnam to punish it for its aggression. Moscow was unwilling to risk war with China by coming to the aid of its ally.

This mixed record of Soviet activism had not prevented the administration of President Jimmy Carter from proceeding with strategic arms negotiations. With great difficulty, a SALT II agreement was hammered out and signed at a summit between Carter and Brezhnev in Vienna in June 1979. The limits set in the treaty froze a status quo that gave the USSR more powerful missiles with a greater throw weight than any possessed by the United States, while leaving the latter with a superiority in the total number of warheads. The main benefit of the treaty was in reducing the risk of war by adding to the stability of the deterrent relationship, making each side's second strike forces more secure. The limits would also permit both sides to reduce their defense budgets.

But the SALT II treaty was never ratified, as it and the remaining fragments of detente fell victim to the Brezhnev regime's most dramatic demonstration of lack of restraint—its invasion of Afghanistan in December 1979. The crisis began with a Soviet-instigated coup d'état in which Afghanistan's Marxist president, Hafizullah Amin, was murdered. At the "invitation" of Amin's Soviet-installed successor, Babrak Karmal, Soviet troops entered the country to put down a widespread Islamic insurrection that had been incited by Amin's radical social and economic policies. As the Kremlin saw it, failure to preserve a pro-Soviet government in Afghanistan would have created the specter of a third (with Khomeini's Iran and Zia's Pakistan) anticommunist Islamic republic on the periphery of Soviet

Central Asia. But even though Afghanistan was headed by a Marxist government with which a treaty of friendship had been signed, the invasion was the first time Moscow had sent combat forces into a country that was not actually a part of the Soviet bloc. This was the critical distinction that shocked world opinion more than the Soviet invasion of Hungary in 1956 or the Warsaw Pact invasion of Czechoslovakia in 1968. The United Nations General Assembly in January 1980 voted 104 to 18 to deplore the invasion, and a conference of thirty-six Islamic states later in the month did likewise.

The reaction of the United States was strong. President Carter lamented, "This action of the Soviets has made a more dramatic change in my own opinion of what the Soviets' ultimate goals are than anything they've done in the previous time I've been in office."[25] As punitive measures, he announced the curtailment of U.S. grain sales, suspension of high-technology exports, deferral of cultural and economic exchanges, and a boycott of the 1980 Moscow Olympics. In his State of the Union address, he warned Moscow against pushing further, stating that the United States was prepared to go to war to defend vital oil supply routes in the Persian Gulf. In summary, he said, "The Soviet Union must realize that its decision to use military force in Afghanistan will be costly to every political and economic relationship it values."[26]

The price paid by the Soviet Union for its occupation of Afghanistan was much greater than it anticipated. Like the United States in Vietnam, Moscow learned that conventional military superiority was no guarantee of success against guerrilla forces. By the time of Brezhnev's death in 1982, more than 110,000 Soviet troops were in Afghanistan, but the resistance— using bases in Pakistan, and covertly supplied by the United States—was fiercer than ever. The Afghan government's army had virtually disappeared through defections, and Soviet officials were overseeing almost every function of administration in the country.

Its heavy casualties were not the only costs to the USSR. The collapse of detente had led to a new tension in relations with the West—and especially with the new and stridently anti-Soviet administration of U.S. President Ronald Reagan, which initiated a major build-up in military power. Virtually cut off from Western trade and technology, the Soviet economy continued to decline, deepening the country's social unrest, and the technological development of its weaponry began to slip well behind that of the United States.

Beset with an even deeper economic crisis, communist Poland was faced with a workers' movement led by Lech Walesa, which managed in the fall of 1980 to topple party leader Edward Gierek and achieve recognition of a free trade union, Solidarity. When the crisis threatened to dislodge the communist regime itself, the Soviet Union hinted at invasion. But the immediate danger passed in December 1981 with the declaration of martial law by General Wojciech Jaruzelski, the commander of the Polish armed forces, who also had assumed the posts of party leader and premier. Nevertheless, the experience of neighboring Poland had to serve as a chilling reminder to the aging Soviet leaders of the limits of popular patience with economic and social deprivations.

The Twilight of the "Old Thinking"

In the sixty-five years between the Bolshevik revolution and Leonid Brezhnev's death in November 1982, the Soviet regime had experienced only three real leadership successions: the protracted conflict among Stalin and his various rivals following the illness and death of Vladimir Lenin; the succession to Stalin; and the succession to Khrushchev, which differed from the others in that the incumbent leader was removed not by death but by a coup d'état. In stark contrast, the USSR had three successions during the twenty-eight months (November 1982 to March 1985) that followed Brezhnev's death. The significance of this brief period goes beyond the fact that three general secretaries of the CPSU died in less than three years, being rooted in a much more profound changing of the aging Kremlin guard. The generation of Brezhnev, Kosygin, Gromyko, and their Politburo colleagues had enjoyed an unusually long tenure in high offices, with most of them rising to positions of command in their thirties as the result of the liquidation of their elders. Thus, the multi-stage succession to Brezhnev was part of the first thoroughgoing generational change in the Soviet leadership since the Great Purge of the 1930s. The other point that was underscored by the unusual string of successions was that the Soviet Union still had no regular constitutional means by which to replace its top leader. Indeed, even in cases where the top leader had left an heir-apparent, power was inherited by another.

Quite likely, some of the drift and immobility of the latter period of Brezhnev's administration was related to the age and physical condition of the ruling elite. His successor, Iurii Andropov, the long-time head of the security police (KGB), who had only recently moved into the party secretariat, was thought to be intellectually superior to his colleagues. But an initial period of vigorous activity in domestic and foreign affairs came to an early end with the failure of Andropov's health.

Andropov had sought to wake up the stagnant Soviet economy by campaigning against the widespread inefficiency and corruption, but only short-term improvements were possible in the absence of a fundamental restructuring of the system of centralized economic decision-making. Although he presided over the removal of some of the oldest and most inept members of the regional party elite, Andropov was either unable or unwilling to introduce radical change in the Soviet system.

During the first part of 1983, the new leader was able to produce modest improvements in Soviet relations with both China and the United States. But Soviet-U.S. relations re-entered the deep freeze in September, when the Soviets shot down an unarmed civilian airliner (Korean Airline flight 007) that had strayed over their territory. In the aftermath, the Soviets compounded international outrage by denying responsibility, lying about the facts, refusing to compensate the families of victims, and accusing the United States of using the plane for espionage.

It was also during the final months of Andropov's brief term that Soviet-U.S. arms control negotiations suffered a severe setback. The arms race had intensified, with both sides concerned about weapons developments by the other and worried that they might suffer politically from perceptions that they were falling behind in strength. In order to replace older missiles that had become vulnerable to more accurate U.S. weapons, the Soviets in 1977 had deployed a new intermediate range missile (the SS-20), which was mobile, solid-fueled, accurate, and MIRVed. Perceived by NATO as not only survivable but also a potential first-strike weapon, the missile appeared capable of upsetting the European balance of power unless matched by NATO. Accordingly, in 1979 the alliance had decided to persuade the Soviets to remove the SS-20s or face deployment by 1983 of a modernized intermediate range nuclear force (INF) of 572 Pershing II and cruise missiles in response. As negotiations bogged down, NATO increasingly saw itself facing a political test of its credibility and cohesion against an adroitly managed Soviet "peace campaign" designed to appeal to a nervous European public.

Paralleling the INF talks and equally stalemated were the negotiations to reduce strategic weapons, now referred to as START. Both sides sought to reduce the other's inventory of missiles viewed as capable of destroying their own retaliatory forces in a first strike. After it was announced in March 1983, the Soviets were also intent on forestalling Reagan's Strategic Defense Initiative (SDI)—a space-based ballistic missile defense capable of destroying Soviet missiles before they could reach their targets. Reagan's plans were especially threatening to Moscow, not only because they could destabilize the military balance and force a new round of offensive missile production, but also because the Soviets doubted that they could muster the economic and technological resources to match the U.S. defenses.

When the United States began installing cruise missiles in Britain and Germany in December 1983 as scheduled by NATO, the Soviet reaction was sharp and immediate: it angrily broke off both the INF and START negotiations. Andropov had calculated that the Soviet walkout would force NATO to halt its deployment, especially in the face of an expected popular outcry in Europe. The tactic backfired, leaving the Soviets with the onus of having cut off all possibilities of curbing the arms race.

Andropov's death in February 1984 did not provoke his colleagues to grasp the opportunity to choose a younger and more vigorous leader. Rather, he was replaced by a seventy-two-year-old, visibly ailing Brezhnev crony, the veteran party bureaucrat Konstantin Chernenko. Domestically, there was not even the pretense of reform of Soviet society or the economy along the lines of Andropov. In foreign policy, there were also no bold initiatives or breakthroughs. However, at the very end of his brief term, Chernenko did retreat from his predecessor's demand that the United States cease deploying INF missiles in Europe as a precondition for the resumption of arms talks. Two days before the negotiations were to recommence, Chernenko died.

This time, the majority of Politburo members could not escape recognizing the necessity of an energetic push toward reform. They elected as general secretary their youngest colleague, Mikhail Gorbachev—at age fifty-four younger than any man to assume the office since Stalin. Gorbachev's colleagues thought that they were electing a tough and earnest reformer, but not a radical. The Soviet system that produced him did not promote to high positions people of unorthodox thought or bold action. Only loyalists advanced in the party apparatus, and nothing in Gorbachev's career suggested that he was anything but a loyal communist.

The Soviet economy that Gorbachev inherited in March 1985 had experienced virtually no real growth in over a decade. It was not even one-half the size of the U.S. economy, and yet it was burdened with the need to support a fully competitive military establishment. Agricultural productivity was less than one-fourth that of the United States, and about one-third of Soviet food production spoiled before reaching the consumer—forcing the USSR to become the world's largest importer of grain. Over 10 percent of the country's gross national product was devoted to subsidizing this inefficient agricultural sector, in order to keep food prices artificially low. The housing stock throughout the country was inadequate, especially in the rural areas, where indoor plumbing was still relatively rare. Because of poor diet and low public health standards, the country was experiencing a decline in the average life span of its citizens and an increase in infant mortality. The supply of consumer goods, always irregular, suffered periodic disruptions, resulting in panic buying and in long lines for all shoppers (except the elite, who had access to special stores) whenever goods were available.

During the Brezhnev years, people had been constantly bombarded with the claim that "life is improving," even while they were surrounded with abundant evidence that the country was falling apart. The result of the sharp disjuncture between claim and reality was almost universal cynicism and the search for "private solutions"—which for many citizens meant the black market, and for others meant "dropping out" through alcoholism, drug abuse, or other deviant behavior.

Gorbachev's initial impulse was to continue the approach of his mentor, Andropov, instilling greater discipline into the work force through a combination of exhortation and a law-and-order campaign that included rooting out corruption and drastically cutting down on the availability of alcohol.

The paucity of results brought a recognition that the roots of the problem were deeper, and that what was required was *perestroika* (restructuring)—moderate reform from within the socialist economic system. More resources were to be invested in the domestic infrastructure and in consumer goods, and the military budget was reduced accordingly. In the services sector, some mixing of forms of ownership was allowed. The gigantic state planning mechanism was to be overhauled, the size and power of the central economic ministries reduced, and enterprises throughout the country were gradually to be put on a system of *khozraschet* (an obligation to produce enough value to cover their costs of production). The trouble with this program was that it had all been tried before, in the 1960s, under the sponsorship first of Khrushchev and then of Kosygin, but it had failed to produce the desired results—in part because it had been openly sabotaged by the party and state bureaucracy long enmeshed in Stalinist work habits and the attendant system of perquisites and job security.

Just as the shortcomings of gradual economic reform were not immediately evident to Gorbachev, so also he began his quest for arms control without a fresh (or workable) strategy. His early proposals called for total abolition of nuclear weapons, on which the USSR was less dependent than the West for its security—essentially resurrecting the "ban the bomb" propaganda campaigns of the late 1940s. But his primary emphasis was on derailing Reagan's Strategic Defense Initiative (SDI). At his initial summit encounter with Reagan, in Geneva in November 1985, he emerged with nothing to show toward either goal.

After a year of hard campaigning before Western public opinion on behalf of both proposals, Gorbachev met with Reagan again—this time in Reykjavik, Iceland. Agreement seemed near on a number of important issues: a 50-percent reduction in strategic forces; elimination of all INF in

Europe and deployment elsewhere of only 100 by each side; and obser-vance of the ABM treaty for another ten years. But Gorbachev made every-thing contingent on limiting SDI to laboratory research during the ten-year period. Reagan refused to comply, and the conference collapsed. Even more damaging to Reagan's prestige was the revelation that as the talks pro-gressed he had departed significantly from the prepared U.S. position. First he had proposed, as a condition of the ten-year extension of the ABM treaty, that both sides eliminate all their ballistic missiles by the end of that period, and then he had accepted Gorbachev's counterproposal that not just missiles but all strategic nuclear weapons be eliminated. As a result, the Soviets were able to launch a post-summit propaganda campaign claiming that total strategic nuclear disarmament could have been achieved, had it not been for Reagan's stubborn refusal to abandon SDI.

In Gorbachev's hands, Soviet policy positions were handled more smoothly and energetically in 1985 and 1986, but they were fundamentally the same positions as before. Soviet-U.S. relations continued to be character-ized by sharp rhetoric and public posturing on both sides. Tension in Soviet relations with China was slightly reduced under Gorbachev, but could not be eliminated as long as Soviet troops remained in Afghanistan and Vietnamese forces stayed in Cambodia, and as long as the Sino-Soviet border remained heavily militarized. Gorbachev appeared still to be trying to win a military victory in Afghanistan. Finally, with regard to domestic policies, the Soviet regime's relationship with its own population did not appear to have changed fundamentally under Gorbachev. This was dramatically illustrated by the leaders' failure to give a prompt, full, and honest account of the terrible accident at the Chernobyl nuclear facility in April 1986.

"New Thinking" and the End of the Cold War

Gradually, Gorbachev realized that he must break the power of the bureau-cracy in order to accomplish reform of the economy. At a crucial CPSU Central Committee plenum in January 1987, the definition of perestroika was broadened to include democratization of the country, and Gorbachev began to unleash popular forces that he thought would be his allies in the struggle for economic reform. Profound changes such as greater official tolerance for religion, the opening up of new avenues of cultural expression, and the revision of interpretations of prior Soviet history were introduced not as ends in themselves, but as devices intended to mobilize public pres-sure against the Soviet bureaucracy, so as to break its resistance to the freeing up of economic forces in the country. The intent of the *glasnost* (openness) campaign was not to open up an attack on the legitimacy of the party or its Marxist-Leninist ideology, but to attack the pillars of the Stalinist system. Similarly, the democratization of political institutions was not originally intended to end the communist party's monopoly on power. Rather, it was to be guided from above to bring about swifter changes in middle-level party leadership, by forcing unpopular party bureaucrats to face the wrath of the voters, and by utilizing local and national legislatures to put pressure on a conservative party bureaucracy.

The necessary companion to these evolving ideas about domestic reform was a new approach toward changing the confrontational relationship between East and West. What came to be known as the "new thinking" in foreign policy proceeded from the premise of the "interdependence of states and peoples," an idea much discussed in the West, but less familiar in the communist world. In an interdependent world, Gorbachev reasoned, national security could not be based on the use or threat of nuclear weapons. Rather, security for the superpowers must be mutual, and must be ensured by political means. Enormous sums of money and attention had been squandered by prior regimes on the military competition, he acknowledged, to the neglect of possibilities for cooperation.

In the new spirit of glasnost, pointed references to the errors and shortcomings of the Brezhnev-era "old thinking" began to appear in the Soviet press. One writer described the decisions to deploy SS-20 missiles and to introduce Soviet troops into Afghanistan as examples of "solutions of a subjectivist nature oriented toward the use of military-force tactics in foreign policy" which did great "moral and material damage" to the USSR.[27] Another condemned the "incompetent approach of the Brezhnev leadership," which had neglected the country's vital national interests by trying to keep up with the United States in an unproductive arms race. "Our true interest," he wrote, was in ensuring an international atmosphere that would allow "profound transformations" in the country's economy and its social and political systems.[28] As the advocates of "new thinking" saw it, economic strength was proving more decisive than military strength in resolving many global issues, and thus only by reversing its precipitous economic slide and establishing linkages to the international economy could the USSR qualify as a true "superpower."

Gorbachev was at pains to stress that the "new thinking" did not amount to an abandonment of the classic principles of Marxist-Leninist doctrine—the "greatest revolutionary worldview." But the ideology had to be adapted to new circumstances: "Loyalty to Marxist-Leninist teaching," he said, "lies in its creative development on the basis of accumulated experience."[29] It was left to Gorbachev's new foreign minister, Eduard Shevardnadze, to announce the most far-reaching change in interpretation of the Marxist-Leninist doctrine—a renunciation of the concept of class struggle as the fundamental guide to foreign policy. At a conference of senior Soviet diplomats and scholars convened in July 1988, he said that in the nuclear age it was no longer justifiable to see peaceful coexistence as a special form of the class struggle. Rather, "the struggle of two opposing systems is no longer the decisive tendency of the contemporary age."[30] A few days later, the Politburo's chief conservative, Egor Ligachev, attempted to rebut this notion. But the last word was given to Gorbachev's close associate, Aleksandr Yakovlev, who wrote in *Pravda*—Lenin's own paper and still the party's authoritative voice—this extraordinary interpretation of Marx's doctrine:

> Marxism as such is the interpretation of the common interests of mankind from the point of view of history and the perspective of the development of all mankind, not only that of individual countries or classes, peoples or social groups. In placing in the forefront the interests of the downtrodden and exploited . . . can it be said that the founding fathers of socialism placed the interests of that class against the interests of all the others? Of course not. The thesis of the priority of the common interests of mankind . . . helps us look realistically and soundly at the idea of the coexistence of countries with different political structures as a requirement of history and a manifestation of the internationalist tendencies of global development.[31]

In stark opposition to the positions articulated by Brezhnev and Arbatov during the detente of the 1970s, Gorbachev and his spokesmen were attacking the very foundations of communist ideology.

Simultaneously with this change in doctrine and the movement toward democratization, Gorbachev executed a momentous shift in Soviet foreign policy positions. In February 1987, he made the first of several significant concessions on the INF issue. This quickly led to a treaty, signed at a summit in Washington in December, in which the two sides agreed to eliminate the entire class of Soviet and U.S. medium-range and short-range missiles. The agreement removed a dangerous threat to European security, while resolving a dispute that had poisoned Moscow's relations with Washington for a decade.

The last years of the 1980s witnessed Soviet initiatives to resolve some of the regional conflicts in Asia, Africa, and Latin America that had been so divisive in Soviet-U.S. relations. The American public had been especially concerned about the extent of Soviet assistance to revolutionary movements in Central America. The Sandinista regime in Nicaragua had received massive military and economic aid from the Soviet Union and its allies. In 1989 Gorbachev communicated to President Bush that the military aid would be terminated. While the Soviets were undoubtedly shocked by the Ortega government's overwhelming electoral defeat early in 1990, Gorbachev was probably pleased to be rid of this burdensome Third World conflict. The long-standing Soviet-Cuban involvement in Angola was terminated through negotiations that were concluded in 1988. In the Middle East, the Soviets joined with the United States in sponsoring a 1987 UN resolution seeking a cease-fire in the lengthy war between Iran and Iraq; when the war finally ended the following year, Moscow moved quickly to improve relations with Iran. At the same time, the Soviet Union adopted a higher profile in urging that international peace talks be initiated, toward resolving the conflict between Israel and the Palestine Liberation Organization.

Most significant, however, was Gorbachev's decision early in 1988 to liquidate the Soviet Union's costly war in Afghanistan. Gorbachev committed the USSR to a phased withdrawal of its troops without assurances that a communist-dominated government would remain in Afghanistan. By January 1989, after suffering casualties in excess of 13,000 killed and 35,000 wounded, all forces of the USSR had been withdrawn, but the disunity of the anticommunist guerrilla forces helped to extend the life of the pro-Soviet government.

Having thereby removed an irritant in relations not just with Washington but also with Beijing, Gorbachev proceeded to encourage Vietnam to withdraw its remaining troops from Cambodia in 1989. With two of China's three conditions for a normalization in relations thus realized, Gorbachev traveled to Beijing in May 1989 for the first Sino-Soviet summit in twenty years. There he addressed the third condition for normalization, announcing a substantial unilateral cutback of about 200,000 troops in the Soviet Far East and proposing demilitarization of the entire Sino-Soviet border. The rapprochement with China was sealed the following year when Premier Li Peng went to Moscow to conclude a ten-year pact for increased economic and scientific cooperation.

Also improving relations on Moscow's other major front, Gorbachev participated in three summit meetings with Presidents Reagan and Bush, in 1988 and 1989, respectively. The fruit of relaxed tensions—benefiting not only world peace but also the Soviet defense budget—was evident in December 1988, when Gorbachev announced in a dramatic speech at the United Nations General Assembly that the Soviet Union would make a unilateral reduction of 500,000 troops and would remove 10,000 tanks, 8,500 artillery pieces, and 800 combat aircraft from the European theater.

As Gorbachev and his reform-minded colleagues began to introduce perestroika, glasnost, and democratization into Soviet domestic politics and "new thinking" into Soviet foreign policy, they were encouraging their communist colleagues in Eastern Europe to join them in the reform program. When they informed the "little Brezhnevs" of Eastern Europe—as early as 1987—that Soviet troops would no longer protect them from their peoples, the Soviet leaders were not anticipating the total repudiation of communism there. Rather, they were hoping that the socialist system in Eastern Europe would be salvaged through the reformist activities of "little Gorbachevs" who would come to power. Justifying Soviet actions in the wake of the dramatic changes of 1989 and 1990, Shevardnadze told the Twenty-eighth CPSU Congress: "We sensed that unless serious changes and reforms were made, matters would reach the point of tragic events. But, proceeding from the principles of the new political thinking, we couldn't interfere in others' affairs. . . . I think that we acted correctly."[32] However, the attempt to save the socialist system in Eastern Europe by reforming it never got off the ground. Throughout the region, spontaneous mass movements, arising out of depressed living standards and widespread alienation and disillusionment, challenged governments that lacked legitimacy.

The movement began in the spring of 1989 in Poland, where negotiations between President Jaruzelski and Lech Walesa produced in June the first partially free elections since the communist takeover. Solidarity won virtually every contested seat. In August, with Poland pledging to stay in the Warsaw Pact, the Soviet Union consented to a noncommunist prime minister there, and in December Jaruzelski was replaced as president by Walesa. Also in the spring of 1989, a reformist communist regime in Hungary, having accepted with Gorbachev's approval the creation of independent political parties, negotiated with the opposition to schedule free elections for the following spring—which it lost overwhelmingly. In the meantime, the Hungarian communists startled the world by tearing down the country's barbed-wire border with Austria. Thousands of East Germans, disillusioned with the lack of opportunities in the "workers' paradise," streamed into Hungary and were allowed in September to cross to freedom in West Germany. Hoping to stem the flow, a desperate East German communist regime received Gorbachev's implicit agreement to replacing its aging dictator. Responding to massive demonstrations across the country, the new leaders announced that travel restrictions to the West would be lifted. As hundreds of thousands of East Berliners poured into the streets, a frightened local communist leader felt he had no choice but to open the hated wall. The delirious citizens of Berlin had a weekend party the likes of which the world never expected to see.

A few days later, more than 200,000 people demonstrated in Prague, where the hard-line communist regime—in a striking reversal of the situation in 1968—had been criticized by the Soviet press as insufficiently reformist. A general strike, organized by students, forced an end to the

Europe

communist monopoly of power in Czechoslovakia and an agreement on free elections. Emerging as the new leader was dissident playwright Vaclav Havel, just released from a Prague prison, who reluctantly accepted the presidency when old-line communist Gustav Husak was forced to resign. In Sofia, Bulgaria, in early December, 50,000 people marched for democracy. In January, the parliament revoked the communist party's monopoly of power, and talks began to prepare the way for free elections in June. Changing its name to the Bulgarian Socialist Party, the former communist party managed to prevail in the elections, though under new leadership.

Romania's revolt under communism was the last in the Soviet bloc, and the only one that became violent. Iron-fisted dictator Nicolae Ceausescu ordered his security police (the Securitate) to fire on demonstrators in Timisoara on December 15. Staging a rally in Bucharest a few days later to condemn "foreign conspirators" for subverting his regime, Ceausescu was loudly booed by students in the crowd. Some demonstrators were killed and others arrested by police. When violence broke out in the capital, Ceausescu and his wife fled. On December 25 they were apprehended, tried, and executed. A provisional government, the National Salvation Front, was formed, headed by Ion Iliescu, a former high-ranking communist who had been ousted by Ceausescu. Its assumption of power was forcibly resisted by the Securitate, which was defeated only after much bloodshed. Iliescu's forces were able to win a landslide victory over anticommunist parties in free elections in May.

Ever since the fall of the Berlin Wall in November 1989, the possibility of German reunification had reappeared as a focal point of East–West negotiations. After Gorbachev publicly accepted the principle of unification at the end of January, NATO and the Warsaw Pact discussed for the next several months what political structure would best guarantee Europe's security: a neutral Germany, a unified Germany in NATO, or a unified Germany in both security systems. These discussions were formalized in the "two plus four" talks among the two Germanys and the USSR, Britain, France, and the United States. Apparently, Gorbachev's initial opposition to the membership of a unified Germany in NATO was a bargaining device, and it succeeded in winning him a good price from West German Chancellor Helmut Kohl: a credit of five billion German marks, together with an agreement that Soviet troops could remain in eastern Germany through 1994, and that NATO forces would not be moved into the former GDR. Moreover, Germany's army would be limited to 370,000 troops, and Germany would be prohibited from possessing nuclear, biological, or chemical weapons. The Final Settlement with Respect to Germany was signed on September 12, 1990, by the two-plus-four powers, followed the next day by a Treaty of

Friendship between Germany and the USSR. The official reunification of Germany took place on October 3.

East Germany's withdrawal from the Warsaw Pact, together with Hungarian and Czech demands for the removal of Soviet troops from their territories, raised the question of the future utility of the alliance. In June 1990, its members declared that the West was no longer an "ideological enemy"—a statement answered the following month by a declaration from NATO that the Warsaw Pact countries were no longer adversaries. The following February, the members of the Warsaw Pact formally voted to disband the military components of the alliance by March 31, 1991.

The reunification of Germany and the end of the system of hostile military alliances in Europe essentially brought the Cold War to an end. A symbolic "peace conference" took place in November 1990, at the summit meeting of the Conference on Security and Cooperation in Europe (CSCE) in Paris, where a Treaty on Conventional Forces in Europe (CFE) was signed. In it, the countries of NATO and the Warsaw Pact agreed to maintain equal levels of conventional forces in Europe, thus formalizing the removal of the decades-long fear that the Soviet Union could overwhelm the continent with its conventional superiority. A few weeks prior to the conference, it was announced that Mikhail Gorbachev had been awarded the Nobel Peace Prize for his contributions toward ending the Cold War.

As the Cold War was ending in Europe, a new crisis broke out in the Middle East that tested the notion, articulated by both the Soviet and American presidents, of a "new world order" in which the powers would cooperate to defend the principle of the non-use of force to achieve national objectives. Soviet-American cooperation was especially tested by Iraq's invasion of Kuwait in August 1990 because of Moscow's long-standing alliance with Baghdad. Gorbachev was subjected to cross pressures from his advisors, some of whom stressed the need for the Soviets to join the emerging global coalition against Iraq, and others of whom counseled against the loss of a position of influence in the Middle East. While condemning Iraq's invasion and suspending arms shipments, as well as supporting the United Nations resolution for an economic and military embargo of Iraq, Moscow refused to withdraw its advisors there and sought to restrain the coalition from using force against Saddam Hussein. Gorbachev sent his special envoy Evgenii Primakov, who had personal ties to Saddam, on missions to Baghdad twice in October and again in February, seeking to persuade Saddam to withdraw from Kuwait. As the deadline neared for President Bush's ultimatum demanding that Saddam withdraw or face ground war, Gorbachev was desperately telephoning world leaders, seeking support for a compromise solution. Although Soviet prestige suffered when these mediation efforts failed, Moscow and Washington both agreed that their cooperative relationship had survived the Gulf War intact.

During the months of the Persian Gulf crisis, Gorbachev was involved in mounting political difficulties at home. Having achieved constitutional changes in March 1990 that ended the CPSU's monopoly of power and established a new executive presidency, he employed the Twenty-eighth Congress of the CPSU in July 1990 to change the party statutes to allow for direct election of the general secretary by the congress, to expand the Politburo to include representatives of each of the USSR republics, and in general to shift responsibility for direct management of the economy from the party to new government bodies. But perestroika had become a hollow slogan as the Soviet economy entered a period of negative growth, and democratization and glasnost—intended to weaken the conservative forces of resistance—had spurred revelations and discussions of unsolved problems, heightening frustrations and stimulating further dissension. The dissent, increasingly targeted toward Gorbachev himself, came primarily from three as yet unorganized sources: (1) the working masses—stolidly conservative proletarian and peasant forces, longing for the relative security and patriotic achievement of the Stalin and Brezhnev eras, angered by growing shortages, and opposing measures that threatened the national "safety net" by introducing unemployment, increased prices, and reduced welfare subsidies; (2) the liberal opposition, grouped around Boris Yeltsin, that sought a radical shortening of the time frame of reforms, more concessions to private enterprise and foreign ventures, more radical decentralization of economic decision-making, virtual elimination of the residual powers of the party, and drastic reduction in the executive powers now concentrated in Gorbachev's hands; (3) secessionist nationality groups, especially in the Baltic states, the Transcaucasus, and Ukraine, emboldened by glasnost, tempted by the spectacle of even greater freedoms newly enjoyed in the neighboring lands of Eastern Europe, and threatening to break up the multinational Soviet state.

In September 1990, Gorbachev backed away from a political compromise with Yeltsin that would have adopted a "500-day plan" for radical decentralization and market socialism. One by one, his more progressive advisors walked away, in sadness or disgust. The last to leave was Shevardnadze, who resigned as foreign minister in December with a dramatic warning that the country was headed toward dictatorship. In picking a new team, Gorbachev found ministers who appeared to be only younger versions of the gray bureaucrats who had run the Soviet system into the ground for the previous three decades. In January, his new team dispatched military forces to the Baltics, ostensibly to enforce Soviet laws on military conscription, but in fact to bludgeon the defiant secessionists into submitting to Moscow's authority. When demonstrators were killed in both Lithuania and Latvia, there was a storm of international protest.

Yet again, the acrobat tilted his political orientation. Gorbachev concluded a surprise agreement in April with Yeltsin and the leaders of nine union republics, establishing a framework for a new Union Treaty that would provide considerable autonomy for the republics. Seeking to regain lost international support, Gorbachev signaled his support for an economic reform plan that would utilize large-scale Western aid to assist a move to a market economy in the USSR, but the West was understandably reluctant to make commitments until details of the plan were in place. Gorbachev pleaded his case for aid at the annual summit of the leading industrial nations (the "Group of Seven," or G-7) in London in mid-July, and with President Bush at a summit in Moscow at the end of that month. The other major feature of the Soviet-American summit was the signing of the long-awaited START treaty—the first arms control agreement to undertake substantial reductions in the size of the strategic nuclear arsenals of the two countries. Under its terms, the United States agreed to reduce its inventory of warheads from 11,602 to 8,592, and the Soviet Union, from 10,877 to 6,940.

Although Gorbachev had assumed the presidency of his country, he had rejected advice that he seek a popular mandate through national elections. The enormity of this error became clearer in June 1991, when his reformist rival, Boris Yeltsin, won election as president of the Russian Republic, drawing 57.3 percent of the vote against several conservative candidates. Yeltsin thus eclipsed Gorbachev by becoming the first popularly elected Russian leader in Russian and Soviet history. A few days after the election, key members of Gorbachev's government—led by KGB chief Vladimir Kriuchkov, interior minister Boris Pugo, defense minister Dimitrii Yazov, and prime minister Valentin Pavlov—attempted a constitutional coup by harshly criticizing Gorbachev's policies before the national legislature and asking it to cede many of his powers to them. Oddly, a victorious Gorbachev took no action against them.

Two months later, the same individuals, joined by four others (including Gorbachev's hand-picked vice president) constituted themselves as a State Committee for the State of Emergency, placing the president under house arrest at his Black Sea dacha and usurping his powers. Ineptly led, the coup collapsed after three days, when important units of the military failed to obey orders to dispel large crowds of resisters who were under Yeltsin's leadership. In the wake of the failure of this effort to resurrect the essential features of the old Soviet political order, the entire system unraveled. The weeks after the coup saw Gorbachev's resignation as CPSU general secretary and the suspension of the party's activities, declarations of independence by the republics, and abandonment of many of the institutions of the central government. As in 1917, the country was ruled for the next several months by a "dual power" consisting of Gorbachev on the one hand and Yeltsin and other key republic leaders on the other. They were ostensibly cooperating to adopt a much-revised Union Treaty that would have preserved most of the former Soviet Union (minus the three Baltic republics, whose independence was recognized in September) as a confederated Union of Sovereign States. However, Yeltsin and the leaders of Ukraine and Belorussia, meeting at the Belovezhskaia forest on December 8, decided instead to create a Commonwealth of Independent States, with Minsk as its capital—leaving no role for a reconstituted USSR or its president. The three leaders telephoned their decision to President Bush before they told the Soviet president. Gorbachev's frantic efforts to save his country and his job went virtually without support. On December 25, 1991, he resigned as president, and on the last day of the year the Union of Soviet Socialist Republics officially went out of existence. In his final television broadcast as president, Gorbachev told his people:

> Our society has attained freedom, has liberated itself politically and spiritually. And that is the major victory, of which we are not yet fully cognizant, undoubtedly because we have not yet learned how to use it. . . .
> We live in a new world: the Cold War is over, the threat of a world war has been averted; the arms race and the insane militarization that distorted our economy, our social consciousness, and our morality have been halted. . . .
> I am certain that, sooner or later, our joint efforts will bear fruit, and that our peoples will live in a democratic and prosperous society.[33]

"The Cold War Is Over"

For decades, as hostile armies stared at each other across the chasm of divided Europe, most observers' estimates of the Soviet Union's strength and its resolve to hold onto its hard-won security zone in Eastern Europe left them firmly persuaded that Moscow would not voluntarily abandon its empire. This assessment seemed credible in light of images from East Germany in 1953, when Soviet armies fired on striking East German workers; or from Budapest in 1956, when Soviet tanks crushed freedom fighters armed only with Molotov cocktails; or from Prague in 1968, when the combined forces of the USSR, East Germany, Poland, Hungary, and Bulgaria squeezed the life out of Alexander Dubcek's effort to build "socialism with a human face." Thus it seemed inconceivable to observers not only in the West but in Eastern Europe itself that communism would crumble in East Germany, Poland, Czechoslovakia, and Hungary without a shot being fired.

For over forty years the United States had led a coalition of Western nations in pursuit of a policy of containment of the spread of Soviet power through the application not only of firm diplomacy but also of enormous and expensive military deterrent forces. In George Kennan's original formulation of the policy in 1947 he had forecast that the steady application of Western resolve and pressure would someday result in the liberalizing transformation of the countries of the Soviet empire. Though Kennan himself felt that the military expression of containment was at times overused, there is no doubt that the events of 1989–90 would not have occurred but for the Western military deterrent that produced an uneasy stability in Europe throughout the long night of the Cold War.

Another key ingredient in producing the transformation of Eastern Europe was the insistence by Western diplomats—led by the United States, during the long years of bargaining that became known as the "Helsinki process"—on the inclusion of a "basket" of human rights principles in any collective treaty that reaffirmed the postwar borders in Europe. When the Soviet Union and its East European allies signed a Helsinki agreement on Collective Security and Cooperation in Europe that contained a statement of the fundamental human rights of all the peoples of Europe, their communist dictators probably reckoned that these ringing phrases were as flimsy as the paper they were written on. To their everlasting consternation, however, human rights groups sprang up throughout the Soviet bloc, seizing on the Helsinki declaration for their moral authority.

In a real sense, however, the seeds of the dissolution of the Soviet empire in Eastern Europe were sown in the very process of its establishment. For the political and economic system that was created there was a virtual replication of the Stalinist totalitarian system which had been imposed on the USSR itself decades before. As an alien system, backed up by the force of the Red Army and managed by puppet regimes, communism throughout most of Eastern Europe lacked the deep roots of legitimacy. Only the determination of Stalin and his successors to hold onto their empire by force kept the system in place despite its manifest unpopularity and its embarrassing economic failures.

Clearly, the indispensable and decisive element in bringing about the swift collapse of these regimes was the changed attitude in the USSR—the unwillingness to continue to support unreformed and unresponsive communist dictatorships. Not even twenty years after it had been brutally articulated, the Brezhnev Doctrine that justified the use of force to protect the "socialist commonwealth" from the wrath of its own people had been unmistakably repudiated by Mikhail Gorbachev. Indeed, when asked in 1987, during the Soviet president's trip to Prague, what was the principal difference between the policies of Mr. Gorbachev and those of Mr. Dubcek, spokesman Gennadii Gerasimov answered with just two words: "Nineteen years."

But explaining the fall of communism in Eastern Europe does not answer the questions as to why it collapsed in the Soviet Union as well, or why the USSR was then itself unable to survive the demise of the Marxist-Leninist system. Much has already been written on this subject, both in the former Soviet Union and elsewhere, and much more research and analysis will undoubtedly follow. An able summary of the explanations that have been put forward was compiled by Jack F. Matlock, Jr., who served as U.S. ambassador to the USSR during much of the Gorbachev period. In his aptly named study, *Autopsy on an Empire,* Matlock suggests several individuals and key events that might be held responsible for the collapse of Soviet communism and the USSR.[34]

The possibly decisive events, as Matlock enumerates them, include the fall of the Berlin Wall (Boris Yeltsin's own suggestion); several events that helped to create a more powerful Russian entity within the USSR (the Russian parliament's declaration of sovereignty in June 1990, the creation of a separate Russian Communist Party later that summer, and Yeltsin's election as Russia's president in June 1991); actions by Gorbachev that caused him to lose the support of the democratic opposition and much of world opinion (his turn to the right in the fall of 1990, and the use of force against Lithuanian and Latvian protesters in January 1991); the August 1991 coup d'état; the Ukrainian declaration of independence in December 1991; and the Belovezhskaia agreement among Ukraine, Belorussia, and Russia, which itself seemed to have been in part a product of the personal feud between Yeltsin and Gorbachev.

The individuals whom Matlock cites as possibly most responsible include Leonid Brezhnev, whose long inertial reign over the "period of stagnation" saw the USSR lose both internal morale and economic capabilities; Ukrainian president Leonid Kravchuk, whose strong opposition to Gorbachev's proposed treaty may have doomed the effort to create a federal or confederal union; and Russian president Boris Yeltsin, who led both the democratic opposition to the rightist coup in August 1991 and the effort by the republican presidents to create the Commonwealth of Independent States as the successor to the USSR.

His own conclusion, however, is that Mikhail Gorbachev bore the greatest responsibility for the fall of the communist system in the USSR, both because of his various initiatives that allowed independent opposition forces to bring an end to the CPSU monopoly of power, and because of his unwillingness—unique among Russian or Soviet rulers—to employ force to save his own regime. It is probable that most of Gorbachev's countrymen would agree with this verdict. More surprising is Matlock's contention that KGB director Vladimir Kriuchkov, as the organizer of the August 1991 coup attempt, was most responsible for the demise of the USSR, since the coup was timed to block the signing of the Union Treaty scheduled for August 20, and since, in the wake of its failure, it became virtually impossible for Gorbachev again to persuade the republics to unite in a voluntary federation. Of the two, history will devote much more attention to Mikhail Gorbachev, who—though reviled by many in his own country for having surrendered the East European empire and for having failed to preserve the unity of the USSR—was hailed throughout much of the world for having played the decisive part in the third, and even more important, dramatic event of this era: bringing about an end to the Cold War.

The Cold War was a state of relations between opposing states or social systems with a constant policy of reciprocated hostility which, nonetheless, was not allowed to escalate to the level of military force. It was a revolutionary era, with conflict between the hostile powers extended to the realms of ideas and economics, with threats a daily fact of life, and with propaganda and subversion omnipresent. And yet there was also moderation, in that there was no use of nuclear weapons after 1945, and there was no direct military clash between the two main opponents—although crises in Berlin and Cuba threatened to boil over into "hot war." There was even on occasion some joint interest by Moscow and Washington in restraining their junior partners and in using the United Nations to extinguish certain dangerous conflicts. Each exercised a degree of prudence in the other's back yard.

The two faces of the Cold War existed alongside each other because of the increased costs of the use of force. Both superpowers came to recognize that nuclear war would be mutual suicide. The very weapons that marked their strength were the least usable. Each could deny gains to the other, but could not achieve its own offensive objectives through the use of force. Ironically, smaller powers seemed freer to act than did superpowers.

Although the East–West conflict that dominated the world scene for forty-five years stopped short of war, these years were nevertheless rife with war and violence. Most notable for the United States were the two protracted wars in which it participated—Korea and Vietnam, in which the USSR was involved only through surrogate communist regimes. But there were numerous regional conflicts in the Middle East, South Asia, and Africa which threatened to drag in the superpowers. There were also innumerable Third World civil conflicts, as well as over a dozen "wars of national liberation" in colonial areas, in which the United States and the USSR were supporting rival contenders. On several occasions, the United States and the Soviet Union resorted to the use of force to quell disturbances in their own neighborhoods: the United States in Central America and the Caribbean, the Soviet Union in Eastern Europe and Afghanistan. Finally, there were several major wars between regional powers in which both superpowers were relatively uninvolved but that they were unable to stop, including the bloodiest of all wars in this era—the Iran-Iraq War of the 1980s.

Although the normalization of the relationship between Washington and Moscow and the disappearance of the Warsaw Pact were of enormous significance, most areas of regional tension, and many root causes of civil conflict and revolution, remained. Ironically, while the prospects of a general war in Europe seemed more remote than at any time in the twentieth century, the ending of the Cold War actually increased the chance of certain forms of ethnic or civil conflict on that continent, as witnessed in both the former Yugoslavia and the former USSR. The Middle East and South Asia also remained volatile.

The end of the Cold War actually seemed to have an adverse impact on the Third World. Moscow's foreign aid programs were cut to the bone, and the U.S. Congress seemed in no mood, absent the Soviet threat, to sustain large programs of economic assistance. On the other hand, Washington and Moscow did not cease sales of military hardware to Third World regimes. Prospects of continuing and escalating economic hardship combined with increasing levels of military force did not bode well for orderly peace and development in these regions.

Despite the ending of the Cold War, there remained dozens of unresolved conflicts, with a variety of causes and with great potential for violence, throughout the world. There also remained enormous arsenals of nuclear and conventional weaponry. And despite rhetoric about a "new world order," the world was in fact no closer to constructing an alternative security system to replace the Cold War alliances—security pacts that did after all bring a certain stability to the postwar world.

4

Domestic Factors in the Making of Russian Foreign Policy

External and Internal Influences on Foreign Policy

When it inherited many of the international rights and responsibilities of the USSR on January 1, 1992, the government of the Russian Federation faced an international system that differed markedly from the one confronted by prior tsarist and Soviet rulers of Russia. The previous chapters have shown how changes in the structure of the international system have influenced the foreign policy of Russia. Such factors as revolutionary developments in military technology, boundary alterations resulting from war or treaty, and shifts in the global distribution of power resulting from changes in states' relative economic and military capabilities have at times produced distinct modifications in Russian policy.

To recapitulate, there were several such changes during the period of the Cold War that had significant impact on the policies pursued by Stalin, Khrushchev, Brezhnev, Gorbachev, and their colleagues. The tight bipolarity of the late 1940s gave way to a multipolar system, as the relative strength of Japan, China, and the states of Western Europe grew during the 1950s and 1960s, and as both the United States and the USSR found themselves competing for favors from relatively powerless Third World regimes. Political conflicts between the Soviet Union and other communist states, beginning in Eastern Europe in 1948 and climaxing in China in the late 1960s, doomed the monolithic communist subsystem to fractious polycentrism and finally to disintegration. Thermonuclear weapons and intercontinental ballistic missiles raised the costs of "hot war" between the chief adversaries to unacceptable levels. But once it had achieved a state of military parity with the United States in the 1970s, the Soviet Union, increasingly hobbled by economic shortcomings, was able to keep up the pace of the arms race only at a cost that proved suicidal. Because the Soviet Union was largely isolated from the global economic system, its superpower status was called into question as military prowess became less and less relevant to international issues in the 1980s and 1990s.

By the time the Soviet Union ceased to exist, at the end of 1991, Mikhail Gorbachev had significantly altered the foreign policy of the USSR, in part as a response to these changes in the international environment. He had played a significant role in bringing about an end to the Cold War and the virtual disappearance of the communist international subsystem. As he hastened to move into Gorbachev's former Kremlin office, Russian Federation President Boris Yeltsin inherited not only these features of a changed international system, but territorial boundaries radically different not only from those of the USSR but also from those of any prior independent Russian state. Coastal territories on the Baltic Sea and the Black Sea, acquired by Peter I and Catherine II through costly warfare, now belonged to units of the former USSR that were no longer under Moscow's control. Except for the province of Kaliningrad, separated from the rest of Russia by independent Lithuania, the Russian Federation had no border with the East European states that had been part of Stalin's postwar empire. Thus pushed back from Europe, a Russia shorn of the Transcaucasian and Central Asian republics was also more distant from the Middle East and South Asia, where nineteenth-century tsars had played the "great game" with Britain and other powers. And although the United States had emerged from the Cold War as the globe's only surviving superpower, the leaders of the new Russia, unlike many people outside the new government, nevertheless perceived no threat from it. Indeed, Russia's rulers faced a more benign environment beyond the borders of the former empire than had been the case for centuries. Far more troublesome for Yeltsin and his colleagues were Russia's newly independent neighbors, the former Soviet republics, relations with which were now matters for foreign—rather than domestic—policy.

It is this last change in the external environment that is largely responsible for producing the tightest mixture of foreign policy and domestic politics that Russia has seen since the earliest months of Soviet power. The bureaucratic structures and personnel that were involved with the foreign policy of the new Russian state, many of which were simply inherited from the Soviet Union, had not been tasked to treat the former Soviet republics as objects of foreign policy. Neither the mechanisms nor the expertise were present in the foreign policy structure—rather, they were spread throughout the domestic bureaucracies. Moreover, these new neighbors encompassed many areas of instability and ethnic conflict, and the resulting military and political concerns for the Russian government were magnified by the fact that twenty-five million ethnic Russians resided in these new states.

In spite of the increased difficulty of untangling external and internal influences on Russia's foreign policy decision-making, we will attempt in this chapter to examine the domestic factors and to describe the institutional and conceptual environment in which the foreign policy of the Russian Federation is being formulated. In so doing, we shall demonstrate that, far from being simply a calculated response to external stimuli on the part of a monolithic state, Russian foreign policy emerges from the interaction of decision-makers representing a variety of personal and institutional perspectives and involved in the simultaneous resolution of a large number of domestic and foreign issues.

In today's Russia, as in the preceding Soviet state, domestic factors constrain and help to determine foreign behavior in two ways. First, internal economic, social, and political plans and policies can rival foreign and defense policies as claimants on limited resources, creating the constant necessity of choosing whether to spend resources on guns or butter, as well as whether to allocate energies and attention to foreign or domestic pursuits. Second, foreign policy decisions can be shaped by the contests for influence among groups and individuals, thus raising to the fore in Yeltsin's Kremlin, not wholly unlike Khrushchev's or Gorbachev's before, the question of *kto kavo* (who is prevailing over whom). For while regular competitive elections are a new part of the institutional landscape in Russia, within the Kremlin struggles over competing policies and struggles for power continue to be closely linked.

The continuity in the operation of these two domestic constraints is heightened by the similarity in Gorbachev's and Yeltsin's views of the role of foreign policy. For both presidents, the domestic challenges of economic and political development were clearly paramount. The primary purpose of foreign policy in the late Soviet and early democratic periods of Russian history has been to create a non-threatening external environment that would be most conducive to this internal development. As was the case in the early decades of Soviet rule, this concentration on domestic development, together with relative shortcomings in military strength, produced a foreign policy of accommodation, retrenchment, and risk avoidance—at least, in Russia's relations with states beyond the borders of the former USSR.

It has certainly not always been the case that Russian rulers have responded to domestic challenges by maintaining a low profile in their external relationships. Our study of the history of the tsarist period, as well as of episodes of Soviet history under Stalin, Khrushchev, and Brezhnev, has revealed ample instances of the contrasting situation, when activist and expansionist foreign policies have been used to strengthen the capabilities of the Russian state at the expense of competing powers. We can learn from this history that simply categorizing the type of regime ruling in Russia—whether imperial, communist, or democratizing—is not a sufficient basis on which to judge how high a priority policy-makers will give to foreign policy or what direction it will take. Rather, to gain a full understanding of the impact of internal factors, we must consider specific features of the ideas and institutions that are dominant at a given time.

Continuity and Change in Russian Ideas on Foreign Policy

In the opening chapters, we have already encountered the impact of ideas on the formulation of tsarist and Soviet foreign policy. Only during the Soviet period have the prevailing ideas been encompassed in an official ideology—Marxism-Leninism, which we have defined and discussed in Chapter 2. In prerevolutionary times, as well as in the post-Soviet period, we encounter not an ideology but *ideas,* understood as broad concepts or paradigms that help both to shape the way that policy-makers view the world around them and to choose policies appropriate to their objectives.

In the late tsarist period, messianic pan-Slavism was such an idea, originating among the intelligentsia but adopted at times by the regime not only as an organizing principle but also as a way of mobilizing popular support for expansionist policies. For the Bolsheviks, Marxism-Leninism provided a different understanding of Russia's international mission, although we have seen that its adherents interpreted it with sufficient flexibility to avoid violating what both they and the tsars perceived to be Russia's national interests. The key precepts of this ideology, as it applied to foreign policy, were rejected before the fall of the Soviet Union, when Mikhail Gorbachev introduced "new thinking." Essentially a variant of liberal internationalism, Gorbachev's foreign policy ideas centered on interdependence, mutual security, cooperative solutions to global problems, the primacy of non-class values, and an understanding of capitalism that rejected the notion of its inherent militarism and the inevitability of war.

Although it was abandoned as a guide to action by Soviet foreign policy-makers before it was officially jettisoned, Marxism-Leninism continues to have some degree of influence on the foreign policy of Russia, not as official ideology but as one of several contending conceptual approaches. This influence is felt not only through the activities of the Communist Party of the Russian Federation—the largest of Russia's political parties—but also through the role that the doctrine had in the political socialization of many members of the current political elite. Accordingly, some elements of Russia's political culture—especially in such conservative strongholds as the armed forces and certain large economic enterprises related to the former "military-industrial complex"—demonstrate significant continuity with the Soviet era.

Nevertheless, the loss of the ideology's official standing, combined with the fall of the CPSU and the disintegration of the USSR itself, left a conceptual void in the foreign policy of the newly independent Russian Federation that raised to the forefront the question of Russia's national identity. Russia had never existed as a nation-state; rather, during both the tsarist and Soviet periods it had been a multinational empire with messianic ambitions. Unlike other European imperial states, the modern Russian nation was not formed prior to the period of colonial expansion. Moreover, the tsars, unlike the rulers of Britain or France, colonized lands that bordered their home territories, thus producing an unusual intermixing of Russian and non-Russian peoples.[1] The Russian Federation remains multinational, but now the proportion of ethnic Russians in the total population exceeds 80 percent, whereas they comprised just over half the population of the USSR, as recorded in its last census in 1989. Further complicating the definition of Russia's national identity is the fact that twenty-five million ethnic Russians live outside the Russian Federation, in the other newly independent states of the former Soviet Union.

Not only are the people of the Russian Federation experiencing new geopolitical confines, but they are also acutely aware of the relative weakness of their state, in comparison to the superpower status enjoyed by the USSR at the height of its power. The dizzying economic decline of the early 1990s produced a profound sense of national humiliation, as Russia's leaders—first Gorbachev, then Yeltsin—were perceived as meeting with Western leaders in the role of supplicants for foreign aid. The combination of a loss of national mission, a wounded national pride, and a confused national identity has rendered more acute the need for a definition of national purpose in the foreign policy of the new Russia. As presidential advisor Sergei Stankevich wrote in March 1992: "Foreign policy with us does not proceed from the directions and priorities of a developed statehood. On the contrary, the practice of our foreign policy . . . will help Russia become Russia."[2]

The task of articulating the basic principles of Russian foreign policy in the early months of 1992 fell to Foreign Minister Andrei Kozyrev, a young professional diplomat who had spent sixteen years in the Department of International Organizations of the Soviet Ministry of Foreign Affairs.[3] On the foundations of the liberal internationalism of "new thinking," Kozyrev—not surprisingly, given his background—constructed a heavy reliance on Russian participation in international institutions. Determined to liberate Russia from the burdens of empire, the messianism, and the over-reliance on military instruments that had characterized both the tsarist and the Soviet periods, Kozyrev developed foreign policy ideas centered on the promotion of human rights and the universal values of global economic, environmental, and nuclear security, realized through a community of democratic states. Since democracies do not attack other democracies, a democratic Russia would have nothing to fear from the West. If the purpose of Russian foreign policy was the creation of the conditions in which the new nation could prosper, Kozyrev reasoned, it would be necessary for Russia to gain membership in the club of developed democratic states and their economic institutions, thus assuming the "fitting place that has been predetermined for us by history and geography."[4] During these early months of 1992, not only Kozyrev but also President Yeltsin and Deputy Prime Minister Egor Gaidar, who was responsible for economic reform, consistently voiced these "liberal westernizing" views of Russia's national interests.[5]

The tradition of expressing the basic principles of policy in a programmatic and officially endorsed statement still runs strong in post-Soviet Russia. Accordingly, Kozyrev was urged to develop a "foreign policy concept" that would be discussed in the government and adopted by the Supreme Soviet and the President, to serve as the expression of a national consensus as well as guidance for diplomats, parliamentarians, and others. The Foreign Minister was under attack from a growing number of critics, who perceived that the quest for Western economic assistance had produced a servile Russian imitation of U.S. positions on such issues as arms control and the war in Bosnia. The drafting of a concept became the occasion for a highly political debate over alternatives to Kozyrev's ideas. Further impetus for the expression of competing ideas was given in the spring of 1992 by the organization of two new foreign policy institutions—the Russian Ministry of Defense and the Security Council, a consultative body of key government officials to advise the president on security policy. At the initial meeting of the latter body on May 20, a draft "Program for the National Security of Russia" was reportedly circulated (but not adopted), stating that the Russian military must be capable of deploying forces "in any region of the world" in order to counteract "possible attempts by the U.S. to achieve unilaterally advantageous conditions in any region of the world."[6]

As competing ideas such as these began to be heard within the Russian government in the spring and summer of 1992, they quickly focused on the question of Russia's identity. For Kozyrev, Gaidar, and other liberals, the Western democracies were the ideal model and partner for Russia. Russia must shed its tradition of distinctiveness and its illusions of serving a "special role" as a "bridge" between Europe and Asia. And it must avoid the temptations of assuming a leading role in the Commonwealth of Independent States, not only because reintegration of Russia's economy with those of the other former Soviet republics would slow market-oriented reforms and integration with Atlantic and European economic institutions, but also because Russia's assumption of a peacekeeping role in the troubled bordering states would restore the privileged status of the military and thereby threaten the tender shoots of democracy in Russia.

Juxtaposed to this "westernizing" or "Atlanticist" orientation of the Foreign Ministry was a "pragmatic nationalist" or "Eurasianist" viewpoint that was expressed by officials in a variety of government and academic institutions. From this perspective, articulated forcefully by presidential advisor Sergei Stankevich, Russia was indeed separate and distinct from the West— even more so with its new boundaries—and did have a special mission to serve as a bridge between Western and Eastern civilizations. Foreign policy must be more than pragmatic opportunism; without displaying messianism, Russia needed a mission—in Stankevich's words, "to initiate and maintain a multilateral dialogue of cultures, civilizations and states. Russia the conciliator, Russia the unifier, Russia the harmonizer.... A country that takes in West and East, North and South, and thus is uniquely capable ... of harmoniously unifying many different elements, of achieving a historic symphony." For Stankevich, Eurasianism was not a rejection of the West, but a balanced policy, although the immediate requirements of balance were to heighten emphasis on the East. With the West, Russia at best could aspire to a role as junior partner, "not worth accepting." But opportunities for displaying great-power leadership were greater among "second-echelon" states such as Mexico, Brazil, South Africa, Greece, Turkey, India, and China. The very first priority for Soviet diplomacy, however, was "to talk in tougher tones"—to defend the Russian population and Russian heritage in the other states of the former Soviet Union from any form of discrimination or attack.[7]

In the first few months after the dissolution of the USSR, it became clear that the Commonwealth of Independent States was not going to maintain unified security forces, and that regional instability—including threats to the rights and status of ethnic Russians in the "near abroad"—was growing. In response, the "pragmatic nationalists" were increasingly vocal in their insistence that Russia exercise hegemony in the region. In August, another advisor to Yeltsin, Presidential Council member Andranik Migranian, wrote, "Russia should declare to the world that the entire geopolitical space of the former USSR is a space of its vital interests." This declaration should not come in the form of a threat to solve problems by the use of force, Professor Migranian added, but rather an announced intention to act as the guarantor of stability in the region.[8] At about the same time, in a paper he wrote for Evgenii Ambartsumov, the chairman of the Supreme Soviet Joint

Committee on International Affairs and Foreign Economic Relations, Migranian likened this proposed declaration to the Monroe Doctrine, and he urged Russia to seek international recognition of its special role in the region, including "special provision for Russia's right to defend the lives and dignity of Russians in the nearby foreign countries."[9]

Although the "pragmatic nationalists" did not go so far as to advocate forcible revision of the boundaries of the Russian Federation, they clearly disagreed with Kozyrev and Gaidar in arguing that Russia should be prepared to make economic, political, and diplomatic sacrifices in order to promote tighter integration of the Commonwealth of Independent States. This point of view—labeled "an enlightened post-imperial integrationist course"—was prominently displayed in a report issued in August 1992 by the new Council on Foreign and Defense Policy. Entitled "A Strategy for Russia," the report had a clear influence on the development of the official foreign policy concept.[10] Among the group's members were Stankevich, Ambartsumov, First Deputy Minister of Defense Andrei Kokoshin, and economist Grigorii Yavlinskii. Another member, Russia's ambassador to the United States, Vladimir Lukin, published a sharp attack on his superior's policies, arguing that preserving friendship with America did not require servile imitation of its policies and "the atrophy of independent thought and action," and advocating the achievement of greater balance in Russian policy than Kozyrev had shown by making "more active use of the potential of other sectors besides the West."[11]

By the end of 1992, this internal criticism was combining with external events—including the disappointing Western response to Russia's requests for economic assistance—to bring to an end the "romantic" phase of Russian foreign policy, and the movement of Russian liberals closer toward the centrist foreign policy views of the "pragmatic nationalists." Another factor contributing to this coalescence was the growing political strength of the "red-brown coalition" of communists and extreme nationalists, whose members voiced an even more sharply critical "fundamentalist nationalist" point of view. Most of the attention given to this orientation was generated by Vladimir Zhirinovskii, leader of the misleadingly named Liberal Democratic Party, a neo-fascist party which showed surprising strength in the parliamentary elections of December 1993. Other proponents included Gennadii Ziuganov, leader of the Communist Party of the Russian Federation, Aleksandr Prokhanov, editor of the extremist newspaper *Den,* and Colonel Viktor Alksnis, leader of the reactionary Soiuz faction in the Congress of People's Deputies. Simply stated, the foreign policy idea expressed by this group sought to recreate the Russian empire—up to and even surpassing the borders of the former USSR—by the use of force, if necessary.

Unlike the "pragmatic nationalists," the "fundamentalists" were openly anti-Western, professing to see Western aid as a conspiracy to weaken the Russian economy, and opposing any further moves to integrate Russia into the world economy. They defined the Russian nation in ethnic rather than civic terms, with some chauvinists openly voicing anti-Jewish and anti-Islamic sentiments. Appealing to many disaffected elements in the military and security establishments, politicians of this orientation advocated the restoration of a strong, authoritarian, imperial state in Russia. More than their "pragmatic" counterparts, these extreme nationalists were the late twentieth-century heirs of the Slavophiles, contemptuously denouncing "westernizers" for thinking that Western culture or political institutions were worthy of imitation, and depicting Russian civilization as distinctive and superior.

In the face of growing criticism in parliament from both centrists and "red-brown" extremists, Yeltsin in October 1992 accepted the resignation of the liberal first deputy foreign minister, Fëdor Shelov-Kovediaev, who had been the most forceful advocate of a "post-imperial" approach by Russia to the former Soviet republics. As the criticism continued unabated, Kozyrev brought Russia's internal debate on foreign policy to international notice in dramatic fashion. Speaking at a meeting of foreign ministers of the Conference on Security and Cooperation in Europe in Stockholm on December 14, the Russian foreign minister declared: "I must amend the conception of Russian foreign policy." He proceeded to assert that Russia, as a Eurasian power, saw limits on its convergence with Western Europe, especially in the face of threatening NATO plans in Bosnia and in the Baltic states. He demanded that sanctions against Serbia be rescinded, and he pledged Russian support to Belgrade. Secondly, he described the space of the former USSR as exempt from CSCE norms and insisted that the former Soviet republics join Russia in a new federation. Finally, he warned those who were hoping for the further disintegration of Russia that "they are dealing with a state that is able to stand up for itself and its friends."

Having shocked the delegates into stunned silence, Kozyrev soon returned to the podium to declare that his speech had been an "oratorical tactic," and that President Yeltsin and he had no intention of implementing its ideas. Indeed, he explained, "the text that I read out before is a rather thorough compilation of the demands that are being made by what is by no means the most extreme opposition in Russia," and the purpose of his extraordinary hoax had been "to show the danger that would be posed if events were to develop differently."[12]

Ironically, within a few hours of Kozyrev's speech, and evidently unforeseen by him, pressure from the Congress of People's Deputies forced

Yeltsin to replace Egor Gaidar as acting prime minister, appointing veteran industrial manager Viktor Chernomyrdin in his place. Simultaneously, he demoted his chief advisor, Gennadii Burbulis, who had played an active role in developing the "liberal westernizing" ideas of Russia's foreign policy in 1992. There was widespread expectation that the foreign minister would resign rather than implement the "pragmatic nationalist" policies that were clearly intended to be adopted in the wake of Yeltsin's turn toward the center. Not only did Kozyrev remain in office, but he became a forceful spokesman for the policies he had denounced in Stockholm, eventually explaining that "as a democrat he felt constrained to take into account public opinion on foreign policy matters."[13]

As might be expected from these harbingers, the official foreign policy concept approved by President Yeltsin in April 1993 reflected the complete abandonment of the "liberal westernizing" idea and the convergence of "establishment" thinking around the "pragmatic nationalist" viewpoint. Even more than the Foreign Ministry drafts circulated in November 1992 and January 1993, the final document—reportedly written by Security Council Secretary Iurii Skokov—emphasized Russia's rights and responsibilities in the states of the former USSR (generally referred to as *blizhnee zarubezhe,* or "near abroad"). By the time it received presidential approval, the concept—described as "not dogma, but . . . a framework for the formulation of a flexible and vigorous foreign policy"—had received input from experts in the Ministry of Foreign Affairs, the Ministry of Foreign Economic Relations, the Ministry of Defense, the Foreign Intelligence Service, the Security Council, and two Supreme Soviet committees—the Joint Committee on International Affairs and Foreign Economic Relations and the Joint Committee on Defense and Security Questions.[14]

Of the nine "vitally important interests" listed in the document, only the third pertained to the world outside the borders of the former USSR. In referring to this domain, the authorized summary of the document mentioned the countries of Eastern Europe ("which are in our historical sphere of interests") and of Western Europe (whose "integration without Russia could do serious damage to the Russian Federation's vital interests") before it referred to Russia's relations with the United States. Evidently seeking to correct the perceived earlier imbalance in this relationship, the summary spoke of common interests that create the preconditions for developing a partnership, but it stressed that U.S.-Russian interests did not always coincide, while complaining about "discriminatory restrictions in the commercial, economic, scientific, and technological spheres."

In the Asian-Pacific region, priority was given to "urgent consolidation of the breakthrough" in relations with China ("from our standpoint, the region's most important state") over "normalizing" relations with Japan, where "the expediency of continuing to search for a solution to the territorial problem" was qualified by the caveat, "but not to the detriment of Russia's interests." The document expressed concern over the threat of nuclear proliferation on the Korean peninsula and on the Indian subcontinent, and it deplored the tensions in South and West Asia from the context of their harmful influence on the former Soviet states of Central Asia and the Transcaucasus. In the Middle East, it called for settlement of the Arab-Israeli conflict, while also envisioning a greater Russian role "in resolving the problems in and around Iraq" and a "stronger Russian presence in the regional arms and raw materials market." Clearly reflecting a reduced global involvement on Moscow's part, the concept document mentioned Central and South America, Africa, and Australia only in the context of "the world community's common efforts to settle regional conflicts."

"Top priority" and "fundamental importance" in Russian foreign policy were reserved to the area of the former Soviet Union. Even while asserting that Russia remained a great power, the concept document stressed its special mission in this sphere:

> The Russian Federation, despite the crisis it is experiencing, remains a great power in terms of its potential, its influence on the course of world events and the responsibility it bears as a result of this. It is responsible not only for the new world order that has arisen since the collapse of the socialist camp, but especially for the creation of a new system of positive relations among the states that used to make up the Soviet Union, and it is the guarantor of the stability of these relations.

In its relations with the former Soviet republics, Russia followed a policy seeking "the greatest possible degree of integration" based on the principle of "strictly voluntary participation and reciprocity." If certain states chose not to cooperate in some spheres, then it was essential to move ahead in developing arrangements "with the interested countries alone." Specific tasks in this realm included the creation of an effective collective security system, ensuring Russia's status as the only nuclear state in the CIS, securing the external borders of the Commonwealth, and developing and improving the peacekeeping mechanism "on the basis of a mandate from the UN or the Conference on Security and Cooperation in Europe." Special urgency was assigned to the "problems of ensuring military security that have arisen as a result of the Soviet Union's disintegration."

Judging from the published summary, the tone of the concept statement fell short of the open hostility toward the external world that was typical of Marxist-Leninist pronouncements and that is still evident in the expressions of "fundamentalist nationalist" politicians. Nevertheless, the concept bore an uncanny resemblance to the positions sketched out in Kozyrev's "shock therapy" in Stockholm, containing far more references to external threats and discriminatory practices than was common in Russian statements when "liberal westernizing" views prevailed. Clearly, the official statement of guiding policy ideas was less oriented toward participation in multilateral institutions and more forcefully assertive in its enunciation of Russia's objectives than Moscow's foreign policy had been during the previous year.

Andrei Kozyrev remained the target of hostile criticism from parliament and the press—and even, on occasion, from President Yeltsin himself—until after the December 1995 elections, when he resigned as foreign minister to take a seat in the new Duma. His replacement was Evgenii Primakov, an academician whose political career had benefited from the patronage of Aleksandr Yakovlev. Trained as an Arabist, he spent five years as a *Pravda* correspondent (with presumed connections to the KGB) in the Middle East. He defended his dissertation while still with the newspaper, and moved into two positions with leading foreign policy research centers: first, as deputy director of the Institute of World Economy and International Relations, and then, as director of the Institute of Oriental Studies. With Yakovlev's sponsorship, he became a close aide to Gorbachev, serving on his Presidential Council and Security Council. After the August coup, he had been appointed as chief of the reorganized Foreign Intelligence Service, and he retained this post in Yeltsin's government.

Expressing his foreign policy ideas in his first press conference as foreign minister in January 1996, Primakov unmistakably allied himself with the "pragmatic nationalist" and "Eurasianist" viewpoints. He declared that "Russia has been and remains a great power, and its policy toward the outside world should correspond to that status," while echoing his predecessor in saying that Russia's policy should create "an environment that would, to the greatest extent possible, be favorable to the development of the economy and the continuation of democratic processes in Russian society."

Russia's relations with its Cold War adversaries, he emphasized, must be "an equitable and mutually advantageous partnership that takes each other's interests into account." Expressing the need to "diversify" Russia's foreign ties, he made special mention of the Middle East and the key states of Asia (not coincidentally, the subjects of his academic specialization). Primakov enumerated four foreign policy tasks which would be given top priority:

1. The creation of the best external conditions conducive to strengthening the territorial integrity of our state.
2. The strengthening of centripetal tendencies in the territory of the former

USSR. Naturally, this does not and cannot mean the rebirth of the Soviet Union in the form in which it used to exist. The sovereignty obtained by the republics is irreversible, but this does not negate the need for reintegration processes, first of all in the economic field.

3. The stabilization of the international situation at the regional level. We have achieved great successes in the stabilization of the international situation at the global level, having jointly won—I want to put special emphasis on the point that there were no victors or vanquished here—jointly won the Cold War. Now things depend on the settlement of regional, nationality-based, interethnic, and interstate conflicts. Russian foreign policy will do everything possible to settle such conflicts, first of all in the CIS and in the Yugoslav crisis.

4. The development of fruitful international relations that will prevent the creation of new hotbeds of tension, and especially the proliferation of means or weapons of mass destruction.[15]

In a later interview, Primakov, repeating the formula that "Russia doesn't have permanent enemies, but it does have permanent interests," described these four tenets as Russia's "permanent interests." Looking ahead to the future state of international relations, he foresaw a world fifty years hence in which the concept of "balance of power" would be different. "Then there won't be any question of who will balance whom or who will outweigh whom." Describing a process of internationalization, he concluded: "There won't be any 'world government,' and states will maintain their sovereignty, but everyone will be so closely connected by production and the economy that it will be hard to speak of a division or balance of power or the other things we've grown accustomed to hearing."[16]

A generation older than Kozyrev, Primakov proved a more experienced manager of the foreign ministry and a more adept politician. The liberal press characterized him as a "moderate reformer," with a steady style and immense organizational talent, who "appears to personify a relative foreign policy consensus." One article quoted Yakovlev's declaration that Primakov, though "not a conservative," would pursue a policy that "will constantly remind the Americans of Russia's existence."[17] Primakov's relative immunity from the sharp criticism that had plagued Kozyrev was due in no small part to the fact that the foreign policy ideas he expressed found support among broad segments of the Russian political elite, while his assertiveness in promoting Russia's national interests seemed to restore a measure of pride in Russian foreign policy. In the wake of Primakov's successful intervention in the Iraq crisis in November 1997, Andrei Grachev, Gorbachev's last press secretary, wrote admiringly of the change in policy, using an especially vivid metaphor:

During the Kozyrev stage, Russian diplomacy, like a bruised, disoriented boxer who has been knocked down, clung helplessly to its American partner, compelling the rest of the world to applaud the single victor. . . . Therefore, Russia's return to the world ring today is being loudly welcomed by everyone who missed the bouts between genuine professionals. Especially since, under the new rules of play, what we are seeing is not the previous brawl between the superpowers, but something like "fair play" between gentlemen, in which Russia plays a role that is new for it: a referee urging everyone to show restraint.[18]

As shown in Jeffrey Checkel's study of Soviet and Russian foreign policy behavior at the end of the Cold War, the degree of success enjoyed by the promoters of particular foreign policy ideas in a highly politicized setting can depend significantly upon their political skill. Checkel points to Evgenii Primakov and Aleksandr Yakovlev as exemplars of the politically savvy policy entrepreneur, while he attributes Kozyrev's relative lack of success to his "lack of political acuity." Checkel's study mobilizes evidence, including interviews of key policy-makers and academicians, to support a series of propositions regarding the effect that ideas can have on foreign policy. Under conditions of great international uncertainty or foreign policy crisis, he argues, decision-makers are likely to search for information and be more receptive to new ideas. These conditions create "policy windows"—linkages between international events and domestic politics—in which policy entrepreneurs can promote their ideas. The period of perestroika in the USSR and the period just after the Russian Federation achieved independence are identified by Checkel as "policy windows." Centralized states (such as the Soviet Union) have fewer pathways by which ideas can reach decision-makers. Adoption of new ideas in such states is thus more difficult, although once adopted, ideas stand a better chance of being implemented. In less centralized states (such as democratizing Russia), there are more pathways for ideas to reach elites. Initial adoption of new ideas is easier in these settings, but once adopted, their lasting implementation is problematic. Finally, he argues, policy entrepreneurs will play a critical role in empowering new ideas in centralized states because many of the other pathways for effecting change (parliaments or public opinion, for example) are blocked or less important. In decentralized states, entrepreneurs lose their comparative advantage as the insulation of policy elites diminishes. In such a context, the greater the political skills of the entrepreneur, the greater the chance of success.[19]

Foreign Policy Decision-Making: The Institutional Context

During both the tsarist and Soviet periods of Russian history, foreign policy was conducted by a highly centralized and authoritarian state. The absolute power of the tsar was exercised through a powerful central bureaucracy, which tightly controlled the Russian economy and society at large. The secret police and the state censors combined to restrict political participation and political expression. Until the introduction of limited parliamentarianism following the 1905 revolution, there were no regularized channels through which countervailing pressures could be brought to bear on policymakers. The politics of foreign policy making was largely confined to the imperial court.

After the October Revolution, the communist party played the primary role in making foreign policy decisions and exercising control over their implementation. For almost three-quarters of a century, until constitutional changes were made in 1990, the party was "the leading core of all public and state organizations" and the guardian of the purity of Marxist-Leninist doctrine. Throughout most of its history, the Communist Party of the Soviet Union (CPSU) was a tightly organized hierarchy under strong central direction. In theory—and, as late as 1930, in practice as well—policy on foreign relations, international revolutionary strategy, and domestic issues was debated and decided by the party congress, to which delegates were elected by party organizations throughout the country. But, under Stalin, as it grew larger and met less frequently (only three times between 1930 and 1952), the party congress became more and more a creature of its executive organs, which technically were responsible to it. The Central Committee of the CPSU, charged with directing policy between sessions of the Congress, was also diluted in authority during Stalin's rule. It became a sounding board and legitimizer of the policies and personnel decisions offered for its unanimous approval by its executive committee, the Politburo.

Throughout most of Soviet history, it was the Politburo that functioned as the chief decision-making body of the CPSU—and thus, of the USSR itself. The chief exception was during the period that Stalin exercised true one-man rule, personally making all major decisions. After Stalin's death, the Politburo (called the Presidium from 1952 to 1966) again functioned as a collective body—the one political organization in the country where a vote really decided something. Comprised of between twelve and sixteen members and six to eight nonvoting members, from 1973 until 1990 it included the prime minister and the ministers of foreign affairs and defense and the director of the secret police (KGB), as well as the most important functionaries of the party apparatus. Not all members were equally involved in foreign policy matters; often, these were referred to subcommittees, of which the most important was the Defense Council. In 1990, as part of the creation of the executive presidency in the USSR, Gorbachev introduced changes in the party rules that changed the composition and reduced the importance of the Politburo. The functions of its Defense Council were largely preempted by a new USSR Security Council.

The other top organ of the CPSU was the Secretariat, which was responsible for formulating the issues and alternatives that constituted the agenda of the Politburo, overseeing the implementation of its decisions, and (with the Politburo) controlling appointments in the party bureaucracy, the government, and the key institutions in society. Since Stalin's time, the general secretary was able to translate his dominance of the Secretariat into a role as *primus inter pares* in the Politburo itself and, ultimately, as the top Soviet spokesman on both foreign and domestic policy. Among the staff agencies of the Secretariat (the "central apparatus") were several with foreign policy responsibilities. Chief among them were the Department for Liaison with Communist and Workers Parties of the Socialist Countries, which conducted Soviet relations with other communist states, and the International Department, which was responsible for CPSU relations with nonruling communist parties.

In the last three years of his regime, Gorbachev sponsored changes that reduced the authority of these agencies—and of the communist party itself—and invigorated the foreign policy role of the institutions of the government of the USSR. In the eyes of the would-be coup-makers of August 1991 (as well as of many outside observers), these changes in long-standing party institutions prepared the way not only for the fall of communism in the USSR, but for the disintegration of the USSR itself.

When the communist party, even in its diminished state, was banned in Russia by Yeltsin's decree the week after the attempted coup, there was no longer an effective mechanism at the center for coordinating foreign policy. Indeed, the two institutions of government which had been created in 1990 to assume the responsibility for implementing Soviet foreign and defense policies—the Security Council and the Cabinet of Ministers—were also abolished in the wake of the failed coup, because their leading members had participated in the plot or tacitly supported it. In their place, Gorbachev formed a State Council, comprised of himself and the presidents of all the republics, which had the responsibility for overseeing foreign policy and national defense during the remaining months of the Soviet Union's existence. Finding an effective substitute for the party as a coordinating mechanism continued to be a major challenge also for the Yeltsin administration.

The other major change in the conduct of foreign policy that began in the latter period of Gorbachev's rule and has continued in the Yeltsin years is the opening of the policy process to wider participation and greater public visibility. Prior to the initiation of glasnost by Gorbachev, extreme secrecy was the norm in the decision-making processes of the USSR, and sensitive foreign policy issues were discussed and decided by a relatively few high-ranking officials within the top leadership. Public discussion, even in parliamentary forums, took the form of after-the-fact justification and ratification of decisions, the basis for which was rarely if ever discussed with completeness and candor. To a limited extent during Gorbachev's last year or two in office, and to a much greater degree in Yeltsin's democratizing Russia, the foreign policy debate has become more public, and more open to the participation of a variety of groups representing more diverse viewpoints.

The Presidency, Its Advisory Councils, and the Coordination of Foreign Policy

Since the creation of the executive presidency in the USSR in 1990, and continuing in independent Russia, the office of the president has been the institutional centerpiece of Moscow's foreign policy decision-making. Prior to 1990, the Soviet "presidency" was a ceremonial position—head of state but not of the government. Formally, the title was Chairman of the Presidium of the Supreme Soviet of the USSR, and only after Brezhnev assumed it in 1976 was it customarily paired with the top position in the party (General Secretary of the CPSU). With the changes in 1990, Gorbachev's presidency resembled that of France, with constitutional powers to head "the country's entire system of bodies of state administration." Although the office was intended to be popularly elected, Gorbachev chose not to subject himself to an electoral test and was instead selected by the Congress of People's Deputies. The Soviet president also headed two new institutions with foreign policy responsibilities: the Council of the Federation, which included the presidents of the union republics and gave them a voice in issues of all-union significance, and the Security Council.

This presidential dominance of foreign policy has been even more pronounced in the Russian Federation, especially since the adoption of the new constitution in 1993: Articles 80 and 86 of this document give the president the power to exercise "leadership of the foreign policy of the Russian Federation," within the framework of the constitution and laws of the country.[20] The earlier, Soviet-era constitution of the Russian republic (written in 1978 and—though much amended in its last years—continuing in force until 1993) gave the Russian parliament the formal right to determine the main lines of foreign policy and approve ministerial appointments, but efforts by the legislative body in 1992 and 1993 to turn this formal power into reality were stubbornly resisted by Yeltsin.

The formal or official powers of the Russian president under the new constitution are greater than those of any previous Russian leader since the tsar. Of course, unlike the tsar's powers, those of the president have been granted by a vote of the Russian people. However, while the constitution was approved by a 58- to 42-percent margin, only 54 percent of the eligible voters participated in the December 1993 vote.

Unlike its predecessor, the 1993 constitution clearly gives the president control of the government. The president nominates the prime minister, and if the lower house of the parliament, the State Duma, rejects the nomination three times, the president may dissolve the Duma and call for new elections. The State Duma may vote no confidence in the government, but the president is entitled to reject this vote rather than call for the government's resignation. A second vote of no confidence within a three-month period will lead either to resignation of the government or to new elections of the Duma. On the other hand, the president may demand the government's resignation without the Duma's approval, as Yeltsin did in March 1998. In accordance with the constitution and federal laws, the president determines the basic guidelines of domestic and foreign policy; serves as commander-in-chief and appoints and dismisses top commanders of the armed forces; approves military doctrine; may declare martial law and states of emergency (with the approval of the parliament's upper house, the Federation Council); and may issue binding decrees and directives (providing they do not contradict the constitution or federal law).

Given these considerable powers, it is not surprising that the president has a large staff, directed by the Head of Administration, and several advisory bodies comprised of experts from inside and outside the government. Initially, the most notable of these bodies was the Presidential Council, which included a number of foreign policy specialists. However, following the military invasion of Chechnia in December 1994, when a large number of its members voiced their public protest of the action, the Presidential Council virtually ceased to function.

The presidential staff also includes an Assistant to the President for International Affairs. This position was filled during Yeltsin's first years in office by a career diplomat, Dimitrii Riurikov. An expert on international law and former head of the Soviet foreign ministry's Middle East department, Riurikov was dismissed in April 1997, reportedly for poor staff work on the Russia-Belarus Treaty. He was replaced by another career diplomat, Sergei Prikhodko; simultaneously, it was announced that coordination of foreign policy in the presidential administration would be overseen by presidential spokesman Sergei Yastrzhembskii, who was Russia's ambassador to Slovakia from 1993 to 1996.

Yeltsin's direct role in foreign policy making is further enhanced by the fact that the foreign minister and the "power ministers" of Russia—the ministers of defense and interior, and the heads of the intelligence and security services—report to the president directly rather than through the prime minister. With so many responsible officials having direct access to the president—and given that Yeltsin's style, like the former provincial party secretary that he is, is to keep his hands directly in so many matters—it is not surprising that there has been an endemic messiness in Russian foreign policy.

The creation of the Security Council in April 1992 was an attempt to bring the top foreign policy and national security officials together to deliberate and prepare decisions for the president to implement by decree. Its permanent (voting) members initially included the president, the vice president (until 1993), the prime minister, the Security Council secretary, and (as of January 1995) the speakers of the State Duma and the Federation Council. Its nonvoting members included the foreign minister, the defense minister, the interior minister, the director of the Federal Security Service, the director of the Foreign Intelligence Service, the commander of the Border Troops, a deputy prime minister, the justice minister, the minister for civil defense and emergencies, and the nationalities minister.[21] A reorganization in August 1996 added the foreign minister, defense minister, and director of the Federal Security Service as permanent members, and the finance minister, minister of atomic energy, and minister of the defense industry as nonvoting members. Much of the work of the Security Council is conducted by interagency commissions, on which each relevant ministry is represented by a deputy minister.

Six men—five of them prominent political figures—have held the position of Secretary of the Security Council during its brief existence. The initial occupant of the position, Iurii Skokov, was a conservative stalwart of the defense industry, identified in the liberal press as the "undisputed leader of the antimarket lobby," and the new council was at first suspected of being an "alternative state structure or shadow cabinet" modeled on the Politburo, or even on the August 1991 coup plotters' State Committee for the State of Emergency. In December 1992, Yeltsin declined to appoint Skokov prime minister, even though he received more votes in the parliament than Viktor Chernomyrdin; but Skokov's appointment to head a new interdepartmental Foreign Policy Commission of the Security Council was seen as a further enhancement of his power and as a harbinger of Kozyrev's imminent resignation. In fact, however, it was Skokov who was soon out of office—removed by Yeltsin just days after his approval of the new foreign policy concept in April 1993, reportedly because of the president's growing doubts about Skokov's loyalty.[22]

In June, Yeltsin appointed Marshal Evgenii Shaposhnikov as Skokov's replacement. Shaposhnikov had become USSR minister of defense in August 1991 after the failure of the attempted coup, and he had been appointed commander-in-chief of the Commonwealth of Independent States after the USSR dissolved. It had been apparent for many months that this was a position without a function, given the failure of the CIS members to create unified armed forces, and so Shaposhnikov's appointment as Security Council secretary helped Yeltsin solve an awkward problem. According to one report in the Russian press, some Western diplomats were speculating that—since "every department to which Yeltsin has appointed Shaposhnikov has soon lost any real influence and subsequently been abolished"—the Security Council would soon be abolished or reduced in importance. The prediction was not far off the mark, for the hapless marshal resigned only two months later, complaining that he had had virtually nothing to do and no access to Yeltsin. He reportedly realized that all that had been required of him was political loyalty to Yeltsin and a minimum of activity, and that "the Security Council is no more than a part of the President's staff that is intended to organize conferences" between the president and certain ministers.[23]

In filling the vacancy, Yeltsin again turned to a loyal supporter whom he was removing from another position for political reasons. The new secretary, Oleg Lobov, was being ousted from the positions of first deputy prime minister and minister of economics, which he had held for less than six months. This action was taken, apparently at Chernomyrdin's insistence, to make way for the return of reformist Egor Gaidar to Yeltsin's government. Like Iurii Skokov, Lobov was a conservative and a close associate of defense industry enterprise directors, but he was of undoubted loyalty to the president—having spent twenty-seven years working with Yeltsin in Sverdlovsk—and was said to be his "oldest friend and comrade-in-arms." Lobov brought his interest in economic matters to his new position, recruiting as his aides several former members of the staff of the USSR State Planning Committee (Gosplan) who had worked for him at the Ministry of Economics. Together they worked on developing a concept of economic security that, in one journalist's opinion, "looks very much like the old system of centralized economic management."[24] Further signs that the Security Council was now concentrating on economics rather than on foreign and defense policy came in October 1994, on "Black Tuesday," when the Russian currency collapsed, and Yeltsin named Lobov to head a commission to investigate the causes. But at the end of 1994 the council's attention was dramatically refocused on a pressing matter of internal security—the threatened secession of Chechnia. The Security Council, with its concentration of "power ministries," became the primary vehicle for decision-making concerning the armed suppression of the Chechen rebellion, and Lobov was named in August 1995 as Yeltsin's personal representative to Chechnia—making him, in effect, the top Russian official there. The liberal press again began to write about the Security Council as a shadowy body wielding "inordinate power," acting like "a junta that came to power without a military coup. . . . For several months now, real power in Russia has been in the hands of a small group—politicians, generals, or bureaucrats—whom no one elected and who are under no one's control."[25]

The Security Council's profile loomed even larger on the Russian political scene in the summer of 1996, when Aleksandr Lebed became its secretary. Having finished third in the first round of the presidential elections in June, the former paratroops general was brought into the government by Yeltsin, who was evidently seeking the support of Lebed voters to provide him the margin of victory in the runoff election with communist candidate Gennadii Ziuganov. Born in 1957, Lebed was a career soldier, having been educated in military institutions, and he had commanded a battalion in Afghanistan. He served in the sensitive position of deputy commander of the airborne assault forces at the time of the August 1991 coup attempt, and he was named commander of the Fourteenth Army in 1992, where he conducted highly visible (and highly independent) actions in the secessionist Trans-Dniester region of Moldova. In 1995 he left the army to enter politics full-time; in the Duma elections that December, he was the second-listed candidate in Iurii Skokov's party, the Congress of Russian Communities. A charismatic and supremely self-confident candidate for the presidency, the general swaggered into Yeltsin's administration with the attitude of presumed heir apparent. When Yeltsin suffered a heart attack just prior to the July voting and lapsed into seclusion thereafter, Lebed quickly became the dominant figure in Russian politics, clearly impatient for the top position.

Lebed's appointment as Security Council secretary coincided with the removal of General Pavel Grachev as minister of defense, and it was followed quickly by the dismissal of a powerful troika of Kremlin "hawks"—General Aleksandr Korzhakov, director of the presidential bodyguards; General Mikhail Barsukov, director of the Federal Security Service; and First Deputy Prime Minister Oleg Soskovets.[26] Lebed was highly visible in these maneuvers, and he claimed that the dismissed officials had been preparing to forestall the second round of elections, even by staging a military coup. Lebed immediately began a highly public lobbying campaign to expand the role of the Security Council. Yeltsin obliged, issuing decrees on July 10 that expanded both the powers of its secretary and the council's functions—broadly redefining national security to include questions of "domestic, foreign, and military policy in the area of ensuring the security of the individual, society, and state."

Not satisfied with this, Lebed reportedly was seeking the creation of a military council under the Security Council's domain, with troops from all power-wielding agencies in the country subordinate to it. Shortly thereafter, a new decree did create a Defense Council—but it was not the body that Lebed had sought. Rather than an operational mechanism under the Security Council, it was an advisory body to the president, to coordinate strategic issues of military development in the power-wielding agencies—supposedly an important component of the expanded function of the Security Council. Although Lebed was among its members, he was not second in rank to the president. Chernomyrdin was the vice-chair, empowered to preside when Yeltsin was absent, and the president's former advisor for national security affairs, Iurii Baturin, was named secretary of the Defense Council.[27] Moreover—as if to further underscore that Lebed was not being given significant authority over the military power of the country—the membership of the new council was virtually identical to that of the Security Council.

As the summer of 1996 progressed, and Yeltsin's precarious state of health was publicly acknowledged, Lebed became embroiled in more struggles with his rivals in the government. He scored a highly visible success in his mission to engineer a peace settlement in Chechnia—helping to propel him to the top of public popularity polls—but he was highly critical of the performance of interior ministry troops and commanders there. At one point, he ostentatiously offered Yeltsin his resignation, but the president refused to accept it, instructing him to try harder to get along with his colleagues. Finally, in the midst of public accusations of coup-plotting between Lebed and interior minister Anatolii Kulikov, Yeltsin's patience was exhausted, and he appeared on television on October 17 to affix his signature to a decree dismissing Lebed.

Lebed's successor as secretary of the Security Council was Ivan Rybkin, the former speaker of the State Duma, who had lent his support to Yeltsin during difficult times in October 1993 and thereafter. The former leader of the Agrarian Party, he had been asked by Yeltsin in 1995 to assist in the creation of a two-party system, by forming a center-left coalition bloc to counterbalance Chernomyrdin's center-right party, Our Home Is Russia. However, Rybkin's party had failed to garner sufficient votes to enter the Duma elected in December 1995. As an apparent consolation prize, he had been appointed in June as head of the Political Consultative Council—a "pre-parliament" incorporating all political parties, formed as a legislation-drafting body—which had faded into quick obscurity. In the eyes of the liberal press, whereas Lebed had tried to turn the Security Council into an unconstitutional military-police agency, Rybkin would demilitarize it and restore it to its constitutional place, overseeing a complex of problems in the realm of "economic, ecological, agricultural, and industrial security."[28]

A presidential decree in January 1997 yet again defined a new organizational structure for the Security Council, intended to make it possible "to organize systematic and comprehensive studies of external threats and challenges to the Russian Federation, prepare conceptual documents on national security problems, develop scientifically substantiated recommendations, and consider decisions and monitor their implementation." The council's agenda for 1997 was strikingly devoid of international security issues; rather, it was said to give primary attention to security issues associated with social problems—"the nonpayments crisis, holdups in the payment of wages and salaries, public health, and demographic problems." The staff had been reduced 20 percent, to 207 individuals, and it had been organized into five administrations, each headed by a deputy secretary. These were: the Economic Security Administration; the Public and Federal Security Administration, "to ensure that the state's territorial integrity is preserved"; the Information Security and Forecasting Administration, to support operations of the council's Situation Center; the Defense Security Administration, to ensure cooperation with CIS agencies and with the Defense Council, to participate in the drafting of a "national security concept," and to help resolve the situation in Chechnia; and the International Security Administration, which pointedly "does not supplant the Russian Ministry of Foreign Affairs."[29]

One of Ivan Rybkin's last achievements as secretary of the Security Council was issuing the long-awaited National Security Concept. Drafting of this document had begun in the late Soviet period. Following discussions in the Security Council, the government, the Duma, and the Federation Council, it emerged for Yeltsin's approval only in December 1977. It described the major threats to the country's security and enumerated the primary objectives that were deemed necessary to strengthen Russia's position. Concluding that the country faced no immediate risk of large-scale aggression, the concept identified the gravest security threat as internal: the nation's economic distress, which had exacerbated its political, ethnic, and cultural tensions. In these conditions, Russia was justified in directing resources away from the defense sector and toward rebuilding the economy.

Within the military realm, the strategic forces were said to be of greatest importance. Contrary to the "no first use" pledge that had been made by Gorbachev, Russia was prepared to use nuclear weapons to deal with any armed aggression that might threaten its existence as an independent sovereign state. With respect to conventional forces, Russia had abandoned the goal of parity for one of "realistic deterrence." Finally, the concept restated Moscow's opposition to enlargement of NATO, and it called for a greater role for both the United Nations and the Organization for Security and Cooperation in Europe (OSCE) in ensuring international security. As a sign of its continuing international activism and influence, Russia would seek a role in future international peacekeeping missions.[30]

In March 1998 Rybkin was appointed deputy prime minister in charge of relations with the Commonwealth of Independent States. In his place as secretary of the Security Council, Yeltsin appointed Andrei Kokoshin, a defense intellectual who, unlike his predecessors, possessed neither military experience nor an independent political base. A former academic secretary of the USSR Academy of Sciences Institute for the Study of the USA and Canada, he was highly regarded as a specialist in U.S.-Soviet strategic stability. Appointed first deputy minister when the Ministry of Defense was reconstituted in 1992, he had succeeded Iurii Baturin as secretary of the Defense Council and had assumed the leadership of the new State Military Inspectorate in 1997. From these positions Kokoshin oversaw the implementation of military reform. He performed so well that Yeltsin's appointment statement hailed him as "a hero of our time." With this new appointment, the largely redundant Defense Council was simply abolished, and the State Military Inspectorate was incorporated as a separate division of the Security Council. A decree issued by Yeltsin on March 28 ordered that the size of the total staff of the combined agencies be cut to no more than 200 positions.[31]

The many twists and turns in the short history of the Security Council make clear that some of its secretaries (the politically ambitious Skokov, Lobov, and Lebed) have sought to inflate its authority, turning it into a powerful decision-making body with broadly defined operational responsibilities, but that President Boris Yeltsin has resisted, evidently sensing that such a body—reminiscent of the post-Stalinist Politburo—would dilute his own power. Nevertheless, the concurrent existence for a while of the Security Council, the Defense Council, and a Foreign Policy Council created by Yeltsin in December 1995, spoke to the persisting problem of lack of coordination in Russian foreign and defense policy.

According to a well-informed journalist, Yeltsin remarked privately, at the time he was asked to approve the creation of the Foreign Policy Council, "I'm already up to here in these councils." As Pavel Felgengauer described it, "He laughed then, and approved it all with a decree."[32] Created just prior to Kozyrev's resignation as foreign minister, the council was chaired by the president and included the ministers of foreign affairs, defense, foreign economic relations, and finance; the directors of the three branches of the security services; and the president's assistant for international affairs. A press report at the time of its creation noted that "none of those invited has any firm idea as yet of its objectives and structure," though its purpose was reportedly "to analyze and make forecasts about the international situation, study public opinion, and coordinate the interactions among federal services." Although there were no reports of its activities in the meantime, this seemingly superfluous council continued to exist a while longer, and its membership was reconfirmed in a presidential decree of January 1997, at which time the prime minister and presidential chief of staff were added to the previous list.[33]

Despite his willingness to approve new coordinating councils in the realms of foreign and defense policy, Yeltsin has on several occasions decreed that the Ministry of Foreign Affairs should play the leading role in the coordination of Russian foreign policy. The first such occasion was in November 1992, when the Ministry of Defense and the Security Council had emerged as major competitors of the foreign ministry, and Yeltsin decreed that the foreign ministry "will be entrusted with the function of coordinating and monitoring work by other Russian ministries, committees, and departments to ensure a unified political line" for Russian foreign policy.[34] As we have seen, Skokov's apparent success the following month in usurping the coordinating role by having himself named to head an interagency foreign policy commission under the Security Council was short-lived, and little was heard of the commission after Skokov's dismissal.

Despite Yeltsin's decree, Kozyrev's ministry continued to have problems asserting its primacy, especially on issues relating to foreign economic relations, which were handled by a separate ministry and were often a concern of the prime minister's as well. In March 1995, Yeltsin—hearing the complaints in a meeting with foreign ministry officials—again offered assistance, approving by decree a new Statute on the Russian Ministry of Foreign Affairs. This decree made the ministry accountable directly to the president, who would henceforth also appoint its deputy ministers (bypassing the prime minister). The statute declared that the foreign ministry determines the overall strategy of foreign policy and implements policy, coordinating and monitoring the relevant activities of other agencies "to ensure the conduct of a uniform Russian policy line." The press reported that the decree "dispelled once and for all" rumors of the possible creation within the president's staff of a new interagency coordinating body, and concluded that "not since World War II have we had a Foreign Minister who has wielded such broad power." And yet at a press conference barely half a year later, the president was complaining that Kozyrev "can't deal with other ministers," and again spoke of the need to "step up the work of coordinating international and foreign-economic activity at the level of the President."[35]

Indeed, as we have already seen, the Foreign Policy Council—a coordinating body "at the level of the President"—was soon formed. But almost immediately thereafter, Kozyrev resigned and was replaced by Primakov, and the president soon issued yet another decree stating that, within the executive branch, the Ministry of Foreign Affairs "shall be the principal agency" in foreign policy "and shall exercise overall supervision of the fulfillment of Russia's international obligations." The decree added that, in Russian embassies, the ambassadors were to assume responsibility for coordinating the activities of all government offices represented in the embassy. Finally, and most specifically, the decree prohibited the presidential staff from accepting for consideration any proposal from an agency regarding foreign economic relations unless the proposal had first been cleared with the foreign ministry, and it declared that official statements on foreign policy might be made only by the president, the prime minister, and the foreign minister (or by others only when instructed by one of these officials). One commentator, noting that this decree resembled the one of the previous year, and that it failed to make any structural changes that might ensure the subordination of foreign economic activity to the foreign ministry, observed that what Yeltsin was attempting "is the coordination of not so much foreign policy as foreign policy rhetoric."[36]

Whether caused by the repeated decrees or, more likely, by the improvement in top-level organizational and political skill, the foreign ministry's ability to achieve a coordinating role over Russian foreign policy increased markedly under Evgenii Primakov. In September 1996, with Lebed still in office at the Security Council and with the new Defense Council in existence, Primakov spoke confidently in an interview of the primacy of his ministry over the making of foreign policy. As he described it, the basic parameters of policy were set by the president, on the basis of which the ministry prepared proposals for his approval. The ministry also could initiate certain concepts and formulate policy, subject to "correction" by the president. The military, Primakov said, had influence on foreign policy, although "interdepartmental accommodation" was more effective now (presumably meaning after Grachev's removal) than before, and the March decree had also helped in this regard. As for the Security Council, "it is not dealing with foreign policy issues at this time, for all practical purposes."[37]

Further evidence of Primakov's dominant role appeared in the last half of 1997. In September, he was named head of a Security Council commission on international security. Shortly thereafter, Yeltsin decreed the elimination of ten consultative bodies in his office, including the potentially troublesome Foreign Policy Council. The number of officials responsible for foreign policy on the presidential staff was reduced from twenty-five to fifteen. A new structure, the President's Foreign Policy Administration, was created, but according to Yeltsin's Assistant for International Affairs, Sergei Prikhodko, its functions were limited to such roles as polishing Yeltsin's speeches. Contrary to rumors, he said, it was decidedly not a re-creation of the CPSU Central Committee Secretariat's International Department. The responsibility for formulating foreign policy, according to Prikhodko, rested with the foreign minister, who had unimpeded and regular access to the president, and who "confers with the president by telephone more than I do."[38]

The Ministry of Foreign Affairs

From the time of the Bolshevik Revolution until the dissolution of the USSR, only ten men held the position of Soviet foreign minister, and they were widely varied in their influence and personalities. The original occupant, Leon Trotsky, held the position from the time of the revolution until April 1918; he surrendered it gladly, regarding it as beneath his talents. Like Trotsky, four others—Molotov, Vyshinsky, Shepilov, and Shevardnadze— were high-ranking members of the CPSU leadership at the time they took over the foreign affairs portfolio. Two (Chicherin and Litvinov) acquired membership in the Central Committee only after serving for a while as foreign minister, and they never rose above that level. (See Table 1.)

The longest-serving of the Soviet foreign ministers, Andrei Gromyko—a product of the career foreign affairs bureaucracy—was initially regarded as a technician. He became a member of the Central Committee in 1956 and of the Politburo in 1973, after which he assumed a more prominent role in policy-making—eventually playing a critical role in the selection of Gorbachev as general secretary in 1985. A few months later, Gromyko was "kicked upstairs" to the then ceremonial position of president (formally, chairman of the Presidium of the Supreme Soviet), clearing the way for Gorbachev to place his close ally, Shevardnadze, in charge of the foreign ministry. Under his direction, the entrenched "old guard" of the Gromyko generation was eliminated from the foreign policy bureaucracy. A massive overhaul of the foreign ministry structure and personnel accompanied the introduction of "new thinking" into Soviet foreign policy.

From the time of Chicherin, it was clear that the Soviet foreign minister was not the chief foreign policy maker; he advised and implemented, but unless he held a job in the top councils of the party, his decision-making role was relegated to secondary matters. Also from the time of Chicherin, it

Table 1

Foreign Ministers During the Soviet Period

Name	Period of Service
Leon Trotsky	November 1917–April 1918
Georgii Chicherin	1918–1930
Maksim Litvinov	1930–1939
V.M. Molotov	1939–1949
Andrei Vyshinsky	1949–1953
V.M. Molotov	1953–1956
Dimitrii Shepilov	June 1956–February 1957
Andrei Gromyko	1957–1985
Eduard Shevardnadze	1985–January 1991
Aleksandr Bessmertnykh	January–August 1991
Boris Pankin	August–November 1991
Eduard Shevardnadze	November–December 1991

was clear that the Soviet foreign ministry was by no means the sole instrument employed in the foreign affairs realm by the Soviet Union. As we have seen, there was a long rivalry and tension between the foreign ministry, as the instrument of more traditional diplomacy, and the Communist International (Comintern) and its successor agency, the International Department of the Central Committee Secretariat, as instruments of world revolution. Indeed, from the establishment of communist regimes in Eastern Europe after World War II until their collapse in 1989, the primary responsibility for conduct of Soviet relations with other communist states was not even lodged in the foreign ministry, but rather in the CPSU Secretariat's Department for Liaison with Communist and Workers Parties of the Socialist Countries.

An example of the traditional tension within Soviet foreign policy and the lack of integration of various instruments under the Ministry of Foreign Affairs was the Soviet Mission Abroad. The Soviet Embassy housed not only the overseas presence of the foreign ministry itself, but also the foreign representatives of numerous other agencies. A great many of these—often between one-half and two-thirds of the total embassy staff—were intelligence agents, not accountable to the ambassador or the ministries in Moscow, who used their official titles only as cover for espionage activities on behalf of the KGB or GRU (the separate intelligence service within the armed forces). Only in the context of this long-standing Soviet practice is it possible to understand the significance of the inclusion, in the March 1995 Statute on the Russian Ministry of Foreign Affairs, of the provision making the ambassador responsible for all personnel in the Russian embassy.

By no means was this change the only alteration in the organization or practice of Moscow's diplomacy in the post-Soviet period. Although Gorbachev and Shevardnadze already had initiated many changes in foreign ministry structure and personnel, Yeltsin and Kozyrev oversaw an even more thorough housecleaning at the Smolensk Square headquarters of the ministry, which was taken over in its entirety by the Russian Federation. Under the Soviet constitution, a foreign ministry had existed in each of the republics. Kozyrev was appointed as Russian foreign minister by Yeltsin in 1990, and by August 1991 had dismantled the party organization in the Russian ministry and staffed the top echelon with recent graduates of the Moscow Institute of International Relations, together with a few transfers from the Soviet ministry, like himself. When the Soviet ministry was taken over, its "deideologization" (and consequent rejuvenation) followed a similar course; all of Shevardnadze's deputies were replaced, and many other experienced diplomats either resigned or were removed. Some of the non-Russian personnel left to join the foreign ministries of the other post-Soviet states.

But the new Russian foreign ministry was not a streamlined operation; whereas at the end of 1991 the Soviet ministry had employed 3,700 persons and the Russian ministry 240, by October 1992 the size of the reorganized Russian ministry was 3,200 employees.[39] Initially, there were thirteen departments, including seven dealing with geographic regions, and nine functional administrations. One of the new departments handled relations with other members of the Commonwealth of Independent States—a task for which trained or experienced personnel were mostly unavailable. In November 1993, bilateral relations with the post-Soviet states were shifted to the established regional bureaus, where the level of staff talent was deeper. By mid-1995, there were twenty-seven departments, as shown in Table 2. In addition to these departments, there were an Executive Secretariat, which included a Coordination and Analysis Group, and various ambassadors-at-large with special responsibilities in the realm of conflict resolution.[40]

A holdover from the Soviet organizational norms was the ministry collegium. Its members included the minister, deputy ministers, and department heads, and its function was to ensure that responsibility was shared among the leaders, especially responsibility for internal administrative matters. The March 1995 statute provided for decisions of the collegium to be made by majority vote. In case of disagreement between the minister and a majority of the collegium, the minister could implement his own decision, and the dissenting opinion would be transmitted to the president or the government. These provisions apparently were intended to give the impression of shared leadership, although—as one journalist wrote—"[i]t would be interesting to see a member of the collegium (especially one appointed by the minister

Table 2

Departments of the Russian Ministry of Foreign Affairs (mid-1995)

Europe (4 departments)
Department for Security and Cooperation in Europe
First European Department (Southern and Western Europe)
Second European Department (Baltic States and Northern Europe)
Third European Department (Central and Eastern Europe)

Asia (4 departments)
First Asian Department (China, Taiwan, Korea, Mongolia, Kazakhstan, Kyrgyzstan)
Second Asian Department (Australia, New Zealand, southeast Asia, Japan)
Third Asian Department (South Asia, Tajikistan, Turkmenistan, Uzbekistan)
Fourth Asian Department (Caucasus, Turkey)

Department for North America
Department for Central and South America
Department for North Africa and the Near East
Department for Africa
Department for CIS Affairs
Department for International Organizations and Global Problems
Department for Disarmament and Monitoring of Military Technologies
Department for Non-Proliferation, Arms Transfers, and Conversion
Department for International Humanitarian and Cultural Cooperation
Department of International Scientific and Technological Cooperation
Department of Information Technology
Department of Regional Cooperation and Economic Problems
Department of International Economic Problems
Department for Liaison with Subjects of the Federation, Parliament, and Political and
    Public Organizations
Legal Department
Historical Department
Personnel Department
Information and Press Department
Consular Service

Source: Neil Malcolm, Alex Pravda, Roy Allison, Margot Legold, *Internal Factors in Russian Foreign Policy.* Oxford: Oxford University Press, 1996, pp. 122–23.

and confirmed by the government) who decides to make his dissenting opinion known to the President."[41]

In addition to these trappings of internal democracy in the foreign ministry, Kozyrev also made a point of consulting various advisory groups about the direction of Russian foreign policy. In October 1991 he held a round-table meeting with private businesses; in July 1992, he established a Council on Foreign Policy to advise the ministry. This group, comprised of senior officials in the foreign ministry, businesspeople, and specialists from research groups, was purely advisory, and quite different in purpose from the similarly named presidential council set up by Yeltsin in 1995. Yet another constituency was drawn into the consultative process in December

1994, with the establishment by the ministry of a Consultative Council of Russian Federation Subjects on International and Foreign Economic Relations, intended to create a coordinated channel for the increasing number of local and regional foreign policy and trade initiatives.

With the establishment of a direct reporting link from the foreign minister to the president, the formal foreign policy role of the prime minister and his government has been reduced. From the time of Lenin until 1990, when the executive presidency was introduced in the USSR, the prime minister, or head of government, typically played a prominent role in the conduct of Soviet diplomacy. Occupants of this position were members of the CPSU Politburo, usually with significant power bases of their own. Stalin, from 1941 until his death, and Khrushchev, from 1958 until his ouster in 1964, held the post of Chairman of the Council of Ministers simultaneously with the leading position in the party Secretariat. Formally responsible to the legislature (the Supreme Soviet) for the administration of affairs of state, the Council of Ministers had among its formal powers the prerogatives to grant and withdraw recognition of foreign states; to establish or break diplomatic relations; to order acts of reprisal; to appoint negotiators and supervise the conduct of negotiations; and to appoint, supervise, and direct Soviet diplomatic representatives abroad. Even after Gorbachev assumed greater executive powers in 1990, the new Cabinet of Ministers retained constitutional powers to "safeguard the country's defense and state security" and to implement its foreign policy. The new constitution of the Russian Federation grants these responsibilities directly to the president.

Nevertheless, the Russian prime minister and his government—and not the Ministry of Foreign Affairs—have been delegated the executive responsibility for the increasingly important function of overseeing Russia's foreign economic relations. Reversing a consolidation that Shevardnadze had accomplished in the fall of 1991, Yeltsin's government created a Ministry of Foreign Economic Relations outside the Ministry of Foreign Affairs, and gave it the primary responsibility for negotiating trade agreements, establishing tariffs and import controls, and promoting exports. The large and sensitive sphere of economic relations with the other former Soviet republics was assigned to yet another body, the Ministry for Economic Cooperation with the Member States of the CIS. In April 1998 both ministries were abolished, their duties split between the foreign ministry and a new Trade and Industries Ministry.

The close relationship of the foreign and defense ministries to the president and their relative insulation from the prime minister and the rest of the government were again demonstrated in March 1998. Almost immediately after his dramatic announcement that he was dismissing Prime Minister

Viktor Chernomyrdin and his government, President Yeltsin let it be known that his foreign and defense ministers would not be affected by the action. The performance of these ministries thus proceeded relatively smoothly during the lengthy interval in which Yeltsin sought and finally obtained Duma approval of Sergei Kirienko—the young and inexperienced minister of Fuels and Energy—as Chernomyrdin's successor.

The Military, the Intelligence Services, and the Making of Foreign Policy

As we have already noted, the creation of the Russian Ministry of Defense in the spring of 1992 reintroduced a powerful rival to the foreign ministry. Especially during the Brezhnev years, the Soviet defense ministry had established itself as a major player in the making of Soviet foreign policy, reflecting the tremendous upsurge in military capabilities in the 1960s and 1970s as well as the growing technical sophistication of weaponry and strategy in the nuclear age. On matters of military strategy and force posture, the judgment of military professionals went unchallenged. Through the minister of defense, these professionals had regular access to the party Politburo. The combination of expertise and access produced a high degree of influence on such issues as budgetary allocations, arms control negotiations, and the use of military capabilities as an instrument of foreign policy.[42]

Nevertheless, the role of the professional military establishment remained restrained and subordinated to the political control of the CPSU. Although the minister of defense was himself a member of the party Politburo and its Defense Council, political supervision of the military was reinforced through the Main Political Administration of the defense ministry, which reported directly to the Central Committee Secretariat. In fact, however, during the period between Khrushchev and Gorbachev, there were such close personal ties and similarities of outlook among the top party and military leaders that the differences of opinion that occasionally came into view paled into insignificance against the backdrop of broad programmatic consensus on Soviet national security policy. In other words, military interests were so well regarded by the civilian leadership that the defense establishment did not need to mount a challenge to party dominance.

In the post-Brezhnev succession, the military sought to maintain this symbiotic relationship. Minister of Defense Dmitrii Ustinov played a major role in the selection of Iurii Andropov and Konstantin Chernenko as successors to Brezhnev, and had he not died before Chernenko, it is possible that he could have blocked Gorbachev's rise to the top. There were signs in 1985 and 1986 that the new political leadership was seeking to reduce the foreign policy influence of the military elite. The opening for a dramatic change came in May 1987, when West German teenager Matthias Rust flew his small single-engine plane past vaunted Soviet air defenses to land in Red Square in Moscow (ironically, on Border Guards Day). A furious Gorbachev immediately sacked Minister of Defense Sergei Sokolev and an air defense chief, and he advanced to the top job his own candidate, Colonel General Dmitrii Yazov, over more senior claimants. Politically weaker than his predecessors, Yazov nevertheless grew concerned about the deep cuts Gorbachev was making in Soviet defense budgets, partly as a result of arms control agreements that stirred unease among the armed forces, and about the collapse of the Soviet security system in Eastern Europe. The armed forces chief of staff, Marshal Sergei Akhromeev, engaged in a dramatic protest by resigning in December 1988, on the same day that Gorbachev announced unilateral cuts in Soviet military strength. Other military figures, such as General Boris Gromov, the last Soviet commander during the war in Afghanistan, ventured into electoral politics, using the democratization initiated by Gorbachev to gain a platform to condemn his policies. The military was also increasingly involved in the suppression of nationalist and separatist movements within the USSR.

Thus it is not surprising that Yazov was among the coup plotters in August 1991, but his inability to maintain unity in the armed forces contributed significantly to the coup's collapse. Two generals who were close to Yeltsin and had rendered critical aid to coup opponents, air force commander Evgenii Shaposhnikov and paratroops commander Pavel Grachev, became USSR minister and deputy minister of defense after the collapse of the coup. In November, Yeltsin banned activities of the CPSU and the Russian Communist Party within the territory of the Russian Republic, leading to the "de-partification" of the defense ministry and the armed forces. The collapse of Marxist-Leninist ideology, with its strong prohibitions against overt military interference in politics, and the demise of the Main Political Administration as the instrument of party control in the armed forces, removed important restraints on free-wheeling political activity in the Soviet military. At the beginning of December 1991, there were widespread rumors that top-ranking military officers were plotting a coup to prevent the collapse of the Soviet Union.

Yeltsin moved quickly to try to reassure the military and gain its support. On December 5 he announced a 90-percent pay increase for all officers, and—in light of the virtual bankruptcy of the USSR—he promised that Russia would pay the salaries. Two days later, he met with the Ukrainian and Belorussian presidents to form the Commonwealth of Independent States. The haste with which this action was taken might well have resulted

from the presidents' desire to reassure the Soviet military that a new security structure would be created to replace the USSR. On December 10, in a
desperate attempt to save the USSR, Gorbachev met with a group of high-
ranking military officials and asked them to support him as commander-in-
chief and to endorse his plans to preserve the union. The following day,
Yeltsin met with the same group, asking their support of the CIS, and he
clearly prevailed in this critical contest with Gorbachev.

At the first summit meeting of the CIS heads of state, on December 30,
Yeltsin's plan to retain unified armed forces was set back by the demands
of Ukraine, Azerbaijan, and Moldova to form their own national armies.
But at the February CIS summit, a joint command was established, responsible for control over strategic nuclear arms, coordination of military doc-
trines, and resolution of armed conflicts within the CIS and along its
borders, and Shaposhnikov was named commander-in-chief of the joint
forces. However, efforts to create a common security system proved unsuccessful. In March 1992, Yeltsin created a Russian defense ministry, naming
himself the acting minister, and in May he created an independent Russian
army, with General Grachev as minister of defense. In September, the parliament passed a Law on Defense that imposed strict state control over the
Russian military, but reformers failed to gain approval for a provision that
would require a civilian minister of defense.

Despite the principles contained in the new law, imposing control on the
military proved extremely difficult, now that prior constraints had been
removed and a number of the military's leaders had plunged into political
activity. The opinions of military professionals were significantly out of
step with the country's civilian leadership, as shown by a January 1992
survey indicating that 71 percent of officers favored restoration of the Soviet state, and a summer 1992 poll that showed that two-thirds would prefer
a military-based regime. Ironically, a rallying point for much of this discon-
tent was to be found in Russia's vice-president, Major General Aleksandr
Rutskoi, whom Yeltsin had hand-picked as his running mate in June 1991,
in an effort to secure military support for his election. Rutskoi had played
an important role in defeating the August coup, personally piloting the air
force plane that returned Gorbachev to Moscow. His ambitions ignited, he
demanded in October that Yeltsin name him as Russian prime minister, and
in December he bitterly criticized Gaidar and the other young reformers on
Yeltsin's new team, calling them "young boys in pink shorts, red shirts, and
yellow boots." He also was sharply critical of Kozyrev's "liberal westernizing" policies, voicing statist and interventionist views that apparently were
widely shared by his former military colleagues. As Yeltsin's conflict with
the Russian parliament escalated in 1993, Rutskoi openly allied himself

with the speaker of the Supreme Soviet, Ruslan Khasbulatov, in opposing Yeltsin, and in the October 1993 confrontation he appealed to the Russian military to support the anti-Yeltsin forces.

Initially, Minister of Defense Grachev was hesitant to commit Russian troops to support Yeltsin against the armed parliamentary supporters who stormed the main television station and the municipal administration building. But Grachev yielded to pressure, and Rutskoi, Khasbulatov, and their supporters were forcibly ousted from the Russian White House, after bloody fighting that left 145 persons dead and 733 wounded. More than ever before, Yeltsin was in the debt of the military leadership; after the "October events," Grachev seemed to enjoy an expanded influence on Russian policy on such issues as the CFE treaty, NATO enlargement, and peacekeeping activities in the CIS. However, the military did not succeed in fulfilling all its wishes, and was notably disappointed in its budget allocations. Nor was Grachev himself a popular political figure, as he became the scapegoat of critics of widespread corruption in the armed forces.

Divisions within the military leadership were once again evident in December 1994, when the decision was taken to send armed forces to Chechnia to put down the secessionist movement. The collegium of the Ministry of Defense was reportedly not even consulted about the decision, which was publicly criticized by several deputy defense ministers, including the chief of staff, General Gromov. Popular both with the public and with army officers, Gromov was removed from his post, but to avoid making him a martyr, Yeltsin transferred him to the Ministry of Foreign Affairs, to serve as "chief military expert." There he was to oversee military aspects of Russian foreign policy, including the implementation of the START and CFE arms reduction treaties. Rather than an effort to create a meaningful linkage between the foreign and defense ministries, this move was undisguised political exile. In the words of an experienced journalistic observer, "If a person has to be gotten rid of, but for some reason it is awkward to fire him on the spot, a high but meaningless post outside the real power hierarchy is specially created for him."[43] The politically ambitious general did not remain long in his place of exile. In December 1995, he was elected to a seat in the State Duma, and soon thereafter he became a candidate for the presidency. Gromov's timing was poor, however, for he was considerably outshone by another would-be Bonaparte—General Lebed.

The evident results of Grachev's performance as defense minister—the miserable performance of the armed forces in Chechnia, the high-level corruption and widespread theft of weapons and equipment for resale, and the wretched living conditions of vast numbers of troops—were a favorite target of Lebed's during his presidential campaign, and thus it was not surprising that the minister's dismissal was the first fruit of Lebed's temporary alliance with Yeltsin. The new defense minister, General Igor Rodionov, had been closely associated with Lebed, having once been his commander and having become his political supporter. Since 1989, Rodionov had been commander of the General Staff Academy, where his professional and intellectual strengths were much admired by the top officers who studied under him. But he had been sent to the academy with his brilliant military career seemingly in ruins, because it was General Rodionov—as commander of the Transcaucasus Military District—who had been blamed, as "the butcher of Tbilisi," for the massacre of civilians at a separatist rally in the Georgian capital in 1989. The action remained highly controversial, however; in Pavel Felgengauer's words, "Granted, the military contends to this day that the troops acted in self-defense . . . and, furthermore, that they were carrying out oral directives from political leaders, who then quickly made themselves scarce and put all the responsibility on the general."[44]

But it was not long before Rodionov suffered the same fate as Lebed. He proved to be too slow for Yeltsin's tastes in implementing a military reform that would allow further reductions in Russia's defense spending. Yeltsin voiced his outrage on May 22, 1997, at the televised opening session of a meeting of the Defense Council. He fired both Rodionov and the chief of the General Staff, General Viktor Samsonov, replacing Rodionov with General Igor Sergeev, commander of the Strategic Missile Forces since 1992. There were rumors that Anatolii Chubais and Boris Nemtsov, the "young reformers" brought in as first deputy prime ministers earlier in the year, had pressed for Rodionov's dismissal; and on the very day it occurred, their growing influence over security matters was confirmed by Yeltsin's announcement of their appointment to the Security Council.

The issue of the use of the military to quell internal political disturbances—increasingly sensitive during the Gorbachev years—became acutely controversial in the period surrounding the October 1993 confrontation between Yeltsin and the parliament. Although Grachev and his colleagues had reportedly resisted, the acceptability of this practice was incorporated in the new military doctrine that was adopted by the Security Council and the president in November 1993. Although the document, "Basic Provisions of Russian Military Doctrine," remained classified, it was discussed with the press on November 3 by General Grachev and Oleg Lobov.[45] According to the Security Council secretary, the document spelled out the circumstances under which the military could be activated in internal conflicts: "Proceeding from the premise that the security of Russian

Federation citizens and the state as a whole is paramount, the doctrine provides for the use of Army units, Ministry of Internal Affairs internal troops, border troops and other forces in situations in which all other means and capabilities have been exhausted."

In addition to the "traditional missions" of the armed forces in "deterring and repulsing aggression," the doctrine envisioned an additional mission— "conducting peacekeeping operations . . . within the CIS and, by decision of the UN Security Council and other international bodies, outside the Commonwealth . . . provided they are not in conflict with Russian's interests and Russian law." The possibility of maintaining Russian troops and bases on the territory of other countries was not ruled out, "on the basis, of course, of bilateral and multilateral agreements with the countries in which they would be located." Seeing the chief danger to peace in local wars, the doctrine emphasized the need to create mobile forces that could be dispatched quickly to danger spots. As for the danger of nuclear war, it was said to be considerably reduced, and nuclear weapons were viewed, in Grachev's words, "primarily as a political means of deterring aggression, not as a means to conduct military operations." Accordingly, the military doctrine reversed Gorbachev's earlier pledge that the country would not be the first to use nuclear weapons. That declaration, now identified as mainly a "propaganda thesis," was said to have justified enormous conventional forces and a quest for attaining a superior nuclear potential. These military attributes were no longer necessary in the new circumstances, in which Russia "does not regard any country as its adversary." However, in order to discourage other CIS members from retaining or acquiring nuclear weapons, the Russian doctrine extended the "nuclear umbrella" to all members of the Commonwealth's Collective Security Treaty "and guarantees their territories against any invasion by any country that is an ally of any nuclear power."

On the whole, in its emphasis on mobile units and peacekeeping responsibilities, especially in the CIS, the new Russian military doctrine clearly envisaged the armed forces as an instrument of the country's foreign policy. And by giving the professional military leaders a major role in developing the political element of the doctrine—as he did in a well-publicized meeting of the Security Council in February 1993—Yeltsin was underscoring the military's significant influence on the formulation of national security policy.[46] As the internal crisis in the military continued, exacerbated by the memory of its inept and demoralizing performance in Chechnia, General Sergeev played a highly visible role in the intensifying national debate on the critical questions of further refining the military doctrine, funding the armed forces budget, and taking steps toward military reform.

Only two months after Sergeev's appointment, Yeltsin issued the first decrees describing the proposed military reform. The total size of the armed forces was to be cut by half a million, to 1.2 million; conscription was eventually to be abolished, but not by Yeltsin's original target date of 2000. Future annual military spending was to be limited to 3.5 percent of GNP, down from a 1991 level of 7.2 percent. In the first stage of reductions, 300,000 civilian jobs were to be cut, and various activities not directly related to defense (such as road construction) were to be transferred to civilian agencies. Expenses of the administrative apparatus of the defense ministry were to be limited to 1 percent of the total defense budget. There was no announced plan, however, to reduce the ratio of officers to enlisted men from its current level of 1:1.

Given Sergeev's prior position as commander of the Strategic Missile Forces, it was not surprising that he recommended merging into it the Military Space Forces and Antimissile Defense Forces, to create unified Missile Forces. In 1998, the Air Force and Air Defense Force were to be combined, leaving a total of four branches in the armed forces. Also reflecting Sergeev's background was the proposal to abolish the high command of the Ground Forces and replace it with an administration within the ministry, transferring the function of territorial management to military districts (which were to be reduced in number from eight to six). Moreover, the Ground Forces would take the deepest cuts. Most controversial of all was the proposal to put all troops, including the sizable forces of the border guards and the interior ministry, under the command of a single, general-purpose troop commander within each military district. Costs of providing for discharged servicemen and of the proposed doubling in officer pay were to be provided from funds received from the sale of surplus military equipment to foreign buyers.[47]

Internal resistance within the military to Sergeev's reform proposals was considerable. Quick condemnations were issued by retired Generals Lebed and Rodionov, as well as by General Lev Rokhlin. The latter officer, who led the defense of Grozny during the war in Chechnia, had been elected to the Duma in December 1995, becoming chairman of its Defense Committee. In 1997 he broke away from Chernomyrdin's political party, noisily denouncing Yeltsin's policies and forming the All-Russia Movement for Support of the Army, Military Science, and the Defense Industry. By the end of the year, Rokhlin had gathered considerable support and was concentrating his fire on the proposed military reform, transparently threatening a military coup to prevent the further deterioration of Russia's armed forces and defense industry.

Yeltsin rewarded Sergeev's reform initiatives by promoting him to the rank of marshal. But in light of the heavy political opposition—including that of the powerful heads of the Interior Ministry and Border Guards—and the declining prospect of needed funds in the wake of the growing financial crisis, there was considerable doubt that the military reform could be carried out. Whereas a successful reform could at best bring stability to a risky and unpredictable situation in Russia's military, a failure could have drastic consequences—with possible scenarios including not only the breakup of Russia's military into semi-autonomous regional units or its co-optation by criminal gangs, but also an outright attempt to seize political power.

Together with the military, the intelligence service is another "power-wielding" institutional actor that regularly found a place at the table when foreign policy decisions were made in the Soviet Union. It continues to do so, without having undergone significant reform, in democratizing Russia. In the USSR, the Committee for State Security (KGB) played an important role not only in conducting intelligence activity in support of foreign policy, but also in the policy-making process. Almost continuously since 1973, the director of the KGB had been a member of the key decision-making body, the CPSU Politburo. Indeed, Iurii Andropov, who held this position from 1967 to 1982, managed to succeed Brezhnev as general secretary of the CPSU—a mark of the prestige and importance attained by the KGB in the post-Khrushchev period. And Vladimir Kriuchkov, whom Gorbachev appointed director in 1988, again underscored the key role of his agency by leading the attempted coup of August 1991.

In the implementation of foreign policy, the First Chief Directorate of the KGB had primary responsibility for espionage, including the collection and dissemination of intelligence, the surveillance of Soviet citizens abroad, penetration of "anti-Soviet agencies" abroad, and the coordination of the intelligence efforts of other agencies. As we have seen, it frequently used diplomatic and journalistic "covers" for its agents, and some Soviet embassies were reported to have had two-thirds of the members of their staffs on the KGB payroll. The other components of the KGB were responsible for counterintelligence, military counterintelligence, transportation security, anti-terrorism, economic crime and corruption, surveillance, communications, security guards, and border guards.

The best available evidence on the role of the intelligence and security services in post-Soviet Russia demonstrates that Yeltsin has not truly curbed the powers of these agencies, but rather has chosen to co-opt their support, not only to perform foreign intelligence functions, but also to assist him in his struggle against his political opponents.[48] The price he has paid for these services is that the successors to the KGB continue to play a significant policy-making role. No longer do intelligence personnel perform their functions as a single agency, however. Largely in response to public pressure after the August coup, Gorbachev placed the KGB under the direction of one of his reformist colleagues, Vladimir Bakatin, who presided over a reorganization that split it into three separate agencies. As was the case with the post-coup Soviet foreign ministry and military, this institution was simply transferred to Russian control. After further reorganization, by the end of January 1992 there were five agencies: the Ministry of Security, which absorbed the six KGB directorates responsible for internal security and counterintelligence; the Federal Agency for Government Communications and Information; the Foreign Intelligence Service; the Main Guard Directorate, later renamed the Federal Protection Service (out of which the Presidential Security Service was created as a separate agency from November 1993 through June 1996); and the Committee for the Protection of the Russian Border. This last agency, responsible for the border guards, was soon put under the command of the Ministry of Security. But in December 1993 it again became a separate agency, called the Federal Border Service. The Ministry of Security itself was renamed at the same time, becoming the Federal Counterintelligence Service; its name changed again, after April 1995, when it became the Federal Security Service.

The dispersal of KGB functions into five agencies and the dizzying succession of different names has not really diminished the power of the security apparatus or disguised the fact that most of its personnel were inherited from the KGB. Under the prior constitution, the agencies were subject to parliamentary oversight through the Supreme Soviet Committee on Defense and Security. But the deputy who headed the committee was himself a security official—hardly an effective watchdog mechanism. A law on the powers of the security services, passed in July 1992, was strikingly similar to the law on the KGB that had been passed by the USSR Supreme Soviet the previous year.

The vacillating behavior of the "power ministries" during the "October days" of 1993 led to another reorganization, but the new constitution provided for even less legislative oversight than before. Yeltsin's emphasis in 1994 on combating crime, together with the invasion of Chechnia at the end of that year, produced a situation in which the investigative powers of security agencies were expanded and safeguards of individual liberties were further constrained. A new law on the security services, passed in April 1995, confirmed this broadened authority, under the president's direct control, and resulted, in the opinion of a Western scholar, in "a security apparatus whose legal powers more than matched those of the KGB."[49]

The directors of four of the security agencies—the Federal Security Service, the Federal Border Service, the Foreign Intelligence Service, and the

Federal Protection Service—are members of the Security Council, and the first three were also members of the short-lived Defense Council and Foreign Policy Council. On these councils, they clearly played a role in advising the president on issues of foreign and defense policy. Indeed, from the time the Security Council decided upon military action in Chechnia in December 1994 until their dismissal in June 1996, two of these officials—General Aleksandr Korzhakov, the chief of Yeltsin's bodyguards, and General Mikhail Barsukov, head of the Main Guard Directorate and then of the Federal Security Service—seemed to exert especially strong and wide-ranging influence upon Yeltsin.

The security agency that has the most direct operational impact on foreign policy is the Foreign Intelligence Service (FIS), which was headed first by Evgenii Primakov and then—after he became foreign minister—by his former deputy, General Viacheslav Trubnikov. Both had previously been employed overseas as Soviet intelligence operatives under journalistic cover—Primakov in the Middle East and Trubnikov in South Asia—and both achieved a degree of professional respect that helped their agency remain less controversial than the other security services. Under the Law on Foreign Intelligence, passed in August 1992, the agency reports directly to the president, with little parliamentary oversight. Under Primakov's guidance, the FIS produced major assessments which took strong positions on three important foreign policy issues: warning about the dangers of nuclear proliferation, pointing out the likely adverse effects of NATO enlargement on Russia's security, and warning against Western opposition to efforts to promote CIS economic and political integration.

In April 1994, Yeltsin made an unusual appearance at the headquarters of the FIS at Iasenevo, giving the agency a strong endorsement and making it clear that it would play a key role in designing and implementing foreign policy. At a time when the military budget was being cut, he told the FIS staff, their agency had become the most important guarantee of the country's security. He made special mention of its role in achieving economic security, in combating organized crime, and in cooperating in the international efforts to curb terrorism, nuclear proliferation, and drug trafficking. Not least important was the objective of acquiring "preemptive information" on the plans and intentions of the West toward the states of the CIS, and of monitoring the situation along the country's borders.[50]

The Federal Border Service also plays an important foreign policy role, since it has assumed responsibility for guarding the outside borders of the entire Commonwealth of Independent States. Russia alone shares borders with eighteen countries, five of which are in the CIS, and has over 60,000 kilometers of borders to protect. But Russian security doctrine is based on the premise that it is the outer borders of the CIS that are most vital to Russia's security, and since most CIS countries lack the manpower or resources to secure their own borders, the Russian Federal Border Service— which was taken over from the KGB Border Guards—has assumed the function. With respect to the borders it shared with CIS countries, Moscow sought to establish a minimal border regime—"transparent borders"—with Belarus, Kazakhstan, Ukraine, Georgia, and Azerbaijan. This proved to be more manageable with the former two states than with the others. Ukraine created its own border troops and has disagreed with the Russians on the extent of patrolling on their common border. And conflict in the Caucasus, especially after the outbreak of war in Chechnia, has required tighter border controls on the movement of personnel and goods on the borders with Georgia and Azerbaijan.

Parliament, Political Parties, and Public Opinion

For most of the Soviet period, the form of government prescribed in the constitution was parliamentary, with the administrative organs of the Soviet state responsible to the USSR Supreme Soviet. Until changes were made in 1989, this bicameral national legislature, comprising a total of 1,500 deputies elected to four-year terms, met for only a few days each year. Between sessions, the Supreme Soviet's powers were exercised by its Presidium, a body of some three dozen members that served as a collective head of state for the USSR, and that was empowered to receive foreign ambassadors, ratify or abrogate treaties, and declare war.

The changes made under Gorbachev created a 2,250-member Congress of People's Deputies, which met in a brief annual session to approve the state plan and budget and to consider constitutional amendments. More routine legislative functions were performed by a permanently sitting bicameral inner parliament—the Supreme Soviet—with 542 deputies, chosen from the Congress membership. Sitting in two sessions per year, of three to four months each, the Supreme Soviet became a forum of genuine debate and legislative power. Standing joint committees had responsibilities for the oversight of government ministries, including those that dealt with foreign and defense policy. Gorbachev chaired the new legislature in its initial year, but with the creation of the executive presidency, the government assumed a presidential rather than parliamentary form. Following the August coup, the Congress of People's Deputies was summoned to Moscow and virtually ordered by Gorbachev and Yeltsin to dissolve itself, in favor of the interim State Council.

The legislatures of the republics, including Russia, were modeled on the

USSR legislature. Thus, when the Russian Federation became independent, its legislative branch consisted of the Congress of People's Deputies, which had the power to determine the general lines of foreign and domestic policy, to impeach the president, or to amend the constitution; and a two-chamber Supreme Soviet—often meeting as a single unit—which considered legislation and controlled the government. The Congress met only a few times a year, and had more than one thousand members, but the Supreme Soviet sat from six to eight months and had 250 members. The legislature was elected in 1990—when the CPSU still dominated Soviet politics—for a five-year term, and thus seemed destined to clash with Yeltsin's policies. Nevertheless, Yeltsin was granted emergency powers in August and October 1991, and on November 2 the Congress gave him the power for one year to bypass the legislature in appointing ministers and passing economic decrees. Yeltsin appointed himself as prime minister and formed a "reform cabinet" whose "shock therapy" on the economy soon aroused parliamentary opposition.

There ensued a titanic struggle between legislature and executive that dominated Russian politics in 1992 and 1993. Ruslan Khasbulatov, an ethnic Chechen hand-picked by Yeltsin to succeed him as chairman of the Presidium of the Supreme Soviet ("speaker") at the time of his election to the Russian presidency, utilized the presidium's right to issue decrees to establish a strong power base in opposition to Yeltsin, and he urged the establishment of a parliamentary republic with a weak presidency. The parliament's obstructionist tactics occasionally extended beyond questions of domestic politics and economic reform and into the realm of foreign policy—both on issues relating to the "near abroad," such as disputes with Ukraine over the Crimea and the Black Sea fleet, and those connected with the "far abroad," such as the START II treaty and the conflict in Yugoslavia. But for the most part, the International Affairs Committee of the Supreme Soviet—chaired by centrist politicians Vladimir Lukin and Evgenii Ambartsumov—while critical of Kozyrev's foreign ministry, was more moderate and less confrontational in its behavior.

Yeltsin convened a Constitutional Assembly in the summer of 1993, hoping that adoption of a new constitution would force new parliamentary elections; but he did not succeed in pushing the draft through to adoption. On September 21, he issued a decree dissolving the Supreme Soviet and the Congress. The resistance mounted by Khasbulatov and his ally, Vice President Rutskoi, was defeated in a bloody confrontation, badly damaging Yeltsin's reputation in the process.

The constitution adopted in the December 1993 referendum created a bicameral Federal Assembly: an upper house, the Federation Council, with

178 representatives chosen from the eighty-nine units of the federation; and a lower chamber, the State Duma, with 450 deputies. The Federation Council, which includes many regional and republican political officials, has special powers on matters affecting the regions and republics, but it also is given sole power to approve the use of the armed forces outside the Russian Federation. The upper house has three committees that deal with foreign policy matters: International Affairs; Security and Defense; and CIS Affairs.

Both houses must pass a bill by majority vote for it to become law, but a two-thirds vote of each house is required to override a presidential veto or to cancel a presidential decree. The Duma, half of whose membership is elected by a proportional party-list method and half from single-member districts, does much of its work in committees. Five of these relate to international issues: the Committees for International Affairs; Security; CIS Affairs and Links with Compatriots; Defense; and Geopolitical Questions.

The 1993 constitution, as we have seen, grants most of the foreign policy-making power to the president. Among the limited formal powers of the Duma and Federation Council in this realm is the power to ratify and denounce treaties. Nevertheless, to the consternation of the president and the occasional confusion of foreign states, the State Duma has been inclined to pass non-binding resolutions stating positions contrary to those of the government on sensitive foreign policy issues—particularly territorial issues with other post-Soviet states. Yeltsin bluntly addressed this matter at the March 1997 CIS summit:

> I want to stress that Russia's foreign policy, including that with regard to the other CIS countries, is determined by the President. Official foreign policy statements can be made, in addition to myself, by the Chairman of the Government and the Foreign Minister. I beg you to proceed from this fact. . . . It goes without saying that we could raise the issue of the unpleasant remarks made by parliamentarians, governors, politicians, and bureaucratic officials. We do not do this and are not going to do this in the future. We know behind whose words the policy of the state is.[51]

On the whole, parliamentary influence on Russian foreign policy has been quite limited. If anything, its impact is more indirect than direct, for by serving as a forum for the articulation of dissenting opinions that are widely shared among politicians and elements of the public, parliament helps shape the political climate in which executive decisions must be made, and it may thereby influence the tone and tactics, as opposed to the basic directions, of foreign policy.[52]

As we noted earlier, the greater openness of the political process in Russia, and the requirement that political elites engage in genuine electoral competition, has made policy-makers pay more attention than ever before to public opinion on international issues. But Russia is still far from being a mature, functioning democracy, and the channels through which public attitudes are transmitted into the political process are in their infancy. Political parties, in particular, remain too undeveloped as organizations to have any major impact on foreign policy. While the opposition parties that have dominated the Dumas elected in 1993 and 1995—Zhirinovskii's Liberal Democratic Party and the Communist Party of the Russian Federation— have attempted to capitalize on the public's confusion about Russia's national identity and its sense of national humiliation, surveys have shown the public to be less nationalistic and less favorable to the use of force than are the party elites. Moreover, election polls have shown that there is a wide variety of foreign policy viewpoints among each party's voters, making it extremely difficult to predict a voter's party choice on the basis of his attitudes about Russia's external relations.[53]

Similarly, interest groups in Russia initially appeared to be poorly organized and fragmented. While it was possible to identify certain economic interests with particular policy preferences—for example, defense industrialists with protectionism and higher defense spending—early research studies of the lobbying activities of interest groups concluded that they had been of limited effectiveness.[54] However, by 1996 several large financial-industrial groups were exerting increasing influence on the policy-making process. Most of these groups had been built on the foundation of large banks, which had prospered through government favoritism, having been authorized to handle (and profit from) deposits of government funds. As participants in the "loans for shares" stage of privatization in 1995, the owners of these banks had parlayed relatively small investments into controlling shares of large enterprises, especially in the fields of energy and metals. Acquisition of major shares of newspapers, magazines, and television networks further enhanced the political power of this small group of Russian businessmen.[55]

Six of the most powerful of these emerging oligarchs had coordinated with Anatolii Chubais to organize and finance Boris Yeltsin's reelection campaign in 1996. But by mid-1997, their interests had begun to diverge; not only were the leading "clans" quarreling among themselves, but some were also using their media outlets to attack decisions made by Yeltsin's government. Chubais, now first deputy prime minister and the powerful leader of the government's economic reform program, became embroiled in an especially bitter controversy with Boris Berezovskii, reputedly the wealthiest of the "new Russians." Having himself been appointed deputy secretary of the Security Council, Berezovskii had special responsibilities for economic reconstruction in Chechnia. In November 1997 Chubais apparently persuaded Yeltsin to dismiss him on grounds of conflict of interest. Berezovskii fired back by revealing that a large payment had been made by a rival oligarch to Chubais and four of his associates, in the form of an advance on royalties for a proposed book. Badly weakened by the ensuing scandal, Chubais was singled out for dismissal when Yeltsin fired the entire government in March 1998.

Although it appeared, as the 2000 elections approached, that the major clans had not been able to maintain their unity, it was nevertheless clear that these business oligarchs, who collectively control over one-fourth of Russia's economy, would exercise considerable influence on the choice of Yeltsin's successor. But their political power was not limited to the electoral arena. Of equal interest for our purposes is the fact that several of them have in effect developed "foreign policies" in support of their financial interests. Thus, for example, Gazprom—Russia's largest company, formerly managed by Viktor Chernomyrdin, former prime minister and announced presidential candidate—has clearly sought to influence Russia's dealings with countries with which it has natural gas supply, exploration, or distribution contracts. As described in the Russian press by a source close to the government, Gazprom was "demonized" by Bulgarian interests and portrayed as a tool of Russian imperialism in the Balkans after it demanded that Bulgaria pay for its gas in convertible currency. Active lobbying to influence Russian energy policy can be expected to increase in the wake of the proposed merger of Boris Berezovskii's Sibneft with Mikhail Khodorkovskii's Yukos. The resulting company, Yuksi, potentially the world's largest oil company, is likely to rival Gazprom in influence over Russia's foreign energy policy.[56]

Russia's history of strong executive leadership—perpetuated in the 1993 constitution, with the extensive powers it gives to the president—together with the rudimentary development of parties and interest groups, makes the personal attitudes and political skills of the top leader and his closest associates of particular importance. This factor should have produced a strong and coherent vision for Russian foreign policy, smoothly and effectively implemented. That it has not done so is, at least in part, the result of several important internal features of Russian politics. In a sense, foreign policy has become hostage to the two types of bitter political struggles that Russia has endured in its first years of independence.

The most visible realm of political struggle—that between Yeltsin and his parliamentary and political opponents—has been able to affect foreign policy primarily because of the openings created by the second realm: the messy struggles within the government itself. And clearly, the greatest impact of these influences from outside the executive branch has been on those issues of foreign policy relating to the "near abroad," the former republics of the USSR that so suddenly became objects of foreign rather than domestic policy. But even in this realm, one major study has concluded that "the fitful incursions of other political forces into foreign policy have accentuated its meanderings more than they have altered its overall direction."[57]

Ironically, it is in the realm of internecine political conflict—the unceasing struggles for power and allegiance within Yeltsin's top entourage—that the greatest impact on foreign policy has been felt. Clearly, the president's personality and political style have encouraged this political infighting. The constant cabinet realignments and bureaucratic reorganizations; the creation of coordinating councils, one after another; and the endless procession of ministers and advisors have contributed greatly to the lack of clarity and coherence in Russian foreign policy. While Yeltsin's fragile health and his personal habits have accentuated these tendencies, at root has been his failure to articulate his own clear and consistent vision of Russia's national interests and to enforce sufficient discipline on his own government team to translate this vision into effective policy.

5

Russia and the Near Abroad

The term "near abroad" (*blizhnee zarubezhe*) refers to the fourteen non-Russian former Soviet republics which became independent states when the Soviet Union collapsed. Since 1991 relations with these states have become an increasingly important focus of Russian foreign policy. As we saw in the previous chapter, initially there was confusion among Russians regarding their relationship to the "near abroad." For some it was psychologically difficult to think of these countries as independent states. Even many of those who accepted the separation of Russia from its "internal empire" thought of it as temporary. The idea that boundaries which earlier had been interior—and in many cases, quite arbitrarily drawn—would become international borders seemed to Russian nationalists to be unnatural, if not bizarre. Fundamentally the issue involved the nature of the Russian state itself. Thus to many Russians (and non-Russians alike) the relationships among the former fifteen union republics were more issues of domestic policy than foreign policy.

Gradually, however, the realization took hold that these former vassals of the Kremlin were in fact independent countries and that they had become the concerns of foreign, not domestic, policy. But what has yet to be resolved is the nature of the relationship between Russia and the "near abroad." More specifically, what has yet to be determined is the degree of hegemony Russia is to exercise over these newly independent states.

A central fact about the "near abroad" is its diversity. Each state is unique, though they can usefully be considered in several groups. The Baltic states (Estonia, Latvia, Lithuania), for example, are in a class of their own because of the intensity of their nationalism and their determination to break as sharply as possible from Russian control. Alone among the Soviet republics, the Baltic states were independent as late as 1940, and they were never reconciled to their status as component parts of the USSR. It is safe to say that among all the former Soviet republics (with the possible exception of Belarus) there exists a determination to remain independent, but that determination is clearly strongest among the Baltic states. They were the first to break away from the Soviet Union—having their secession formally approved by Gorbachev's State Council in September 1991—and they alone among the fourteen non-Russian states have consistently refused to join the Commonwealth of Independent States (CIS).

Thus we can identify as a second group the eleven states that have affiliated with Russia as members of the CIS. Within that group, there are also subgroups. The first would be Ukraine and Belarus, the two Slavic states that agreed with Russia on December 8, 1991, to form the original membership of the Commonwealth of Independent States. Then there are the three Transcaucasian states—Georgia, Armenia, and Azerbaijan—and the five Central Asian states of Kazakhstan, Kyrgyzstan, Uzbekistan, Turkmenistan, and Tajikistan. (One could also group Azerbaijan with the five Central Asian states, because they share a common Muslim heritage.) In a category of its own is Moldova, a territory largely carved out of prewar Romania. But no matter how they are grouped, it must be stressed that in terms of culture, level of economic development, resources, and history, each of the states of the "near abroad" is unique.

The Commonwealth of Independent States

Eleven of the former Soviet republics are joined with Russia in the Commonwealth of Independent States. They constitute the core of the "near abroad." The CIS is an organization whose birth was accidental and whose future remains as uncertain now as it did at its birth. Those who founded the CIS really wanted a different type of union.

In the aftermath of the failed August 1991 coup, both Boris Yeltsin and Mikhail Gorbachev recognized that the Soviet Union would have to be replaced by a new type of union. Gorbachev wanted a union which would give its republics more autonomy, particularly in the economic sphere, but one which would retain considerable powers for the center, particularly in the realm of foreign policy and national security. Essentially Gorbachev wanted a redesigned federal system, which he proposed to call the Union of Sovereign States.[1] Boris Yeltsin also wanted a new union, but he wanted a decentralized system that would give the central government only those powers which the component members were willing to cede. In a word, Yeltsin favored some type of confederation.[2]

In late 1991 there was some uncertainty regarding which republics would join a new union, but Gorbachev and Yeltsin were in agreement that Ukraine would have to be included. Ukraine was the birthplace of the Russian state in the ninth century, when several Slavic tribes were united into an independent polity identified as "Kievan Russia."[3] Few in Russia contemplated the idea of an independent, sovereign Ukrainian state. But equally few grasped the strength of Ukrainian nationalism. On December 1, 1991, a referendum in Ukraine sealed the fate of a new union when 90.3 percent of the voters opted for independence.

Boris Yeltsin was forced to improvise quickly. A week after the Ukrainian referendum the Russian president met with Leonid Kravchuk and Stanislau Shushkevich, his counterparts in Ukraine and Belarus, and on December 8 at Belovezhskaia Pushcha (a forest preserve near Minsk) agreed to create the Commonwealth of Independent States. The Commonwealth was less of a union than Yeltsin had wanted, but Leonid Kravchuk insisted that Ukraine would not participate in any kind of a federation. A loose commonwealth was the only arrangement Kravchuk would accept.[4]

The majority of the other republics wanted some form of affiliation with Russia, and accordingly the CIS was expanded on December 25, 1991, with the signing in Alma-Ata of a protocol admitting Kazakhstan, Kyrgyzstan, Uzbekistan, Turkmenistan, Tajikistan, Moldova, Armenia, and Azerbaijan. Of the fifteen union republics, only the Baltic states and Georgia chose not to join. Within Azerbaijan and Moldova strong domestic opposition to the Commonwealth prevented their national parliaments from ratifying their membership. Azerbaijan withdrew from the CIS in October 1992. As we shall see, pressure from Russia subsequently forced Georgia to join, Azerbaijan to rejoin, and Moldova to ratify its membership. Of the fifteen union republics, only the Baltic states are not members, and the Yeltsin administration has evidenced no intention to force them to join.

The CIS is an instrument of Russian foreign policy in two ways. It serves as a means of coordination of policies among its members. It is also a mechanism for asserting Russian hegemony over the other eleven states. Both goals have been pursued simultaneously. Initially prominence was given to the former, but with the passage of time the latter has become an important feature of Russian policy. According to the text of the original agreement, the members agreed to coordinate foreign policy activities. They specifically committed themselves to creating a "common military-strategic space" under a joint commander, including a unified control over nuclear weapons. That commitment, along with an agreement to create a "common economic space," was abandoned within two years.[5]

Among the many international organizations in existence, the CIS is unique. The CIS is neither a political alliance nor an economic community, though its activities have elements of both. It is a loose federation with no independent powers of governance. There is provision for central institutions—principally a Council of Heads of State and a Council of Heads of Government—but these councils lack authority to impose CIS decisions on

Commonwealth of Independent States

any member. Decisions require the unanimous consent of all those voting. And as a matter of practice, most of the decisions reached have not been put into effect. Not infrequently several members fail to appear at scheduled summit meetings. By failing to participate in a CIS decision, a member is free to opt out of compliance. But even those members participating in decisions and agreeing with them are not obliged to comply and often do not. President Nursultan Nazarbaev of Kazakhstan, one of the most ardent supporters of integration, complained in 1994 that of 452 agreements signed within the CIS framework, most were never implemented.

Behind the failure of the CIS to become the integrated system Yeltsin and other Russians wanted it to be lay the determination of each state to preserve its newly acquired independence and sovereignty. This was true of each member without exception, though there were considerable differences in the degree to which some states were determined to maintain their distance from Russia.

Perhaps Ukraine and Belarus represent the poles of sentiment within the CIS regarding a willingness to integrate with Russia. If the Commonwealth was weak, it was because of Ukraine's determination to keep it that way. Leonid Kravchuk wanted no common law, no common citizenship, and no status for the CIS in international law. It is generally believed that he viewed the Commonwealth basically as a step toward complete separation from Russia. Other members who opposed the creation of strong coordinating structures and close cooperation with Russia were Azerbaijan, Moldova, and Turkmenistan. Those favoring more integration and cooperation were Armenia, Belarus, Kazakhstan, Kyrgyzstan, Tajikistan, Uzbekistan, and, of course, Russia itself.

No issue better illustrated the bitter struggle between those forces pressing for and against integration than the effort to create a unified CIS military command. As noted above, one of the expressed objectives of the Commonwealth was the creation of a "military-strategic space under a joint command." But from the very beginning, differences emerged over the issue of establishing unified armed forces. At the first CIS summit on December 30, 1991, Ukraine claimed the right to create a national army under Ukrainian command. President Leonid Kravchuk also demanded Ukraine's control over military units on its territory, including the Black Sea fleet, which was headquartered in the Crimean city of Sevastopol. One of Kravchuk's first acts as president was to require all military personnel in Ukraine to take an oath of allegiance to the Ukrainian state. At the time, the army was only 40 percent ethnically Ukrainian and was commanded by an officer corps that was 75 percent Russian. Clearly Kravchuk perceived that the lack of control over the armed forces on Ukraine's territory was a serious threat to its sovereignty.

Russia's military leaders opposed the idea of national armies—also being sought by Moldova and Azerbaijan—among CIS members, hoping instead to place the bulk of the former Soviet armed forces under a unified CIS command. The opponents of integration prevailed, however, and the CIS leaders agreed to permit those states which so desired to create their own armies. But they also agreed to establish a Council of Defense Ministers, headquartered in Moscow, and to make Russian General Evgenii Shaposhnikov commander-in-chief of the CIS Joint Armed Forces. While there was no agreement on the size and composition of the so-called Joint Armed Forces, there was no doubt initially that the nuclear forces of the former Soviet Union would be under the CIS Joint Command. It soon became evident, though, that the concept of a joint command—even over nuclear forces—was illusory. Not only Ukraine but also several other members were suspicious that the CIS Joint Command was in effect a surrogate for the Russian High Command. These suspicions were heightened by the close personal relationship between President Yeltsin and General Shaposhnikov.

If Moscow could not unify the armed forces of CIS members, it could take measures to establish control over former Soviet armed forces stationed outside the territory of the Russian Federation. That is what it did on May 7, 1992, when the Russian government announced its decision to create an independent Russian army. Unable to prevent military decentralization, Russia had no choice but to create its own national command. For about a year the CIS Joint Command continued to coexist with the Russian High Command, though the exact responsibilities of the former were unclear. In theory, the CIS Joint Command might have been utilized to control nuclear weapons, but in fact, Yeltsin concurred with the Russian military that all nuclear weapons would be controlled by Russia. By mid-1993, all support for a unified CIS command had dissipated, and on June 15, its abolition was announced in Moscow.[6]

Moscow's decision to take control over nuclear weapons was reached with difficulty and required a period of several years to accomplish. It was made possible in part with the strong support—financial and political—of the United States. When the CIS was created, nuclear weapons were deployed in four states: Russia, Belarus, Kazakhstan, and Ukraine. Those weapons included both tactical and strategic bombs. Tactical bombs are designed for use on the battlefield and held little value for Ukraine, Kazakhstan, and Belarus. Thus agreement was easily reached among the three to remove all tactical stockpiles from their territory. Strategic weapons proved to be a more difficult issue to resolve. All three states committed themselves in principle to ridding their territory of all nuclear weapons, but as Ukraine soon found itself enmeshed in a series of contentious issues with Russia, Leonid Kravchuk balked at the idea of turning strategic nuclear weapons over to Russia. Additionally the question of compensation for the nuclear fuel in these weapons was raised.

With the evident collapse of the CIS Joint Command, Russia demanded that all nuclear inventories be transferred to Russia. In this Moscow had the strong support of the United States, which viewed the problem as a serious nuclear proliferation threat. The United States and other Western governments pressured the three new "nuclear states" to adhere to the Nuclear Nonproliferation Treaty and to ratify the START I Treaty. In pursuit of that goal U.S. Secretary of State James Baker met with the foreign ministers of the four states in Lisbon, Portugal. On May 23, 1992 they signed a Protocol to the START I Treaty providing that Belarus, Kazakhstan, and Ukraine would ratify the Nonproliferation Treaty "in the shortest possible time."[7]

Russo-Ukrainian relations during 1992–93, however, were frequently antagonistic, and Kravchuk, pressured by domestic forces demanding retention of nuclear weapons, balked at carrying out the terms of the Lisbon Protocol. Ukrainian nationalists clearly saw these weapons as a useful bargaining tool. Kravchuk wanted as a *quid pro quo* for total nuclear renunciation security guarantees from the United States and financial compensation. During 1992 and 1993, Russia, Belarus, and Kazakhstan ratified the START I Treaty, leaving Ukraine as the only holdout. As of late 1993, Ukraine still possessed 1,656 nuclear warheads. In early September Yeltsin met with Kravchuk at Massandra in the Crimea and negotiated an agreement to cancel a portion of Ukraine's huge debt to Russia in exchange for the transfer to Russia of Ukraine's nuclear weapons. That deal collapsed in a firestorm of criticism which Kravchuk encountered on his return to Kiev. So he again reneged. To appease the United States, from which he was seeking financial assistance, Kravchuk promised not to aim Ukraine's nuclear weapons at the United States.[8] This was little consolation to Russia.

In the aftermath of the collapse of the Massandra Accords the new administration in the United States renewed efforts to stop Ukrainian nuclear proliferation. President Bill Clinton, Kravchuk, and Yeltsin met in Moscow on January 14, 1994, to resolve the issue. Concessions were made on all sides. Ukraine, Belarus, and Kazakhstan were promised financial compensation for the highly enriched uranium in the warheads, and Ukraine was given security assurances by both Russia and the United States. A Trilateral Agreement was signed committing Ukraine to bring START I into force and to "accede to the Nuclear Nonproliferation Treaty as a nonnuclear-weapon state in the shortest possible time."[9] Even this agreement encountered resistance in Kiev. In June 1994 Kravchuk was replaced as president by Leonid Kuchma, who succeeded in November in obtaining overwhelming parliamentary approval of the Nonproliferation Treaty. But that removed only one of the several problems in Russo-Ukrainian relations.

Russo-Ukrainian Discord

The nuclear problem reflected Ukraine's deep sense of insecurity. Fundamentally Kiev had no need for nuclear weapons and indeed could not even afford the cost of their upkeep. But in Ukrainian public opinion the suspicion was rampant that Russia did not accept the permanence of Ukrainian independence. Two issues which contributed to that fear involved the Black Sea Fleet and the status of Crimea.

The Black Sea Fleet, a naval force of approximately 300 ships, was one of the four fleets of the Soviet Union. It is headquartered in the Crimean port of Sevastopol, a city under Ukrainian sovereignty but populated largely by ethnic Russians. In a very provocative move, in January 1992 the Ukrainian Minister of Defense laid claim to the bulk of the Black Sea Fleet. Ignoring the existence of a CIS Naval Command, Kravchuk appointed a Ukrainian naval commander for the fleet. Not surprisingly, the Russian response was outrage, particularly from the military, but including the voice of Vice President Aleksandr Rutskoi. President Yeltsin's response was moderate. He rejected the Ukrainian claim out of hand, but nevertheless indicated a willingness to negotiate the issue. Within Russia there was consideration of putting the fleet under CIS control, putting it under Russian control, or sharing control with Ukraine. As the prospects for the CIS Command declined in 1992, sentiment in Moscow shifted to the latter two alternatives.

There were nationalist elements in both Kiev and Moscow who took an extreme position on the Black Sea Fleet issue. But Yeltsin was anxious to avoid a rupture with Ukraine, and even Kravchuk understood that in the end he would have to compromise. Over a period of several years the two leaders met often in an attempt to settle the controversy. Four separate agreements were signed between 1992 and 1994, but the issue was not resolved, although the differences were narrowed considerably.[10] Agreements at Dagomys and Yalta in the summer of 1992 provided for division of the fleet and for joint financing until the proportions due for both countries could be established. A year later in Moscow the two presidents agreed on an equal division of the fleet on the condition that agreement could be worked out for the basing of the Russian part of the navy on Ukrainian territory.

This issue of basing rights has been the source of bitter exchanges between hard-liners in both countries. On July 9, 1993, the Russian Supreme Soviet resolved that the port of Sevastopol was a Russian city and therefore part of the Russian Federation. This decision, repudiated by Yeltsin, inflamed Ukrainian public opinion and made even more difficult Yeltsin's efforts at compromise. He professed to be "ashamed of the decision."[11]

Another attempt was made at Massandra in September. This meeting sought simultaneously to resolve the issues of Ukraine's nuclear weapons and of the Black Sea Fleet by turning both the nuclear weapons and the fleet over to Russia in exchange for the cancellation of Kiev's debt to Russia (largely incurred by energy imports). It appeared that Moscow had achieved a coup of sorts, but the Massandra deal went the way of earlier agreements when nationalist elements in Kiev forced the government to back down. Kravchuk's last deal before leaving office in 1994 was an agreement in April that the Black Sea Fleet would be divided on an equal basis, after which Ukraine would sell part of its share to Russia.

The Black Sea Fleet issue was never really a security problem, but an expression of the larger political differences between the two states. One of these differences was territorial. Russian authorities, particularly in the legislature, claimed the Crimean peninsula and especially the city of Sevastopol as part of Russian territory. Boris Yeltsin himself never endorsed those territorial claims, but in December 1996 the upper house of the parliament, the Federation Council, called on Yeltsin to impose a moratorium on any agreement on the Black Sea Fleet until a special commission examined the status of Sevastopol. Supporting this position was Moscow's popular mayor, Iuri Luzhkov. President Leonid Kuchma, Leonid Kravchuk's successor, insisted that the loss of Sevastopol would mean the end of Ukrainian independence.

A related and potentially more serious issue is the status of the Crimean peninsula. Crimea was until 1954 a Russian oblast (region). According to the last Soviet census in 1989, 67.04 percent of its population were Russians, while Ukrainians comprised only 24.75 percent. Almost half of the Ukrainians speak Russian as their native language.[12] In 1954 Nikita Khrushchev arbitrarily transferred Crimea from the Russian SFSR to the Ukrainian SSR to mark the three hundredth anniversary of the unification of Ukraine with Russia. In the Soviet period the shifting of an oblast from one republic to another meant little, because all political power was concentrated in Moscow. But when Ukraine became an independent state the magnitude of the loss to Russia quickly became apparent. Russia's nationalistic Supreme Soviet voted overwhelmingly to examine the constitutionality of Khrushchev's transfer. On May 21, 1992, the Supreme Soviet went further and resolved that the transfer of Crimea to Ukraine in 1954 "had no legal force from the moment it was adopted."[13] The Russian parliament called for negotiations between Russia and Ukraine and representatives of Crimea. Ukrainians were furious and rejected out of hand the idea of negotiations. Extremist rhetoric was heard from both sides. One Russian member of parliament threatened war between the two countries, to which a Ukrainian legislator replied, "the Crimea will be Ukrainian or it will become totally depopulated."[14]

The presidents of both countries were anxious to prevent this issue from forcing a rupture in relations and took steps to cool passions. Fundamentally, as on the issue of the port of Sevastopol, Yeltsin was not prepared to press Russian territorial claims against Ukraine. At a Russo-Ukrainian summit in Dagomys, Yeltsin and Kravchuk reached agreement on a number of contentious issues including the division of property, the opening of state borders with visa-free access, and the principle of dividing the Black Sea Fleet. Political concessions were made on both sides. Kravchuk affirmed his country's intention not to withdraw from the Commonwealth of Independent States, and both presidents agreed that neither country had a territorial claim on the other. Tacitly Russia acknowledged that Crimea was an integral part of Ukraine.

Boris Yeltsin's administration has smothered but not completely suppressed Russian claims to Crimea. In Russian nationalistic circles, the claim to Crimea is reasserted periodically not only by extremists in the parliaments but even by some liberals, such as Anatolii Sobchak, the former mayor of St. Petersburg. Former Russian Vice President Aleksandr Rutskoi was a strident defender of Russia's claim to Crimea. Furthermore, within Crimea itself there is a domestic constituency for reuniting Crimea with Russia. In January 1994 the first presidential elections ever held in Crimea resulted in the victory of a Russian nationalist who had made reunification with Russia one of the planks in his campaign platform. Pro-Russian sentiment in Crimea remains strong, but the government in Kiev has succeeded in enforcing the Ukrainian claim to sovereignty over Crimea. However, in a concession by Kiev, Crimea has succeeded in acquiring a significant degree of autonomy under the Ukrainian constitution, including the right to establish Crimean citizenship.

Political turmoil within Russia and Ukraine in 1995 and 1996 made impossible a resolution of these differences. Following his re-election in 1996 and the improvement of his health in 1997, Yeltsin was able to reassert his executive authority. Though on many foreign policy issues the hard-line nationalists of the State Duma mirrored their predecessors in the Supreme Soviet, Yeltsin's increased political clout in 1997, together with the strong powers over foreign policy under his tailor-made constitution, permitted the Russian president to override domestic opposition and come to terms with Ukraine. A compelling motive for him to do so was the movement within NATO to expand into Eastern Europe. Russia's leverage against the powerful forces of NATO was meager, but one instrument to bolster its defense was to strengthen the weak bond between the two Slavic states.

This Yeltsin did in the spring of 1997. In late May an accord was finally reached on the Black Sea Fleet. For appropriate compensation Russia was permitted to station its portion of the Black Sea Fleet at the port of Sevastopol for twenty years. This accord set the stage for President Yeltsin to make his first visit to Kiev, where he and Leonid Kuchma signed a treaty of friendship. Moscow agreed to write off most of Ukraine's huge oil debt to Russia. At the ceremony Yeltsin publicly observed, "We respect and honor the territorial integrity of Ukraine."[15]

A resolution of Russian–Ukrainian differences was important to Yeltsin and Kuchma for economic as well as political reasons. Russians were eager to invest in Ukrainian enterprises converted from state to private ownership. Kiev in turn desperately needed Russian assistance for its ailing economy. Ukraine has been plagued since independence with financial and currency problems compounded by a chronic shortage of energy.

Early in 1998 Kuchma reciprocated the Kiev summit with a visit to Moscow, where he and Yeltsin signed a ten-year agreement on economic cooperation. A joint statement at the conclusion of the summit proclaimed, "The Presidents reaffirmed that Russian–Ukrainian relations are of a special nature and are a top priority for both states."[16] Formally, good relations were affirmed, but in both countries suspicions remained regarding the ultimate intentions of the other. For the Kremlin, concern about the Black Sea Fleet agreement was heightened by the fact that the Ukrainian parliament refused to ratify the agreement and because many in Kiev contended that the May 1997 agreement violated the Ukrainian constitution.

CIS Integration

The failure of the CIS to create a common "military strategic space" was paralleled by its inability to forge a "common economic space." Politically the CIS is not a federation, and economically it is not a common market. Even though until 1991 the former Soviet republics were governed as a unitary state with a command economy, as independent states they have achieved less genuine economic integration than the European Union.

Expectations of economic cooperation were initially high, because as parts of the Soviet Union the former republics were in fact economically interdependent. The non-Russian republics were dependent upon Russia for their supplies of energy, particularly oil and gas. Ukraine provided grain and other foodstuffs and rolled ferrous metal. Central Asia supplied cotton for the clothing industries in the western republics. It made economic sense for the CIS states to agree upon rules to govern the exchange of goods and services among themselves. In addition, at independence the ruble was the common unit of currency for each republic. Russia was in the dominant position, because all of the presses for printing rubles were within its domain. If the ruble were to remain a common unit of currency, there would need to be created a central bank and policy-making institutions to maintain a uniform fiscal policy. But these incentives for economic integration were not strong enough to create workable economic institutions. In the end, each republic chose to create its own currency.

During the early years of the Commonwealth, there were unsuccessful attempts to establish a viable economic framework for CIS members. Ironically, it was Russia, the strongest proponent of economic integration, which in practice severely undermined the possibilities. President Yeltsin's top domestic priority was radical economic reform (the so-called "shock therapy"), which he introduced in January 1992. According to CIS principles, Russia was obligated to consult with its CIS partners regarding economic policy. Yeltsin did not do so, despite the fact that his policy of price decontrol had ruinous impact on all those states using the ruble for their currency. Ukraine, for one, was outraged. But Russia was not alone in its disregard of its neighbors. Several CIS members placed restrictions on the export of goods to the Russian Federation, which in turn led to retaliation by Moscow.

Illustrative of the economic chaos within the CIS were the conflicting monetary policies of the member states. In 1992 the Russian Central Bank adopted rules governing the settlement of accounts with banks outside of Russia which forced Russian enterprises to demand hard-currency payment from buyers in non-Russian republics lacking a positive credit balance with the Central Bank. Non-Russian banks had no control over the amount of rubles in circulation because the presses were in Russia. In this chaotic environment, Russia was often the victim as well as the perpetrator. Inflationary policies pursued by CIS governments had their impact inside Russia.

Russia's unilateral monetary policies created a crisis for the "near abroad" countries relying on the ruble. In July 1993 the Russian government introduced a currency restriction prohibiting the use of pre-1993 ruble notes in Russia and permitting only Russian citizens and enterprises and foreign visitors to exchange old rubles for new ones. When this reform was introduced, nine of the CIS republics still relied on the ruble. Eventually each state came to the conclusion that national sovereignty required it to abandon the ruble for its own national currency. Ukraine, Belarus, and Kyrgyzstan were among the first to do so.

Notwithstanding the reluctance of the Commonwealth members to align their economic policies, their leaders continued to engage in the rhetoric of economic integration. Typical of the gap between rhetoric and behavior was the agreement signed in Bishkek, Kyrgyzstan, on October 9, 1992, creating a Unified Monetary System. Going even further, in May 1993 a declaration of intent was signed calling for an increase in economic integration and envisioning a common market. Later that year Russia, Ukraine, and Belarus announced their intention to integrate their economies into a "single economic space." None of these agreements have been realized.

Early in 1997 the CIS Heads of Government yet again approved an overall concept for CIS economic integration, but Russian Minister for CIS Affairs Aman Tuleev admitted that several states would not go along with the concept. The Russian press contemptuously referred to proposals for unified CIS trade, labor, transport, customs, and currency systems as being in the CIS tradition of "paper creativity."[17] Nevertheless, it is significant that the pressures for sovereignty and independence among the "near abroad" countries have not entirely extinguished the idea of unity.

Belarus

The failure of CIS integration did not prevent Russia from successfully pursuing its policy objectives toward the "near abroad." Sometimes Moscow worked through CIS bodies and at other times actions were taken on a bilateral basis outside the CIS framework. In every case Moscow's strategy depended upon the special circumstances affecting the country or region.

Belarus was unique because of its closeness to Russia. Ethnically and culturally the people of Belarus are similar to Russians. Belarus before 1991 had never been an independent state. Its history was one of incorporation into various empires: the Lithuanian domain, the Polish-Lithuanian Commonwealth, the Prussian empire, the Russian empire, and finally the Soviet Union. The people of Belarus had a weak sense of national identity. For that reason its leaders were more supportive than those of other republics of Gorbachev's efforts to unite in a new union. Economically Belarus was dependent upon Russia. It depended upon Russia for its security. It was home to a large concentration of military facilities that had been part of the former Soviet Union's defense infrastructure (including nuclear forces).

Thus it was natural that Belarus was anxious to participate in the CIS as an original founding member.

While closer to Russia politically and culturally than any other member of the Commonwealth, Belarus under its first president Stanislau Shushkevich quickly acquired a taste for independence and ruled out any thought of subordinating its sovereignty to Russia. What Shushkevich wanted was close cooperation without merging with Belarus's giant neighbor. In 1992 the parliament of Belarus voted to create a ministry of defense and to subordinate all former Soviet troops on its territory to Belarusian authority. Officially the country defined its foreign and security policies as neutralist. Accordingly, President Shushkevich initially chose not to sign the CIS Collective Security Treaty, which we discuss below. This decision, however, proved unpopular with the Belarus parliament, which voted in April 1993 to seek entry into the Collective Security Treaty. In June 1994 Shushkevich reversed himself and agreed to affiliation.

Russian pressure had contributed to the change in Belarus's position, as Moscow threatened to charge non-signatories of the Collective Security Treaty for officer training. Shortly after Belarus's adherence the two countries signed a comprehensive military agreement providing for joint training, the maintenance of a joint air defense system, and cooperation in arms development and export.

Belarus's first presidential election in 1994 was won in a landslide by pro-Russian Aleksandr Lukashenko. To bolster his program for closer ties to Russia, Lukashenko submitted a referendum asking the public to endorse integration with Russia and recognition of Russian as equal in status to the Belarusian language. Voting on May 14, 1995, the public approved both propositions by a solid 83.3 percent. Immediately thereafter the two countries abolished customs checkpoints along their common border.

Russia's interest in Belarus was not without important qualifications. Security interests were primary. In particular Moscow wanted legal authorization to station Russian troops on Belarusian territory. This it received in a treaty on cooperation and friendship, signed on April 12, 1994, which the Belarusian parliament ratified in April of the following year. But Lukashenko initially wanted much closer economic relations, to bolster his own weak economy, and on this issue Moscow was hesitant. The Belarusian economy was in such bad shape that integration could only end up as a burden on Russia (as the German Democratic Republic proved to be when it merged with the Federal Republic of Germany). Additionally, under both Shushkevich and Lukashenko, Belarus remained a command economy resistant to economic reform. Lukashenko's ideas on economic reform differed sharply from those of Yeltsin. Consequently

Yeltsin resisted the lifting of trade barriers and rejected plans for a monetary or customs union between the two countries.[18] Lukashenko's suppression of the media at home and the increasingly authoritarian nature of his
administration, not to mention a mercurial pattern of behavior, put off many
in Russia who were trying to nurture a fledgling democracy.

Strong sentiment remains in Russia, particularly among communists and
nationalists, for the creation of a union with more teeth than the CIS. During the presidential campaign of 1996, Yeltsin found himself in a bitter
struggle with his communist opponent Gennadii Ziuganov. Starting the
campaign as an underdog, the incumbent attempted to win over as large a
segment of the pro-union electorate as possible. As a part of the strategy,
Yeltsin signed two agreements pledging integration between Russia and
three other CIS members. On April 2, Russia and Belarus signed a treaty
creating a "Community of Sovereign Republics." And on May 29, Russia,
Belarus, Kazakhstan, and Kyrgyzstan agreed to a "Treaty on the Deepening
of Integration in the Economic and Humanitarian Fields." Echoing the goals
of the CIS, this new community envisaged the formation of a "single economic space" including a common market. Suggesting that this nucleus of
states could expand to include others, Kazakh President Nursultan
Nazarbaev—always a proponent of integration—termed the treaty "the 4 + n"
document.

Both treaties were little more than vague commitments to integrate. There
was clearly no intention to merge into a new state. The treaties explicitly
affirmed that all the parties would retain their national sovereignty. Reference was made to the coordination of foreign policies, synchronization of
economic reforms, and a common currency and budget, but no bodies were
created to implement these goals nor were any precise timetables established
for integration. The treaty between Russia and Belarus permitted either party
to opt out with six months' notice.[19] Although no one has opted out of the
treaty yet, neither have steps been taken to breathe real life into either agreement. If electoral considerations were paramount to Yeltsin, then the treaties
paid off in his success in the June voting and the July runoff. Lukashenko
has not wavered in his rhetorical support for the idea of integration, but he
has steadfastly avoided taking any measure that would subordinate power in
Minsk to that in Moscow. In November 1996, Lukashenko engineered a
referendum which greatly expanded presidential powers and gave him virtual
control over parliament. Moscow has not interfered with the increasingly
authoritarian trends in Belarusian politics. In part this is because Belarus's
foreign policy is fully compliant with that of Russia, and in part it is a result
of the stasis in Russian politics that has accompanied the health problems of
Russia's president in 1996 and 1997.

Central Asia

The newly independent states of Central Asia—Kazakhstan, Kyrgyzstan, Uzbekistan, Tajikistan, and Turkmenistan—also lacked a history of independence. Since the eighteenth century the peoples of this vast region have been governed by the tsars, and after them, the Soviets. One scholar described the independence of these states in 1991 as an "unsolicited gift."[20] These countries share a Muslim religious heritage and—with the exception of the Tajiks, who are of Iranian origin—have a common Turkic ethnic origin. National identities in this region were not strongly established. In Gorbachev's 1991 referendum on the future of the union, the strongest support in favor of preserving the USSR came from the voters of the five Central Asian republics. One reason was the high degree of economic dependence of the region on Moscow. Both the August coup and the Soviet collapse in 1991 confronted the Central Asians with unpopular choices. They were unprepared for independence, and they welcomed admission to the CIS as founding members.

Another important factor linking the new states to Russia is the large Russian minorities living in some of them. According to the 1989 USSR census, in Kyrgyzstan 21.5 percent of the people were Russian. Kazakhstan's population was 37.8 percent ethnic Russian, almost equal in number to the indigenous Kazakh population. It was thus not surprising that Nursultan Nazarbaev, Kazakhstan's president, was an outspoken advocate of keeping the union together and, when that proved impossible, of integrating the CIS as much as possible. Even those regional leaders who advocated independence for their countries acknowledged that close cooperation with Moscow was a necessity for survival. And yet, as weak and dependent as they were, the leaders of Central Asia soon acquired a taste for independence and a determination not to be mere puppets of Moscow.[21]

Russia's vital interests in Central Asia are both political and economic. In a general sense Moscow has sought to maintain a degree of hegemony over the entire region, an equivalent of the U.S. Monroe Doctrine in the Western Hemisphere. Indeed, as we saw in the previous chapter, the parallel was made directly in an article by Andranik Migranian, then a member of Yeltsin's Presidential Council.[22] A major consideration behind such thinking was security. Moscow wanted to deploy its troops in the "near abroad" and to maintain an air defense system that would cover not just Russia but the outer borders of the former Soviet Union. Moscow was also concerned about the growth of Islamic fundamentalism in Central Asia and its possible spread to the Russian Federation itself.

Instability in Central Asia also posed the danger of encouraging the migration of large numbers of Russians back to a country then unprepared to absorb them. According to the 1989 census, some 9,500,000 Russians lived in Central Asia. Even though many of these Russians came originally as colonizers, they were not as discriminated against in Central Asia as in some other parts of the former USSR, such as the Baltics. But the fact that on average only 3 percent of the Russians knew the titular language of their country of residence indicated a less than complete level of assimilation and the ever-present possibility of a migration back to the mother country. Indeed, there has been a substantial migration of Russians from Central Asia, notwithstanding that none of the states in the region denied Russians the rights of citizenship. But—with the exception of Turkmenistan, which has a small Russian population—the Central Asian states have rejected the Russian demand that Russian-speaking people be given the right to maintain dual citizenship.

Economic objectives also played a role in Russia's relations with Central Asia. For a time an effort was made to keep these countries in a "ruble zone" so as to maintain a measure of fiscal control over them; but a deadlock in negotiations in 1993 forced the states to rely on their own resources and their own currencies. Independence did not bring economic prosperity to Central Asia—just the opposite. For the entire region the post-Soviet period has been one of economic hardship. The reasons are several, including the economic incompetence of Central Asia's governing elites. But adding to their woes was the end of Russian subsidies and Moscow's pursuit of policies almost exclusively to Russia's own advantage. Those countries possessing abundant natural resources, such as Kazakhstan, were pressed to share them with Russia. For example, Russia insisted that the Tengiz oil field in western Kazakhstan be open to Russian participation before the government of Kazakhstan was able to mobilize a consortium of foreign investors. In summary, the relations between Russia and Central Asia in the years following independence could be described as "uneasy cooperation."[23]

Regional Stability and Russian Hegemony

The failure of the CIS to integrate economically or militarily did not prevent Russia from using the organization to establish its dominance over the former Soviet territorial space. During the early period of his administration, Yeltsin was anxious to demonstrate to his new partners in the West that Russia's imperial period was a thing of the past, and Moscow moved slowly and cautiously in its relations with the "near abroad." But as the number and intensity of conflicts among CIS members grew, and as domestic political pressure for asserting Russia's authority increased, the Yeltsin administration increasingly adopted a tougher strategy toward the "near abroad."

Andrei Kozyrev, Russia's first foreign minister, focused his efforts on developing relations with the West. He did not even bother to make a tour of the "near abroad" until the spring of 1992. Responsibility for relations with the former Soviet republics was initially entrusted to Fëdor Shelov-Kovediaev, a young first deputy foreign minister. In a report entitled "Strategy and Tactics of Russian Foreign Policy in the New Abroad," Shelov-Kovediaev made the case for a more active Russian policy of promoting the integration of the former Soviet republics. While categorically rejecting the use of force in the region, he insisted that Russia had "special interests" which required recognition by the international community. One of the most vital of these interests was stability and the prevention of the spread of regional conflicts from bordering states into the Russian Federation itself. Though Shelov-Kovediaev was not to last the year in his post, his ideas were in part embodied in the Russian foreign ministry's "foreign policy concept" published in December 1992 and ultimately adopted by Yeltsin in April 1993. As we have seen in the prior chapter, special emphasis in the "concept" was placed on the need to defend the external borders of the CIS. By early 1993 President Yeltsin was firmly committed to an active policy of intervention in the "near abroad." In a speech before the politically important Civic Union on February 28, Yeltsin declared:

> Stopping all armed conflicts on the territory of the former USSR is Russia's vital interest. The world community sees more and more clearly Russia's special responsibility in this difficult undertaking. I believe the time has come for distinguished international organizations, including the UN, to grant Russia special powers as a guarantor of peace and stability in the former regions of the USSR.[24]

The problem confronting Russia was how to use the CIS to build an effective mechanism for security. Integration was not working, so other means had to be devised to achieve the desired ends through multilateral cooperation. An attempt toward that end was the Collective Security Treaty. Originally, the idea of a collective security force had been worked out bilaterally between Russia and Kazakhstan. However, the idea appealed to other CIS members, so at a CIS summit in Tashkent on May 15, 1992, six states (Armenia, Kazakhstan, Russia, Tajikistan, Turkmenistan, and Uzbekistan) signed a formal pledge.[25] In principle the treaty created a defensive alliance whose ultimate decision-making authority was to be a Collective Security Council.

But there were serious limitations with the mechanism for collective security. To begin with, it was far from comprehensive. Notably absent were the Slavic states of Ukraine and Belarus, as well as Azerbaijan and Georgia (not yet in the CIS), and Moldova and Kyrgyzstan. Indeed, this treaty revealed a split within the CIS, with Russia allied primarily with the Central Asian states. The Collective Security Treaty also was limited structurally. Essentially a defensive alliance, the treaty could come into force only when one sovereign entity attacked another. It did not cover conflicts that arose between groups within one state. And with the exception of the war over Nagorno-Karabakh between Armenia and Azerbaijan, the conflicts that plagued the CIS were essentially internal struggles or civil wars.

An alternative mechanism which was to prove more efficacious was peacekeeping. Developed by the United Nations, the institution of peacekeeping involves the use of collective armed force to intervene when invited by the warring parties to monitor a truce or cease-fire. Within the United Nations, peacekeeping developed as an alternative to peacemaking (i.e., the use of armed forces to curb aggression). Originally, peacekeeping by the United Nations was designed to limit interstate conflict, but with the end of the Cold War, peacekeeping operations increasingly dealt with intrastate fighting or civil wars.[26] It was in this kind of conflict—internal wars within states bordering on Russia—that peacekeeping offered the greatest prospects.

Moscow was concerned about the outbreak of ethnic and national conflicts in the newly independent states bordering Russia for several reasons: (1) in several of the regions there were Russians who might need protection; (2) conflict might spread to the Russian Federation; (3) the success of separatist groups outside of Russia might encourage separatism within Russia; (4) Islamic fundamentalism might spread to Russia's southern neighbors and then to Russia itself; and (5) a belief that its status as a "great power" obligated Russia to assume responsibility for keeping the peace in the region. To these considerations might be added a sixth: hegemonic aspirations—the desire of Russia to re-establish control over the territory once dominated by the Soviet Union.[27]

Interestingly, the initiative for creating a CIS peacekeeping force came from the president of Kazakhstan, Nursultan Nazarbaev, a strong believer in the idea of CIS integration. At a CIS summit in Kiev on March 20, 1992, he proposed to establish a corps of military observers and collective forces to maintain peace among CIS members.[28] Approving the plan were ten CIS states: Armenia, Belarus, Kazakhstan, Kyrgyzstan, Moldova, Russia, Tajikistan, and Uzbekistan, with Azerbaijan and Ukraine signing on the condition that their parliaments must approve. The agreement specified that CIS peacekeeping forces would be used only under the following conditions: (1) only states not involved in the particular conflict would send troops; (2) forces would be volunteers recruited on a contractual basis; (3) command would be joint; (4) use of peacekeeping forces would require approval of the CIS Council of Heads of States; and (5) the belligerent parties had to agree to troop deployment. Basically, the principles of CIS peacekeeping were modeled on United Nations principles. An attempt was made in July to organize a peacekeeping force in advance that could be called upon in case of a crisis, but no such force ever materialized (as was the case with similar UN efforts in the 1940s).

Russian Peacekeeping in Operation

Peacekeeping operations were organized or planned for five conflicts that developed in the "near abroad." Not one of these operations was carried out as specified in the CIS agreement or in accordance with UN principles. The five conflicts were the civil war in Tajikistan, two secessionist movements in Georgia (South Ossetia and Abkhazia), the war over Nagorno-Karabakh in Azerbaijan, and the independence struggle of the Trans-Dniester region in Moldova.

In Central Asia the major conflict was the civil war in Tajikistan. It was a complex war, in which the antagonists differed over political, ideological, ethnic, and regional issues. The war began in late 1991 when a coalition of forces which included groups seeking democracy, Islamic forces, and ethnic Pamirs and Garmis challenged the authority of the government of Rakhmon Nabiev. Bitter fighting during the war took a large toll in lives, produced widespread atrocities, and generated over a half million refugees. In December 1992 Nabiev was replaced by his communist ally, Imomali Rakhmonov, who appealed to Russia and other CIS states for assistance against the opposing forces. That appeal was received sympathetically in Russia, Kazakhstan, Uzbekistan, and Kyrgyzstan, because of widespread fear that the civil war in Tajikistan would spread instability throughout the region and possibly enhance the prospects of spreading Islamic militancy. Russian involvement was virtually inevitable because of the presence in Tajikistan of Russian (former Soviet) forces, which found themselves caught between warring factions. In 1993 Russian troops were sent to guard the border between Tajikistan and Afghanistan. That same year the leaders of Russia, Kazakhstan, Kyrgyzstan, Tajikistan, and Uzbekistan formally authorized the formation of a CIS peacekeeping force.[29] This operation, controlled by Russia and not invited by the Tajik insurgents, reached a size of approximately 25,000 troops. Russia was accused of using peacekeeping as a pretext for establishing its control over Tajikistan, and indeed, for all practical purposes, while the war lasted the country was a Russian protectorate. But Moscow made a genuine effort to bring both sides to the negotiating table, and ultimately it succeeded. In June 1997 the presidents of Russia and Tajikistan and the leader of the Tajik insurgency signed a Moscow-brokered pact formally ending the war.[30]

Russia's relations with Central Asia remain in flux. All of the region's leaders accept some form of greater integration as inevitable—a prospect which is fully in accordance with Moscow's wishes. That will involve a strengthening of the CIS. Economically these countries are weak and dependent on Russia. Politically too they are weak and vulnerable and are inclined to look to Moscow for support. Thus they are prepared for the time being to accept Russian hegemony. But the idea of national sovereignty has caught hold, and none would accept anything like the return of Soviet-style control or even the subordination that characterized the old Warsaw Pact alliance.

The problem is that there is a consensus in Russia that it is heir to the USSR and as such is entitled to be the regional hegemon.[31] What remains to be determined is the balance between Russian aspirations and Central Asian compliance. For example, Russia has been pressing these states to grant dual citizenship to Russians living in them. They are reluctant to comply, viewing that concession as an infringement on national sovereignty. So long as Boris Yeltsin wielded power in Moscow, Russia avoided backing its demands with force. Yeltsin was not averse to using military power when he felt it necessary (witness the war in Chechnia), but he clearly preferred diplomacy to coercion. There are some waiting in the wings in Russia who would be far less restrained in the use of force should they come to power.

The Caucasus

No region of the former Soviet Union is more prone to ethnic violence than the Caucasus. All of the conflicts that engulfed the region had their origins during the years of Soviet rule, but they were largely contained by the instruments of state power centered in Moscow. That power was bitterly resented by the diverse nationalities of the region, perhaps nowhere more so than in Georgia. The military suppression of a Georgian nationalist demonstration in Tbilisi in April 1989, which resulted in nineteen deaths and many more casualties, shocked many in Moscow, including the USSR's Georgian-born foreign minister and Gorbachev's ally, Eduard Shevardnadze. The Tbilisi massacre not only spurred Georgian demands for independence, but sparked nationalist emotions throughout the Caucasus.[32]

In October 1990, parliamentary elections in Georgia were won by a nationalist bloc headed by Zviad Gamsakhurdia, and in May 1991 he was elected as Georgia's president. An extreme nationalist who had been repressed as a dissident by Soviet authorities, Gamsakhurdia proved an erratic and repressive leader. He was passionately anti-Soviet and anti-Russian. Georgia joined the Baltics as the only former Soviet republics to reject outright membership in the CIS. Relations with Russia deteriorated under his leadership. Gamsakhurdia even gratuitously offended Moscow by supporting the demands of the Chechens to separate from the Russian Federation. As president, Gamsakhurdia was inept, corrupt, and oppressive. After a brief reign he was overthrown by domestic opponents who reportedly received weapons from Russian military forces in the region.[33] He was succeeded as Georgia's leader by Eduard Shevardnadze, who was invited by the Georgian parliament in March 1992 to return to his native country. Shevardnadze has proven to be a tough leader—not a compliant partner of Moscow—but willing to work with the Yeltsin administration.

Since Georgia attained independence from the USSR, its domestic and foreign politics have been dominated by its struggle with secessionist movements in South Ossetia and Abkhazia. Gamsakhurdia's extreme nationalist policies exacerbated longings for independence among the peoples of these two autonomous republics. Within a month of Gamsakhurdia's parliamentary victory, South Ossetia and Abkhazia both declared themselves sovereign republics.

South Ossetia is a province of Georgia which borders on North Ossetia, an autonomous republic within the Russian Federation. Georgians are Orthodox Christians, while the Ossets are predominantly Muslim. According to the 1989 census only 14 percent of South Ossetians were fluent in the Georgian language. Because they share ethnicity with the North Ossets, many South Ossets sought political union with their brethren in the north. Fearful that the secessionist movement would spread to its own territory, Moscow refused their demands. President Shevardnadze, though noted as a champion of democracy while serving in the Gorbachev administration, also was sufficiently nationalistic to oppose any measure that would lead to the disintegration of the Georgian state.[34]

Fighting between South Ossetian and Georgian forces broke out late in 1990, intensifying over the next two years. Russia became involved because large numbers of refugees fled north, and because of its concern that the fighting might spread to North Ossetia. Under pressure from Moscow, Shevardnadze agreed to meet with Russian President Boris Yeltsin as well as representatives from North and South Ossetia. In June 1992, at Dagomys near the city of Sochi, the negotiators agreed to a cease-fire and the deployment of a joint peacekeeping force.

This mission in no way involved the Commonwealth of Independent States. It was a first of its kind, organized on a trilateral basis between Georgia, Russia, and South Ossetia. The initial objective was to enforce a cease-fire by separating the warring sides. Nominally under a joint command, the force was effectively subject to Russian authority. This operation was successful in keeping the peace, though it did little to resolve the underlying conflict. The practical effect of the cease-fire was to freeze in place territorial conquests won in battle. Shevardnadze has conceded a degree of autonomy to South Ossetia, but the Ossets want more. In view of the unsettled status of Chechnia in the North Caucasus, Russia continues to view outright secession as a bad precedent for the region.

A more serious threat to Georgian territorial integrity is the secessionist struggle of Abkhazia. Located between the Black Sea and the Caucasus mountains, Abkhazia is a province in northwest Georgia. Abkhazians, predominantly Muslims, constitute only 17 percent of the population of the province, although they dominate its government. In August 1990 the Abkhazian Supreme Soviet declared its independence (at the same time as South Ossetia). The brief but repressive administration of Zviad Gamsakhurdia had the same impact on Abkhazia that it did on South Ossetia: it heightened tensions, which ultimately led to bitter fighting. Eduard Shevardnadze was confronted in 1992 and 1993 with a military insurrection by forces loyal to Gamsakhurdia, as well as a war of secession in Abkhazia. The pressure of both forces on his government led to disaster in the fall of 1993. Fierce Abkhaz assaults on Sukhumi, the provincial capital, led to the city's fall and heightened fears that Georgia might disintegrate. In desperation Shevardnadze appealed to Russia for assistance.

Although accounts vary regarding how much responsibility the Russians bore for Shevardnadze's predicament, it is widely believed that Russian forces gave significant aid to Abkhaz leader Vladislav Ardzinba. What is less clear is how much of that assistance was authorized by the Russian president. Ardzinba had important supporters in Moscow, including Vice President Aleksandr Rutskoi and Ruslan Khasbulatov, speaker of the Russian parliament. Furthermore, the Russian military despised Shevardnadze because it held him responsible (along with Mikhail Gorbachev) for the collapse of the Warsaw Pact and the Soviet Union. Shevardnadze's biographers contend that Ardzinba's forces were aided by volunteers from the North Caucasus.[35] Although the evidence is inconclusive, Georgians are certain that Russians were involved in the bombing missions in support of the Abkhaz rebels.[36] Whatever Yeltsin's views, and they were at times apparently ambivalent, he failed to prevent members of the Russian armed forces from helping the separatists. Fearing that the fighting might spread, Yeltsin in late 1992 intervened to mediate a cease-fire. When Abkhazian forces, reinforced with Russian equipment, violated the cease-fire, Russia did nothing to stop the secessionists.

The Georgian military fiasco in 1993 occurred at about the same time that Moscow was in political crisis. Yeltsin's defeat of his political enemies in the parliament—under the leadership of Khasbulatov and Rutskoi—worked to Shevardnadze's advantage, in that it strengthened the Russian president's resolve to stop the fighting in Georgia. But Shevardnadze had to pay a price. In return for Russian assistance against both Abkhazia and the forces of Gamsakhurdia, Shevardnadze had to agree to join the CIS and accept Russian military bases on Georgia soil. "I sent a telegram to Moscow," Shevardnadze said, "saying Georgia will join the Commonwealth of Independent States, which I was against until the last moment."[37] On February 3, 1994, Boris Yeltsin arrived in Tbilisi to conclude a Treaty of Friendship and Cooperation and a status-of-forces agreement with Shevardnadze. Russia received the right to maintain three military bases in Georgia with a troop strength of 23,000. Russia also acquired access to ports on the Black Sea, including Poti, a major terminus of rail lines and roads from Tbilisi.

The net impact of Russian intervention had been to prevent either side from achieving outright victory. Abkhazia could not become independent, but Tbilisi had to concede autonomy for the province. When Moscow rescued Georgia in the fall of 1993, Andrei Kozyrev assured Shevardnadze that Russia opposed the dismemberment of Georgia.[38]

The Abkhaz rebellion was the first conflict in the region to involve the United Nations. While recognizing Georgia's territorial integrity, the United Nations was not prepared to send forces to guarantee it. UN Secretary General Boutros Boutros-Ghali proposed that a CIS peacekeeping force be deployed in Georgia, with UN monitors overseeing the force. On July 2, 1994, the Security Council welcomed the "contribution made by the Russian Federation . . . of a peacekeeping force."[39] At the same time the Security Council authorized 136 UN military observers to monitor the Russian peacekeepers.

Russian peacekeeping in Georgia clearly has served the foreign policy interests of Moscow. Shevardnadze has been forced to accede to a Russian role in the affairs of Georgia. In the face of a persistent deadlock over Abkhazia, the Georgian president has sought support from both the United States and the United Nations for a multinational force to replace the Russians. But neither the United States nor the United Nations has been willing to take a stand in opposition to the Yeltsin administration. In the meantime, UN-sponsored talks in Geneva in 1997 focused on direct negotiations between the parties in an attempt to end the impasse.

Nagorno-Karabakh

Russia has used the conflict between Armenia and Azerbaijan over the region of Nagorno-Karabakh to exert influence over both countries. Moscow played little role in sparking the initial dispute, but it has vigorously monopolized the mediation and peacekeeping efforts to settle the conflict.

Nagorno-Karabakh is an autonomous oblast in Azerbaijan, the inhabitants of which are primarily Armenian. Predominantly Christian, the non-Slavic Armenians have a long history of animosity with the Muslim Azeris. Like many inter-ethnic antagonisms in the former Soviet Union, this one was exacerbated by Soviet nationality policy. Typical of its divide-and-rule practices, the Bolshevik government in 1921 placed Nagorno-Karabakh, whose population was 94 percent Armenian, under the administrative control of Azerbaijan. Even during the height of Soviet rule, political demonstrations between Armenians and Azeris led to violent clashes. The conflict flared up during Gorbachev's rule, defying his efforts at settlement. When Azerbaijan declared its independence in 1991, the government of Nagorno-Karabakh proclaimed itself an independent republic. Fighting again flared up between Nagorno-Karabakh Armenians and Azeris, and when Armenian military forces joined their brethren, an undeclared war between Armenia and Azerbaijan ensued. Militarily the Armenians won on all fronts—within Nagorno-Karabakh itself, taking control of the land between Armenia proper and the oblast, and also occupying territory deep into Azerbaijan east of Nagorno-Karabakh. In the scale of military action and the number of victims, the war over Nagorno-Karabakh was larger than any other conflict in the former Soviet Union. And it was second to none in viciousness. Atrocities were committed by both sides.[40]

The Armenian-Azerbaijani conflict is both an interstate war and a war of secession. Before the Soviet collapse many in Armenia and Nagorno-Karabakh shared the belief that Nagorno-Karabakh would unify with Armenia. After Armenia and Azerbaijan became independent, the idea of unification declined and was superseded by the notion of an independent Nagorno-Karabakh republic. As the aggressor in the war against Azerbaijan, Armenia found itself under international pressure to withdraw from occupied territory. In April 1993 the UN Security Council demanded the withdrawal of Armenian troops from Azerbaijan.

An earlier and more extended international effort to stop hostilities was

made by the Conference on Security and Cooperation in Europe (CSCE—
later to become the OSCE). In March 1992 it established the "Minsk
Group" (Belarus, France, Germany, Hungary, Italy, Russia, Sweden, and
Turkey) to mediate the conflict and plan for a CSCE peacekeeping operation. A CSCE observer group arrived in the region in April 1993.

Russian involvement has complicated the CSCE effort to mediate the
conflict or to deploy peacekeepers. Moscow claims the right to play the
leading role. Russian mediation succeeded in May 1994 in producing a
cease-fire and an agreement for a peacekeeping force. Armenian president
Lev Ter-Petrosian sought Russian peacekeepers; Nagorno-Karabakh Armenians wanted no Turkish troops in the force; and Azerbaijani president
Gaidar Aliev balked at the idea of a Russian/CIS-dominated force and
insisted that only a CSCE-mandate force could operate in his country.

An apparent breakthrough on the principle of an OSCE peacekeeping
force was reached at the Budapest summit in December 1994. A force of
3,000 troops was proposed, but the specifics of which countries would con-
tribute were unresolved. To date the force exists in principle only. Meanwhile Armenia continues to occupy Azeri territory, and Nagorno-Karabakh`
maintains a *de facto* but unrecognized independence. Nevertheless, the
agreement in principle on an OSCE peacekeeping force is more than Russia
had previously conceded toward permitting outside forces to engage in
peacekeeping and mediation in any of the "near abroad" countries.

The Yeltsin administration made clear that Russia must play the dominant role in managing conflict in the Transcaucasus. In this sense democratic Russia continues the historic policy of the Soviet Union and Imperial
Russia in viewing the Transcaucasus as a "dagger pointed toward the heart
of Russia." Unlike the other CIS conflicts, the issue here does not involve
protecting ethnic Russians, because few live in the region. Instead, Moscow
is motivated by a number of economic and geopolitical factors. Of considerable importance is the question of Azerbaijan's cooperation in the exploitation of Caspian Sea oil and the pipelines to bring the oil to Western
markets. Russia voiced reservations over the signing in September 1994 of
the "deal of the century" to exploit three Caspian Sea oil fields. In the deal,
Azerbaijan negotiated a $7.4 billion contract giving eight Western oil com-
panies a 70-percent share in the project. To appease Moscow, Lukoil, the
Russian oil giant, was granted 10 percent of Azerbaijan's initial 30-percent
stake. Russia has pressed for a larger share. The number and location of the
pipelines to deliver the oil to Western markets also remain unresolved.[41]

Azerbaijan's President Gaidar Aliev, a former KGB general and Soviet
Politburo member, has maneuvered shrewdly in his dealings with Russia.
Where necessary he has made concessions to Moscow, as on the issue of oil

production. He also agreed to rejoin the CIS after a brief withdrawal. But alone among the leaders of the "near abroad" he has resisted the stationing of Russian peacekeepers or military bases on Azerbaijan's soil. Aliev also has carefully exploited Russia's concerns about the influence of Turkey, a traditional rival, and Iran, a center of militant Islam, in the region. In 1994 Aliev signed a ten-year Treaty of Friendship and Cooperation with Turkish President Suleyman Demirel. He also has concluded several political, economic, and cultural agreements with Iran. Undoubtedly, however, Aliev's politics are constrained by the knowledge that Moscow helped to destabilize the administration of his predecessor, the intensely nationalistic and pro-Turkish leader Abulfez Elchibey. Though potentially one of the richest of the former Soviet states, Azerbaijan remains vulnerable to Russian pressure—which Moscow has not hesitated to exert.[42]

Moldova

Moldova is another case of Russian intervention in the "near abroad" to establish control over territory it believes to be within its sphere of influence. The circumstances of this Russian intervention, however, differ from the others in the degree to which Russian forces have been guided by policy from Moscow. Russian military forces in Moldova were not always completely under Moscow's control, with the result that policy toward the area often had a schizophrenic character.

Moldova is confronted by a secessionist movement in a region referred to by its leaders as the Trans-Dniester Republic. The territory involved is a small strip of land on the eastern bank of the Dniester River between Ukraine and the rest of present-day Moldova. At the time of the 1989 census, the region contained 546,000 people, or 12.6 percent of Moldova's population. Of that number 40 percent are Moldovan, 28.3 percent Ukrainian, and 25.4 percent Russian. Thus the Russians, like the Abkhazians in their territory, are a minority, but they too dominate the politics of the region. The Trans-Dniester territory had always been ruled from Moscow; its history was different from that of the west bank, or Bessarabia, which had been a part of the Russian empire but became a part of Romania after 1917. Bessarabia was returned to Moscow's control as part of the Nazi-Soviet Pact of 1939.

In the period leading up to the collapse of the USSR, the nationalist-minded government in Chisinau adopted laws making Romanian/Moldovan the state language and replacing the Cyrillic with the Latin script. The east bank Russians strongly opposed these measures, believing they would lead to a subordinate status for Russians, and that they heightened the possibility that Moldova would merge with Romania. In addition to the ethnic issues between Chisinau and the east bank capital of Tiraspol, there were sharp political differences. The Trans-Dniester Russians were strong supporters of the Soviet system and welcomed the August 1991 coup in Moscow. Moldova's leaders by contrast opposed the coup and backed Gorbachev. In August 1991 Moldova declared its independence from the Soviet Union, and a week later Trans-Dniester seceded from Moldova, declaring itself a constituent republic of the USSR, with Tiraspol as its capital.

Moldova's efforts to stop the secession and enforce its authority in the Trans-Dniester region led to widespread fighting in 1992. The rebellious Russians were aided by the 14th Army, which as a component of the Soviet armed forces had been based in Tiraspol. With its active support, the Dniester troops were able to hold off Moldovan forces and establish effective control over the entire east bank of the Dniester River. In the spring of 1992 Boris Yeltsin put the 14th Army under Russian control, and in June he appointed General Aleksandr Lebed to be its commander.

Defeated on the battlefield, Moldova had no choice but to involve Russia in negotiations for a cease-fire.[43] Moldova sought a peacekeeping force under international supervision and requested the OSCE to send such a force. When the OSCE declined, Chisinau had no choice but to accept Russia's proposal for a joint force of Russian, Moldovan, and Trans-Dniester troops to monitor a truce.[44] (Although the contingent was referred to as a CIS peacekeeping force, the CIS members who expressed a willingness to participate ultimately chose not to do so.)

On July 21, 1992, Yeltsin and Moldovan President Mircea Snegur signed an agreement creating the trilateral force and a security zone on both sides of the Dniester. As a step toward a political settlement, the two presidents agreed on the territorial integrity of Moldova and the gradual withdrawal of the 14th Army. As a concession to the Trans-Dniester inhabitants, the region was to be given autonomy, and in the event that Moldova and Romania were to unify, the Trans-Dniester region would have the right to secede.[45]

The joint force successfully kept the peace, but—as so often happens with peacekeeping—little was achieved toward a lasting settlement. Trans-Dniester remains a semi-sovereign state in all but name. It has a government, passports, and a postal system. While Lebed commanded the 14th Army, he supported Trans-Dniester independence, though he severely criticized the leadership in Tiraspol. He even ran successfully for the Trans-Dniester parliament in 1993. Indeed, during the period of Lebed's command, the Russian government had only partial control over the activities of the 14th Army. Yeltsin's administration was constrained by the fact that the Trans-Dniester cause had attracted strong support among Russian nationalists. However, Yeltsin himself had good reason to oppose the secessionists' cause. The Russians in the region were politically closer to his enemies than to him. During the October 1993 crisis, Moldova supported Yeltsin, while most of the Trans-Dniester leaders sided with Rutskoi and Khasbulatov.[46] And as elsewhere, Yeltsin was sensitive to the implications of Trans-Dniester independence for independence-minded regions within Russia.

In part, the reversals of Russian policy have reflected the tug and pull of diverse domestic political forces. Particularly contentious issues were the timetable and conditions for withdrawal of the Russian 14th Army. On October 2, 1994, Russia and Moldova signed an agreement for these forces to withdraw over a three-year period. The withdrawal, however, was made conditional on a political settlement providing a "special status" for the Trans-Dniester regime.[47] Aleksandr Lebed opposed withdrawal, as did many in the Russian Duma. Yeltsin was pulled in one direction by strong international pressure against Russia's intervention in the internal affairs of a sovereign state, and in another direction by his own military. In April 1995, Yeltsin challenged Lebed, who threatened to resign. Many did not expect Yeltsin to accept the resignation of so popular a military leader, but he did. Lebed went on to challenge Yeltsin in the 1996 presidential election, and then to serve briefly in his administration, but the Trans-Dniester issue has continued to defy resolution. As late as mid-1998, the Russian parliament had not ratified the October 1994 agreement to withdraw Russian forces from Moldova.

The Baltic Republics

Among the states formed from the former Soviet republics, Latvia, Lithuania, and Estonia are the most determined to remain independent of Russia's control. Not only did they reject membership in the CIS, but they vigorously sought political and economic integration with Western Europe. There remains among many of the Baltic peoples a residual bitterness over their forced incorporation into the USSR following the Nazi-Soviet Pact and the brutal treatment inflicted upon them by Stalin. They contend that their incorporation into the Soviet Union was never legally valid, a perspective which permeates their relations with Russia.

Demographics is another factor, and it cuts two ways. Estonia and Latvia have such a large percentage of their population who are not of the titular nationality that there is concern over national survival. At independence approximately 40 percent of the population of Estonia consisted of non-Estonians. In Latvia the proportion of non-Latvians was even higher, 48 percent. The situation is different in Lithuania, where according to the

1989 census Lithuanians accounted for almost 80 percent of the total population. In 1994 the percentage of Russians in these three republics was estimated at 29.4 percent for Estonia, 33.5 percent for Latvia, and 8.5 percent for Lithuania.[48] As a consequence of these demographics as well as resentment over a half century of Soviet (viewed by many Balts as Russian) domination, there was a strong movement in Estonia and Latvia to deny citizenship rights to non-Estonians and non-Latvians and to make the acquisition of citizenship difficult.[49]

From the Russian perspective, the presence of some 1,725,000 ethnic Russians in the Baltic republics imposed on the Russian government an obligation to protect the civil rights of the diaspora Russians. Indeed, Yeltsin's government was under considerable domestic pressure to act on behalf of the 25.3 million Russians in the "near abroad." Russian refugees from the Baltics were among the organizers of the Congress of Russian Communities, which at its second Congress in 1994 demanded, *inter alia*, "protection of the interests of Russian citizens regardless of their place of residence."[50] The Congress of Russian Communities, with General Aleksandr Lebed among its leaders, became a potent force in Russian politics.

Russo-Balt antagonism did not necessarily mean cooperation among the Baltic states on all foreign policy issues, nor did it preclude considerable accommodation between Russia and the Baltic states. Despite their common struggle for independence, the Baltic republics worked toward common objectives in a very modest way. Close ties were imperiled by preoccupation with domestic problems, competition for Western investments, and often just plain mutual suspicion. Lithuania's relations with Latvia were worse than its relations with Russia, due to an unresolved dispute over the demarcation of Lithuanian and Latvian waters. Latvia and Estonia quarreled over fishing rights. Meetings among leaders of the three states through the Baltic Assembly and the Baltic Council of Ministers were often perfunctory. Though each state has sought admission to NATO, they have never agreed to a mutual assistance alliance among themselves.[51] Politically, Lithuania tends to look toward Poland, while Estonia and Latvia feel stronger ties to Finland and Scandinavia. In terms of economic and security interests, all three are inclined to look to Germany rather than to each other.

Whatever suspicion exists toward Russia is muted by economic dependence and the realization that tiny states must make accommodation with neighbors who happen to be great powers. For decades, non-communist and democratic Finland illustrated the limits of an independent foreign policy toward the Soviet Union. Baltic military forces are small and poorly armed. The Baltic states are dependent upon Russia for natural gas and other sources of energy. Russia is their largest trading partner, and Russian cooperation is necessary for the transit of goods to any of the other CIS states to the east and south.

Nevertheless, relations have often been contentious. Fundamentally that tension reflects Moscow's determination to keep the region within Russia's sphere of influence and the resistance of the Baltic states to Russian hegemony. The dialectic between the benefits of cooperation and the struggle for power have produced relations which were often fluid and changing. Initially the greatest Baltic concern was the presence of some 130,000 Russian troops in the three countries. Moscow used the issue of withdrawal as a bargaining chip to obtain greater political rights for the Russian minority in the Baltics. Of the three countries, Lithuania's citizenship law was the least restrictive. A combination of pressures (some economic) from Moscow and concessions by Vilnius induced the Yeltsin government to agree to withdraw all Russian forces by August 31, 1993.

Another military problem with political implications for Lithuania involved the transit of Russian military equipment and personnel from the Kaliningrad oblast (a region separate from Russia, on the Baltic Sea south of Lithuania) to Russia. Disagreement over the terms of transit had embittered Russo-Lithuanian relations, until a compromise was reached in June 1995 which made it possible for Russian troops to cross Lithuanian territory on terms acceptable to both sides. This agreement illustrated the efforts on both sides to normalize relations as much as possible. However, in the mid-1990s a new issue arose—NATO expansion—which put the two countries on irreconcilable paths.

Latvian and Estonian relations with Russia have been particularly strained. The slowness of Russian troop withdrawal and the restriction on Russian citizenship rights were powerful sources of antagonism. Both Latvia and Estonia adopted citizenship and naturalization legislation which the Yeltsin government considered discriminatory. In October 1991 the Latvian Supreme Council ruled that automatic citizenship would be granted only to people who had been citizens of Latvia in June 1940 and their descendants. In November 1993 the citizenship law was modified to include a system of annual naturalization quotas for noncitizens. Russia's position was that all inhabitants of the country should be granted citizenship. Hard-fought negotiations failed to produce an outcome satisfactory to either party. The international community, particularly Europe, exerted pressure on both sides to modify their positions. The OSCE, European Union, and Council of Europe wanted the Baltic states to liberalize their citizenship rules, and the international community wanted Russian forces out of the Baltics.

A partial breakthrough was reached in late 1993, when Russia agreed to withdraw its forces from Latvia by August 1994 if Latvia would permit Russia to retain its radar station at Skrunda for six years and if Russian military pensioners were given social guarantees. These terms, which did not give full satisfaction to either side, were formalized in April 1994 when Presidents Boris Yeltsin and Guntis Ulmanis signed a treaty in Moscow.[52]

However, problems of citizenship and language continued through the decade to poison relations between Latvia and its giant neighbor. Like its Russian counterpart, the parliament in Latvia is the repository of strong nationalist sentiment. In early 1998 the Latvian parliament considered legislation to make the exclusive use of the Latvian language mandatory in state institutions and in the private sphere. Not only did Moscow condemn the idea as discriminatory to Russian-speakers in Latvia, so did the OSCE's high commissioner of Human Rights.[53]

A few weeks before his dismissal as Russia's prime minister, Viktor Chernomyrdin warned while visiting in Riga, that "without a change in the situation of the Russian-speaking populations, and above all, without a fundamental acceleration of the process of granting Latvian citizenship to Russian-speakers, no early progress should be expected in other spheres of bilateral cooperation."[54] His warning failed to deter a downturn in relations in the spring, when, as a result of the forceful suppression of a demonstration of thousands of ethnic Russians in Riga on March 3, Moscow threatened to impose economic sanctions on Latvia. In an effort to ward off a crisis in the region, the Clinton administration pressured Riga to modify its citizenship laws. In April the Latvian cabinet agreed to grant citizenship to all children born in Latvia after August 21, 1991.[55] Parliamentary approval of that measure would not solve all the problems of the 450,000 ethnic Russians in Latvia, but it would be a step toward promoting a dialogue between Moscow and Riga.

Of the three Baltic states, Estonia has had the most contentious relations with its giant neighbor. It simply ignored Russian demands that citizenship be granted to all Estonian residents. Laws adopted in late 1991 and early 1992 granted automatic citizenship only to those who had been citizens of the prewar republic and their descendants. Estonia angered Moscow also by demanding a revision of its border with Russia, based upon the 1920 Treaty of Tartu. This revision would have transferred more than 2,000 square kilometers to Estonia. Russia refused to recognize the validity of the Treaty of Tartu. As in the Latvian-Russian dispute, outside pressure was exerted on both sides to make concessions. The United States Senate, much to Moscow's displeasure, threatened to block aid to Russia if Estonia were not freed of foreign troops. On July 26, 1994, Yeltsin and Estonian President Lennart Meri signed agreements providing for the withdrawal of Russian troops by August 31 and committing Estonia to provide some 10,700 military pensioners the same rights as Estonian citizens.[56] But the border differences were not resolved, nor did Moscow obtain its full objectives regarding citizenship rights for ethnic Russians.

One option that is available to all diaspora Russians is to return to live in Russia as citizens. Relatively few Baltic Russians have chosen to do this, in all likelihood because economic conditions are better in the Baltic states than in Russia, and a move would probably lower their standard of living.

We will see in the following chapter the importance of the issue of NATO expansion in East-West relations. Russia saw NATO expansion from the beginning as a threat to the balance of power and to its prestige as a great power. In the end Moscow was unable to reverse the decision made at Madrid to admit the Czech Republic, Hungary, and Poland to NATO. But the issue of the "near abroad" states was another matter. And the focus of that struggle was the Baltic states.

It is no exaggeration to describe alignment with Western Europe as the central foreign policy objective of each of the Baltic states. They view being part of Europe as central to their security and sovereignty. That has meant membership in the European Union and NATO. On June 9, 1994, the Baltic states were given "associate partner" status in the Western European Union.[57] At the same time several free trade agreements were signed with the European Union. Although economic reform has taken hold in the economies of the Baltic republics, particularly in Estonia, there was little serious expectation that the Baltic republics would be eligible for full membership before the year 2000, although all of them were included on a December 1997 list of candidates promised eventual membership by the EU. Russia has taken no steps to prevent the expansion of the EU into this region.

But NATO is another matter. As determined as the Baltic states are to join NATO, Russia is determined to keep them out. When NATO initiated its "Partnership for Peace" program in early 1994 as a preliminary step toward possible full membership, the Baltic states quickly joined the bandwagon. Lithuania was the first to join on January 27, 1994, and Estonia and Latvia followed soon thereafter. During the intense debate in 1996 and 1997 over which countries would be among the first to be invited into NATO, there was never any doubt that the Baltics would not be among them. U.S. Secretary of Defense William Perry warned in September 1996 that the Baltic states were "not yet ready" for NATO. So their exclusion at Madrid in July 1997 came as no surprise.

As we will see in chapter 6, Russia was unable to prevent NATO invitations to three former Warsaw Pact states, but it did attempt to influence the parameters of NATO expansion. One of the limits demanded by Moscow was that NATO not incorporate any of the states of the former Soviet Union. And Moscow's greatest concern was the Baltics, which were the only former Soviet states actively seeking admission to NATO. Moscow's policy was formally described in a "conceptual outline" published by the Ministry of Foreign Affairs on February 13, 1997. In it the Russian government acknowledged the inevitability of NATO expansion but insisted that such expansion could not include former USSR republics, "especially the Baltic countries." Admitting the Baltics to NATO would create a "serious barrier" between them and Russia. In compensation Moscow announced its willingness to offer its neighbors some kind of security "guarantees."[58]

Prior to the NATO decision, negotiations were begun in January between Foreign Minister Evgenii Primakov and NATO Secretary General Javier Solana. Primakov took a strong line against Baltic membership in NATO. He publicly warned of the consequences if that were to happen:

> Russia cannot remain indifferent to the factor of distance—the Baltic countries' proximity to our vital centers. Should NATO advance to new staging grounds, the Russian Federation's major cities would be within striking range of not only strategic missiles, but also tactical aircraft. . . .
>
> In other words, as soon as the Balts took such a path . . . our dealings with NATO would be over. There would still be bilateral relations with the Western countries as such, of course, but in other respects Russia's foreign policy would diversify noticeably and be stepped up in the eastern and other sectors. It goes without saying that additional defensive measures would also have to be taken.[59]

The question of whether and when East European states will be admitted to NATO remains an open one. So in fact is the future status of Russia's relations with the "near abroad." A strong core of Russian opinion, both elite and mass, supports the idea of greater integration among the former Soviet republics. That opinion is matched by similar views among a portion of the populations of some of the CIS states, particularly in Central Asia. But among all of the newly independent states (with the possible exception of Belarus) there is a strong determination to preserve the independence and sovereignty won in 1991. Boris Yeltsin wants greater integration and, at the very least, Russian hegemony. So far, Yeltsin has shown a preference for diplomacy over coercion in the "near abroad." But Yeltsin's presidential term ends in 2000, and what tactics his successor will choose is also an open question.

6

Russia and the West

A Changed Orientation

The collapse of the Soviet Union in 1991 changed the structure of the international system. Throughout the Cold War the international system was bipolar. A bipolar system, as contrasted with a multipolar system, is one dominated by two great powers or by two blocs, each led by a great power. Although bipolarity had characterized regions of the world before—e.g., Athens and Sparta in the fifth century B.C.—never before had it existed at the global level.

Political science theorists have described a bipolar world as a confrontational one in which both sides view the other as a deadly adversary and in which each "pole" views any gain by the other as its own loss. In the language of game theory, the bipolar struggle was a "zero-sum game."[1] It cannot be established with certainty whether bipolarity contributed to the Cold War or whether the dual structure of the international system happened to be dominated by strongly antagonistic states. In either event, by the beginning of the 1990s, the United States was clearly the dominant world power. For the moment, the international system appeared to be "unipolar."[2] And with the new system came a respite in great power rivalry.

In both Washington and Moscow, a new perception of the other emerged. The two rivals became partners. We observed the beginning of this change in the Gorbachev period, as he liquidated one by one the sources of contention between East and West: in the arms race, Afghanistan, Africa, Eastern Europe, Germany, Cuba, and elsewhere. But Gorbachev was a man of contradictions. He could never fully divest himself of the spirit of competition between socialism and capitalism. As he expressed it in his book, *Perestroika: New Thinking for Our Country and the World:* "Economic, political, and ideological competition between capitalist and socialist countries is inevitable."[3] We can only speculate how far the rapprochement between East and West would have gone had Gorbachev remained in power.

Gorbachev's successor, Boris Yeltsin, went beyond rapprochement with the United States. He began his administration with a genuine attempt to build a partnership with the United States, even though differences emerged between Moscow and Washington as early as during his first term as president. What explains the transformation in Russian foreign policy? In chapter 4 we noted the shift in the perceptions of the political elite of Russia. Ideology was completely abandoned, ending the worldview of an inherent conflict between political systems. Yeltsin did not just modify communist doctrine, as did Gorbachev; he jettisoned it completely.

Earlier we described the debate in Russian politics between the "Atlanticists" and the "Eurasianists." Yeltsin, and especially his first foreign minister, Andrei Kozyrev, actively trumpeted the Atlanticist position. The Russian president stated his views at a special summit meeting of the United Nations Security Council on January 31, 1992:

> Russia sees the U.S., the West, and the countries of the East not merely as partners but as allies. This is a highly important prerequisite for, and, I would say, a revolution in, peaceful cooperation among the states of the civilized world.
>
> We rule out any subordination of foreign policy to ideological doctrines or a self-sufficient policy. Our principles are simple and understandable: the supremacy of democracy, human rights and liberties, legality, and morality.[4]

Before a joint session of the U.S. Congress on June 17, 1992, Yeltsin reaffirmed his wish to join "the world community."[5]

But clearly more than ideology or perceptions was involved. Russia was impelled by its domestic condition to seek outside assistance, and no country was better positioned to aid the new administration than the United States. Yeltsin made the transformation of Russia's economy his number one domestic priority. In the words of Anders Aslund, a Swedish economic advisor to Yeltsin, "When the Soviet Union broke up in December 1991, the Russian economy was in a crisis as complex as it was profound."[6] Foreign help was essential. In an extraordinary speech on October 28, 1991, Boris Yeltsin discussed at length and in detail the need for Western assistance and cooperation, and he even promised to give the West whatever information it would want to facilitate aid.[7]

Western support for Yeltsin had an importance beyond economics. It was also important for him politically. Yeltsin understood that he could count on the support of Washington when he confronted domestic reaction. The value of this support became clearly evident during the failed coup of August 1991.[8] And later, during the parliamentary crisis in October 1993, Yeltsin sought and received support from the West.[9] In sum, the shift in

Russian foreign policy toward a pro-Western orientation reflected conviction, necessity, and self-interest.

Arms Control

Russian commitment toward cooperation with the United States began with the issue of arms control and weapons reduction. We have noted above that in the late Soviet period Gorbachev's "new thinking" had redefined the country's national security requirements, placing less emphasis on nuclear weapons and more on arms control. The result was a number of negotiated reductions in weapons, of which the most important were the Intermediate Nuclear Forces (INF) agreement of 1987, the Conventional Forces in Europe (CFE) treaty in 1990, and the Strategic Arms Reduction Talks (START) treaty in 1991.[10] The arms race during the Cold War had been one of the factors which undermined economic growth in the civilian sector. Not surprisingly, Yeltsin immediately pushed for arms cuts, particularly of nuclear weapons. Reducing nuclear weapons, he announced in January 1992, "would make it possible to save substantial amounts of money. This money would be channeled toward civilian objectives and toward implementation of reform."[11]

But cooperation with the United States in arms control offered more than just economic benefits. Yeltsin was attracted to an idea introduced by President George Bush for a scheme known as GPALS (Global Protection Against Limited Strikes). Bush proposed that the United States and Russia jointly deploy a limited number of non-nuclear missile defenses to protect both countries against limited ballistic strikes, whatever their source. Speaking before the United Nations in January 1992, Boris Yeltsin unexpectedly expressed interest in GPALS. Cooperation on missile defense appealed to him because it provided an opportunity to strengthen the foundations of Russian-U.S. cooperation, particularly in a field where Russia would be a genuine partner and not a supplicant. When the two leaders met in a Washington summit in June, they signed a statement in support of the GPALS plan.[12] But nothing ever came of GPALS, because of strong opposition to the plan in both countries. In Russia there was fear, particularly within the military, that GPALS might endanger the Anti-Ballistic Missile (ABM) Treaty and become a stalking horse for the Strategic Defense Initiative (SDI).[13]

A much more important issue confronting Moscow and Washington was a follow-on treaty to the START agreement. Under the terms of the START I treaty, the United States and the Soviet Union had agreed to reduce their strategic nuclear forces from 11,602 to 8,592 for the United States, and from 10,877 to 6,940 for the Soviet Union. Further reductions were to be made in succeeding agreements. Negotiations for a START II treaty were begun in the winter of 1992 and completed in the remarkably short time of five months. Two issues dominated the negotiations: the number of strategic nuclear warheads to be permitted each side and which delivery systems were to be destroyed. In January, Boris Yeltsin proposed reducing nuclear warheads on strategic missiles to between 2,000 and 2,500. President Bush wanted a ceiling of between 4,500 and 5,000.[14] The range ultimately agreed to by both was between 3,000 and 3,500.

From the U.S. perspective the major benefit of START II was that it prohibited land-based Intercontinental Ballistic Missiles (ICBMs) with multiple warheads. The bulk of the Russian strategic arsenal—the SS-18s, SS-19s, and SS-24s—were of the type outlawed by the START II treaty. For years the United States had sought to prohibit these "MIRVed" missiles because they were considered "first strike" weapons. A portion of the U.S. strategic inventory does consist of precisely this type of missile (the Minuteman III and MX missiles), but the bulk of the U.S. missiles with multiple warheads are in submarines, deep in the oceans. U.S. doctrine viewed the submarine-launched ballistic missiles to be less prone to use in a "first strike," because they could not be destroyed in a surprise attack and were not accurate enough for a "first strike." Thus, there would be no incentive to use them preemptively in a crisis.

The major concession made by Russia in START II was agreement to eliminate all land-based ICBMs armed with multiple warheads—the backbone of its strategic force—while the United States was permitted to retain the heart of its strategic force—multiple-armed warheads in submarines. The date for completing the reduction in warheads and prohibited missiles was 2003.

For the first time since the beginning of the nuclear arms race, Russia abandoned its goal of parity with the United States. "We are departing from the ominous parity," Yeltsin explained, "where each country was exerting every effort to stay in line, which has led to Russia . . . having half of its population living below the poverty line." He acknowledged that Russian concessions were made to give tangible "expression of the fundamental change in the political and economic relations between the United States of America and Russia."[15] START II was agreed upon at the June 1992 summit and signed on January 3, 1993.

Not all Russians were prepared to accept the asymmetrical terms of START II. There was disquiet within the military. *Pravda,* an organ of the opposition, suggested that the treaty could be a "hasty, unwarranted concession to Washington and Russia's final loss of the status and importance of a superpower." And it predicted, "this will evoke sharp debates in the Russian Supreme Soviet during the ratification of the agreement."[16] That prediction was an understatement. Five years after its signing, START II remained unratified by Russia.

For almost three years, ratification was linked to the problem of Ukraine's refusal to ratify the START I agreement. START II could not be implemented until all the former Soviet republics possessing nuclear weapons—Russia, Ukraine, Belarus, and Kazakhstan—agreed to ratify the START I treaty and the non-proliferation treaty. We have noted in chapter 5 the antagonism in Russian-Ukrainian relations during the early post-Soviet period. Responding to strong domestic opinion, Ukrainian President Leonid Kravchuk resisted giving up the "nuclear card" as a bargaining chip in negotiations with Russia over a variety of issues, including the status of the Crimea, the Black Sea fleet, and financial compensation for returning its nuclear weapons to Russia. A prolonged effort was made by Russia and the United States, acting in concert, to pressure Ukraine to ratify START I. U.S. Secretary of State James Baker negotiated an agreement, concluded on May 23, 1992, in Lisbon, Portugal, that committed Ukraine to START ratification. But the Ukrainian president failed to follow up on his commitment.

The U.S. effort continued under a new administration. At a Moscow summit in January 1994, Presidents Bill Clinton and Boris Yeltsin induced Leonid Kravchuk to sign a trilateral agreement in which Ukraine would take measures to bring START I into force in return for financial compensation and security guarantees from both Russia and the United States.[17] Even that commitment was stymied because of Ukrainian domestic politics, and final Ukrainian parliamentary approval was not given until later in the year. By that time, Leonid Kravchuk had been succeeded as president by Leonid Kuchma.

Although the accession of Ukraine, Belarus, and Kazakhstan (as well as Russia) to START I legally opened the way to move on Russian ratification of START II, new obstacles developed both in Russian domestic politics and in Russian-U.S. relations. As we will see below, a sharp change in Russian foreign policy resulted from a nationalist surge in Russian politics and the takeover of Russia's legislature in 1993 by nationalist and rightist forces. And in 1994, a new issue emerged—NATO expansion—which made ratification of START II even more problematical.

An issue related to arms control was the problem of the security of nuclear and chemical weapons in the arsenals of some of the newly independent states. Fearful that these weapons might fall into the hands of terrorists or governments supporting terrorism, Congress in late 1991 enacted legislation creating the Cooperative Threat Reduction program

(CTR), sometimes referred to as the Nunn–Lugar program after its Senate sponsors. The program was intended to give Russia, Belarus, Ukraine, and Kazakhstan financial and technical assistance for dismantling or safely storing nuclear and chemical weapons. Toward that end, projects were financed for defense conversion, housing for former military officers, jobs for scientists, storage of nuclear weapons, improvement of security for transportation of nuclear weapons, and destruction of chemical inventories. The CTR program is scheduled to end in 2001.

War in the Balkans

At about the same time that the Soviet Union collapsed, the Yugoslav state fell apart, precipitating Europe's first major post–Cold War conflict. The assertion of independence by Croatia and Bosnia-Herzegovina, two of Yugoslavia's constituent republics, led to bitter fighting between Croats, Serbs, and Muslims. The most bitter and prolonged part of the fighting took place in Bosnia-Herzegovina, as each of these three communities fought for control over territory in the newly independent state. The Serbs (who comprised 31.3 percent of the Bosnian population) and the Croats (who were 17.3 percent) opposed a unified, independent Bosnian state whose dominant population was Muslim (43.7 percent). The Serbs and Croats wanted instead a loose confederation in which they would be essentially self-governing or free to unite with their brethren in Croatia and Serbia.[18]

Fighting in Bosnia began in the spring of 1992 and continued until a peace agreement brokered by the United States was signed in November 1995. The Bosnian war created a strain in Russian-U.S. relations because the sympathies of the two countries were with different parties to the conflict. Russia was traditionally an ally of Serbia. As we saw in chapter 1, historically Russia had assumed the role of protector of the Orthodox Christian Slavs in the Balkans. This feeling of kinship between Russians and Serbs resonated throughout Russian society. The United States found itself sympathetic to the Bosnian Muslims because they were the victims of widespread Serbian atrocities associated with the policy of "ethnic cleansing" (forcible displacement from territories seized by the Serbs). Both Moscow and Washington were constrained in their support for their respective sides. Russian Foreign Minister Andrei Kozyrev made no attempt to defend Serbian aggression, and the West recognized that atrocities had been committed, albeit on a lesser scale, by Croats and Muslims also. Nevertheless, throughout the war, Yeltsin found himself having to weigh the benefits of supporting traditional friends with those of cooperation with the West. His dilemma was not unlike that which confronted Mikhail Gorbachev in 1990–91 as a result of Iraq's aggression against Kuwait.[19]

While Yeltsin's policies vacillated over time, reflecting the changing pressures on his administration, he carefully avoided a rupture with the United States. His general strategy was to concede to the United States those points which Washington pressed, while at the same time working to soften the blows inflicted on the Serbs. Thus at a Helsinki meeting of the CSCE in July 1992, Russia joined those governments voting to suspend Yugoslavia's membership because of its aid to Bosnian Serbs who were accused of aggressive actions. Even more important was the debate at the United Nations over the question of imposing economic sanctions against Yugoslavia. Andrei Kozyrev argued that negotiations were preferable to punishing Yugoslavia. Yeltsin was scheduled to meet with President Bush in an upcoming summit, and he was confidentially advised by the Russian ambassador to the United Nations that it was "very important not to oppose on this point the Western countries and the United States, where public opinion is strongly against Milosevic [the president of Yugoslavia]."[20] In the end, Russia—which had the power of the veto—voted with the majority to impose unprecedented, strict sanctions against Yugoslavia.

Yeltsin's Yugoslav policy encountered strong conservative opposition at home. Reminiscent of the USSR Supreme Soviet's condemnation of the United Nations vote to use force against Iraq, the Russian Supreme Soviet demanded a moratorium on United Nations sanctions against Yugoslavia. Typical of right-wing opinion was the criticism in the newspaper *Sovetskaia Rossiia* that "the consistent antinational policy pursued by the current Russian leadership has found its logical conclusion in the open and unconcealed betrayal of the fraternal people of the allied republic of Yugoslavia." *Pravda* charged, "Moscow . . . does not have a policy course of its own."[21]

Under the leadership of Radovan Karadzic, the Bosnian Serbs ruthlessly pursued their policy of "ethnic cleansing." Though sympathetic to the Serb cause, the Russian government condemned Serb atrocities as well as Yugoslav support for Bosnian Serb aggression. That aggression led to Serb control of approximately 70 percent of the territory of Bosnia-Herzegovina. In August 1992 the issue of using military force to guarantee the delivery of humanitarian aid came before the UN Security Council. Russia, notwithstanding its dislike of coercion against the Serbs, supported resolutions authorizing the use of force if necessary. At the Forty-eighth General Assembly session, the Assembly voted to expel Yugoslavia. Again, the Russian delegate to the Security Council made no effort to use the power of the veto to prevent the expulsion of Yugoslavia from the United Nations.[22] The Yeltsin administration was careful to avoid drifting too far from the mainstream of international opinion on Yugoslavia and Bosnia.

Arms Reductions and Arms Sales

One constituency which Yeltsin could not afford to disregard was the military. He carefully involved the Ministry of Defense in the negotiations for START II, and notwithstanding some criticism from the right, Yeltsin was able to secure a degree of political cover with the endorsement of START II by Minister of Defense Pavel Grachev and Chief of the General Staff Mikhail Kolesnikov.[23] Two issues on which the military pressed Yeltsin and received the president's support were revision of the CFE Treaty and arms sales abroad. On both issues, Yeltsin pressed the West for accommodation. The CFE Treaty, signed in November 1990, established allocations for a variety of conventional weapons in the NATO and Warsaw Pact states. It contained restrictions on the internal distribution of forces in Russia, specifically in the Military Districts of Leningrad and the North Caucasus, which the Russian military considered too restrictive for post-Soviet Russia. Before the Soviet collapse, these districts were rear-echelon regions, but with the collapse of the Warsaw Pact and the breakup of the USSR, they unexpectedly emerged as part of Russia's first line of defense. Opposition to the CFE within the national security elite was strong even during the Soviet period. That antipathy intensified with the change in Russia's geopolitical position. The limitation in the Leningrad District posed no immediate problems, but instability in Georgia, Armenia, and Azerbaijan, and the use of Russian peacekeeping forces in the Caucasus, required an upward adjustment of limitations. Defense Minister Pavel Grachev first expressed dissatisfaction with the flank ceilings in March 1993. In September Yeltsin formally proposed amending the CFE Treaty. There was strong resistance in NATO to this Russian demand, particularly from Turkey, the member of NATO most affected. Russia remained adamant, arguing not only the threat to stability in the region and the long-term danger of Islamic fundamentalism, but also concern for the cohesion of the Russian Federation itself. Facing the possibility of Russian denunciation of the CFE Treaty altogether, NATO agreed to negotiate the issue.[24]

Arms exports were another contentious issue. The military wanted government support for arms exports in order to keep munitions and weapons factories in business. The government desperately needed arms exports as a source of hard currency. Yeltsin's arms export policies balanced elements of cooperation with competition with the West. In order not to antagonize Washington, Yeltsin forfeited billions of dollars in arms sales by cooperating with UN sanctions against Libya, Iraq, and Yugoslavia. For this he suffered strident criticism from nationalists at home. On the other hand, Yeltsin was unwilling to abandon the lucrative market in other regions of the world. He pushed his government to expand arms sales in the Middle East and Asia, where for decades the West had been the dominant supplier.

As we will see in detail in the following chapter, some of the larger sales created strains in Russian-U.S. relations. A deal to sell India cryogenic rockets brought protest from Washington and eventually had to be modified to meet some of the U.S. concerns. In 1993 Russia negotiated a large sale to Malaysia of eighteen MiG fighters. The bid overcame competition from the McDonnell-Douglas Company in the United States. As the Russian press noted, "The time has come to acknowledge that where arms exports are concerned, we and the West—particularly the U.S.—are not partners but competitors, both economically and politically."[25]

Russia's Shift to the Right

For about two years the Yeltsin administration maintained a pro-Western orientation in the conduct of foreign policy. Russian-U.S. summits in 1992 and 1993 demonstrated an unprecedented rapport between the leaderships of the two countries. At the Washington summit of June 1992, Yeltsin and Bush signed a Charter of Russian-American Partnership and Friendship affirming "the indivisibility of the security of North America and Europe" and a common commitment to "democracy, the supremacy of law . . . and support for human rights."[26] In Vancouver, Canada, Yeltsin and President Clinton agreed to create a Russian-American Commission on Questions of Technology (popularly known as the Gore-Chernomyrdin Commission, for its co-chairmen). In Canada Yeltsin received a pledge of an immediate assistance package of $1.6 billion, and the Paris Club granted Russia a ten-year deferral of its debt obligations due in 1993.

As we saw in chapter 4, the "Atlanticist" consensus within Russia's governing elite, led by Foreign Minister Andrei Kozyrev, was by no means universally shared throughout Russian society. Yeltsin was in almost constant conflict with the parliament inherited from the Soviet period. Both in the parliament and in non-government circles, Yeltsin was attacked by nationalists for his support of U.S. policy in Yugoslavia, and for such actions as the 1993 U.S. air strike against Iraq. *Pravda* chided Yeltsin, saying, "The role of Washington yes-man is unbecoming of any country, especially Russia, and it inevitably conflicts with national interests."[27] Andrei Kozyrev served as a lightning rod for much of the criticism of the Yeltsin administration. The Supreme Soviet called in vain for his removal.

Nationalists in Russia held Yeltsin as responsible as Gorbachev for the disintegration of the Soviet Union, and they hated him for it. They had a diffuse agenda ranging from the restoration of the USSR to the protection of Russians throughout former Soviet territories. Other foreign policy issues promoted by nationalists were support for the Dniester Republic in Moldova, the protection of civil rights of Russians in the Baltic states, retention of the Kurile Islands seized from Japan in 1945, and restoration of Russian sovereignty over the Crimea.

For Boris Yeltsin these pressures imposed a careful balancing strategy. His record as a whole justifies the conclusion that his commitment to partnership with the West reflected a genuine conviction. And indeed, though there were significant swings in Russian foreign policy over the course of Yeltsin's two terms, the underlying rationale never changed. But to understand the swings it is necessary to consider both the political calculations of the governing elite, especially the president, and the evolving political and economic conditions within Russia.

Certainly a factor in the evolution of Russia's policy was popular disillusionment with the fruits of economic reform. "Shock therapy," begun in January 1992, led to severe economic hardship for millions of ordinary people. By virtually every economic index, production declined during the early post-Soviet years. Economic assistance from the United States proved to be disappointingly smaller than most Russians expected. Those critical of Yeltsin to begin with belittled U.S. aid. "For a year and a half," noted *Pravda* after the Vancouver summit, "we have been fed cock-and-bull stories about the inevitable 'rain of gold' from the West to back up Yeltsin's reforms."[28] Nor was disillusionment with U.S. aid limited to hardened anti-Yeltsinites. In late 1993, polls showed that by a two-to-one margin Russians were convinced that the West's economic advice represented a deliberate effort to weaken Russia. This margin increased in 1995 and 1996.[29]

Yeltsin's own views changed with those of the electorate. To say this is not to suggest that Yeltsin shifted with the fluctuating winds of public opinion as measured by polls. But as president, he felt an obligation to be "comprehensible, controllable, and dependent upon public opinion. He must listen."[30] To many, Yeltsin has the reputation of an authoritarian leader. His repudiation of Mikhail Gorbachev in the waning days of the Soviet Union, his use of force against an intransigent parliament in 1993, and his attempt to suppress the Chechens by military measures sustained that reputation. But there is a different and equally consistent element in his political modus operandi, and that is his willingness to compromise and to find common ground with his critics and opponents. This tendency was evident in his negotiations with Gorbachev before the August coup; it was clear in repeated attempts to find common ground with his enemies in the Supreme Soviet and Congress of People's Deputies; and it revealed itself in his re-election campaign. In short, as the broad contours of public opinion shifted, so did Yeltsin. This could be viewed as political expediency or as the democratic response of a leader to his people.

Zhirinovskii's success in the December 1993 parliamentary elections was a bad omen for the president. Although the Liberal Democratic Party lacked a cohesive or comprehensive program, the rhetoric of its leader was that of an extreme nationalist. Many thought of Zhirinovskii as a fascist. Zhirinovskii condemned the dissolution of the USSR and promised to restore Russia to its status as a great power. He offered his leadership as the protector of the twenty-five million Russians living outside the Russian Federation. Specifically, he promised to recover for Russia lost territories in Ukraine, the Baltic states, Kazakhstan, Turkmenistan, and Finland. In one of his less considered statements, he even suggested the return of Alaska to Russia.[31]

Russia began 1994 with a new constitution and a new parliament. The fact that Yeltsin confronted another antagonistic parliament, as he had prior to the constitutional crisis in 1993, did not mean that he was as constrained as before. As we have noted in chapter 4, the powers of the president were significantly greater under the new constitution. Indeed, with regard to foreign policy Yeltsin had virtually a free hand. He could, should he choose, run roughshod over the parliament, but in so doing he would be going against what appeared to be the popular will.

Russia's new constitutional order shares certain features with that of France. Both nations' constitutions were drafted by strong leaders in times of crisis. In 1958 Charles de Gaulle wrote the constitution for the French Fifth Republic, to give himself the power to deal with the crisis caused by war in Algeria. Both constitutions combine elements of presidential and parliamentary systems. As in all parliamentary systems, the government is subordinated to parliament; but unlike other parliamentary systems, in France and Russia an independently elected president chooses the government. Another similarity is that the potential for stalemate exists in both regimes, if the forces controlling parliament are hostile to the president. That was the situation in Russia in the mid-1990s, as it was with France under François Mitterrand in the 1980s and 1990s.

In France this potential conflict was avoided by a policy of cooperation between the president and parliament which became known as "cohabitation." To the surprise of some, Yeltsin in 1994 engaged in his own form of cohabitation by demonstrating a willingness to compromise with opponents in the State Duma. In domestic politics this meant a slowdown in the economic reform. In foreign policy it meant a shift to the right.[32]

The War in Chechnia

No issue so dramatized the shift in Russian politics—both domestic and foreign—as the war in Chechnia, which erupted in December 1994. Chechnia is one of the ethnic republics that make up the Russian Federation. It borders on the independent state of Georgia in the Caucasus and has a Muslim population with a long history of resistance to central authority. Some Chechen units collaborated with German forces invading the Caucasus during World War II, provoking Stalin to deport large numbers of Chechens to Central Asia. In 1991 the Chechen Republic declared itself independent, but its independence was recognized neither by the Russian government nor by any other state. During the early years of his administration, Yeltsin avoided a direct confrontation with Chechen forces led by President Dzhokhar Dudaev, but he did give assistance to a dissident force organized as a "Provisional Council" headed by Umar Avturkhanov. Its effort to take control in Chechnia failed.

Reports of impending warfare in Chechnia were heard throughout 1994.[33] On December 11, Russia sent armed forces into Chechnia for the purpose of overthrowing President Dudaev and establishing Russian authority in the country. Ostensibly, the reason for the invasion was to establish constitutional order—the Russian constitution denied any of its eighty-nine subjects the right to secede unilaterally—and to suppress widespread crime and corruption in Chechnia. What was not made clear at the time was why Yeltsin had chosen that particular time to act. Why had Yeltsin not attempted to negotiate a special constitutional arrangement with the Dudaev government, permitting a degree of republican autonomy, as he had with other republics?[34]

Russia's opaque political system rendered difficult a clear analysis as to whether the decision to invade was made by military leaders not fully responsible to the Russian president, or whether perhaps Yeltsin himself was moving sharply toward a more nationalist, hard-line policy. Either way, the consequences were a significant shift in Russian foreign policy. Yeltsin's political move had some similarities to the rightward move of Mikhail Gorbachev in 1990. As the Soviet president had done that fall, Yeltsin abandoned his political ties with many of his former democratic allies in favor of associates on the political right. The attack on Chechnia was supported by a so-called "war party" consisting of Defense Minister Pavel Grachev, Interior Minister Viktor Erin, Chief of the Federal Counterintelligence Service Sergei Stepashin, Nationalities Minister Nikolai Egorov, Security Council Secretary Oleg Lobov, and the chief of Yeltsin's bodyguards, Aleksandr Korzhakov.

Evidence that the war in Chechnia was part of a broader change in Russian foreign policy was provided by Yeltsin's dramatic behavior at the Budapest meeting of the OSCE, which convened just days before the outbreak of fighting. Speaking against the expansion of NATO, Yeltsin warned of a new "cold peace" in Europe. His allusion to the United States was unmistakable when he observed, "History proves that it is a dangerous delusion to think that the fates of continents and of the world community as a whole can be controlled from a single capital."[35] Just days earlier, Foreign Minister Andrei Kozyrev had stunned the members of the NATO Council meeting in Brussels with an unexpected announcement that Russia would not join the Partnership for Peace Program pushed by Washington.

The West did not question the right of Russia to establish, even forcefully, its authority in Chechnia, but it did object to the brutality of Russian forces fighting in the war zones, and particularly to the killing of civilians and indiscriminate bombing of the capital city of Grozny. Russian forces were both wantonly destructive and at the same time totally ineffective in winning the war.

As a result, the prestige of the Russian military declined, and with it the popularity of the Russian president. Chechnia was the first televised war ever viewed by the Russian people, and as the U.S. administration learned in Vietnam, popular viewing of a losing war generates strong domestic opposition. A national poll early in 1995 found a 72-percent disapproval rate of the Kremlin's policy in Chechnia and only a 16-percent approval rating.[36] In February 1995 polls showed that Yeltsin's approval rating had fallen to 8 percent. Particularly significant was the loss of support among many of his former democratic allies. Ironically, Yeltsin's war policy was supported primarily by right-wing nationalist elements, precisely those forces least likely to support his overall foreign or domestic policies.

The war in Chechnia was the most divisive security policy issue in Russian politics during the election years of 1995 and 1996. Its impact was felt in the 1995 parliamentary elections and in the presidential elections the following year. Efforts were made in the State Duma to force an end to the war by legislative means, but they failed because of the refusal of the nationalist parties to attack Yeltsin on that issue. The only parties consistently supporting an anti-war position were Russia's Choice, Yabloko, and Women of Russia, which together could not mobilize a majority in the legislature.[37]

However, in the summer of 1995 a terrorist attack on Russian soil by Chechen forces galvanized public opposition to the war. A gang of 200 guerrillas led by Shamil Basaev seized some 2,000 hostages in the Russian city of Budënnovsk. Russians were outraged that such a large-scale operation could be undertaken in a city almost 100 miles from the Chechen border. Compounding the humiliation of the raid was the inept performance of the military effort to rescue the hostages. A desperate attempt to storm the hospital where the hostages were held not only failed, but led to casualties among the hostages. In the end the Russian hostages were saved only by negotiations led by Prime Minister Viktor Chernomyrdin, who had to agree to permit Basaev and his guerrillas to escape. So angered were critics of the war in the legislature that the State Duma voted its first motion of no confidence in the government on June 21, by a vote of 241 to 72 (with twenty abstentions).[38]

Politics in Russia during the second half of 1995 was dominated by the election campaign for a new Duma scheduled for December 17. Yeltsin's policies were under attack from both the left and right. The principal vehicle for supporting the president's policies was the party "Our Home Is Russia," headed by Chernomyrdin. The parliamentary elections turned into a political defeat for the administration. Half the Duma was elected by proportional representation from party lists and half by direct election from districts. Our Home Is Russia garnered only 10.13 percent of the proportional vote. The major parliamentary winner was the Communist Party of the Russian Federation, which won 22.3 percent of the popular vote for the party lists; Zhirinovskii's Liberal Democratic Party was second with 11.18 percent, and Grigorii Yavlinskii's Yabloko Party won 6.39 percent. In the proportional representation vote, no other party among the forty-three registered to participate gained the necessary 5 percent minimum for representation in the Duma. Overall, Yeltsin ended up with a parliament no more sympathetic to him than its predecessor. Those who constituted the opposition—a coalition of leftist and nationalist elements—were potentially in a position to mobilize a majority in the parliament. Thus foreign policy decisions which required the support of the Duma—such as ratification of START II—were problematical at best. However, the fundamental constitutional fact remained that foreign policy was made by the executive branch, not by the parliament.

Almost immediately after the parliamentary elections in December 1995, politics in Russia began to focus on the presidential election scheduled for the following June. As we have seen, one of the casualties of the nationalist upsurge embodied in the new Duma was Foreign Minister Andrei Kozyrev. As one of the longest-serving members of the administration, Kozyrev came to symbolize better than anyone else the liberal, democratic, and pro-Western features of Yeltsin's presidency. As such, he had been for years the point man of bitter criticism from statist, nationalist, and leftist elements in Russian politics. The fact that Gennadii Ziuganov, the head of

Russia's Communist Party, welcomed the replacement of Kozyrev with Evgenii Primakov meant that Yeltsin would have more clout with the Duma and at the same time not be quite as vulnerable to criticism of his foreign policy from both the left and right. Some saw the Primakov appointment as an indication that Yeltsin intended to run for a second term.[39] And in February Yeltsin did indeed announce his candidacy for re-election.

Boris Yeltsin's campaign turned out to be a spectacular come-from-behind race. From the beginning his main opponent was Ziuganov, who in January was supported by 20 percent of those who indicated to pollsters their intention to vote, compared to 8 percent who supported Yeltsin.[40] Yeltsin's low rating was due largely to domestic conditions; foreign policy proved not to be an important factor in the campaign, due in part to Primakov's ability to neutralize it as an issue.

Although it was not a campaign issue, the war in Chechnia contributed significantly to popular dissatisfaction with the incumbent. The Russian military simply could not subdue the Chechens. Occasional truces would be signed, only to be violated and followed by renewed fighting. In January Russia was shocked by another Chechen terrorist assault on Russian territory. Four hundred militants under the command of Salman Raduev, the Chechen president's son-in-law, seized a hospital in the city of Kizlar, taking some 2,000 hostages. Intensive negotiations led to an agreement to permit Raduev to leave the city with 165 hostages in eleven buses. When the convoy reached the town of Pervomaiskoe, they were surrounded by Russian troops who attempted to storm the Chechen positions. After several days of fighting in which dozens were killed on both sides, Raduev managed to escape into Chechnia with some of the hostages. The incident embittered both sides, further dispirited Russia's military, and intensified popular dissatisfaction with the war.

Yeltsin's conundrum was that Russia could neither fight nor negotiate its way out of the war. President Dzhokhar Dudaev never wavered from his demand that Russia unconditionally recognize Chechnia's independence. That Yeltsin was not prepared to do. On March 31, Yeltsin unveiled a new "peace plan" for Chechnia. Admitting that "the Chechen crisis is Russia's gravest problem," Yeltsin proposed an immediate cessation of military operations to be followed by parliamentary elections in the war-torn republic, followed in turn by negotiations to determine "Chechnia's status within the Russian Federation."[41] Though unwilling to meet directly with Dudaev, he offered to enter into talks with the Dudaev side through intermediaries. The problem with this strategy was that it had been tried before without success. Several truces had previously been announced, only to be violated. Yeltsin's March peace plan met the same fate, as fighting continued through the spring and summer.

The presidential campaign and the war in Chechnia were closely linked. Like U.S. presidents Lyndon Johnson and Richard Nixon in Vietnam, Yeltsin wanted the political benefits of ending the war but feared the political consequences of paying the price Dudaev demanded for peace. Chechens, including Aslan Maskhadov, the man who would succeed Dudaev, viewed the March peace initiative as no more than a Russian ploy. Some believed that their prospects for getting out of the Russian Federation would be improved if Yeltsin were to lose the presidential election.

Yeltsin won re-election in spite of the war. In the first round of voting on June 16, he received 35 percent to Ziuganov's 32 percent. Aleksandr Lebed, former commander of Russia's 14th Army in the Trans-Dniester region, came in third with 14.7 percent. In a shrewd political move, Yeltsin made Lebed a member of his administration, appointing him secretary of the Security Council and assistant for national security. Though there was no direct connection between this appointment and the war in Chechnia, Lebed's brief tenure was to significantly influence Russian policy. One of his first accomplishments was to secure the dismissal as defense minister of Pavel Grachev, a strong proponent of military victory in Chechnia. Yeltsin's political strategy paid off with a victory in the second round of voting in July, when he obtained 54 percent of the vote.

Militarily, the situation in Chechnia deteriorated. Within a month of the election, Chechen insurgents had retaken Grozny, the capital. Sent to the scene of battle, Lebed was appalled by the condition of Russian troops, and he concluded that Russia had no choice but to withdraw. Yeltsin, who was in poor health at the time, appointed Lebed as his primary agent to negotiate an end to the fighting. President Clinton and several NATO governments urged Moscow to forgo the option of storming Grozny and to negotiate a settlement with the rebels. Moving swiftly, Lebed did just that. On August 31 he signed an accord with Aslan Maskhadov, Chechen chief of staff, which called for an end to the fighting and the withdrawal of Russian and Chechen forces from Grozny. On the all-important question of the legal status of Chechnia, the agreement deferred the decision for five years.[42] Lebed proclaimed, "The war is over."

Thus began a new phase in the Russian-Chechen struggle. Both sides, in agreeing to defer a determination of the final status of Chechnia, had compromised politically. Russia interpreted the agreement to mean that until a decision was made otherwise, Chechnia was a part of Russia. But by agreeing to withdraw its forces from the country it lost *de facto* control over the republic. The rebel government claimed independence but could not obtain recognition from Russia (or any other government) and was in fact largely dependent upon Russia for economic recovery. But Lebed's agreement did mark the end of active warfare in the country.

Neither President Yeltsin nor Prime Minister Chernomyrdin was involved in the negotiations at Khasaviurt of the agreement that ended the war, and it is uncertain whether they approved of what the impetuous Security Council secretary had done. Moscow was in the grip of a political vacuum brought on by a serious deterioration of Boris Yeltsin's health following the strenuous re-election campaign. In late summer Yeltsin announced that he would undergo heart bypass surgery. Through the remainder of the year, as the terms of Lebed's agreement were debated, Yeltsin was forced to delegate much of his authority to others, leaving the government open to the tug and pull of ambitious politicians. In the debate over the Khasaviurt agreement, leftist and nationalist leaders such as Ziuganov and Sergei Baburin condemned the agreement, while liberal spokesmen were more supportive. But overwhelmingly, Russian spokesmen insisted that Chechnia had to remain a part of the Russian Federation.

Aleksandr Lebed himself did not survive the resolution of the debate as a government official. In October Yeltsin fired his Security Council secretary because of Lebed's inability to work cooperatively with other members of the administration. Politically ambitious, Lebed had challenged the authority of others in the cabinet and undertaken measures which members of the government considered beyond his authority.

A satisfactory resolution of the Chechen issue has eluded Russian authorities. Yeltsin's decision in November 1996 to withdraw the 101st brigade of Interior Ministry troops and the Defense Ministry's 205th brigade from Chechen territory ended any possibility of keeping Chechnia in Russia by force. For all practical purposes, Chechnia operates as an independent state. On November 23 Chernomyrdin and Maskhadov signed an interim agreement on final steps toward peace between Chechnia and Russia, but the language permitted both sides to maintain their previously held positions regarding the republic's constitutional status.

On January 27, 1997, elections were held in Chechnia for a new president. The winner was Aslan Maskhadov. Although an ardent nationalist, he was respected by the Kremlin as a relative moderate. Some Russians believed that Maskhadov would prove more tractable on the issue of sovereignty than his unyielding predecessors, but they were mistaken. Indeed, it is unlikely that the Chechen population would have accepted such a concession by their leader. Referring to his country by its ancient name of Ichkeria, Maskhadov promised in his oath of office to "strengthen this independent state."

An attempt to square the circle was made by the two presidents with the signing of a peace treaty on May 12, 1997. Yeltsin officially recognized the independence of the Republic of Ichkeria, while Maskhadov conceded that his country was not seceding from Russia. For the Chechen leader, the central provision of the treaty was Russia's commitment "to build their relations in accordance with generally recognized principles and norms of international law."[43] Both sides also formally renounced the use of force in their relations.

For Russia, Chechnia is important not only because of the constitutional issue and its international prestige. There are vital economic issues at stake, the chief of which concerns oil. A central objective of Russian foreign policy is retention of control of the pipelines transporting the enormous quantities of Caspian Sea oil to the world market. Chechnia has been a vital link in the flow of oil from Baku, Azerbaijan, to the Russian Black Sea port of Novorossiisk. That line is now in Chechen hands, and Russia will be compelled to negotiate with Grozny over the terms and conditions for transporting oil through the country. The instability in Chechnia has stimulated among oil producers the prospect of building alternative pipeline routes through Georgia, Turkey, and even Iran. These prospects are profoundly threatening to Russia, and are a strong inducement for Moscow to come to terms with the regime in Grozny.[44]

War and Peace in Bosnia

Russia's shift toward a more nationalistic foreign policy produced in Moscow a stronger defense of the Serbs in their war against the Muslims and Croats in Bosnia. In the face of Western pressure to assist the Muslim-controlled government of Bosnia, Russia successfully blocked efforts in the United Nations to have the arms embargo in Bosnia lifted. It also strenuously opposed military intervention by the West.

Yeltsin's inclination to support the Serbs, however, was curbed by his determination to avoid drifting too far from the mainstream of international opinion. He thus supported Western political initiatives to negotiate a settlement of the war. During 1993 Cyrus Vance and David Owen, on behalf of the United Nations, devised a plan to create a weak confederation in Bosnia-Herzegovina organized around ten ethnically based cantons. Moscow endorsed the plan, as did Milosevic in Belgrade, but the Vance-Owen Plan was rejected by Bosnia's Serbs.

Russian diplomacy in the Balkans was constrained by the fact that its allies were guilty of the larger atrocities committed by the belligerents, and thus the preponderance of world opinion sided with the government of Bosnia. An incident early in 1994 gave Moscow an unexpected opportunity to take the diplomatic initiative. On February 5 a mortar attack on a public market in Sarajevo killed sixty-eight people and wounded 200 more. Though both sides denied responsibility, the general assumption was that the Serbs had committed the atrocity. Public opinion, especially in the West, was outraged and demanded a military response against the Serbs. NATO, which up to this point had moved cautiously, issued an ultimatum to the Bosnian Serbs, demanding that they remove their heavy weapons twenty kilometers from Sarajevo or place them under UN control. The ultimatum was backed with a threat of air strikes.

The situation posed a dilemma for Moscow. Opinion in Russia over-whelmingly opposed NATO military action against the Serbs. Yet the atroc-ity in the Sarajevo marketplace seemed to demand a response. However, many in Russia believed that the mortar attack on February 5 was in fact a Muslim provocation. There had been repeated instances of deliberate provo-cations by the Bosnian government. Foreign Minister Andrei Kozyrev in-sisted that no military action be unleashed without specific authorization by the UN Security Council, where Russia had the veto. Yeltsin consulted with U.S., German, and British leaders, after which he appealed to the Serbs to withdraw their artillery from Sarajevo, as demanded by NATO. To assuage the Serbs, Yeltsin promised to send a contingent of 400 Russian soldiers to join UN forces in the combat zone. This was sufficient cover for Slobodan Milosevic and Radovan Karadzic to bow to NATO's ultimatum. Yeltsin's initiative defused the crisis and enhanced Russian prestige all around. Even domestically the Russian president benefited. As a leading newspaper put it, "In this production President Yeltsin collected quite a few foreign policy dividends, both in the West and within our country."[45]

Russia's diplomatic triumph was short-lived. Barely two months after the shelling in Sarajevo, another crisis arose as a consequence of an assault by Serb forces on the Muslim-held city of Gorazde. UN Security Council Resolution 836, which had been adopted unanimously, had declared Gorazde a United Nations–protected safe area. Russian spokesmen insisted that it was the Muslims who had begun combat operations in Gorazde, but the Foreign Ministry was quick to condemn the Serb assault on a UN-protected city which contained UN and International Red Cross personnel. Russians across the political spectrum, however, were angered that NATO air strikes were carried out on April 10 and 11 against Serb artillery posi-tions without consultations with Moscow. "Trying to make such decisions without Russia is a big mistake and a big risk," warned Andrei Kozyrev. "The bombing of Serbian positions near the city of Gorazde is a slap in the face of Russia's prestige," claimed Deputy Prime Minister Sergei Shakhrai.[46] But Moscow understood the culpability of the Serbs and re-sented the position in which they had put Russia. Vitalii Churkin, Kozyrev's deputy, vented his spleen to journalists: "The Bosnian Serbs must understand that in Russia they are dealing with a great power, not a banana republic. Russia must decide whether a group of extremists can be allowed to use a great country's policy to achieve its own aims. Our answer is unequivocal: 'never.' "[47]

The crisis in Gorazde illustrated the paradox of the Balkan war for Russian foreign policy. Russia's national interest dictated that NATO forces not be used against the Serbs, so as to prevent NATO from becoming the guarantor of peace in Europe, but Serb war tactics were provoking NATO military strikes, and Moscow was unable to control its nominal allies. The optimal solution for all parties would be a negotiated settlement. Yeltsin proposed a summit meeting that would include Russia, the United States, and the European Union, but nothing came of it. Instead the locus of diplomatic efforts became a group of five nations—Russia, the United States, France, Great Britain, and Germany—known as the "contact group." Their goal was to devise a political solution to the Bosnian civil war.

In July the contact group proposed a new peace plan to the Croats, Muslims, and Serbs. Under the plan, Bosnia-Herzegovina would be divided into two political entities. Fifty-one percent of the country would be governed by a Croat-Muslim Federation and 49 percent would be governed by Bosnian Serbs. This plan would have required the Serbs to give up part of the 70 percent of the country they controlled. Notwithstanding a personal appeal from Yeltsin to Radovan Karadzic, the Serbs rejected the idea. The Bosnian Serb intransigence led Moscow to abandon relations with the Serb hard-liners in Bosnia and to focus on Milosevic in Belgrade to exert pressure on Karadzic. Although unsuccessful at the time, this plan contained some of the ingredients of the Dayton Accords that ultimately ended the fighting. Meanwhile Russia continued its policy of opposition to lifting the arms embargo against the Muslim-dominated government of Bosnia and the use of NATO forces against the Serbs. Moscow was unsuccessful in persuading the West to lift economic sanctions imposed on Serbia.[48]

As the pace of fighting picked up in Bosnia in late 1994, the pressure on the West to restrain the Serbs increased, undermining Russia's efforts to prevent NATO from becoming involved militarily. In November NATO planes attacked an airfield in the Serb region of Krajina, in retaliation for a Serb assault on the Muslim city of Bihac, designated by the United Nations as a safe area. Anti-U.S. rallies were held in Moscow, but that did not dissuade Yeltsin and Kozyrev from condemning the Krajina Serbs for provoking the air strikes. Russia's State Duma condemned the NATO action as unwarranted. In December, responding to domestic pressure to provide greater support for the Serbs, Russia vetoed a UN Security Council resolution on the grounds that it was excessively critical of the Bosnian and Krajina Serbs.

By the spring of 1995, Russia's Bosnian policy began to fall apart under its contradictions. Serb military action reached a level of aggressiveness which the West could not ignore. The consequence was an escalation of NATO air strikes against Serb military positions. Moscow could not stop the air strikes nor Bosnian Serb military actions which provoked them. Russia found itself in the humiliating position of being ignored by both sides, by its ostensible friends. In May the Serbs unleashed a massive artillery attack against five UN "safe havens"—Sarajevo, Tuzla, Gorazde, Bihac, and Srebrenica. When NATO, with UN authorization, retaliated against Bosnian Serb positions near the Serb capital of Pale, Serb forces seized more than 300 UN military observers and peacekeepers (including some Russians) as hostages. Even Belgrade condemned the hostage-taking.

Yeltsin was deeply offended that NATO air strikes were unleashed without any consultation with Moscow. At the same time, in frustration, he publicly acknowledged that the Serbs "got what they deserved."[49] Karadzic's forces eventually released their UN hostages, but that did not prevent the UN from sanctioning the creation of a NATO "rapid reaction force" for use in defense of the Bosnian Muslims. Russia, while criticizing the decision as "overly hasty," abstained (along with China) on the Security Council resolution, which was adopted by a vote of 13–0. Boris Yeltsin still believed that the war could be resolved by allowing the Bosnian Serbs to form a confederation with Belgrade. He unsuccessfully pressed that argument with G-7 leaders meeting in Halifax, Nova Scotia.

In August the war in the former Yugoslavia turned decisively against the Serbs. Assaulted by NATO air strikes, Serb positions weakened in both Croatia and Bosnia. A Croatian offensive against Serb-held territory in Krajina led to the occupation of the region by Croatian government forces (and the expulsion of several hundred thousand Serbs). The so-called republic of Serbian Krajina, which had been in existence for four years, collapsed in two days. Moscow protested Croatia's action in vain. Nor could Russia get support from the contact group, because both Washington and Bonn wanted more, not less, pressure put on the Serbs. In desperation, Yeltsin turned toward diplomacy, inviting Croatian President Franjo Tudjman and his Serbian counterpart Slobodan Milosevic to meet in Moscow for talks. That initiative, too, proved to be futile when Tudjman refused to go to Moscow. A follow-on proposal for a trilateral meeting including Alija Izetbegovic, Bosnia's Muslim leader, was no more successful. Finally, Yeltsin proposed a meeting in Moscow of the heads of the "leading states," the opposing sides in Bosnia as well as the presidents of Yugoslavia, Croatia, and Bosnia-Herzegovina. Russia's press blamed the West for sabotaging this idea.[50] Politically Russia's Balkan policies had become bankrupt, giving rise to increased criticism of Yeltsin by his domestic enemies. Combined with the war in Chechnia, the war in Bosnia was pushing Russian foreign policy more than ever before toward an isolated, anti-Western position.

The NATO strikes steadily took their toll on the Bosnian Serb positions on the battlefield. A particularly devastating series of air strikes, the largest conducted by NATO since its formation in 1949, hit Bosnian Serb military installations in late August, in the aftermath of another brutal shelling of civilians in Sarajevo. Nationalists in Russia screamed that NATO was "unleashing a war in the Balkans." Russia's State Duma voted to end participation in the United Nations sanctions against Yugoslavia and called upon Russian volunteers to go to the aid of the "fraternal Serbian people." At the same time it asked Yeltsin to fire Foreign Minister Kozyrev and suspend Russia's participation in the Partnership for Peace program (described below). As in the past, the Russian government protested the NATO air strikes, but Yeltsin vetoed the Duma law seeking to force withdrawal from sanctions against Yugoslavia. (President Clinton, in a symmetrical action, vetoed U.S. congressional moves to force a lifting of the arms embargo on Bosnian Muslims.)

By early fall a combination of military and diplomatic pressure induced the leaders of all the principal parties to agree to a cease-fire, which became effective on October 10. A new stage in Bosnia-Herzegovina's civil war began when Presidents Izetbegovic, Milosevic, and Tudjman agreed to meet in the United States to work out a peace settlement. As a sop to Russian prestige, Moscow was given the honor of hosting the ceremonial opening of the talks on October 30, but immediately thereafter the serious business moved to the Wright-Patterson Air Force Base in Dayton, Ohio.

Even before the terms of an agreement could be worked out, a difficult political issue had to be resolved regarding Russia's participation in the peacekeeping operation to enforce the truce in Bosnia. Russia was determined to participate in the force, and NATO agreed that Russian involvement was important to guarantee peace and stability in the Balkans. The problem was that Moscow would not permit Russian troops to be subject to NATO's command, and the United States found unacceptable any arrangement for a dual command. Addressing the General Assembly, Yeltsin proposed a monitoring force that would operate under UN command. Given all the weaknesses that had already been exposed with UN authority over NATO operations in the Bosnian war, there was no possibility that a UN command would be acceptable to Washington. While in the United States for the fiftieth anniversary of the United Nations, Yeltsin met with President Clinton to resolve the issue. This summit convened in Hyde Park, amidst a generally congenial atmosphere. The outcome, finalized days later in Brussels, was a compromise which conceded to Washington the substance of the issue, but offered to Moscow a face-saving appearance. Dubbed by some "operation fig leaf," the plan called for Russian troops participating in Bosnian peacekeeping operations to report to a U.S. general rather than to NATO's commander. For domestic political reasons, both presidents were anxious to see that their ninth summit be seen as successful. (Russia was in the midst of a parliamentary political campaign, and Clinton was facing a re-election campaign.) At a luncheon, Yeltsin affirmed, "Our partnership is designed to last not for one year, not for a decade, but for centuries, forever."[51]

Under the firm guidance of the United States, in the person of Assistant Secretary of State Richard Holbrooke, the negotiations in Dayton produced an agreement which transformed the military struggle in Bosnia into a political one. The structure of government created by the Dayton Accords was a complex one reflecting a balance—though not necessarily equal—of concerns of the three parties. The principle of a unified, sovereign Bosnian state was maintained in the creation of a central government with a Bosnian parliament and a three-headed presidency. This state would consist of two autonomous parts, a Croat-Muslim confederation occupying 51 percent of the land, and a Serb republic with 49 percent. The Dayton Accords demarcated the territorial lines of the two autonomous regions, with the exception of the corridor around Brcko, which connected the eastern and western parts of the Serb republic. The fate of Brcko was left for later arbitration. Refugees from all parts of Bosnia-Herzegovina were to be permitted to return to their original homes. Those individuals who had been indicted as war criminals by the Special United Nations Tribunal at The Hague were to be turned over to the tribunal.

To ensure compliance with these terms and to enforce the peace, the Accords established a special NATO Implementation Force (IFOR). Originally the IFOR comprised some 60,000 troops. Of these, 1,600 came from the Russian Federation. Russia's participation in the IFOR was approved by the Council of the Federation in January 1966. The IFOR was intended to last only one year, but the ongoing antagonism among all three communities in the country forced NATO to extend its peacekeeping operations.

In one important sense the Dayton Accords were successful. Forty-two months of warfare and brutal atrocities were ended. Daily life for the peoples on all sides became peaceful, and a semblance of normality returned for many. But peace did not bring national reconciliation, and those features of the peace agreement intended to establish unified institutions of government have been observed in form but not substance. The parliaments of the two halves of the country are populated largely by intransigent nationalists.

In effect Bosnia remained divided, not only between the Serb and Croat-Muslim parts, but also within much of the Croat-Muslim federation. Of the two million refugees created by the war, most have not been repatriated because of the opposition of local populations to their return. The ethnic and religious hatreds which gave rise to the war have not been resolved by the Dayton Accords.[52]

Bosnia has continued to be a source of contention between Russia and the West, but on a smaller scale than during the war. Peace resolved two of the bitterest sources of contention between Moscow and Washington. No longer was there an issue of NATO air strikes against the Serbs. And neither was there a problem of economic sanctions against Belgrade: in return for Milosevic's support and participation in the Dayton Accords, the UN agreed to lift its embargo against Yugoslavia.

In the post-Dayton period, Moscow became preoccupied with a new set of domestic issues, including elections to the parliament in 1995 and presidential elections in 1996. There was still a war going on in Chechnia, as well as the ongoing problems associated with economic reform. But in Russia's relations with the West, the biggest issue of contention in the post-Dayton period became the proposal to expand NATO to include former members of the Warsaw Pact.

NATO Expansion

The decision by the North Atlantic Treaty Organization to include within its membership some of the countries of Eastern Europe that formerly had been members of the Warsaw Pact became the single most contentious issue in Russian-American relations in the 1990s. Of the many issues related to NATO expansion, the most general and fundamental concerned what type of European security system would replace the alliance structure of the Cold War period. From Russia's perspective, the basic question was how Russia would fit into a system of European security. Would it be accepted as a great power, or simply as another European state? Would it be viewed as a partner or as a potential adversary? And what institutional mechanism would govern decision-making for security issues in Europe?

For nearly all Russians, NATO was stigmatized by the history of the Cold War and was viewed as an adversarial organization. Russian political elites much preferred as a mechanism for European security the more politically neutral OSCE. But there was more involved in the expansion of NATO than just vital national interests. National prestige was also an important consideration. Russia has yet to come to terms with its loss of status as a superpower. Indeed, many Russians question whether their country can even be ranked as a "great power." An expansion of the military alliance which played a vital role in the defeat of the Soviet Union was viewed by many as rubbing the Russian nose in the Soviet defeat—a national humiliation.

Besides the questions of foreign policy raised by NATO, there were considerations of domestic politics. One reason the Clinton administration supported the idea was because of its appeal to many American voters who had close ties to Poland, the Czech Republic, and Hungary. During his campaign for re-election, Bill Clinton delivered a speech in Detroit which called for expanded NATO membership by 1999 and which had the political purpose of attracting the support of some twenty million voters of Central and East European ethnic origin. Presidential candidate Robert Dole was also a strong supporter of NATO enlargement, removing the subject as an issue of debate in the campaign.

Conversely, Russians opposed the admission of former Warsaw Pact members into the Atlantic alliance. As a domestic political issue in Russia, NATO expansion had relatively low salience among the public at large; but among the nation's political elite there was overwhelming opposition, nowhere stronger than in the military. Spokesmen for Russian nationalists used the issue to criticize the Yeltsin administration for not doing enough to block the plan. "Atlanticist" leaders like Andrei Kozyrev were put on the defensive over the issue.

Both sides of the debate over NATO expansion shifted their positions over time. One reason was the abstract and remote rationale for expansion. NATO was a military alliance created to prevent a Soviet invasion of Western Europe. Even if one accepted as valid the glib summary of NATO's purpose offered by its first secretary-general—"to keep the Americans in, the Russians out, and the Germans down"—there seemed little doubt that NATO's objectives either had been achieved or were, after the Cold War, irrelevant. Nobody considered Russia in the 1990s to be a threat. The military arguments for extending the protection of Article V of the Treaty to the countries of Eastern Europe were unpersuasive. Conceivably a future Russia might be a threat to Eastern Europe, but that contingency hardly required expanding NATO in the 1990s. By the same token, NATO was no threat to Russia and should not have been perceived as such. There was, in short, a shadow-boxing quality to the debate, however serious the issue was in Russian-Western relations.

Two broad considerations moved NATO toward enlargement. One was the need for a new mission and *raison d'être* in the aftermath of the Cold War. Some within the alliance came to the conclusion that NATO would survive only by expanding and becoming a security force for all of Europe. This view was strengthened by NATO's decision in June 1992 to move "out of area" and place its military forces at the disposal of the United Nations and the OSCE for peacekeeping operations in the Balkans. Another stimulus to enlargement was the desire of several East European governments, led by the "Visegrad" states (the Czech Republic, Hungary, Poland, and Slovakia) for security guarantees from the West. The December 1993 Russian elections, which led to the spectacular victory of the ultra-nationalist forces of Vladimir Zhirinovskii, raised concern in Eastern Europe about the long-term dangers of a nationalist regime in Moscow.

Russia responded negatively to the idea of NATO expansion. Although Boris Yeltsin had spoken favorably of Poland's interest in NATO during a visit to Warsaw in the summer of 1993, he quickly reversed himself under pressure from members of his administration, particularly the military. Just before the parliamentary elections in December 1993, Evgenii Primakov, then director of Russia's Foreign Intelligence Service, issued a blistering critique of NATO expansion. He noted that historically NATO and the former Soviet Union had viewed each other as enemies and that "this psychological mind-set cannot be broken painlessly." An expansion of NATO to Russia would create a "new geopolitical situation that is extremely disadvantageous to Russia." This would lead Russia to rethink its defense concepts and restructure its armed forces. He concluded, "If the countries of Central and Eastern Europe join that organization, the objective result will be the emergence of a barrier between Russia and the rest of the continent."[53] Moscow's alternative to NATO expansion was a proposal that NATO and Russia jointly guarantee East European security, an idea that appealed neither to NATO nor to the Visegrad states.

An attempt to satisfy the security interests of Russia and the states of Eastern Europe was a proposal developed by the Clinton administration, known as the Partnership for Peace (PFP). First proposed at a meeting of NATO defense ministers in October 1993, the PFP was designed to be a stepping stone to eventual membership in NATO. It had several objectives: (1) to satisfy the security concerns of the Central and East European states; (2) to avoid destabilization of the delicate political environment in Russia; and (3) to buy time.[54] The PFP was designed to establish cooperative military relations between the members of the partnership through consultation, joint exercises, planning, and training.

The offer of partnership was extended to every member of the OSCE, including Russia. Although they much preferred full membership in NATO, the Visegrad states accepted the offer quickly. By February 1994, agreements to join the Partnership for Peace were also signed by Romania, Lithuania, Estonia, Ukraine, Bulgaria, Latvia, Moldova, and Albania. Moscow's initial response was positive, because it viewed the PFP as an alternative to NATO expansion. But from the beginning there was ambivalence in Moscow. Russians understood only too well that both NATO expansion and the PFP were based upon the fear of Russian aggression, and thus were essentially a continuation of the Cold War policy of containment.

Throughout 1994 the Yeltsin administration wavered in its policy toward the PFP. At a summit meeting with the U.S. president in June, Boris Yeltsin endorsed the PFP initiative. But within the newly elected Russian parliament, opposition to the PFP mounted. Concern within the military intensified as a result of NATO military activity in Bosnia in the winter and spring. Air strikes against the Serbs were made without consulting Russia, giving rise to the feeling in Moscow that Russia was not being accorded the great-power status to which it was entitled. Russia wanted NATO to acknowledge a special strategic partnership, closer than that provided under the PFP. After considerable bargaining, Andrei Kozyrev signed the PFP framework document on June 23, along with a protocol affirming that "Russia and NATO have agreed to prepare a wide-ranging individual program of partnership, in keeping with Russia's size, importance, and potential."[55] The vagueness of the protocol and its lack of a legally binding force failed to satisfy Moscow that Russia was in fact being accorded geopolitical parity with the United States.

If Yeltsin expected the PFP to serve as a barrier to NATO expansion, that hope was dashed in the aftermath of the November 1994 congressional elections in the United States. Republican control of Congress brought renewed demands for NATO expansion, which were endorsed by the Clinton administration. That along with the passage of the Brown Amendment, permitting the Visegrad states privileges in logistics and weapons acquisitions normally reserved for NATO members, increased Russian suspicions.[56] In December Moscow shocked the West with a sharp reversal of the June decision on the PFP. Andrei Kozyrev, the most pro-Western member of the administration, stunned a meeting of the NATO Council in Brussels by postponing Russian participation in the PFP. Boris Yeltsin followed that up with a harsh speech before an OSCE summit in Budapest, warning that pushing NATO up to Russia's borders risked plunging Russia into a "Cold Peace."[57]

Pressed by his military, Yeltsin sought to persuade the United States and Europe to accept an alternative to NATO for Europe's security. One concept advanced by Kozyrev was to subordinate NATO to the CSCE. Early in 1994 Kozyrev proposed

> that the North Atlantic Cooperation Council (NACC) be transformed into an independent structure of military-political cooperation, but one that is closely

linked to the CSCE. Under this proposal, the CSCE is assigned the role of coordinator of the efforts of NATO, the European Union, the Council of Europe, the Western European Union, and the CIS in the areas of strengthening stability and security, peacekeeping, and protecting the rights of national minorities in Europe.[58]

NATO flatly rejected the scheme. As it became increasingly evident in 1995 that NATO expansion was inexorable, Moscow focused on the preconditions which it would demand for acquiescing to the inevitable. Among the preconditions advanced were a favorable revision of the CFE Treaty, the nondeployment of military bases and nuclear weapons in the newly admitted countries, exclusion of the former Soviet republics (especially the Baltic states) as candidates for NATO membership, and recognition of Russia's security system with the CIS states.[59]

But Moscow was playing with a weak hand. What Kozyrev was attempting to do was to obtain Western agreement on a European security system that went beyond mere consultation and detente. And NATO, while willing to offer some assurances on the deployment of bases and nuclear weapons in Europe, was unprepared to formalize any substantive concessions. Yeltsin relied heavily on Kozyrev's credibility with the West, but the hapless foreign minister was unable to produce the desired results. This failure was not the only reason for Kozyrev's replacement as foreign minister early in 1996, but it was a factor. NATO's leaders tried to soften Moscow's resistance through various diplomatic formulations. President Clinton suggested "a broad, enhanced NATO-Russia dialogue and cooperation going beyond PFP," and France proposed in April a NATO-Russia non-aggression pact, but Moscow remained unappeased.[60] Nevertheless, Moscow signed on to the PFP on May 31, 1995, even as it continued to oppose NATO expansion.

Foreign Minister Evgenii Primakov was, if anything, even more vehement than Kozyrev in his critique of NATO's moving eastward as a military alliance. In April 1996 he proposed that NATO and Russia jointly guarantee the Visegrad states as an alternative to their membership in NATO. Neither Washington nor the states involved were interested. Primakov also objected to NATO membership for Austria, the Baltic states, Finland, and Sweden. Recognizing that Kozyrev's plan for the OSCE to be the structure for Europe's security was not gaining support, Primakov abandoned the idea. Ever the realist, he acknowledged that NATO expansion was inevitable and directed his efforts in 1996 toward securing some concessions for his country, in the form of special arrangements for Russia with regard to NATO decision-making. But here also Washington would not budge.

The Clinton administration, mindful of Russian resentment, sought a solution to the impasse that would preserve some measure of prestige for Russia, give support to Yeltsin, and defuse the issue for nationalists. The year 1996 was particularly critical for the Yeltsin administration, beginning with the presidential campaign and concluding with a paralysis of government caused by the president's heart condition. On September 6, Secretary of State Warren Christopher proposed in Stuttgart, Germany, that a "NATO-Russian Charter" be worked out in conjunction with invitations in 1997 for new members in NATO. United States policy was to concede to Moscow a voice but not a veto on sensitive security issues. Aleksandr Lebed, then secretary of the Russian Security Council, argued that a NATO-Russian Charter was not sufficient unless it was "very specific in terms of its legal implications" and that it should be embodied in a legally binding treaty. Lebed pressed his argument before NATO Secretary-General Javier Solana in Brussels, but he admitted afterward, "We did not come to terms."[61]

President Clinton had determined that NATO expansion would be a centerpiece of his foreign policy. Following his election to a second term, he decided to move rapidly on this issue. He announced that invitations would be formally extended to the first batch of new members at the NATO summit in Madrid in July 1997. Intensive negotiations in the spring of 1997 were conducted to obtain Russian acceptance of the inevitable. On March 12 Moscow dropped its demand that a NATO-Russian Charter take the form of a legally binding treaty, accepting in its place an executive agreement. On May 27 Boris Yeltsin and Javier Solana signed the "Founding Act on Mutual Relations, Cooperation, and Security between NATO and the Russian Federation." This act created a NATO-Russian Council which would meet periodically to consider security problems as they arose in Europe. The Council would operate by consensus, but NATO remained free to act without Council approval. As a concession to the Russians, NATO stated that it had "no intention, no plan, and no reason" to deploy nuclear weapons on the territories of its new members or to significantly increase troop levels on their territories. Evgenii Primakov put the best face possible on the pact, calling it a "big victory for Russia," but in a television interview on the night of the signing Yeltsin acknowledged that Russia "was playing a weak hand."[62] In July NATO invited the Czech Republic, Poland, and Hungary to apply to become members.

No event since the end of the Cold War symbolized the new world order more than the expansion of NATO. For Russia it was a major blow to its national prestige. The invitations extended in the summer of 1997 did not remove this bone of contention between Russia and the West. It marked only a new stage in the Russian struggle to contain NATO. At Madrid, Western spokesmen made clear their intention to go beyond the first three invitations. Madeleine Albright specifically promised Lithuania, Latvia, and Estonia that they would be future candidates for membership. In reply, a spokesman at Russia's Ministry of Foreign Affairs said, "We are put on guard by the Madrid declaration's mention of the states in the Baltic region, a reference that, although indirect, nevertheless was in the context of prospects for further NATO expansion. I want to emphasize once again that such a decision has been and remains unacceptable to Russia."[63]

Russia and Europe

In the initial period after the collapse of the USSR, President Yeltsin and Foreign Minister Kozyrev pursued the effort to "join the West" as the highest priority of Russian foreign policy, making no particular differentiation among the democratic market societies and associated international institutions whose partnership they sought. Like Gorbachev before them, they knocked on many doors, concluding treaties of friendship and cooperation with individual Western states, seeking membership for Russia in that most exclusive of Western "clubs," the G-7, and pursuing opportunities to cooperate with (and ultimately join) selective organizations such as the European Union, the Council of Europe, the Paris Club, and the London Club, as well as broader financial associations such as the General Agreement on Tariffs and Trade (soon to be succeeded by the World Trade Organization), the European Bank for Reconstruction and Development, and the International Monetary Fund. In the security realm, the Russian parliament quickly ratified the Treaty on Conventional Forces in Europe—initially concluded in 1990, together with a Charter for a New Europe, which emphasized an undivided "greater Europe" (or, as Gorbachev liked to put it, a "common European home"). Seeking a pan-European security framework, Russia became an enthusiastic participant in the Conference on Security and Cooperation in Europe (later renamed the Organization for Security and Cooperation in Europe), which included the United States and Canada as well as most of the states of Europe.

Heavily criticized by the mounting nationalist opposition for "slavish" imitation of Western policies, stung by the strong showing of Vladimir Zhirinovskii and other "national-patriotic" forces in the December 1993 elections, and disappointed by the lukewarm embrace and hesitant financial support of most of their would-be Western partners, by 1994 Yeltsin and Kozyrev not only had shifted their priorities to the "near abroad" but also had adopted a more differentiated approach toward the West. Not only political extremists but "establishment" figures were asking whether Russia should be in such a hurry to join the "European-Atlantic" system, thereby binding itself with rules not of its own making and restricting its freedom of action elsewhere.[64]

Quarrels were erupting with the United States over policy in Bosnia, the proposed enlargement of NATO, continuing U.S. trade restrictions, and Russia's planned weapons exports to anti-U.S. regimes, which led to complaints about the United States's "hegemonic" behavior. Particularly after the outbreak of war in Chechnia, Russia's relations with the EU soured and its progress toward membership in the Council of Europe slowed, accentuating Moscow's growing isolation and stimulating tendencies to play Western states off against one another. By the end of 1997, Yeltsin was talking openly in European capitals about the need to reduce U.S. influence in "our Europe."

In its initial enthusiasm for forging links with the countries of Western Europe, Russia during its first year or so of independence clearly neglected its ties with its former Warsaw Pact allies in Eastern Europe. In its new geographical configuration, Russia no longer shared borders with Romania, Hungary, or Czechoslovakia, and only its enclave-province of Kaliningrad had a border with Poland. Some degree of tension in relations resulted from the history of past Soviet offenses against Poland, Czechoslovakia, and Hungary. Yeltsin wrote of "certain psychological difficulties" in relations with Lech Walesa and Vaclav Havel—understandable, he conceded, because "hanging over us is the cursed legacy of the USSR."[65] Further complications arose from Moscow's difficulties in complying promptly with the demand of these countries for a complete withdrawal of Red Army forces.

Another major source of difficulty was in the economic realm. Even before the formal dissolution of the Council for Mutual Economic Assistance in mid-1991, trade between the USSR and Eastern Europe had declined sharply, as a result of the decision in the late 1980s to settle accounts in hard currencies rather than in "transferable rubles." Furthermore, Moscow had begun to demand world prices for the oil and gas it sold to Eastern Europe, hoping thereby to build a trade surplus with the region. However, the collapse of industrial production in the USSR created imbalances in the other direction. Short of hard currency and unable to pay even the interest on the Soviet debt, Russia refused to pay in fuel, for which it could earn hard currency on the world market.[66] The resulting impasse, combined with the eagerness of both the East Europeans and the Russians to reorient their economies to Western Europe, produced further sharp declines in regional trade with Russia; indeed, the total volume dropped by half between 1989 and 1993.

By the end of 1993, the influential political commentator Stanislav Kondrashov was concluding that Eastern Europe now ranked only fourth or fifth in Russia's priorities, having been transformed from a zone under Russian influence to one of "coldness and distrust." Complaining that the potential of the East European "Russian lobby"—established by the Soviet intelligence services and a half century of ideological coexistence—was being squandered, he asked how Russia could hope to function as a great power if it failed to re-establish friendly relations with these former partners.[67] But in fact relations had probably not yet reached a low point, as the results of the December 1993 elections—the "Zhirinovskii factor"—stimulated fears in Poland and elsewhere of a new security threat. East European leaders began pressing for prompt admission of their states to NATO, much to the displeasure of Russia, with whom relations took on a character—in one journalist's words—of "controlled mutual antipathy."[68]

The concerns of Poland, the largest and most strategically located of Moscow's former allies, illustrate the difficulties in Russia's relations with Eastern Europe. Warsaw's trade with the Soviet Union had almost completely collapsed prior to 1992, and a trade agreement signed with the Russian government in September 1991 failed to halt the decline; annual trade volume dropped from $14 billion in 1989 to $2.7 billion in 1992. The two states were deadlocked for three years on issues related to settlement of mutual debts, finally agreeing early in 1995 to a mutual write-off of indebtedness. President Walesa visited Moscow in May 1992 to sign a treaty on friendship and cooperation, but his trip occurred only after repeated postponements resulting from disagreements on the document's wording, and the atmosphere of the visit was marred by reports that Poland was siding with Ukraine in its territorial conflicts with Russia. Yeltsin's return trip to Poland also was postponed amid the furor over a remark by Kozyrev that all Moscow had lost in Eastern Europe were "false allies we never trusted anyway."[69] It was August 1993 before the Russian president finally journeyed to Warsaw. The visit was marked by several gestures of Russian goodwill: Yeltsin pledged to withdraw the last Russian army units from Poland by October 1, three months early; he handed over to Walesa material from the CPSU Politburo archive that was intended to disprove the suspicion that the Soviets had planned to send troops into Poland prior to General Jaruzelski's declaration of martial law in 1981; and he surprised all observers by inserting into the joint declaration a statement (later reversed) that Poland's decision to join NATO was not in conflict with the interests of Russia.

Despite these gestures and a Russo-Polish agreement on construction of a gas pipeline from the Yamal peninsula to Germany, relations continued to be strained during the following year. A planned visit to Poland by Viktor Chernomyrdin in November 1994 was postponed in protest of alleged mistreatment by Polish police in Warsaw of Russian passengers on a Moscow–Brussels train. The prime minister's visit took place in February 1995, but the Russians were again distressed when Lech Walesa was a notable absentee from celebrations in Moscow in May of the fiftieth anniversary of the Allied victory in Europe. The Russians were encouraged by former communist Aleksei Kwasniewski's victory over Walesa in the December 1994 presidential elections. Moscow's ambassador to Warsaw noted in a press interview that the new president's professionalism and intelligence "far outstrip" Walesa's and that "he knows us and will refrain from stirring up historical matters that are irritants in Russian-Polish relations."[70] When Yeltsin met with the new Polish president on his first state visit to Moscow in April 1996, he hailed the prospect of improved relations (despite Kwasniewski's persistence in maintaining Poland's earlier stance on NATO), remarking that "lately something hadn't been right between us and Walesa."[71] Poland's relations with Russia did appear to improve in the post-Walesa period, brightened in part by the approaching completion of the first stage of the ambitious pipeline project. This improvement was noted on the occasion of the visit to Moscow in November 1997 of Prime Minister Jerzy Buzek, who pledged that his new government would devote particular attention to building a partnership between Poland and Russia.

As indicated in Yeltsin's memoirs, relations between Russia and Czechoslovakia also were burdened by the legacy of the past, though the presidents of the two countries were evidently able to "break the ice" more successfully (over a beer in a Czech cafe, Yeltsin notes) than were Yeltsin and Walesa. Vaclav Havel visited Moscow in April 1992 to sign a treaty of friendship and cooperation—a document which included a reference to the 1968 Warsaw Pact invasion of Czechoslovakia as an unjustified use of force. The two sides also settled financial issues relating to the withdrawal of Red Army forces, with Havel agreeing to supply materials for building housing in Russia for the demobilized troops, in return for Russia's turning over real estate in Czechoslovakia that had belonged to the Soviet forces.

As was the case with Poland, however, economic relations were slow to recover. The debt issue was still unresolved in August 1993, when Yeltsin visited Prague and Bratislava to sign new bilateral treaties with the now-separated Czech Republic and Slovakia. The new Russian-Czech treaty lacked an apology for the 1968 invasion (a concession to the heightened assertiveness of parliamentary sentiment in Moscow), but Yeltsin and Havel finessed a delicate situation by laying wreaths both at the grave of a Soviet tank crew member killed in the 1945 liberation and at that of a student killed in the 1968 invasion. The atmosphere during Yeltsin's visit to Slovakia was notably warmer, and the trip produced an unexpected agreement on military cooperation between the two countries. Not until May 1994 did Russia and the Czech Republic reach agreement on repayment of Moscow's $3.5 billion debt, partly through transfer of the property of privatized Russian enterprises. In keeping with the direction signaled earlier, Chernomyrdin announced during a two-day visit to Bratislava in February 1995 that the $1.7 billion debt to Slovakia was to be repaid principally with Russian weapons, including six helicopter gunships, and with Russian assistance in the construction of two nuclear power plants.

Issues in Russian-Hungarian relations essentially followed the Polish and Czech patterns, although they were resolved somewhat earlier. Yeltsin visited Budapest in November 1992, where he was able not only to sign a new treaty of friendship and cooperation, but also a financial settlement relating to troop withdrawal and an agreement on repayment of Russia's $1.7 billion debt, half of which was to be paid with weapons (MiG-29s and armored personnel carriers). Prompt settlement of the debt issue allowed Russian trade with Hungary to rebound more quickly than did its trade with Poland or Czechoslovakia. It reached an annual volume of $2.7 billion in 1994, though it was heavily imbalanced in Russia's favor due to Hungary's dependence on imported Russian natural gas. Finally, in the symbolic realm, the Russian president was generous: during his 1992 visit to Budapest Yeltsin laid a wreath at the grave of Imre Nagy, turned over documents from party and KGB archives relating to the 1956 invasion, and apologized to Hungary for the Soviet intervention. But a paragraph in the bilateral treaty condemning the 1956 invasion caused the Supreme Soviet early in 1993 to withhold ratification.

These four East European states (Poland, the Czech Republic, Slovakia, and Hungary) formed the "Visegrad group," and were thought to be the states most likely to be included in the first round of NATO's expansion. Soon after his appointment as foreign minister, Evgenii Primakov made a point of visiting all four states to discuss Russia's opposition to NATO expansion. As the momentum built toward the Madrid summit of NATO in July 1997, threatening noises were occasionally heard from Russian representatives. Thus, for example, Moscow's ambassador to Prague suggested that Czech participation in NATO could have negative consequences for Russian deliveries of natural gas. Despite a foreign ministry disavowal and direct reassurances from Chernomyrdin during an April 1997 visit, the prudent Czechs hastened to reduce their dependence on Russia by agreeing to import gas from Norway.

Not surprisingly, given its slower progress toward democratic and market reforms (and its notably more pro-Russian policies), Slovakia was not included in the first wave of prospective new members of NATO. Expressing its relief, the Russian newspaper *Segodnia* hailed Slovakia (along with Serbia) as a "bulwark" of Russian policy in Eastern Europe, having resisted temptations to turn westward and instead having made Russia "the main reference point" in its foreign policy. The newspaper noted with favor that trade turnover with Slovakia had climbed to $2.2 billion in 1996, with cooperation at its deepest in the natural gas industry, and that thanks to Slovakia's willingness to take repayment in military hardware rather than hard currency, Russia's debt would be completely repaid within six or seven years.[72]

Romania, another aspiring member of NATO, had distanced itself from the USSR during the long reign of Ceaucescu, and relations with Russia after the fall of his regime showed no particular improvement. Not until September 1993 did the Romanian head of government travel to Moscow, where agreements were concluded on restoring economic ties, which had virtually collapsed. But Romania continued to be distinguished as the only East European country with which Russia failed to conclude a bilateral political treaty. Reportedly, the primary obstacle was not debt—Romania was the only East European country not owed money by Russia—but rather Bucharest's insistence that such a treaty include a joint condemnation of the Nazi-Soviet Pact, under which the Romanian province of Bessarabia was assigned to the Soviet sphere. Already concerned about a possible future union of Romania and Moldova, Moscow evidently feared that condemning the 1939 treaty would legitimize a possible Romanian claim on former Soviet territory.

Bulgaria, in contrast, had traditionally enjoyed closer relations with Moscow, and its geographical setting made it a less likely military or economic partner for Western Europe. President Zhelyu Zhelev had sensed the shifting political winds earlier than his East European counterparts, having traveled to Moscow in October 1991, pointedly not meeting with Gorbachev, but issuing a joint declaration with Yeltsin on the establishment of diplomatic relations between Russia and Bulgaria. A formal bilateral treaty on friendship and cooperation was concluded during Yeltsin's return visit in August 1992, during which an agreement was reached also on cooperation between the two defense ministries. But economic relations between the two states were anything but cooperative. Not until May 1995, during a visit to Sofia by Chernomyrdin, did they agree on terms for repayment of Russia's $100 million debt, half of which was to be repaid with spare parts for Bulgaria's armed forces. By that time trade between the two had fallen 90 percent since 1990—from $14.4 billion to $1.8 billion—primarily because of disputes over gas prices. Relations warmed following Bulgaria's agreement to participate in a gas pipeline extending from Russia to Greece, and its expression of interest in being part of a future oil pipeline route. But continued sensitivity over economic relations was evident early in 1996, when the government in Sofia officially protested Yeltsin's mention of Bulgaria as a country that might want to join the new economic union among Russia, Belarus, Kazakhstan, and Kyrgyzstan.

For the countries of Eastern Europe, as for Russia itself, the dominant foreign economic concern was not re-establishment of the trade patterns that had prevailed in the region since the end of World War II, but rather the construction of a relationship with Western Europe that would open its enormous markets to their goods, while attracting investment capital to their emerging market economies. The biggest target of these efforts was the European Union, which now comprised fifteen members. Talks between EU representatives and the new Russian government began in the spring of 1992. That this was by no means a negotiation between economic equals was evident later that year, when the EU extended to Russia and the other members of the Commonwealth of Independent States the same tariff preferences it gives to developing countries. President Yeltsin traveled to Brussels in December 1993 to sign a political declaration on partnership and cooperation, but the difficult bargaining on economic relations continued. Whereas the EU had agreed quickly to freer trade with the East European states, a draft partnership agreement with Russia was reached only in the spring of 1994 and signed by Yeltsin in Corfu, Greece, in June of that year, after eight official rounds of talks. The provisional agreement would free the movement of services and capital but only gradually liberalize trade. Restrictions would continue on Russian exports of steel, textiles, and uranium. Though still a nonmember, Russia would obtain the right to demand compliance with GATT practices in its trade with the EU (provided it also complied), and Russia could protect its market through an exemption for five years from strict implementation of most-favored-nation status (MFN) with respect to the EU states, though it would be allowed to extend MFN to the countries of the CIS. Restrictions recently imposed by Russia on the operation of foreign banks in the country would be immediately waived for five major European banks and eventually rescinded altogether.

However, signing of the interim agreement by the EU was postponed after the invasion of Chechnia, which the European Parliament harshly condemned. A delegation consisting of the French, German, and Spanish foreign ministers was dispatched to Moscow in March 1995 to explain the EU position. In the words of two *Kommersant-Daily* correspondents, the action signified that Europe was no longer willing to accept Yeltsin's reassurances, "and it appears that Chechnia will become the turning point at which both Europe and the world as a whole will start to regard 'counting on Yeltsin' as an anachronism."[73] Nevertheless, in July the interim agreement was finally signed by the EU, relieving "the unpleasant feeling of isolation" that intensified with the military operation in Chechnia, and paving the way for Russia's further integration with the world economy.[74] When the Agreement on Partnership and Cooperation with the EU was finally ratified by the Duma in October 1996, the influential deputy Vladimir Lukin declared that the agreement was no less important than START II. The treaty would have the effect of lowering EU tariffs on Russian exports by two-thirds, while allowing Russia to maintain considerably higher tariffs on European products; it would thus facilitate Russia's gradual integration into the EU's single market. After further delay, the agreement entered into force only in December 1997, by which time the EU was accounting for 40 percent of trade and investment in Russia. However, Russia was still not certified as a "market economy," allowing the EU to retain antidumping restrictions on fifteen products.

Russia's admission to the Council of Europe, an organization of democratic nations focusing on social and political issues, was an even lengthier process. The states of Eastern Europe and the three newly independent Baltic states were admitted with relative ease, but Russia was confronted with a varied and changing list of obstacles to membership. When the initial Russian application was filed in May 1992, the primary obstacle was said to be the continuing presence of Russian troops in the Baltic states of the former Soviet Union. A year later, the list of conditions was expanded to include free parliamentary elections and a new democratic constitution for the Russian Federation. By this point, despite loud complaints from Moscow over Estonia's treatment of its Russian minority, Estonia had been admitted to the Council of Europe—an action which Kozyrev protested by canceling his attendance at the council meeting.

In September 1994, having held elections and adopted a constitution, and having virtually completed all troop withdrawals, Moscow learned from the visiting Council secretary-general that it would need to bring its human rights legislation into harmony with European standards. The invasion of Chechnia by Russian troops caused the Council of Europe to "freeze" Russia's application—an action considered insulting by Russian politicians from various camps. Not until January 1996 did the Council's parliamentary assembly finally vote to admit Russia, despite a report from its commission on legal and human rights issues, stating that Russia was not yet a law-governed state and was unlikely to become one in the near future. However, even this much-delayed action was not without conditions; the resolution stipulated that Russia must sign the European Convention on Human Rights (an act that would give Russian citizens legal standing before the European human rights court), and must complete the process of adapting its legislation to European standards, including abolishing the death penalty and curbing the powers of the Federal Security Service. The resolution even advised Russia to cease referring to its neighbors as the "near abroad."

In the security sphere, Russia pinned its hopes for becoming part of a pan-European system on the Organization for Security and Cooperation in Europe (OSCE), a group of fifty-two member countries, spanning the globe from North America to Central Asia. Although the organization sent observers to conflict zones in the former Yugoslavia and USSR, it struggled to achieve consensus for the operation of actual peacekeeping forces on the continent. Yeltsin traveled to Budapest early in December 1994 to address the summit of the OSCE. In the face of mounting discussion about enlarging the membership of NATO, the Russian president warned that Europe was in danger of being plunged into a state of "cold peace," due in part to the "dangerous delusion" that "the fates of the continent and of the world community as a whole can be controlled from a single capital." Creation of an all-European institution with a "reliable legal foundation," which could assume tasks of conflict resolution and peacekeeping, had become a "vital necessity," and plans to expand NATO were at variance with this objective. As for Russia, it sought partnership with the OSCE and the United Nations in the political and material responsibilities of peacekeeping operations in the former Soviet space, though "of course, not to the detriment of effective operations."[75] The summit's decision in principle to create a peacekeeping force of 3,000 for Nagorno-Karabakh was hailed by *Izvestia* as an action that "should go down in history as the birth of a new peacekeeping institution, second in importance only to the United Nations."[76] But Russia failed to gain acceptance of its initiative to change the structure of the OSCE or to obtain a mandate to conduct its own peacekeeping operations in the CIS, leading *Nezavisimaia gazeta* to a far more pessimistic (and ultimately more accurate) conclusion: "Russia, with its claims to OSCE supremacy in peacekeeping in the region, had the unrealizable nature of its hopes pointed out to it in a completely unambiguous way."[77]

Only five days after Yeltsin's return to Moscow from Budapest, he launched the invasion of Chechnia, bringing a hailstorm of European criticism down on his head. The OSCE stiffly reminded Russia of its requirement for a six-week advance notification of major troop movements. The organization sent a three-man delegation to Moscow with an offer to send observers to Chechnia to mediate the conflict. Its chairman, calling for a humanitarian truce and early elections, declared that the use of armed force on such a scale was in violation of OSCE principles and of the principles of human rights. Frostily rejecting such interference in its internal affairs, Russia charged that the violations of human rights were in fact being committed by the Chechen rebels. Clearly, however, the Russian government's actions in Chechnia further damaged its prospects for being accepted into the Western community of nations.

Throughout the 1990s, the primary advocate in regional forums on behalf first of Soviet and then of Russian integration into Europe has been Helmut Kohl's Germany. As phrased by Germany's ambassador to Russia, Bonn's role is "somewhat like that of a defense lawyer for Russia in the construction of the new Europe."[78] Antagonists in two world wars and the Cold War, Germany and Russia have come to recognize their mutual stake in preventing conflicts in their common neighborhood that might again cast them in adversarial roles. As we have seen earlier in this volume, since the time of the Treaty of Rapallo in 1922 the two states have engaged in periodic efforts to act as partners in an altered balance of power in Europe.

Bonn had acquired a considerable stake in Gorbachev's success, given the agreements it had forged with him on German reunification and withdrawal of Soviet forces. Yeltsin's initial visit to Bonn as Russian president took place in November 1991, when Gorbachev was still in the Kremlin, and Germany was cautious in discussing diplomatic and economic ties. Kozyrev's follow-up visit in January formalized the understanding that existing treaties between the USSR and Germany would be honored by the Russian Federation. Bonn was particularly interested in the fate of the Russian citizens of German origin whom Stalin had forcibly resettled from the Volga region in 1941, and for whose relocation needs Germany had already committed significant funding. Kohl had no particular wish for large numbers of these "Volga Germans" to emigrate to Germany, and he urged Moscow to establish an autonomous republic for them in the Volgograd region. Given that Germany then accounted for 57 percent of all foreign investment in the CIS economies, and that it has contributed more than half of all foreign economic assistance received by Russia, its wishes carried weight in Moscow.[79]

Chancellor Kohl's first visit to Yeltsin's Russia came in December 1992, at a time when Yeltsin was engaged in a momentous showdown with the Congress of People's Deputies, having been forced to abandon his nomination of Egor Gaidar as premier. In this context, Kohl's reassuring words and actions were viewed in the Russian press as a "life preserver" for Yeltsin, reassuring the "world community of Russian reforms and their continuation." The two leaders signed eight agreements, including a promise by

Germany to give an eight-year respite on repayment of Soviet debts to the former GDR, and a pledge of an additional 550 million marks (bringing the total to 8.3 billion marks) for construction of housing in Russia for troops withdrawn from Germany. Yeltsin promised in turn to complete the troop withdrawal four months early (by August 1994), and to provide ten billion rubles in the Russian budget for setting up new "national districts" for the Volga Germans. At the conclusion of his visit, Kohl termed Russia Germany's "major partner in the East."[80]

The harmony between Bonn and Moscow was briefly disturbed in August 1994 by a sensational case of alleged nuclear smuggling, which was played up in the Western press as evidence of lax Russian security. After a German "sting" operation caught a Spaniard and a Colombian carrying 300 grams of plutonium-239 on a plane arriving in Munich from Moscow, the Russian atomic energy ministry hotly denied that the nuclear material was of Russian origin. Discussions between the two nations' security services resulted in an agreement to open offices in each other's capital to facilitate their cooperation in combating illegal trafficking and terrorism.[81]

At the end of August Yeltsin returned to Germany, accompanied by virtually his entire government team, for a ceremony marking the completion of the withdrawal of Russian troops. Yeltsin drew considerable attention to himself when he seized the conductor's baton and led an army chorus in song; a German magazine reported on his "unsteady gait" at the parade ground. All told, about a half million troops and more than 100,000 weapons and pieces of equipment were pulled out of Germany within four years. There was considerable grumbling about the pace, since despite Germany's provision of significant funds for housing the forces in Russia, more than 25,000 military families were said still to lack accommodation. On the eve of the fifty-fifth anniversary of the start of World War II in Europe, the Russian president solemnly declared, "This Russia and this Germany will never fight each other again."[82] In an interview with *Izvestia*, he said:

> Germany is no longer a threat to peace. The exhausting cold war is over. Therefore the withdrawal of Russian troops is a natural step whose time has come.... An era of enmity, distrust, and suspiciousness is ending in the history of Russia and Germany, and in the history of Europe.... Russia and Germany have no significant unresolved problems or disagreements.... In many spheres we are partners.[83]

The state of Russo-German relations was not entirely insulated from the effects of Moscow's invasion of Chechnia; to cite one example, Defense Minister Pavel Grachev was uninvited by his German counterpart to a Munich forum on European security scheduled for March 1995.[84] But given the stakes Bonn had in Yeltsin, the estrangement was neither deep nor lasting. Helmut Kohl was back in Moscow at the beginning of the Russian presidential campaign to describe Yeltsin as a "reliable partner," a "tried and true friend of Germany," and the best president for Russia, with "absolutely no reservations."[85] In April 1997, following his reelection and his return to health, Yeltsin journeyed to Germany. The sole major issue then pending between the two states concerned the status of some 200,000 items of "trophy art" removed from Germany by Soviet troops following World War II. Yeltsin had promised Kohl that it would be returned to Germany, but an outraged parliament passed a law declaring it to be Russian state property. Yeltsin's veto was overridden by the Duma just prior to his visit to Germany, but a more diplomatically sensitive Federation Council delayed its vote to override until after the visit had been concluded. As if to soften the impending blow, Yeltsin reminded Kohl that the issue cut two ways, noting that occupying German troops had done $1.3 trillion worth of damage to Russian cultural property. In the end, however, the parliament held firm, refusing to allow Yeltsin to return the property to Germany.

Second only to Germany in Russian priorities in Europe is France. French and Russian diplomats fondly recall the historic Franco-Russian alliance of 1893 and their common struggle against German armies in two world wars. As their Soviet predecessors did from the time of Charles de Gaulle, on occasion Russian leaders have subtly reinforced France's continuing rivalry with Germany and its resentments at Washington's perceived wish to dominate Western Europe. While Yeltsin's personal relations with President Mitterrand never approached the level of warmth he exhibited with Chancellor Kohl, the personal dimension in diplomacy has loomed larger since the election in 1995 of Jacques Chirac as France's president.

Although French economic aid to Russia did not approach the level of German assistance, France did grant economic credits in 1992, announced during Yeltsin's February visit to Paris. In 1994, the two countries signed agreements on military cooperation—Moscow's first with a West European state—including projects for joint development and production of weaponry, which were intended in part to allow the two countries to compete more effectively with the United States in the arms export market. By the time of Kozyrev's visit to France in November of the same year, a more explicit anti-American tone was being heard. Neither state was speaking approvingly at this point about NATO expansion, and they pointedly discussed possible initiatives with respect to Bosnia and Iraq that would undercut the perceived unilateralism of Washington's approach to these conflict areas. Mitterrand underscored the need not to isolate Moscow but rather to build Europe with Russian participation, and Kozyrev chimed in, stressing that Russia's cooperation with France, Germany, and Britain "will not be a partnership against the U.S. but a partnership with it, but in such a way that Europe's voice is heard independently, and that Moscow's voice in the European chorus is also sufficiently distinct."[86]

Yeltsin's first direct talks with Chirac, during a stopover on his way to the United Nations in October 1995, again focused on NATO expansion and Bosnia; in the view of a pair of Russian journalists, they displayed a "proximity of views based on a certain anti-Americanism."[87] During the following year, an exchange of visits by the two prime ministers led to closer relations in the economic and technical spheres; a bilateral commission was set up (modeled on the Gore-Chernomyrdin commission), a new French credit was granted, and agreement was reached on Russian repayment of tsarist debts. Further talks between Chirac and Yeltsin in 1997 (with Yeltsin going to Paris once and Chirac traveling three times to Moscow) produced final agreements on questions of debts, clearing the way for Russia's admission to the Paris Club of creditor nations. In September, on the last of these visits, Chirac was accompanied by twenty French businessmen, who engaged in wide-ranging talks on trade expansion. It was noted that while French exports to Russia had increased 30 percent, France still ranked eighth on the list of Russia's trade partners. Political talks between Yeltsin and Chirac again focused on topics on which the two took positions distinct from that of the United States. As if to underscore the warmth of the relationship, Yeltsin presented Chirac with the Order for Services to the Fatherland, First Class (the first time such an award had been presented).[88]

Given its greater geographical distance and the closer proximity of its foreign policy to that of the United States, Britain was a less prominent object of Russian courtship than the two major continental powers of Western Europe. Yeltsin's initial trip to London as Russian president in January 1992 was undertaken with full awareness of the importance to Gorbachev's international reputation of Margaret Thatcher's commendation in 1984: "One can do business with Mr. Gorbachev." Knowing that foreign visits had been an area of triumph for his predecessor, Yeltsin was pleased with his reception. Prime Minister John Major declared that "Yeltsin made a very good impression on me," and the British agreed to increase economic aid to Russia.[89] During a second visit later in the same year, Yeltsin signed a bilateral treaty and an economic agreement, and he was given the opportunity to address the British parliament.

An exchange of visits between Major and Yeltsin in 1994 featured good atmospherics but very little in the way of bilateral accomplishment. In London in September, Yeltsin failed to get British backing for his project to expand peacekeeping responsibilities for the OSCE, but on all other issues the two were reportedly in agreement. But the more important trip that year was purely ceremonial—Queen Elizabeth II's visit to Russia in October was the first visit by a British monarch since the Bolshevik revolution. The change of governments in Britain had little effect on the course of Anglo-Russian relations; a visit to Moscow by Prime Minister Blair in October 1997 focused on economic relations, with attention being given to the fact that Britain now ranked second to Germany among foreign investors in Russia.

Other European capitals visited by Yeltsin included three in the south: Rome (December 1991), Athens (June 1993), and Madrid (April 1994). In each case, Russia has signed a bilateral treaty on friendship and cooperation as well as multiple trade and economic agreements, but only in the case of Italy has the economic relationship appeared significant. Indeed, Yeltsin made a second visit to Italy in February 1998, where he signed contracts worth $3 billion, primarily for oil and gas deliveries and for a joint venture in automobile production. By this time, Italy ranked as Russia's second largest European trading partner.

In contrast, for reasons of geography and history, Russia's relationships with the countries of northern Europe have been more intense. Moscow has participated in the Council of Baltic Sea States established in March 1992 by Russia, Germany, Poland, Sweden, Denmark, Finland, Norway, Lithuania, Latvia, and Estonia. Intended to coordinate policies in the realms of the economy and environment, transportation, energy, law enforcement, and tourism, the council also was a forum in which Russia voiced its complaints about the treatment of Russian minorities in the three Baltic states of the former Soviet Union.

Next to Lithuania, Latvia, and Estonia, whose relations with Moscow were discussed in an earlier chapter, Finland has been the northern European neighbor most closely tied to Russia. Formerly under the tsar's rule, Finland practiced an anxious neutrality during the Cold War, tilting far enough toward Moscow in its foreign and domestic policies to escape outright incorporation into the Soviet sphere. Echoes of this uneasy past have occasionally been observed in current Russo-Finnish relations. Relations began well, with Finland being the first European state with which Yeltsin's Russia signed a bilateral treaty. On his first visit, Yeltsin laid a wreath at the monument to Finnish soldiers who fell in the Winter War of 1939–40, and documents normalizing economic ties were signed. The approach of Finnish elections the following year brought concerns, however, with the Russian press noting that some presidential candidates were violating the agreement on mutual renunciation of territorial claims by raising the "Karelian question." A considerable stir was raised in Finland when the same Russian ambassador who often lectured the country during the Soviet period issued a harsh protest just days before the election about the behavior of two Finnish nationalist parties. Bilateral economic relations improved following an agreement on repayment of Russia's debt of $1.3 billion, most of which was to be repaid through arms deliveries. By 1997, Russia ranked fifth among Finland's trade partners, with an annual volume of $4.7 billion, much of it in the sphere of energy. Opening a section of a highway in October 1997, Prime Minister Lipponen announced a plan for expanded "northern cooperation" and spoke of Finland as a bridge between Russia and Western Europe.

Yeltsin's last foreign trip of 1997 was a highly publicized visit to Sweden, notable less for its diplomatic achievements than for several embarrassing mistakes made by the Russian president. At one point, Yeltsin evidently believed he was in Finland; on another occasion, he referred to a "Swedish" oil deal that actually had been concluded with Norway. Blurting out a confusing offer for a unilateral reduction in nuclear arms—later disavowed by his staff— he mistakenly identified Germany and Japan as nuclear powers. In this context, observers were uncertain of the status of a declaration he made in a speech to the Swedish parliament—later confirmed by his defense minister and evidently intended to reassure the Baltic states that their membership in NATO would be unnecessary—promising a 40-percent cut in Russian ground and naval forces along the country's northwestern border by 1999. In any event, Yeltsin's strange behavior was later blamed by his staff on fatigue and a developing cold, and he was hospitalized upon his return to Russia.

More diplomatically significant, and symbolic of the growing differentiation that had occurred in Russian policy toward the West, was a trip Yeltsin made a little earlier in the fall of 1997, to a summit meeting of the Council of Europe in Strasbourg. The Russian president seemed at pains to underscore the extent to which Russia regarded itself as part of a Europe that was increasingly resistant to U.S. domination. "We do not need an uncle from somewhere," he declared in an interview before the summit. "We in Europe are capable of uniting ourselves to live normally." In addition to its fears that the United States was seeking to redivide Europe to Russia's disadvantage through expansion of NATO, Moscow resented continuing U.S. refusal to grant most-favored-nation trade status, Congress's threats to cut off aid (regarded as niggardly in any event) in retaliation for a parliamentary act regulating religious practice in Russia, and Washington's announced intention to retaliate against Russia and France for their cooperative project to develop gas fields in Iran.[90] Within a few weeks, Russia again displayed its independence, joining with France in resisting the tough American stance on UN sanctions on Iraq. In a move clearly aimed at emphasizing that his main Western partners were in Europe, Yeltsin announced at Strasbourg that he would hold annual summits with the French and German leaders to review the state of the European continent.

7

Russia and
the "Non-West"

As we saw in chapter 3, the international system at the end of World War II was perceived in both the United States and the Soviet Union as rigidly bipolar. In 1947, both the Truman Doctrine and Andrei Zhdanov's speech at the founding conference of the Cominform portrayed a struggle between two camps, each united around its own ideology. As the great colonial empires collapsed in the postwar period, new nations in Asia, the Middle East, Latin America, and Africa joined the few already independent states in those regions, unwillingly cast in the role of an arena for the competition of the two blocs.

During the period of the Cold War the developed states of West and East were depicted as the First and Second Worlds, and the less-developed countries became known as the Third World. Although the breakup of the Soviet bloc rendered the familiar labels obsolete, Russian foreign policy in the post-Soviet period has continued to differentiate among three "worlds"—the West; the former USSR ("near abroad") and Eastern Europe; and that large grouping of countries in Asia, the Middle East, Africa, and Latin America that we will call (for lack of a better term) the "non-West."

As we have seen, Khrushchev revived the Leninist perception of the developing world as the "vital reserve of imperialism," and he initiated a relatively low-risk Soviet challenge that sought ideological victories for "socialism" as well as strategic benefits in the economic and military spheres. The initial Soviet forays became a broader-based investment under Brezhnev, as the USSR sought to counter Western (and Chinese) influence in all areas of the Third World, establishing in the process facilities that allowed Soviet military power to be projected on a truly global basis. But Soviet influence reached its high-water mark in the mid-1970s, after which it lost some of its hard-won beachheads, while also failing to persuade the United States that expansionist and revolutionary activities in the Third World were compatible with superpower detente.

As the Soviet economy faltered, Gorbachev began, even before the end of the Cold War, to liquidate some of the USSR's most costly and unproductive Third World investments. Soviet troops were withdrawn from Afghanistan, and Moscow cooperated in arranging negotiated solutions to long-standing regional conflicts in Asia, Africa, and Latin America. As their global competition ended, both the Soviet Union and the United States sharply cut back their economic and military assistance programs in these regions.

In chapter 4 we examined the domestic political controversy that arose in Russia in 1992 as a result of the initial emphasis given by President Boris Yeltsin and Foreign Minister Andrei Kozyrev to relations with the West, seemingly at the expense of Russia's ties to the "near abroad" and the "non-West." In his critics' eyes, Kozyrev's alleged fixation on the West and slavish imitation of Western positions on international issues came at the expense of specific economic and security interests of Russia. Just as important to the advocates of a more nationalistic foreign policy, Kozyrev's "Atlanticist" policies also permanently relegated the country to a "junior partnership" at best, thereby sacrificing Russia's role as a great power and a global leader—even if only of "second-echelon" countries. The "Eurasianists"—advocates of a more forceful Russian role in the former USSR and in the "East" generally—gained additional ammunition for the campaign to counter a Western-oriented policy when plans for expanding NATO into the former Soviet empire threatened to further isolate Russia from democratic Europe. When Evgenii Primakov, much of whose career had been spent in the Middle East, replaced Kozyrev in 1996, further impetus was given to the reorientation of Russian foreign policy.

At least since the adoption of Russia's official foreign policy concept by President Yeltsin in April 1993, top priority has been given to the "near abroad." Accordingly, the main objective of Russia's policy in the "non-West" has been to ensure the security of the territories of the former Soviet lands, insulating them from the harmful effects of regional conflicts such as the struggle for control of Afghanistan, or from threatening movements such as Islamic extremism. Given the strategic nature of energy resources in the Caucasian and Central Asian republics, Russia has tended to define its security interests in these areas to include preventing outside powers from gaining leverage over these resources. Setting its overall priorities in this way has pointed Russia toward East and South Asia and the Middle East as the zones of greatest concern. These are also the regions where there is the greatest danger of a broader but no less potent threat to Russia's security interests—nuclear proliferation.

With the recent emphasis on the role of foreign policy as a contributor to economic development, it is not surprising that another major objective of

Russia's policy toward the countries of the "non-West" is economic. These regions constitute an enormous and growing market, where Russian goods—be they raw or semi-processed materials, lower-quality consumer goods, or the more sophisticated products of Russian science and engineering—have a somewhat better chance of obtaining a competitive advantage than they do in Western marketplaces. And imported products from Asia, Africa, and Latin America have potential benefit for Russian manufacturers and consumers, especially if they are obtained in partial payment of the enormous debts that some countries in these regions have accumulated as a result of their transactions with the former Soviet Union.

The combined total of debt owed to Russia by developing countries was estimated in September 1997 at a staggering $112.7 billion (all but $1 billion of which dated from the Soviet period). Of fifty-one debtor nations, only India was currently repaying its debt in full. The largest debts were owed to Russia by Cuba, Mongolia, India, and Vietnam. Moscow's admission to the Paris Club of creditor nations put international pressure on the debtors to repay. And while the Russians agreed to discount the debt, in amounts ranging from 35 to 80 percent, the repayments were to be made in hard currency. The effect, according to First Deputy Prime Minister Anatolii Chubais, would be to triple the volume of annual debt payments to the Russian government from developing countries.

Whereas prior to the end of the Cold War, aid and trade transactions between the Soviets and the Third World had been heavily subsidized by Moscow for political reasons, cash-strapped Russia, forced to abandon "soft" credit terms, found its goods far less attractive than they had been. As a consequence, trade with most of the "non-West" in the immediate post-Soviet period fell sharply. Reflecting these realities, Russia cut back its costly overseas trade-promotion efforts, which were often a front for espionage activities during the Soviet period. Whereas Moscow operated 130 organizationally distinct trade missions abroad in 1991, the number had been cut to forty-seven by 1996, with trade counselors in Russian embassies taking over the responsibilities in the countries with less-promising markets.

As was the case during the Soviet period, Russia's main export to the "non-West" has been weaponry, and a major beneficiary of renewed activity in these regions has been the underemployed military-industrial complex of Russia. The depression in Moscow's arms industry actually began in the Gorbachev period, as a result of cuts in Soviet military budgets that accompanied the arms control agreements with the United States, combined with the negotiated settlements of regional conflicts in the Third World.

By 1991, the last year of the Soviet period, the market for arms in the developing countries had dropped to $28.6 billion, down sharply from $61 billion in 1988. It continued to decline in the post-Soviet years, reaching $15.4 billion in 1995.[1] The Soviet Union and its allies dominated the Third World arms market until the late 1980s, but their share of a declining market began to plummet in the latter years of Gorbachev's rule and continued to do so in the first post-Soviet years, reflecting Moscow's shrinking political profile as well as the withdrawal of subsidies for arms purchases. Between 1984 and 1994, the world market share of the countries of the former Warsaw Pact dropped from 38 percent to 9 percent, while that of the United States rose from 25 percent to 57 percent. The drop in value of Moscow's arms sales to the Third World was even more precipitous: from $28.8 billion in 1986 to $5.9 billion in 1991 and $1.3 billion in 1992.[2]

As a result of a determined sales effort, Russia reversed the decline, and in 1995 its sales totaled 65 percent higher than the previous year. Although cash receipts in that year were only about $3 billion, Russian sources claimed that this was still twice the amount that actually flowed into state coffers in 1987, when announced sales of $20 billion were almost entirely financed with "soft" credits. As an indicator of the importance of rebounding arms exports to the Russian economy, exports were said in 1995 to constitute half of the industry's total revenues.[3]

The following year, Russia announced figures that would have propelled it to third place in world arms sales, with $4.6 billion (behind the United States at $11.3 billion and Britain at $4.8 billion) in a total world market estimated at $31.8 billion. This growth was said to have continued in 1997; Russian arms salesmen claimed to have taken $7.3 billion in orders by September, with another $3.25 billion expected by the end of the year. More than half of Russia's sales were related to aviation, and another one-sixth were naval arms.[4] Later reports, however, adjusted these figures downward, to $3.5 billion in 1996 and only $2.5 billion in 1997. The revisions resulted in part from orders being canceled (e.g., Indonesia and Malaysia) or expected sales not materializing (e.g., Ecuador and Bulgaria). In part, however, they resulted from the discovery by the arms export agency's new management that earlier figures had been inflated for political reasons.[5]

The Russians, moreover, have not moved to a strictly "cash and carry" basis for their arms sales. Only about 60 percent of revised 1996 and 1997 revenues were said to have been collected in convertible currencies.[6] The value of Russian arms transfers to some states (including former Warsaw Pact allies Hungary and Slovakia and NATO member Turkey) has been applied toward paying off debts incurred by the USSR and inherited by the Russian Federation. And some customers—prominently including the two largest, China and India—continue to deal with Moscow on a non-cash basis. Weapons sales to China include a prominent barter component, and credits extended to India are serviced with payments of Indian goods. As a consequence, Russian arms factories are left—in the words of a leading Russian defense analyst—with the burden of unloading Chinese and Indian "junk" on the domestic market.[7]

As Russia has labored to regain a major share of the shrinking global arms market, it has encountered stiff competition, leading Moscow to complain at times about "unfair" competitive tactics. Not surprisingly, Washington has been regarded as the chief culprit. In recent years, Russia has made incursions into arms markets traditionally dominated by the United States—Latin America (Colombia and Brazil) and South Korea—or into areas regarded by the U.S. government as highly volatile (Cyprus and Iran). As the Russians see it, the U.S. response to being out-hustled in the marketplace has been decidedly heavy-handed. Boris Kuzyk, assistant to the president for "military-technical cooperation" (the Russian euphemism for arms sales), told the Russian press that Washington denied an entry visa to Colombian president Ernesto Samper as "revenge" for his concluding a contract in 1996 with Russian arms dealers for the purchase of Mi-17 transport helicopters. (An alternative explanation for the U.S. government's displeasure with Samper was that funding for the helicopters was to come from funds provided to Colombia by the United States for its pursuit of drug dealers, and the Colombian president was alleged to have accepted campaign funds from drug bosses.) Kuzyk also charged that the United States had refused to allow the Russian arms export agency, Rosvooruzhenie, to open an office in New York, where it could more readily bid for contracts with United Nations peacekeeping operations, and that U.S. government pressure tactics had been used to keep the agency's director, Aleksandr Kotelkin, out of the United States and certain allied countries.[8] Kotelkin himself repeated these charges in a separate interview, adding an account about alleged "punishment" by the United States of its ambassador to Cyprus (reassigned to the embassy in Bhutan) and its military attache there, as a result of their failure to prevent the government of Cyprus from purchasing S-300 surface-to-air missile systems from Russia.[9]

The relatively large amount of revenue brought in to the cash-strapped Russian economy by arms exports has sparked a scramble for control of arms sales. Until the practice was ended in 1997, large banks were able to profit from the use of funds deposited from sales, which sometimes never reached the factories that manufactured the weapons. In August 1997, three days after praising his work, Yeltsin replaced Kotelkin as director-general of Rosvooruzhenie, and the agency was put under the supervisory control of a commission chaired by Chernomyrdin and his deputy, Iakov Urinson. In a new division of labor, Rosvooruzhenie was given responsibility to deal with foreign sales of arms and military equipment, while a new agency (Rossiiskie Tekhnologii, or Russian Technologies) was established to sell licenses, and another (Promeksport, or Industrial Exports) to sell obsolete used arms and spare parts.

In addition to Russia's competition with Western arms dealers, another source of vexing rivalry has been the sale of Soviet-designed weapons by the arms factories of former bloc countries such as Bulgaria, Slovakia, and Poland, as well as—most troublesome of all—Ukraine and Belarus. In March 1997 Ukraine delivered the first shipment in a $650 million order from Pakistan for 320 T-80UD tanks. Since India, Pakistan's hostile neighbor, was one of Moscow's best customers, the Russians sought to pressure Ukraine to cancel the order. Key components of the Ukrainian-assembled tank are supplied by Russian plants, and Moscow's minister of foreign trade, Oleg Davydov, threatened to cut deliveries of these parts. Ukraine vowed to obtain alternative supplies from East European sources, and Davydov retreated from his demand, reportedly under heavy pressure from the Russian suppliers, for whom cancellation of Ukraine's orders would mean a $150 million loss. Another reported consideration in the Russian retreat was Ukraine's threat to halt delivery of docking systems that it assembles for the Mir space station.[10] In 1997, Belarus reportedly "grabbed" a Peruvian contract for MiG-29s.[11] The following year Belarus's president visited Syria and Iran in search of further contracts.

Russia's arms dealers also have been on the receiving end of complaints, most notably about the quality of their weapons. Recent combat demonstrations of Russian-made arms—their use by the Iraqi military in the Persian Gulf war and their use by the Russian army in Chechnia—have not inspired confidence in the reliability or technical capacities of certain weapons. But there have been other instances in which purchasers have found numerous cases of defective products or poor servicing of contracts. A detailed account in the Indian press contends that the engines on three-fourths of the MiG-29s purchased from Moscow and put into service by the Indian Air Force in the early 1990s had failed prematurely. Indian engineers discovered a design defect, but India had to shoulder the bill for the lengthy repairs. A 1990 Indo-Soviet agreement to allow overhaul facilities to be established in India took six years to bear fruit. A 1993 $4.3 million contract for an item of naval hardware produced similar frustrations. When the hardware was delivered, it lacked the cables that allowed it to function. Contending that cables were not part of the contract, the Russian firm refused repeated requests by the Indian Embassy either to supply the cables or to take back the equipment; as of 1997, the equipment reportedly continued to sit in storage with no prospect of use. A final example concerned

1991 and 1992 contracts for R-60 MK air-to-air missiles, supposedly guaranteed for twelve months from the date of delivery and having a shelf life of eight years. Upon their arrival in India, the missiles underwent field tests that found at least twenty-three of them to be unserviceable. When the Indian Air Force asked that they be replaced, the Russian firm insisted on sending its own team of specialists—at India's expense—to verify the claim. The article concluded: "Even then, at least eleven missiles are currently lying in stock waiting to be repaired. Indian defense planners should now realize that Russia is just one among arms suppliers. No longer the cheapest. Never the best."[12]

Having surveyed some of the general features of Russia's approach to the "non-West," we now turn to a region-by-region examination of how Moscow's policy has been implemented.

Russia's Relations in the Far East

As the country with which the Soviet Union shared its longest border, China, not surprisingly, occupied a higher foreign-policy priority for Russia than any other non-Western country—all the more so, given the state of high tension on that border in recent decades. As described in chapter 3, Gorbachev took steps in the late 1980s to address the most serious issues in the Sino-Soviet conflict, and his efforts culminated in his May 1989 trip to Beijing, which symbolized the end of the Cold War between the two communist giants. But the Chinese were severely displeased with the domestic political changes that Gorbachev was overseeing in the USSR, especially as Soviet democratization became a beacon for Chinese students, whose dissent was crushed on Tiananmen Square just days after Gorbachev's visit. And although they had reached an accord with Gorbachev's government on 98 percent of their border with the USSR in May 1991, the Chinese rulers barely disguised their support for the coup that sought to topple the Soviet president in August.

As the USSR was breaking up in December 1991, Boris Yeltsin sent an emissary to Beijing to reassure China that Russia would abide by the border accords. The following March, Russian Foreign Minister Andrei Kozyrev was in the Chinese capital for the formal exchange of ratified documents. (However, the validity of the Central Asian sector of the border settlement was now a matter for newly independent Kazakhstan, Tajikistan, and Kyrgyzstan to reaffirm, which they did in October 1992.) Also in March, progress was made in the realms of economic and military cooperation; Russia and China signed a new trade agreement, and the chief of staff of the CIS armed forces concluded an agreement to sell twenty-four SU-27 fighter planes to China. On the ideological front, Kozyrev stated Moscow's wish to avoid confrontation, but signs of tension were not absent during his visit; he expressed Russia's concern for China's human rights behavior, and China brought up the matter of Russia's relations with Taiwan. These relations were complicated in 1992 by the conduct of private diplomacy on the part of Yeltsin's long-time associate Oleg Lobov, who chaired the Moscow-Taipei Coordinating Committee. An exasperated foreign ministry obtained a presidential decree in September that addressed China's concerns by stating that Russian relations with Taiwan would be conducted only on an unofficial level and only with the concurrence of the ministry.

In December 1992 Boris Yeltsin made a state visit to Beijing, and the Russian delegation signed over twenty documents, among them a mutual promise not to enter into any military-political alliance directed against the other state. The Chinese characterized the atmosphere of talks during Yeltsin's visit as "friendly, open and constructive . . . and in a spirit of mutual respect, understanding and trust." The gradual escalation of such rhetorical descriptions of presidential visits over the next several years serves as a barometer of the changed atmospherics in the Sino-Russian relationship—or, at any rate, of the way in which Moscow and Beijing wanted the world to view it. Thus, Chinese President Jiang Zemin's visit to Moscow in September 1994 was said to signify a "qualitatively new level of relations" of "constructive partnership," although not an alliance and not aimed against any other country. Yeltsin, during his visit to China in April 1996, described a "partnership directed toward the twenty-first century" between nations of which there was "no other such pair in the world." And during Jiang's April 1997 visit to Russia, the Russian president reached new rhetorical heights, describing the visit as one of "enormous, and perhaps even historic, significance, inasmuch as we are determining the fate of the twenty-first century." Of the joint declaration signed by the two presidents, Yeltsin declared, "Never before has Russia signed such a document with any other country." Guests at the formal luncheon held during Yeltsin's November 1997 visit to Beijing witnessed not only a warm embrace but singing by the two presidents. Observers could not recall such a cordial atmosphere at prior Sino-Russian summits.[13]

Consistent with the Marxist-Leninist tradition, of which both presidents were well aware, such phrase-mongering is not a casual exercise, but is calibrated to carry a distinct message. In this case, the message is not solely or even primarily to be understood as a description of the actual state of relations between the two states, but rather as an indicator of the extent of their mutual concern over the status and behavior of another—the United States—and of their desire to send a warning to its government. Both sides have been explicit in their opposition to "hegemonism"—the effort to build a unipolar international system. As Yeltsin put it in June 1997, "Someone is always dragging us toward a unipolar world and wanting to dictate unilaterally, but we want multipolarity." Such statements on the part of Russia have been especially frequent since the United States announced its plans for expansion of NATO. The implied countermeasure—a "pairing" of "great Russia" and "great China," as Yeltsin termed it in 1996—was intended to persuade NATO not to undertake expansion, or at the very least to place limits on it. Although China also denounces NATO expansion as "a policy of blocs," Beijing is less directly affected by it, and is more concerned about its differences with the United States on Taiwan, trade, and human rights.

Bilateral relations between the two neighbors have been normalized on several fronts. Further progress was made in 1994 in demarcating the border, leaving stretches totaling less than ten square miles (two islands near Khabarovsk and another in Chita province) still under dispute. Both presidents confidently predicted during Jiang's June 1997 visit to Moscow that these issues would be resolved in 1997, but Yeltsin faced very strong opposition from local authorities to further concessions. Thus, when it was announced during Yeltsin's November 1997 visit to China—his fifth summit with Jiang Zemin—that the 4,200-kilometer border had been demarcated for the first time in the two nations' histories, the fine print on the agreement revealed continued difficulties. Although Russia and China agreed on joint economic use, the legal status of the islands in the Amur River was still unresolved. Moscow apparently was unwilling to further inflame its already heated relations with regional authorities in Khabarovsk Krai by ceding possession. And the work on demarcating the 55-kilometer "western border" at the junction of Kazakhstan, China, and Russia also had not been completed.

Jiang's June 1997 visit to Moscow did provide the occasion for signing a significant agreement with Yeltsin and the presidents of the three Central Asian border states on reductions in the military presence along the border. This treaty sets maximum limits on numbers of ground troops, tactical aircraft, and air-defense aircraft within a hundred-kilometer-wide zone on either side of the border. In negotiations that had taken place over a five-year period, China had pressed for a 300-kilometer-wide zone, but the extensive Soviet military infrastructure had been built so close to the border that the wider zone would have produced considerable disruption. As the treaty specifies, Russia will reduce the strength of its Transbaikal and Far Eastern border forces over a two-year period by 15 percent—a level reportedly already planned by the general staff as part of overall force reductions. China's forces are deployed further inland, and will not need to be reduced.[14]

A Sino-Russian border issue of considerable sensitivity concerns the extensive Chinese immigration—much of it illegal—into Russian territory. The demographic imbalance along the border, with 150 million Chinese crowded into northeast China and only seven million Russians in the vast bordering territories of Siberia and the Far East, has been a source of concern for Soviet and Russian citizens, officials, and journalists for many years. As border tensions eased at the beginning of the 1990s, the scale of illegal immigration increased—rising threefold between 1992 and 1993. This prompted Russia to conclude an agreement with Beijing in 1994 to establish formal border-crossing posts and tighten visa restrictions. The immediate impact was a sharp reduction in Sino-Russian trade, much of which was "shuttled" across the border by Chinese traders.[15] The Russian press continued to provide sensational accounts of illegal immigration (termed in one account an "invasion of Huns"), prompting an advisor to Yeltsin, Emil Pain, to write an article in the government's newspaper stating that "claims about dangerous levels of Chinese immigration and a related real threat to national sovereignty in the Russian Far East are not supported by the actual facts." By his calculations, the "Chinese diaspora" in the Russian Far East accounted for less than 3 percent of the region's population—about half as many as resided there after World War II. Pain pointed out that trade with China is a "life preserver" for the Far East, and he blamed local authorities for whipping up anti-Chinese fears.[16]

As noted above, the reduction in shuttle trade caused the level of Sino-Russian trade, which had reached $7.8 billion in 1993 (second only to the level of Russia's trade with Germany), to fall to $5 billion the following year. It recovered somewhat in 1995, reaching $5.5 billion, and rose to $6.8 billion in 1996—with the Russians enjoying a $3 billion trade surplus. Yeltsin and Jiang set a target of $20 billion by 2000, but the announcement was greeted by skepticism that trade could grow so quickly. However, several ambitious projects have been discussed in recent high-level visits, most notably including a multibillion-dollar gas pipeline from Eastern Siberia to the Yellow Sea, which would eventually supply up to forty billion cubic yards of gas annually, meeting a large part of China's burgeoning energy needs. Additionally, the Russian press has reported agreements for Russian credits to China of $2 billion and $2.5 billion to finance the construction of nuclear power plants in Gansu and Liaoning provinces. While Russia failed to win contracts for engineering work on the huge Three Gorges dam, a $3-billion contract for Russia to develop a nuclear power plant at Lianyungang, left unsigned during Yeltsin's November 1997 visit, was concluded late the following month—and hailed by Russia's atomic energy minister as "the contract of the century."

The Sino-Russian trade relationship is a prime example of one in which armaments constitute the single most important Russian export, accounting for at least $5 billion in the last five years, and reportedly comprising at least one-third of the $7 billion in forward-order sales claimed by Rosvooruzhenie at the beginning of 1997.[17] Combat aircraft have been the chief component of Russian deliveries; China has purchased at least six dozen transcontinental SU-27 fighters, which are capable of making the Beijing-to-Moscow trip in two and one-half hours with one mid-air refueling. Other categories of purchases which have been concluded or which are being discussed include naval vessels (Sovremennyi-class destroyers equipped with supersonic missiles, two Kilo-636 diesel-powered submarines, and less advanced Varsha-vianka submarines), S-300 surface-to-air missile complexes, T-72 tanks, Smerch multiple rocket launchers, and the technology for advanced gas centrifuges used in uranium enrichment and for MIRVed missiles.

According to the Russian air force chief of staff, China concluded the largest military contract in Russia's history in 1995, a $2 billion–plus deal for the technology and licenses to manufacture the SU-27 at a factory in Shenyang province, scheduled to begin production in 1999. The Russian press reported concerns that China would thereby free itself of the need to purchase aircraft from Moscow in the future, and that if China made minor modifications to the plane's design, it might even become a competitor in the export market. Russian officials were quoted as saying that Russia needed the contract to save its defense industry, and that profits from the contract would be plowed back into development of new aircraft technology. But another account claimed that there was no prospect of a new generation of Russian-made planes in the foreseeable future, and that officials were simply trying to cover up a major blunder on the part of Russian negotiators, the circumstances of which were even scheduled to be discussed in a special meeting of the Security Council.[18]

Apart from the prospect that Russia could lose control of its most advanced military technology, there have been other concerns raised about the arms trade with China. As noted above, by no means all of the payment comes in the form of cash, and defense factories find themselves needing to dispose of a variety of bartered products in order to realize their profits. Among the most difficult was the case of the Chinese pigs which were traded for an arms shipment and then banned in Russia by the veterinary inspector, who suspected that they might spread hog plague in the country. In another instance, the Chinese bartered 15,000 low-quality radio-cassette players for three Mi-6 helicopters.[19] However, whereas the barter method initially constituted about three-fourths of Chinese payments, China's growing dollar trade surpluses have enabled Russian negotiators to arrange for hard currency payment in recent contracts.[20]

A far more significant issue is whether Russia is endangering its own long-term security by selling to its giant neighbor its most advanced weapons and the know-how to produce them. Russian military sources have expressed envy that Beijing is receiving more modern equipment than their own units possess. Most Russian analysts appear to believe that China's near-term foreign policy ambitions are directed toward Taiwan and the South China Sea, and that her interests in stability in Central Asia parallel those of Russia. Russian-made equipment may indeed enable Beijing to obtain a regional advantage in force-projection capability in a future Taiwan crisis; the Sovremennyi destroyer's cruise missiles have a combat range of three hundred miles, are reportedly resistant to U.S. air defense systems, and will allow China to test the naval superiority of the United States in the East China Sea. Nevertheless, the Kremlin appears to perceive no danger to Russia in such contingencies.

Expressing this viewpoint, former defense minister Pavel Grachev declared in 1995 that "China poses no threat to Russian security now and will not in the near future," and he asserted that if Russia did not sell arms to China, some other country would. Others have asserted that China was already engaged in privately hiring Russian scientists and engineers to assist in weapons development, and that Russia only benefits from contractually providing such assistance. As journalist Pavel Felgengauer put it, arms sales to China are "not only a way for our hapless military-industrial complex to preserve jobs and earn money, but also the start of a long-range strategic partnership and a new balance of forces in Asia that would favor Russia." The dissenting view, taking note of the demographic imbalance between Russia and China in the Far East, sees a long-range potential for conflict between the two continental powers. Another trouble spot, China's Xinjiang province, whose population is ethnically kin to that of the neighboring post-Soviet states, is troubled by sporadic anti-Beijing rebellions that could potentially spark a cross-border "liberation war." From the perspective of these observers, even with respect to the nearer term, by closely associating with China and by selling it arms, Russia risks upsetting the delicate military balance in Asia and even being drawn into China's territorial disputes with Taiwan, Vietnam, Japan, and ultimately the United States.[21]

Eighteen months after Grachev stated that he saw no threat, his successor included China on a list of potential enemies of Russia—and was hastily corrected by the foreign ministry. But Rodionov seemed to be voicing what many Russians were thinking. Nevertheless, Yeltsin and Primakov seemed to have calculated that they could keep the relationship with China in check, utilizing it as a way of jointly balancing U.S. influence in Asia, while enlisting Beijing's cooperation in preserving stability in Central Asia. If China's military and economic power continue to grow and her territorial ambitions eventually turn back toward the north and west, their successors may find greater safety in again tilting the triangular balance by strengthening Russia's ties with the United States.

Despite the major effort Moscow has made to normalize and strengthen its ties with Beijing, Russia has by no means put all its Far Eastern eggs in the Chinese basket. Following upon Gorbachev's initiatives, Yeltsin also has sought to improve Russia's relations with two strong allies of the United States—Japan and South Korea. In both cases, the ideological direction of the new Russian regime gave reason to expect that the two leading East Asian capitalist powers, both relatively poor in natural resources, would be eager investors in the development of Russia's vast Far Eastern mineral reserves. Russia also hoped to play a role in regional security arrangements that would foster stability and promote expanded trade. But neither Tokyo nor Seoul responded to Moscow's overtures with the degree of enthusiasm for which the Russians had hoped.

One reason that Japan's investment in the Russian Far East has been less than anticipated is undoubtedly the country's continuing political instability, of which Japanese investors are notoriously shy. But Japan would rather concentrate Moscow's attention on another factor explaining its reticence: the continuing absence, more than a half century after World War II, of a peace treaty between Japan and Russia. The obstacle to the conclusion of a treaty is the persisting dispute over the ownership of several small islands— Iturup (called Etorofu by Japan), Kunashir (Kunashiri), Shikotan, and a cluster of tiny islands known as Habomai—which are claimed by the Russians as the southern Kuriles, and by the Japanese as the Northern Territories. First claimed for the tsar by Russian explorers early in the eighteenth century, the Kurile Islands and neighboring (and much larger) Sakhalin Island were the subject of two Russo-Japanese treaties seeking to delineate a territorial boundary between the two countries in the second half of the nineteenth century. The first, signed at Shimoda in 1855, provided for them to share Sakhalin, and it divided the Kurile chain, with Russia getting the islands north of Iturup and Japan receiving the four southern islands. The second, signed at St. Petersburg twenty years later, gave all of Sakhalin to Russia, in return for which it renounced its claims to the Kuriles, all of which became Japanese territory.

The next alterations in the Russo-Japanese boundary came as a result of war rather than diplomatic compromise. The Treaty of Portsmouth in 1905, at the conclusion of the Russo-Japanese War, again partitioned Sakhalin Island, the southern half of which became Japanese. The Yalta Agreement of February 1945 provided for Moscow to enter the war against Japan three months after Germany's surrender, in return for which the southern half of Sakhalin would be returned to the USSR and the Kurile Islands would be handed over. However, the Potsdam Declaration of July 1945, on the basis of which Japan eventually agreed to surrender, did not specifically mention these territories, and the Japanese claim that they cannot be legally transferred without their consent. At the peace conference in San Francisco in 1951, in which the Soviet Union did not participate, Japan renounced "all right, title, and claim to the Kurile Islands and to that portion of Sakhalin and the islands adjacent to it over which Japan acquired sovereignty as a consequence of the Treaty of Portsmouth." Japan contends, however, that there was no reference made to the geographic definition of the Kurile Islands, to which it says the islands of the "Northern Territories" do not belong—a position to which the United States also stipulated at San Francisco—and moreover, that it did not in any event cede sovereignty over any of these territories to the Soviet Union.

Nevertheless, the islands remained in the possession of the Soviet Union, and not until after the death of Stalin was their future discussed directly between Tokyo and Moscow. Following the Geneva Summit, Khrushchev was seeking to lure both the West Germans and the Japanese away from their security ties with the United States, and the Soviets were willing to discuss a territorial transfer as a condition of a peace treaty with Japan. In the October 1956 joint declaration between them, the Soviets agreed "to transfer to Japan the Habomai Islands and Shikotan, the actual transfer of these islands to Japan to take place after the conclusion of a peace treaty between the USSR and Japan." After ratification of this declaration by the two parliaments, the Soviet and Japanese foreign ministers exchanged letters expressing readiness to discuss the status of Kunashir and Iturup as well. But the peace treaty was never concluded, and in 1960 Khrushchev used the excuse of the revised U.S.-Japanese Security Treaty to add another condition: the islands would be returned "only on the condition that all foreign troops be withdrawn from Japan."[22] Nevertheless, the offer to return the two southernmost islands following the conclusion of a peace treaty was secretly, but briefly, put back on the table during a visit to Tokyo by Gromyko in 1972, when the Soviets became alarmed at the rapprochement among the United States, Japan, and China.[23] The Japanese never responded, and the Soviets soon reverted to their position that the territorial issue had been settled at San Francisco.

Contrary to their expectations, the Japanese did not succeed in using the bait of trade and investment to elicit territorial concessions from the proponents of the "new political thinking" in Soviet foreign policy, despite several visits to Tokyo by Shevardnadze and Yakovlev. Indeed, by the time Gorbachev made an official state visit to Tokyo in April 1991, he was politically too weak to be able to deliver such concessions, though he did acknowledge that a territorial issue existed. By this time, however, the Japanese probably thought that they could fare better if Boris Yeltsin were to come to power in Moscow. Yeltsin had traveled to Tokyo in January 1990, when he was still only a member of the Soviet parliament, and during his visit he had proposed the following five-step process of negotiations: (1) formal recognition of the existence of a territorial dispute; (2) demilitarization of the four southern islands; (3) creation of a free enterprise zone with preferential treatment for Japanese investment and a broad cooperation treaty; (4) a formal peace treaty; and (5) a formal territorial settlement. Yeltsin estimated that the process might take a generation to complete, and the Japanese conceded that the islands need not be returned prior to conclusion of a treaty, provided that Japanese sovereignty over them was recognized beforehand.

The dust from the August 1991 coup attempt had barely settled when the Japanese approached the Russian foreign ministry to propose, unsuccessfully, that Yeltsin state his readiness to be guided in a territorial settlement by the 1855 Shimodo Treaty.[24] After the demise of the USSR, Japan continued to show its eagerness to proceed with negotiations, urging an early visit to Tokyo by Yeltsin, but the Russians were in less of a hurry. Thus, in January 1992, when Foreign Minister Watanabe came to Moscow to firm up plans for a Yeltsin visit, the president flew off to the Black Sea without receiving him. In May, however, Yeltsin reconfirmed his commitment to the five-stage resolution of the territorial problem, with a peace treaty to be concluded as early as 1993, and he indicated that all Russian military units on the disputed islands, with the exception of border troops, would be withdrawn.

By this time Yeltsin's foreign policy had become a matter of sharp internal contention in Russia, with critics upset about its excessive softness and unseemly eagerness to please the West. With Yeltsin now scheduled to fly to Tokyo in September, the government's stance on the territorial issue with Japan became a matter of angry and visible debate. General Grachev, newly appointed defense minister, stated that Russian army troops would not be withdrawn from the southern Kuriles, prompting a Japanese demand for explanation. The proffered statement from the foreign ministry only deepened the confusion, and a scheduled meeting of the Russo-Japanese working group on a peace treaty was postponed at Moscow's request. On July 28, the Russian parliament held hearings on the territorial issue; these had originally been scheduled for June but were delayed at Yeltsin's request.

At the parliamentary hearings, the inflammatory nature of the issue was evident. A prominent moderate deputy, Oleg Rumiantsev, flatly declared that if Moscow were to make a concession on the territorial issue with Japan, Russia would no longer be an important factor in world politics. The government, obviously sharply divided, refused to state a position prior to Yeltsin's visit. A memorandum from the general staff of the Russian armed forces to the parliament, refuting the notion that the islands were of little importance, pointed out that the most useful straits for passage to the Pacific from Vladivostok and the Sea of Okhotsk, where much of the Russian submarine fleet is based, lie north of the disputed islands. If the southern Kuriles were in Japanese hands, it was argued, they could be turned into a forward military post facing the Russian coastline, giving a significant advantage to the "enemy" in the event of a conflict.[25] Regional authorities also publicly resisted the idea of a territorial concession, with the Sakhalin governor flatly refusing to implement any such action. But Deputy Prime Minister Mikhail Poltoranin, visiting Tokyo in August in preparation for Yeltsin's visit, declared that the president's position would be based on the 1956 joint declaration agreeing on the transfer of the two southernmost islands.

On August 25, the official report of the Supreme Soviet Joint Committee on International Affairs and Foreign Economic Relations recommended to Yeltsin that, under present conditions, "unilateral recognition of any form of Japanese sovereignty over any part of Russian territory is extremely dangerous." Committee chairman Evgenii Ambartsumov declared that the Russian people would not accept the idea of territorial changes, and the Supreme Soviet would not ratify any such agreements. Another deputy, giving voice to the "domino theory" that undoubtedly lay behind the concerns of many, warned that if Russia were to make a concession, "others who lay claim to Russian lands, of whom there are quite a few, will immediately pounce on us." Yeltsin himself continued to play his cards close to the vest, noting that he had been presented with twelve options, and that he would reveal his own views only to the Japanese prime minister.

In a stunning reversal, Russia announced on September 10 that Yeltsin's trip to Tokyo, scheduled to begin in four days, had been canceled by the president. *Izvestia* declared that the cancellation—"an insulting demarche which falls outside the bounds of civilized behavior in the international arena"—was a sign of internal weakness and of unreliability in Russia's foreign policy. Kozyrev and the democratic wing of the leadership were seen as having been weakened. The foreign minister seemed to agree with this assessment, denouncing "attempts at unprofessional interference by the bureaucracy in foreign policy" and declaring in an interview that "they" were attempting to shake him up psychologically.[26] The strength of the opponents of territorial concessions must truly have been overwhelming, causing a Russian government that was desperate for financial assistance to turn down what Kozyrev later claimed was a Japanese offer of $28 billion for the southern Kuriles.[27]

The failure to agree on the territorial basis for a peace treaty undoubtedly retarded the development of Russo-Japanese relations in other spheres. Trade between Moscow and Tokyo, which had averaged $5.5 billion a year prior to 1991, fell to $4.8 billion in 1991 and $3.1 billion in 1992. Angry quarrels erupted in 1993 over the Russian practice of dumping nuclear wastes in the Sea of Japan, and in 1994 over incidents in which Russian border guards fired on Japanese fishing vessels that had wandered into waters off the southern Kuriles. Even an October 1994 earthquake on the islands occasioned bilateral tensions, with the Japanese claiming that they had done more than the Russians to provide relief, and accusing the Russians of using the disaster to promote schemes for joint rebuilding efforts that flaunted the premise of Russian ownership.

Contradictory signals on the territorial issue continued to emanate from Russia, to the evident frustration of the Japanese. In August 1993 Prime Minister Chernomyrdin declared, on a speaking tour in the Far East, that Russia would never give up its territory. Two days later, a statement from the president's office explained that the premier was speaking about only one possible option. But Chernomyrdin then repeated his statement, adding that if some people wanted to condition their economic cooperation on territorial concessions, so be it; Russia was not a pauper. A few days later former state secretary Gennadii Burbulis, by then supposedly a private citizen, arrived in Tokyo for a ten-day visit. Telling the Japanese media that he was there to prepare for Yeltsin's visit, and that he would be discussing the territorial issue, on which there were many viewpoints in Russia, Burbulis characterized the prime minister's remarks as personal views. Once again the press office in the president's office tried to clear up the confusion, declaring that only the foreign ministry was authorized to conduct talks on the president's forthcoming visit.

President Yeltsin finally made his state visit to Tokyo in October 1993, but there were few practical results. The psychological climate was improved by Yeltsin's apology for Stalin's harsh treatment of Japanese prisoners of war in Siberia. Pressured by his hosts to reaffirm the 1956 treaty commitment to return the two southernmost islands, Yeltsin did so only indirectly, by reaffirming that Russia is heir to international agreements signed by the Soviet Union. The president did announce in Tokyo that Russia at an unspecified future time would withdraw military units from the southern Kuriles, with the exception of border troops, in accordance with his five-stage settlement plan, but the effect of this was negated the following year by denials from General Grachev that any Russian troops would be leaving the Kuriles.

With the passage of time and with changes of personnel in key government positions in both Moscow and Tokyo, there were signs of greater flexibility on both sides of the relationship. Perhaps sensing an opening as a result of diminished economic and political stability in Japan, foreign minister Primakov journeyed to Tokyo in November 1996 with ideas about promoting a thaw in Russo-Japanese relations. In particular, he proposed that the territorial dispute be set aside while Russia and Japan worked to jointly promote investment in the southern Kuriles; he cited as precedent the example of joint British-Argentinian prospecting for minerals on the Falkland/Malvinas Islands that both countries claim. The Japanese, promising to consider the proposal, offered a goodwill gesture in response, freeing $500 million in soft loans that had been frozen for five years. Although Primakov was trying to break the deadlock while allowing both sides to save face, concrete progress was unlikely given Primakov's statement that any "softening" of Russian sovereignty was out of the question, and given Japan's stance of forbidding its businessmen or officials to engage in any activity on the islands involving permits, licenses, or other actions that would even indirectly affirm Russia's rights.[28]

Further progress was made when Yeltsin hosted Japan's Prime Minister Ryutaro Hashimoto for an informal "weekend without neckties" in November 1997 in the Siberian city of Krasnoiarsk. The two leaders pledged their "maximum efforts" to conclude a peace treaty by 2000, based on the 1993 Tokyo Declaration in which Yeltsin had acknowledged the existence of a territorial dispute over the southern Kuriles. However, First Deputy Prime Minister Boris Nemtsov downplayed the possibility that the islands might eventually be surrendered, noting that the Russian constitution upholds the territorial integrity of the country, and the president is the guarantor of the constitution.[29] Rather, signs pointed to some sort of joint economic zone in the southern Kuriles, as Primakov had hinted in his visit earlier in 1977. Despite the lingering ambiguities, the "sauna summit" was said by Yeltsin to have helped break the ice and overcome mutual distrust. The two sides discussed initiatives to increase Japanese investment and trade, including joint development of Siberian petroleum reserves and modernization of the trans-Siberian railroad. This atmosphere persisted in a second "weekend without neckties" summit in Japan in April 1998, where hints of further progress continued to be dropped but without tangible signs that a solution was near.

In the realm of security relations, a significant departure occurred in May 1997 with the visit to Tokyo of Igor Rodionov—the first ever by a Soviet or Russian defense minister. Aside from agreements to develop confidence-building measures and bilateral defense exchanges, the Russian voiced an especially benign view of the Asian-Pacific security situation, declaring that Moscow no longer viewed any country in the Far East as a potential adversary and no longer objected to the U.S.-Japanese security alliance. For their part, however, the Japanese probably took advantage of this opening to voice a less optimistic view, expressing their concern about the threat to the regional balance arising from China's escalating arms purchases from Russia.

Whenever they discuss the regional security situation, Russia and Japan undoubtedly voice their mutual concern over the instability on the Korean peninsula. In the waning months of the Cold War, Gorbachev had initiated a balance in Moscow's relations with the two Koreas. In 1988 he allowed Soviet participation in the Seoul Olympics and opened trade relations with South Korea. Two years later Gorbachev realized his hopes for a financial benefit from his initiative; the establishment of diplomatic relations was soon followed by a lavish South Korean credit of $3 billion to Moscow. An exchange of state visits between Gorbachev and President Roh Tae Woo fanned Soviet expectations for additional South Korean investment, but it also further enraged the North Korean regime, which had been heavily dependent on Soviet military and economic aid. In pursuit of greater self-reliance, Pyongyang stepped up its program to develop nuclear capabilities.

Yeltsin and Kozyrev abandoned any pretense of even-handedness in Russia's relations on the Korean peninsula. When the foreign minister traveled to Seoul in March 1992, the South Koreans welcomed Kozyrev's declaration that relations were moving from normalization to "full-fledged cooperation," and they acceded to his request to reinstate credits frozen after the collapse of the USSR. Announcing that Russia had stopped selling offensive weapons to the North, Kozyrev said that not only would Russia not cooperate in the further development of Pyongyang's nuclear program, but it also supported the complete denuclearization of the peninsula. In a meeting with the South Korean foreign minister in June, Yeltsin declared that the 1961 Soviet–North Korean security treaty "has lost its effectiveness and exists in name only." Later in the year, Russia announced that it had prevented sixty-four of its scientists from leaving for North Korea to assist with the latter's missile program.

Yeltsin's first Far Eastern trip as head of state, in November 1992, was made not to Beijing or Tokyo but to Seoul, where he signed a treaty on the basic principles of Russian–South Korean relations and issued a public apology for the 1983 downing of Korean Airlines flight 007. Yeltsin was disappointed when these symbolic acts failed to elicit any additional loans from South Korea. In retrospect, it probably dawned on the Russians that by virtually abandoning their position of influence in Pyongyang, they had made themselves less valuable to Seoul and less necessary as a participant in future security arrangements in Northeast Asia. They set about trying to remedy this situation early in 1993, with a trip to North Korea by deputy foreign minister Georgii Kunadze. Both sides expressed interest in preserving "normal good-neighborly relations," despite the current ideological differences. But the results of the meeting conveyed little sense of neighborliness. Trade between the two had fallen 50 percent in 1992, to 1981 levels, and North Korea owed Moscow $3 billion. However, there was little chance that economically strapped North Korea could pay this down, given Russia's insistence that future trade, including spare parts for Soviet-built weapons, must be on a purely commercial basis. With respect to their security treaty, the terms of which did not permit renunciation prior to 1995, the sides discussed a possible exchange of letters on their different understandings of Article I, which required military assistance in the case of armed conflict. And finally, on the sensitive question of nuclear development, Moscow stiffly reminded North Korea of its international obligations under the non-proliferation treaty (NPT).

Effectively demonstrating Russia's continuing lack of influence, North Korea announced shortly after Kunadze's visit that it planned to abandon its participation in the NPT. Russia called for an international conference on the issue, and threatened to join in sanctions if the threat were carried out. In underscoring Russia's sense of urgency about the security situation in Korea, Kozyrev went so far as to characterize the peninsula as "the near abroad for Russia, if you will."[30] But an even sharper display of Russia's seeming loss of relevance came in October 1994, when it was announced that the United States and North Korea had agreed on a new nuclear program for Pyongyang, under which North Korea would freeze its nuclear development, dismantle its graphite-moderated reactors, and replace them with light-water reactors. It was eventually agreed that these would be supplied by an international consortium, in which Russia was pointedly not invited to participate. Moscow's sense of exclusion from discussions of Korean security was later magnified, when Washington ignored Russian suggestions for a broader conference and instead promoted quadrilateral talks among the two Koreas, China, and the United States. As one journalist put it, Moscow was being "gently pushed out" of real participation in the

Korean peninsula, and—as it now did in the Middle East—would play "only the role of honored guest."[31]

Russia, however, was in no mood to be excluded, and it reasserted its presence on the peninsula in a familiar way—through the sale of arms. This time, Seoul rather than Pyongyang was Moscow's customer. Other aspects of the trade relationship with South Korea had failed to live up to expectations. Total trade in 1994 was up 40 percent over the prior year, but still amounted to only $2.2 billion. The Russians complained that their exports had been primarily raw materials, often sold at below world prices and resold by Seoul. And in three years, South Korea had invested only $25 million in Russia, spread over thirty projects. Although Chernomyrdin, during a September 1995 visit to Seoul, spoke of possible joint development of gas fields in Irkutsk and Yakutsk and establishment of a Korean technological park in a Nakhodka free economic zone, it was already clear that the greatest potential for reducing the Russian debt to South Korea was through the sale of arms. The first arms-for-debt-repayment deals were concluded in April and July of 1995, amounting to $650 million worth of T-80U tanks, BMP-3 light infantry vehicles, and S-300 defensive missile systems. In November 1996, defense minister Rodionov signed a bilateral cooperation agreement with his South Korean counterpart, calling for military exchanges, naval port visits, and training of some South Korean personnel in Russia; he also expressed hope for future sales of Russian planes. Reports that the Pentagon was objecting to Seoul's purchases from Moscow were met with derision in the Russian press: "In short, the market is the market, and the South Koreans obviously have their own ideas about which systems are preferable."[32]

Understandably more strenuous were the North Korean objections to Russia's arms sales. Itself able to obtain only a small number of military spare parts from Moscow, as part of a trade volume that had dropped below $100 million in 1996, Pyongyang's cooperation with Russia was described in the Russian press as "on the brink of extinction." The succession struggle that followed the death of long-time leader Kim Il Sung coincided with a severe economic crisis that brought widespread famine to the reclusive country. Tensions on the Korean peninsula rose as some observers predicted that the heavily armed Pyongyang regime might lash out militarily at the South in a final attempt at forcible unification of the country. In this context, it was understandable that Russia was reluctant to associate too closely with its former client state. In reaction to Moscow's tilt toward South Korea, North Korea angrily described Moscow's arms sales to Seoul as a criminal act that showed that "Russia itself is all but in the camp of forces hostile to the DPRK." If Russia continued along this road,

Pyongyang warned, "we will have to settle scores with it."[33] However, South Korea's stunning economic collapse at the close of 1997 precluded further purchases by Seoul from the Russian arms industry.

Russia and the Middle East

The southward expansion of the Russian Empire in the eighteenth and nineteenth centuries brought it into frequent conflict with the Ottoman Empire and with Persia, as well as with the competing empires of Britain and France. During the Soviet period, Lenin, Stalin, and their successors engaged in active (and occasionally expansionist) diplomacy in the region, as Moscow competed for territory and influence with the countries of the Middle East and with Western "imperialism." And although, after the collapse of the USSR, the Russian Federation now finds itself geographically separated from the Middle East by the buffer states of the Caucasus and Central Asia, Moscow's vital interests in these former Soviet republics and the vast energy reserves they contain—second only to those in the Middle East itself—have made the region a high priority for Russian foreign policy.

Accordingly, of highest concern in the region are Turkey and Iran—the two states that share a border with the states of the former Soviet Union and that are thus seen as Russia's potential competitors there. Russia's policies toward them have varied, in part as a result of the shifting political winds in Moscow, with Westernizers and nationalists competing over the direction of foreign policy. But there also has been variability in Moscow's perception of threat that Ankara or Teheran is seeking to extend pan-Turkic or Islamic-fundamentalist influence in the Caucasus and Central Asia at Russia's expense. In both cases, Russian policy has swung back and forth from nervous rivalry to a relationship so cooperative that it has included the sale of arms. As an analyst at the Russian Center for Strategic and International Studies described the policy confusion, "The exchange of blows between the proponents of a pro-Turkish and a pro-Iranian orientation in the Russian establishment is more vigorous than the actual rivalry between those two states in the Central Asian and Transcaucasus regions."[34]

Although Turkey is a member of NATO and was the recipient of some rather brutal threats and territorial demands from Stalin, its relations with the post-Stalinist regimes in Moscow were relatively cooperative. In the wake of the breakup of the USSR, Turkey—a secular, democratic, and market-oriented Islamic state—was widely viewed in the West as a potential model for the development of the newly independent Islamic states of the former Soviet Union, much of whose population is ethnically and linguistically related to the Turks. Initially, Turkey was cautious in the region, assuring Kozyrev during his February 1992 visit that it did not view itself as competing with Russia for a sphere of influence. Turkey's sympathies were evident, however, in the regional conflict in Nagorno-Karabakh that had embroiled Armenia and Azerbaijan in war since 1988. Turkey was the first country to recognize Azerbaijan's independence, and a visit to Turkey in January 1992 by the strongly nationalist Azeri president, Abulfez Elchibey, aroused Russia's suspicions. During his visit to Moscow to conclude a treaty on principles governing Russo-Turkish relations in May, Prime Minister Suleyman Demirel was pressed for a commitment that Turkey would not intervene militarily in the conflict. But Moscow's anxiety was heightened by Azerbaijan's mid-1992 withdrawal from the Commonwealth of Independent States in protest of a perceived pro-Armenian stance, together with the marked increase in Azerbaijani-Turkish trade and the extent of the country's penetration by Turkish media.

These concerns were broadened in October, when the leaders of Kazakhstan, Uzbekistan, Turkmenistan, Kyrgyzstan, and Azerbaijan met with the Turkish head of state in Ankara for discussions of a "Turkic Common Market" featuring cooperation in the economic and security realms. Fears of a burgeoning rivalry for influence were revived when the five Central Asian republics met in May 1993 to form the Central Asian Regional Union, which was encouraged by Turkey, amid talk that their energy resources would be directed away from Russia and through Azerbaijan and Turkey. And the second summit of the Turkic-language states in Istanbul in October 1994 occasioned a statement by a Russian foreign ministry spokesman on the "undesirability of a segregation of the Turkic-language countries along national and ethnic lines." In contrast, by the time of the third summit, held in Bishkek in August 1995, there was no official reaction from Moscow. By this time, one journalist noted, it had become evident that the leaders of the former Soviet republics were in no hurry to replace Moscow's patronage with Ankara's, and he wryly observed that three of the six heads of state in attendance spoke not in their native languages, but in Russian.[35]

Moscow's reduced level of anxiety probably resulted from the parallel development of its own economic and security relations with Turkey. In March 1993 the Russians announced a $75 million sale of helicopters and armored personnel carriers to Turkey's national police force, with most of the proceeds to be applied toward Russia's debt. This first-ever Russian arms sale to a NATO member nation was followed in May by the first visit to Turkey by a Russian defense chief in two centuries. A year later Grachev and his Turkish counterpart signed a formal agreement on cooperation between their defense industries, which contemplated joint production of certain weapons systems. An additional sale of Russian military hardware in the summer of 1994, following Germany's suspension of arms sales in protest of Turkish raids on its Kurdish minority, allowed Turkey to demonstrate to the West that it had an alternative source of arms supplies. And in December 1995, a package of economic agreements was signed that included a $350 million Turkish credit and a restructuring of the Russian debt. The two sides noted that their trade turnover in 1995 had reached $3 billion, and that Turkish firms had concluded $5 billion in contracts for construction of facilities in Russia—clear signs that Turkey had become one of Russia's leading trade and investment partners.

However, elections in Turkey that same month provided a less favorable portent for Russia. The success at the polls of the Islamic Welfare Party, followed by the accession of its leader Necmettin Erbakan to the premiership the following June, aroused new fears in Moscow—understandable in light of Erbakan's stated pan-Islamic goals, which included the "liberation" of Azerbaijan and Chechnia. In the ensuing months there were several signs of growing tension between the two countries. In September Russian participation in joint Black Sea naval exercises was canceled, amid expressions of concern over Turkey's growing shipbuilding program. And in December 1996, Foreign Minister Tansu Ciller's visit to Moscow was marred by a whole list of mutual complaints. On the Russian side, these concerned Turkey's restrictions on the passage of Russian tankers through the Bosporus, allegedly for environmental reasons, and the activities of Turkish groups supporting Chechen separatists. On the Turkish side, there were parallel complaints about activities of Kurdish organizations in Russia, and an expression of sharp anger about Russia's announced plans to sell surface-to-air missile systems to the Greek-dominated government of Cyprus. But these incidents were not likely to permanently mar Russo-Turkish relations, and tensions were expected to again decrease as a result of the military-induced resignation of the Erbakan government in the summer of 1997. Indeed, a December 1997 visit to Turkey by Chernomyrdin—the first ever by a Russian prime minister—featured the announcement of a twenty-five-year agreement according to which Turkey would be supplied with thirty billion cubic meters of Russian gas annually, following the completion of a pipeline to be built across the Black Sea.

The Soviet Union's relations with Iran during the 1980s were not nearly as cordial as those with Turkey, but there may be greater potential for long-term future cooperation between Moscow and Teheran. The ideological tensions that accompanied Ayatollah Khomeini's Islamic revolution have largely disappeared, given Gorbachev's decision to withdraw Soviet troops from Afghanistan, the relative moderation of Iran's revolutionary policies after the ayatollah's death, and the subsequent fall of communism and breakup of the USSR, which nominally removed the yoke of communism from the practice of the Islamic religion there. Initial concerns that Iran would promote "Islamic fundamentalism" among the Muslim minority in Russia or in the buffer zone that has been created between the two countries were clearly overblown. With the exception of the Azerbaijanis, most Muslims in the former Soviet Union do not adhere to the Shiite branch of Islam that predominates in Iran. More to the point, Teheran has seemed willing to conduct its relations in ways that do not threaten the interests of Moscow.

The improvement in relations began during Gorbachev's last years in power. A state visit by President Rafsanjani to Moscow in June 1989 was the occasion for signing several agreements, including an important arms deal, under which the Soviets obtained badly needed hard currency for MiG-29 and SU-24 aircraft, needed by Iran to replace heavy losses during the long Iran-Iraq war. Subsequent sales included T-72 tanks and several Kilo-class submarines, and deliveries were estimated to total $1 billion in 1991 and an even greater sum in 1992. The U.S. government put heavy pressure on the new Yeltsin government to cancel military deliveries to Iran, and Moscow did agree to delay the delivery of some of the submarines. But a Ministry of Foreign Affairs spokesman, in an interview with *Izvestia,* frankly acknowledged Russia's dilemma: " 'We understand the U.S.'s concern, and we don't want an arms race to be unleashed in the Persian Gulf, either. But we have our own interests, first of all, our economic interests (convertible currency!). Second, we view Iran as a friendly, neighboring state,' said the Russian diplomat. 'Ignoring its requests in the defense sphere would be unreasonable. Today only enemies are refused deliveries of military equipment.' "[36] When the Yeltsin government followed the American lead, not only was it exposing itself to further ridicule from internal opponents, but it also was ignoring the distinctive security situation Moscow faced. At least at that time, Iran seemed concerned that conflicts within the former Soviet states might spill onto its own territory; it thus appeared to share Russia's desire for good-neighborly cooperation in the interests of stabilizing the region. As long as Iran behaved responsibly in Russia's backyard, Moscow saw no reason to accede to U.S. pressure to cut off arms sales.

These considerations were evident in Kozyrev's March 1993 trip to Teheran. He confirmed Russia's intention to sell arms to Iran and reached agreement on projects in the nuclear field, including the sale of two 440-megawatt nuclear reactors—a deal which he claimed would not put Russia at odds with the United States. Moreover, he discussed a Russian-Iranian "strategic partnership" for ensuring stability in the Caucasus and Central Asia, one immediate fruit of which was Iran's agreement to use its influence over the opposition forces in the Tajikistan civil war to encourage a settlement of the conflict.

Although its primary emphasis was on promoting "cultural Islam" rather than overt political interference in the former Soviet republics, Iran's presence was active enough to keep Moscow on edge. In September 1993, the foreign ministry issued a statement of concern about reports that Iranian troops had crossed into Azerbaijan, and it urged Iran to show restraint in the Nagorno-Karabakh conflict. The following month, a nine-day trip by Rafsanjani to Azerbaijan, Uzbekistan, Kazakhstan, Turkmenistan, and Kyrgyzstan stimulated some alarm in the Russian foreign ministry. And in December of the same year, the Turkish prime minister met the Iranian vice-president to discuss the possibility of coordinated actions—probably in the form of an energy pipeline—to ease Azerbaijan's economic dependence on Russia.

These concerns were not sufficient, however, to deter Russia from concluding a major deal to assist in the development of Iran's nuclear program. In January 1995, the Russian Ministry of Atomic Power and the Nuclear Industry announced a $1 billion contract—reportedly won despite heavy competition from Western firms—to complete a reactor at Bushehr, the construction of which had been halted in 1979. The United States immediately objected, claiming that the reactor would help Iran to build a nuclear weapon, but the Russian ministry said that the project complied with the NPT and would be monitored by the International Atomic Energy Agency. The U.S. Congress prepared legislation that would cut off aid to Russia if the deal went through. A face-saving compromise was announced in May at the Clinton-Yeltsin summit. Gas centrifuges for enriching uranium—supposedly included in the contract without the knowledge of the Kremlin or the Ministry of Foreign Affairs—would be eliminated from the deal, and provisions for training Iranian nuclear physicists in Russia also would be dropped, cutting the value of the deal in half. The other terms of the contract would be analyzed by the Gore-Chernomyrdin commission to verify their conformity with the NPT.[37]

Despite this embarrassing episode, Russia continued to seek increased trade with Iran, but a worsening economy limited Teheran's attractiveness as a customer. Deputy Prime Minister and Minister for Foreign Economic Relations Oleg Davydov, visiting Iran late in 1995, said that the main difficulties in Russo-Iranian trade were not political, but were related to problems of payments that followed the 1992 decision to settle accounts only in freely convertible currency. Total trade volume had dropped 29 percent in 1994, to $520 million, and Iran's overdue debt to Russia had climbed to $582 million (two-thirds of which was owed to the state arms trading agency). Nevertheless, Davydov predicted later in the year that the total volume of Russian exports to Iran could reach $5 billion in another decade.[38]

Russia's interest in participating in Iranian energy projects caused another dispute with the United States in the fall of 1997. A joint French-Malaysian-Russian project to develop Iranian gas fields threatened to trigger U.S. sanctions against the participating companies, apparently jeopardizing a plan by the Russian participant (Gazprom) to raise investment capital on the U.S. market. In December 1997, Gazprom announced that it had withdrawn from these financing plans—but not from the proposed deal with Iran.

In his first year in office, Foreign Minister Evgenii Primakov continued the Russian effort to strengthen ties with Iran. Visiting Teheran in December 1996, he declared that relations between the two were "developing along an ascending curve," in part because of Iran's assistance in arranging a cease-fire in Tajikistan. For his part, Primakov's Iranian counterpart told a Russian journalist that Russo-Iranian relations were the best they had been in two hundred years, causing the journalist to conclude that Moscow's way of working with Iran "i.e., trying to bring its behavior into conformity with generally recognized international norms—can be more effective than the ultimatum-based methods of the Americans."[39] These signs of cooperation on regional problems continued into 1997, as the two countries collaborated on their policies toward the Taliban in Afghanistan, and as Russia sought Iran's help in pressuring Turkmenistan and Azerbaijan to cooperate with Moscow in the exploitation of the considerable petroleum reserves in the Caspian Sea. But whether the relationship could remain relatively trouble-free was in question, given Iran's expressed interest in acquiring additional arms (T-80 tanks, S-300 air defense missile systems, and MiG-20 fighter attack planes) that would likely upset the regional balance in the Persian Gulf and greatly alarm the United States.[40]

Reports appeared in the Western press in September 1997—"taken very seriously" by the U.S. government—that Russia was supplying missile technology to Iran. Primakov hastily denied the reports, and Yeltsin added a blanket pledge that, while limited arms sales would continue, there would be no deliveries to Iran of missiles or missile technology. Pressed again on the subject the following month by Israeli Prime Minister Netanyahu, the Russian foreign minister reportedly cited his prior intelligence background as the basis for assuring the Israelis that Iran would not have nuclear weapons or the means to deliver them any time within the next decade. As for the prospect of unauthorized "leakages," Primakov added "that he personally had promoted the adoption of measures to prevent specialists with access to missile and nuclear secrets from having contacts with Iran."[41] As the subject continued to be pressed by the U.S. government in 1998, Primakov acknowledged that some "brain drain" had occurred, but that it was simply not in Russia's interests to assist its neighbor in acquiring long-range missiles.

No less a threat to stability in the Persian Gulf region, and no less undesirable in Washington's eyes as a possible partner for Moscow, was Saddam Hussein's Iraq. We have seen in chapter 3 how Gorbachev and his personal envoy Evgenii Primakov had tried to salvage the long-standing Soviet investment in Baghdad by negotiating a peaceful resolution to the 1990 Iraqi invasion of Kuwait, and how the failure of those mediation efforts had left the Soviet Union trailing unenthusiastically in the wake of the international effort to rein in Saddam Hussein. In the United Nations Security Council, the representatives of the Soviet Union and Russia have repeatedly voted to support international sanctions on Iraq, but Moscow probably has ranked second only to Baghdad itself in the amount of economic harm it has suffered as a result. Russia has lost a major partner both in energy development and in weapons sales, while holding a debt, estimated as high as $10 billion, that financially strapped Iraq is unable to repay. Given Russia's own economic crisis, Yeltsin's persistence in supporting costly UN sanctions has been prominently used by his domestic political opponents as a prime example of Russia's sacrificing its own interests to satisfy the West.

For both Gorbachev and Yeltsin, Kuwait and the other oil-rich moderate states of the Gulf Cooperation Council appeared to offer an alternative market and source of financial support. Kozyrev visited six of these states during a seven-day tour in April and May of 1992, emphasizing Russia's new-found ideological affinity by stating that "now we prefer to deal with stable, moderate regimes" rather than the USSR's previous partners, Libya, Iran, and Iraq. But Kozyrev encountered a certain reticence deriving from fresh memories of Moscow's recent friendships in the region; and by the end of his trip, only Oman had offered credits to Russia—a $500 million investment in the oil and gas industry and $100 million for modernization of Russia's oil fields. Nevertheless, the primary importance of strengthening cooperation with the Persian Gulf states was reaffirmed in a foreign ministry "concept"—approved by Yeltsin—that was developed in the fall of 1992 to guide Russia's relations with the Arab world. The chief goals identified in this document were: (1) ensuring Russia's national security; (2) preventing the spread of political and military fires in the Middle East to the increasingly unstable regions of the Caucasus and Central Asia; (3) making use of the potential in the Arab states to help solve Russia's economic problems.[42]

In the longer term, despite Russia's continued support of sanctions—
even its dispatch of two ships to the Persian Gulf task force enforcing
them—most of the Gulf states remained wary. However, Russia did manage
a breakthrough with Saddam Hussein's recent victim, Kuwait, which was
busy securing itself against possible future aggression by strengthening economic and military ties with all five permanent members of the Security
Council. In December 1993, Russia signed a military cooperation agreement with Kuwait, calling for joint naval maneuvers and an exchange of
military delegations. The following November, a visit to the Gulf by
Chernomyrdin produced an agreement for a Russian arms sale of $750
million to Kuwait, involving infantry fighting vehicles and rocket launchers, and a $3 billion agreement with the United Arab Emirates for joint
production of SU-37 fighter-bombers.

For the most part, Russia was disappointed with the size and scope of its
economic and military transactions with the states of the Persian Gulf. In
April 1993, as Yeltsin's domestic opponents were increasing their pressure
on him, parliament speaker Ruslan Khasbulatov sent an emissary to Iraq to
explore the possibility of restoring closer relations. The defeat of the parliamentary opposition in October 1993 momentarily eased the domestic criticism of Russia's compliance with the sanctions imposed on Iraq and Serbia,
but criticism resumed after the December elections, with Zhirinovskii in the
forefront. Under the cloak of secrecy, Iraq's deputy prime minister Tariq
Aziz visited Russia in July 1994 to enlist Moscow's help in lifting UN
sanctions, holding forth the prospect of debt repayment and contracts for
Russian firms. Russia lobbied in the Security Council for a gradual lifting
of sanctions as a reward for positive steps that Iraq might take, while it
urged the Iraqi government to announce recognition of Kuwait's independence and borders.

In October 1994, in the midst of Russia's campaign to champion Iraqi
good behavior, Saddam Hussein rekindled the crisis by sending his troops
to the Kuwaiti border. As if to heighten Russia's embarrassment and force it
into a position counter to that of the West, he simultaneously sent his oil
minister to Moscow to discuss future cooperation. Yeltsin sought to salvage
the situation by sending Kozyrev to Baghdad in search of a political settlement. His meetings produced a communiqué saying that Iraq was ready to
recognize Kuwait's sovereignty and border, in return for which Russia
would support a six-month period of monitoring Iraq's compliance with UN
requirements, followed by an unconditional end to the sanctions. This initiative was speedily and angrily rejected by the Western powers, who mus-
tered their forces for a military response to Saddam Hussein. Desperately
seeking to keep his initiative alive, Kozyrev offered assurances that Saddam

had agreed unconditionally to recognize Kuwait's borders, but no high-ranking Iraqi official would confirm his statement, and no other states seemed ready to take Saddam Hussein at his word. Ultimately, once Iraqi forces had been turned back under threat of military reprisal, Kozyrev returned to Baghdad to praise Saddam's wisdom in recognizing Kuwait, and to appeal personally to the Iraqi parliament to ratify the action. Although much of the Russian press praised the initiative as an admirable exercise of independent diplomacy, Vladimir Lukin (the chair of the Duma's foreign affairs committee and former Russian ambassador to the United States) wrote a withering critique of Kozyrev's efforts:

> It is our passion for mere show, the Potemkin village syndrome, that is our undoing. . . . We managed to spoil what we should have been handling with greater care—working relations with the American administration. . . . If our national interest consists in getting Iraq to start paying off its debt as soon as possible while at the same time avoiding any worsening of relations with the West . . . then, as a result of the diplomatic measures we have conducted, the situation has become more difficult on both counts. That's the "bottom line."[43]

Lukin's position was not shared by a majority of his colleagues in the Russian Duma, who continued to chafe under the presumed yoke of Western policy in Iraq. In April 1995, the Duma passed a resolution calling for UN sanctions against Iraq to be lifted, and demanding that the government more actively pursue debt repayment and business investment in Iraq.

The deep rift that had reopened between Russia and the West over the proper response to Iraqi assertiveness appeared again in September 1996, when Saddam Hussein violated UN rules by sending troops into a special Kurdish-inhabited zone in northern Iraq. The United States responded by launching twenty-seven cruise missiles against military targets in Iraq, followed by a second strike with seventeen missiles that completed the destruction of Iraq's air defense system in an expanded "no-fly zone." At the time of the U.S. attack (of which the Russians had advance notification), Deputy Foreign Minister Viktor Posuvaliuk was in Baghdad trying to resolve the crisis. He claimed that he had received assurances from Tariq Aziz that Iraq would withdraw its troops from the special zone, and Posuvaliuk had sought unsuccessfully to forestall U.S. military action. An angry statement from the Russian government—said by Yeltsin's chief of staff to have been fully supported by the ailing president—bitterly denounced the U.S. actions:

> Serious concern is prompted by the fact that Washington is essentially laying claim to the role of supreme arbiter, trying, in effect, to supplant the Security

Council, which, in accordance with the UN Charter, possesses an exclusive right to authorize the use of force. The decision adopted unilaterally by the U.S. and Britain to expand the "no-fly" zone in southern Iraq should also be viewed in this context. These actions, which set a dangerous precedent, are at variance with international law and are unacceptable. The military actions in and around Iraq must be stopped. Russia insistently urges all parties to abandon the logic of force and to embark on the path of a political settlement of the crisis situation that has arisen.[44]

Responding to what the Russian press termed the low point in U.S.-Russian relations in 1996, the U.S. government expressed its disappointment that Russia had not yet learned that Saddam Hussein responds not to diplomacy, but only to force. Nevertheless, with Primakov himself more directly involved in the conversations with his "old comrades" in Iraq, Moscow has continued its search for a way to reduce sanctions in return for "good behavior," in the full expectation (avidly encouraged by Baghdad) that when Iraq resumes normal economic activity, Russia will be the major foreign beneficiary.[45]

Saddam Hussein forced the sanctions issue to the forefront again in the fall of 1997, when he ordered the expulsion of American members of the United Nations inspection team searching for Iraqi weapons of mass destruction. When the entire UN team withdrew in protest, the United States stepped up its military presence in the Persian Gulf region, amid rumors of an impending attack on Iraq. But the diplomatic and military coalition that had prevailed in the 1991 war had fallen apart, first of all within the United Nations Security Council itself, where only Britain among the permanent members gave strong support to the U.S. position. Capitalizing on his personal ties, Foreign Minister Primakov wrested an agreement from the Iraqis to readmit all members of the inspection team. Emerging from a meeting with Yeltsin and Iraqi Deputy Prime Minister Tariq Aziz, Primakov summoned the other "big five" foreign ministers to an extraordinary middle-of-the-night meeting in Geneva to announce his triumph and secure their concurrence.

Insisting to the skeptical Americans that they had made no deal with the Iraqis "behind anyone's backs," the Russians did promise that, on the basis of Iraq's fulfillment of the relevant UN resolutions, Russia would "energetically work for the earliest possible" lifting of UN sanctions. However, the ultimate loophole in the agreement—on the basis of which Saddam Hussein continued to declare "presidential sites" off limits to UN inspectors—was hidden in language that spoke of increasing the effectiveness of the work of the UN special commission "while showing respect for the sovereignty and security of Iraq."

Moscow clearly wanted to push such details to the background, preferring to capitalize on what Primakov termed "a great success for Russian diplomacy . . . achieved without the use of force and without a show of force." In the words of a Russian reporter, the United States was essentially isolated, and Russia strengthened its reputation "as an influential power not only throughout the Middle East . . . but in the world as a whole." Deputy Foreign Minister Viktor Posuvaliuk also saw in the role Russia was playing in the crisis a special significance for broader Russian foreign policy: "The world is increasingly coming to realize that Russia is emerging or has emerged from its period of confusion and major problems, and that it is now oriented toward conducting an energetic and constructive foreign policy. Many countries have confidence in the balanced line we are pursuing." He stressed that Russian diplomats were not acting as "undiscriminating defense attorneys" for Iraq, since they were calling for strict fulfillment of all the UN resolutions. "But at the same time we are saying that Iraq must be shown that there is light at the end of the tunnel. Not fire but light."[46]

When the Iraqi conflict flared up again in January 1998 over Saddam Hussein's refusal to allow UN inspectors access to eight "presidential sites," Yeltsin again sought to gain both international and domestic political prestige by sending Posuvaliuk to Baghdad in search of a solution. Embarrassed when a "deal" announced in Moscow was immediately denied by the Iraqis, an angry Yeltsin warned that continued U.S. military activities in the Persian Gulf could bring dire consequences: "One must be careful in a world that is saturated with all kinds of weapons. By his actions Clinton might get into a world war. They are acting too loudly." Yeltsin's spokesman sought to explain away the president's inflammatory rhetoric by speculating that foreign reporters might not have adequate command of the Russian language. But military action was averted when UN Secretary General Kofi Annan's mediation defused the crisis. Claiming a share of the credit, the Russians again saw in the Persian Gulf crisis some hopeful signs that the ability of the United States to dictate its will was waning, and that "the unipolar world is receding into the past."[47]

A similar, if lower-profile, mix of activities and motives has characterized Russia's diplomacy toward another Middle Eastern pariah state—Libya. The advent of the Yeltsin government had not been welcomed in Tripoli, which refused until 1995 to acknowledge that its $3.8 billion debt to the USSR was now owed to the Russian Federation. When Russia joined with the West in November 1993 in voting for UN sanctions against Libya, in response to the latter's refusal to cooperate against terrorism, Moscow succeeded in obtaining an amendment to the resolution that demanded that Libya repay its debts. Ironically, a Russian trade delegation was discovered to be in Tripoli at that very time, and an embarrassed foreign ministry quickly stated that Russia had every intention of abiding by the sanctions. With the sanctions still in force (and Primakov now in charge at the foreign ministry), a Russian delegation returned to Libya in March 1996 for a discussion of debt repayment and future large-scale economic cooperation. At this point, there were said to be only two hundred Russian specialists remaining in the country—about one-thirtieth the size of the former Soviet contingent. Although Russia claimed that it had suffered at least $7 billion in losses, and though it noted bitterly that some Western companies continued to do business in Libya, Russia nevertheless declared that it would continue to abide by the international sanctions.

Evgenii Primakov, a specialist on the Middle East, was determined that during his term as foreign minister Russia would move back onto the center stage of diplomacy in the region. Having moved forward from the supporting cast in the Persian Gulf conflict, Russia still sought to do the same in the remaining long-running dispute in the Middle East—the Arab-Israeli conflict. During earlier phases, Moscow had been handicapped by its lack of influence with Israel. But this changed—as did so many other features of Moscow's foreign policy—during the late Gorbachev period. By 1988 Soviet restrictions on Jewish emigration to Israel had eased and consular missions were opened. In October 1991 full diplomatic relations, broken after the six-day war in 1967, were restored. At the end of that month Gorbachev attended the Madrid Conference on Middle East peace, which was co-chaired by the USSR.

Yeltsin's government moved quickly to further strengthen Russian-Israeli relations. Vice President Rutskoi visited Israel in April 1992, and the following August Shimon Peres made the first visit to Moscow by an Israeli foreign minister. The following month Peres and Kozyrev signed an agreement calling for closer relations in several spheres. Trade relations between the two countries began to increase at a dizzying speed, moving from only $70 million in 1991 and $280 million in 1993 to about $650 million in 1995. Finally, much to the chagrin of Yeltsin's domestic critics, Moscow demonstrated an unaccustomed even-handedness in the ongoing Arab-Israeli peace process, and Kozyrev was invited to the White House in September 1993 to celebrate the Oslo accords between Israel and the Palestinians.

The strong showing by Zhirinovskii and the nationalist forces in the Duma elections of December 1993 may have motivated Yeltsin initially to play a more independent role in Middle East negotiations, following the disarray caused by the February 1994 massacre of twenty-nine Palestinian worshippers by a Jewish settler in the West Bank town of Hebron. Without consulting Washington, Yeltsin dispatched Kozyrev to Tunis to meet with Palestine Liberation Organization (PLO) leader Yasir Arafat, urged a reconvening of the Madrid conference, and supported the demand of the Arabs for international observers to protect West Bank Palestinians. In April Arafat and Israeli Prime Minister Yitzhak Rabin made separate visits to Moscow for consultations with Yeltsin. Although Moscow was not coordinating its initiative with Washington, it nevertheless remained even-handed. Rabin, a former general, was even invited to lecture at the General Staff Academy in Moscow, and he extracted two promises from the Russians—to use their influence with Syria to help in locating captured Israeli soldiers, and to forgo the sale of any new offensive weapons to Syria.

By this point, Moscow had only limited influence in Syria, which had been refusing to negotiate with the Yeltsin government about its substantial debt ($10 billion) to the USSR. During an April 1994 visit to Damascus, Deputy Prime Minister Oleg Soskovets opened conversations on debt repayment, while agreeing to resume deliveries of spare parts for Soviet-made weapons. A follow-up visit by Kozyrev in October produced a Syrian agreement on a repayment schedule stretching to 2015. This cleared the way for better relations between Syria and Russia, which still had about 2,000 military and civilian specialists working in the country.

The higher Russian profile in the Middle East occasioned an approving article in the Russian press by Karen Brutents, a veteran academic specialist on the area. Whereas Soviet influence in the Middle East during the Brezhnev period had been comparable to that of Washington, and the Arabs had been Moscow's main economic partners in the Third World, he argued, the early Yeltsin policy had curtailed political ties, wanting to destroy everything "sinful" that had been built up over the years. A legacy had thereby been wasted, and Russia had been relegated to a purely ceremonial role in the peace process. Even though the rise of independent states in the Caucasus had pushed Russia farther away geographically, "in some respects, Russian security is now even more closely connected with the Middle East than it was before," and tremors there could have serious repercussions in the "near abroad." The Arab countries remained a promising market for Russia, with possible benefits to stem from coordination of petroleum exporting policies. Finally, Brutents argued, changes for the better were being seen in Russian policy, with Arafat's visit to Moscow and Kozyrev's trips to the Middle East. The key, he maintained, was pursuing an independent policy that was based on a clear understanding of the importance to Russia of good relations with the Arab world.[48]

By the beginning of 1996, the stage was set for a major effort by Primakov, newly appointed foreign minister, to bring Moscow's diplomacy back to the forefront of the Arab-Israeli relationship. The opportunity came in April, when Israel launched "Operation Grapes of Wrath" in response to shelling of northern Israeli settlements by Hezbollah guerrillas in southern Lebanon. Primakov traveled to Israel, Lebanon, and Syria, offering himself as mediator in the conflict, and hinting that Russia would be able to exert influence over forces in both Syria and Iran that could assist in normalizing the situation in Lebanon. His meeting with Prime Minister Peres was described as "difficult," and Peres reportedly told him that Israel was interested only in U.S. mediation. A similar message came to Primakov from Washington, in a telephone call from Secretary of State Warren Christopher, who said, "We can handle this without you."[49] The Russian foreign ministry staff bitterly complained to journalists that U.S. "egoism"—a desire to keep a monopoly on diplomatic activity in the area—was the main reason Russia was even being excluded from the international group formed to monitor implementation of the cease-fire in southern Lebanon. One commentator noted that Russia's increasing efforts to develop ties with Iraq, Iran, and Libya probably contributed to the wariness of the United States, though he found an even more basic reason Russia was being left on the sidelines: "Moscow's basic problem is that, unlike the Americans and the West Europeans, it is unable to provide any material backup for its claims to a special role in the region, which is accustomed to massive financial infusions."[50]

Primakov's chief deputy for the Middle East gave a candid interview in which he expressed the foreign minister's frustration with Washington. According to Viktor Posuvaliuk, Russia was proceeding from the premise that the Madrid process needed to be given fresh impetus, and the best way to do this was to assure "a more energetic role for Moscow." However, he told his interviewer, "You are right when you say that an attempt is being made to prevent Russia from taking an active role in the Middle East." Russia's general line was to strengthen ties with all states in the region; paradoxically, Moscow was being accused on the one hand of associating mainly with countries such as Libya, Iraq, or Sudan, but then hindered when it tried to broaden its ties, especially through the sale of arms. In the next five years, he asserted, the countries of the region intended to buy arms worth up to $80 billion. If Russia did not sell to them, then some other country would: "So our task is to find our own niche in these plans."[51]

Primakov did not let his initial disappointment discourage continued efforts in the region. In October 1996 he embarked on another trip to the Middle East, visiting Syria, Lebanon, Jordan, Israel, and the Palestinian Authority. Recognizing that the Arab world's ardor toward Moscow had cooled, partly because its valve of financial and military support had been shut down, partly because of Russia's war in Muslim Chechnia and its support of Bosnian Serbs, but also because Kozyrev had given far more attention to Israel than to its neighbors, Primakov nonetheless persisted in trying to revive former friendships in the Arab world. By the time Arafat came to Moscow in February 1997, on his first visit as elected president of the Palestinian Authority, Primakov had specific suggestions which—in one journalist's words—"left no doubt that Russia's diplomatic train, which had sat on a siding of the Mideast railway for many years, is back on track." These ideas centered on arranging an expanded conference on a comprehensive settlement; the meeting would be held in Moscow and attended by all Middle Eastern countries. In a joint statement with Arafat, Russia declared that Palestinian aspirations to achieve self-determination did not harm Israel's legitimate interests, that the problem of the West Bank settlements must be resolved, and that the outcome of talks on Jerusalem must not infringe on the rights of any religious faith. As this journalist concluded, "The logic of events allows one to assume that in general Moscow will henceforth speak with a more pronounced Arab accent in talks on the subject of a Mideast settlement: Disillusioned with the West's NATO-related ambitions, it will try to charm the Muslim world again."[52]

There is little doubt that Moscow's Arab accent was being heard in Israel as well. In April 1996 the Russian government had revoked the registration of the Jewish Agency in Moscow, which was heavily involved in arranging the emigration of Russian Jews to Israel. Government spokesmen claimed that the agency had violated Russian laws by circumventing visa procedures, but there were widespread complaints in the press about its active inducements toward emigration, especially of talented young people. In a June interview, Posuvaliuk had strongly implied that re-registration would be possible, but he had also stated, with respect to the bilateral relationship, "The 'honeymoon' in our relations with Israel is over, and now they have entered a time of maturity." This was even more evident the following March, when Prime Minister Benjamin Netanyahu visited Moscow. Although he declared that Israel now considered Russia to be a "friendly state," and announced a $50 million loan for Russian agricultural development, there were evidently serious disagreements between him and his Russian hosts, especially about Moscow's arms sales to Syria and Iran. Primakov assured Netanyahu that Russia was not supplying missiles to Iran, and Yeltsin apparently promised him that Moscow would not sell state-of-the-art weapons to Syria.[53] But once again, Russia's active pursuit of opportunities in the weapons market was being regarded as a major obstacle to its acceptance as a responsible partner by all sides in the regional conflict.

Netanyahu reportedly had told the Russians that "there shouldn't be two chefs in the same kitchen"—in other words, that their help was not needed in efforts to settle the Arab-Israeli conflict. But Egypt's President Hosni Mubarak, visiting Moscow a few months later, clearly was encouraging a greater Russian role in the region. Noting with regret the absence of regular high-level visits during the past decade and the 50-percent drop in Russian-Egyptian trade (to an annual level of only $400 million), Mubarak and Yeltsin agreed to set up a bilateral commission to promote trade and economic cooperation.

The following month, following a New York meeting with Secretary of State Madeline Albright to coordinate U.S. and Russian efforts, Primakov returned to the Middle East for his third tour in less than two years. Visiting Egypt, Jordan, Syria, Lebanon, Israel, and the Palestinian Authority, the Russian foreign minister was well received, but he made no apparent progress in putting the peace process back on track.

Russian Policy in South Asia

In the hands of Leonid Brezhnev and his immediate successors, the policy of the Soviet Union in South Asia was a function of three conflicts: Moscow's bitter rivalries with Beijing and with Washington, and (after 1978) the Soviet war in Afghanistan. When Mikhail Gorbachev succeeded in 1989 in withdrawing Soviet forces from Afghanistan and achieving a rapprochement with China, and when the Cold War ended in the following year, the Soviet approach to the region changed markedly. The breakup of the USSR increased the geopolitical distance between Moscow and South Asia, just as Yeltsin's and Kozyrev's initial orientation toward the United States and Europe effectively expanded the psychological distance. But as we have seen, a combination of domestic political pressures and instability in the "near abroad"—especially in the Muslim-majority states of the Caucasus and Central Asia—heightened Russia's attention to the neighboring Asian states.

In Afghanistan, the communist regime of Najibullah had survived the withdrawal of Soviet troops, largely because of the disunity of the opposition mujahideen forces. Upon assuming control in the Kremlin, Yeltsin cut off military aid and raw material supplies to Najibullah, contributing to the collapse of the Afghan communist government in April 1992. Kozyrev visited Kabul the following month and joined in a statement condemning the imperialistic policy that the USSR had conducted in Afghanistan. The new government in Kabul acknowledged that Moscow's political orientation had changed, but it nevertheless asked for reparations from Russia to help in the rebuilding of the devastated country. In no position to comply,

Kozyrev did offer to supply spare parts for the Soviet-made weapons found in great abundance in Afghanistan.

Repressive policies by the new regime against members of the former government created a stream of refugees from Afghanistan to Russia, estimated by the late summer to number as many as 15,000. With conflict continuing in the capital, the Russian Embassy was closed and sealed and embassy personnel were evacuated. When civil war broke out in Tajikistan—the population of which is ethnically similar to a large part of the Afghan population, and which shares a six-hundred-mile border with Afghanistan—Afghan territory became a base for pro-Islamic forces opposing the government of Tajikistan, which was dominated by former communists. Fearing a "domino effect" in Central Asia and parts of the Russian Federation if Tajikistan fell to Muslim extremists, Russia increased its military involvement in the region. By early 1993, an estimated 65,000 Tajiks were in camps in Afghanistan, and many were being actively recruited to guerrilla warfare training centers. Frequent border violations prompted a formal protest from the Tajik foreign ministry, and Russia—whose troops were patrolling the Tajik-Afghan border—was no less alarmed. As one Russian journalist wrote: "[That border] remains Russia's external border. There is no other border, I was told at the Russian Federation Ministry of Security. Events there have a direct bearing on Russian interests."[54]

Border incidents mounted in the summer of 1993, with heavy casualties suffered by Russian troops. When Yeltsin's chief domestic rival, parliament speaker Khasbulatov, made direct overtures toward a settlement with the Afghan government—demonstrating again the fractured nature of Russian foreign-policy making—the Russian foreign ministry demanded that he break off contacts. Meanwhile, the defense ministry was publicly urging that Russian border troops be reinforced, but the government was understandably concerned about public fears of renewed war with Afghanistan. Kozyrev lodged an official protest with Kabul and threatened rocket attacks against rebel bases in the country, and Yeltsin dispatched foreign-intelligence director Primakov to Kabul and Teheran to seek a resolution to the conflict. In September Kozyrev himself visited Kabul, where it was announced that Russia and Afghanistan had agreed on the process for talks and eventual elections in Tajikistan.

Although tensions persisted, the immediate crisis on the Tajikistan-Afghanistan border subsided—until alarms were again sounded three years later by the apparent victory of the militant Islamic Taliban faction in Afghanistan. Supported by Pakistan—and, at least covertly, by the United States—the Taliban opposition forces burst onto the international scene in the summer and fall of 1996, sweeping through Afghanistan, capturing its capital, and routing the more moderate Hekmatyar government. One of the Taliban's first actions was to execute the former communist president, Najibullah. Frightened by the prospect that its crusading pan-Islamic zeal would propel the Taliban northward, and ultimately across the Tajikistan and Uzbekistan borders, the leaders of the Commonwealth of Independent States held an emergency meeting at the beginning of October to discuss possible measures for collective defense.

An article published in the Russian press in September by Evgenii Primakov—by then foreign minister, but identified in his capacity as a member of the Russian Academy of Sciences—underscored the particular threat that Russia saw in the Taliban's form of Islam. Noting that "Islamic fundamentalism" was on the rise—including among the seventeen million Muslims of the Russian Federation—Primakov distinguished between this movement and "Islamic extremism" of the type exhibited in Afghanistan by the Taliban, which threatened to spill over into Tajikistan.

> And not Tajikistan alone. Many people believe, not without reason, that after Tajikistan such a wave could sweep other Central Asian states as well—an event that would undoubtedly have an extremely negative impact both on Russia's security and on the prospects for the development of the CIS. Russia does not oppose Islam as a religion; rather, it seeks, along with many other states, including Islamic ones, to erect a barrier to Islamic extremism.[55]

Wearing his diplomatic hat, Primakov sent messages to the foreign offices of the United States, Britain, Germany, Italy, and other states, calling for joint action to encourage a political settlement in Afghanistan. Primakov made it clear that Moscow was supporting no particular party in the intra-Afghan conflict, although it had no particular liking for the leaders of the Taliban after their brutal execution of Najibullah. Outside mediation efforts never got off the ground, however, and by May 1997, when it defeated the army of Abdul Rashid Dostum and captured the northern stronghold of Mazar-i-Sharif, the Taliban seemed to be on the verge of capturing all of Afghanistan. For Pakistan and for oil interests in the United States, the prospect of a unified country spurred talk of a possible gas pipeline to be built from the rich fields of Turkmenistan through Afghanistan and Pakistan to the Indian Ocean. But for Russia, it posed not simply the economic threat of competition for the existing pipeline route through Russia, but the more immediate fears of Taliban incursions into Tajik or Uzbek territory. With Afghan refugees streaming into Tajikistan, the Russian government issued a stern warning to the Taliban: "The Russian leadership hereby gives notice that if the borders of Commonwealth countries are violated, the mechanisms of the Treaty on Collective Security of the CIS Member States will be activated immediately. Instructions have been issued to the relevant departments."[56]

But the Taliban overreached in the north, alienating local leaders with their harsh policies and suffering military defeats that pushed them back almost to the gates of Kabul by late July 1997. Although the Taliban were still in control of the twenty or so Pashtun-majority provinces, a coalition of other factions dominated the nine provinces inhabited mainly by Tajiks, Uzbeks, and Hazaras. These groups were supported by Russia, the Central Asian states, Iran, and India—all united in fear of the Islamic extremism of which Primakov had warned. Even Pakistan appeared to be backing away from complete support of the Taliban, in favor of some form of coalition government for Afghanistan. The topic was discussed in June 1997 at a meeting in Islamabad which included a Taliban representative and Russia's deputy foreign minister. With no signs of an imminent compromise, however, the prospect appeared to be for continued fighting in this unfortunate country, which had already lost 1.5 million people in more than two decades of war.[57]

During the 1980s, the Soviet Union's military involvement in Afghanistan had influenced Moscow's relationships in the decades-long conflict between India and Pakistan. The latter country served as the main base for the Afghan opposition forces, as well as the conduit for American and Chinese aid to the mujahideen, and its relations with the USSR during the long war were extremely tense. As for India, although it was uncomfortable with the intrusion of superpower military force into the internal struggles of a Third World neighbor, it was sufficiently nervous about the threat of Islamic extremism to keep its concerns muted, especially in light of its unwillingness to jeopardize Soviet support in its conflicts with Pakistan and China. Nevertheless, it was the Sino-Soviet rapprochement and the end of the Cold War, more than Soviet withdrawal from Afghanistan, that appeared to have the greatest direct impact on Moscow's relations on the subcontinent in the 1990s. Absent the ideological and geopolitical struggles with Beijing and Washington, Moscow's security interests in India were considerably diminished. From the standpoint of trade relations as well, it seemed likely that decline was in prospect. The longstanding problem of a lack of complementarity in their respective economies was exacerbated by a mutual shortage of hard currency and a newly competitive relationship in world capital markets. Even the product which had long been Moscow's chief export to India—weaponry—seemed less appealing to military purchasers in New Delhi after the shortcomings of Soviet-made arms and Soviet war-fighting doctrine had been revealed in the Persian Gulf war.

India had become accustomed to receiving more attention from the Kremlin than any other nonaligned country; it was the only Third World country Brezhnev had ever visited as general secretary (and he went twice), and it also received Gorbachev twice, in 1986 and 1988. Thus the fall-off in attentiveness in Gorbachev's last years in office, which continued in Yeltsin's first year, and which resulted from Moscow's changing perceptions of its security and economic needs, was acutely felt and perceived as neglect by New Delhi. The major topic of discussion between the two governments in 1992 concerned the financial exchange rates to be used in settling their current trade transactions, and the prospects for repayment of India's $6 billion debt to Russia. The two sides worked out a trade protocol that called for trade volume to be maintained at the 1991 level of $2.2 billion, with India providing tea, coffee, spices, medicines, and raw materials for consumer-goods production, and Russia providing oil, metals, copper, newsprint, and arms. India did not have hard currency reserves sufficient to pay in convertible currency, but the credits Russia granted for arms sales were on tougher terms than in the prior period.

The single most troublesome transaction in this period had actually been concluded at the beginning of 1991, when the CPSU Central Committee, against the advice of the Soviet foreign ministry, had approved a deal between the Soviet space agency, Glavkosmos, and the Indian Space Research Organization, for the sale of critical rocket technology. India claimed that it needed the cryogenic engines to launch commercial satellites, but the United States charged that the sale of the engines and the technological information for their manufacture would enable India to assemble ballistic missiles, possession of which would alter the regional military balance. When India was assured by Gennadii Burbulis in May 1992 that the Russian government would honor the $250 million deal, the United States angered both countries by threatening to apply sanctions against them.

President Yeltsin's trip to India in January 1993—said to be characterized by an "extremely warm and cordial atmosphere"—halted the downward slide in relations that had begun in 1990, and among the many reasons it pleased his hosts was his reconfirmation that the rocket deal would go through. A breakthrough was achieved in settling the issue of India's debt; Russia agreed to an exchange rate that automatically subtracted two-thirds of the debt, and the remainder was to be repaid over a period of forty-five years. Russia welcomed a recent thaw in India's relations with China, and India did not object to a replacement of the 1971 Indo-Soviet treaty with a new bilateral treaty lacking security clauses.

Russia's continuing sharp disagreement with the United States over the rocket technology sale reportedly led to cancellation of Chernomyrdin's planned visit to Washington in June 1993. But the following month, at the G-7 meeting in Tokyo, Presidents Clinton and Yeltsin worked out a compromise that allowed Russia and India to save face without endangering the

South Asian nuclear balance, while also helping to keep 15,000 Glavkosmos workers employed. Essentially, it provided for Russia to deliver a number of cryogenic booster units and model units for training, but not the technology. India would pledge to use the equipment for peaceful purposes only and not to re-export it.[58]

A few years later, however, the controversy between the United States and Russia over Russian aid to the Indian nuclear program seemed likely to be replayed. Early in 1997 it was revealed that Russia planned to sell two light-water reactors—valued at $1.5 to $2 billion each—for power plants in southern India. Washington protested that the deal would violate a 1992 agreement among nuclear suppliers, which stipulated that nuclear technology could not be sold to nations that are not formally recognized as nuclear weapons states and that do not allow international inspection of all their nuclear facilities. The Russians claimed that the agreement did not apply, since talks about the sale were initiated in 1987. Privately, they argued that the revenues were desperately needed by the atomic energy ministry in order to meet its budget needs.[59]

Indo-Russian trade, despite the ambitious targets that had been set, actually fell to a record low level in 1992, and though it increased more than 40 percent the following year, it still amounted to barely $1 billion. An exchange of visits by the two prime ministers in 1994 produced a series of agreements that sought to revive the commercial relationship, which by then had refocused on the familiar Russian export: armaments. Although India had shopped in the West, and although—as we have noted earlier in this chapter—it was not entirely satisfied with the quality of Russian arms, its lack of hard currency limited its options for modernizing its fleet of military aircraft, and the Russians proved willing to accept flexible payment arrangements. Moscow agreed in 1994 to cooperate in building a plant in India that would produce an upgraded version of the MiG-29 fighter. In 1996 India agreed to buy forty of the more advanced SU-30 fighters for $1.8 billion, and the Russians agreed to open talks on licensing its production in India. The SU-30 would replace India's aging British Jaguars as the air force's main strike element through 2015, and would counter Pakistan's squadrons of U.S.-made F-16s and French Mirage 2000s.[60]

By the time of Prime Minister Deve Gowda's visit in March 1997, it was announced that India had purchased $3 billion in arms from Russia in the past two years, and that the two sides were discussing potential contracts of another $7 billion—a level that would move India ahead of China in the ranks of Moscow's arms customers. Tensions between India and Pakistan were on the rise, and the appetite for arms on the subcontinent was enormous. Included on India's shopping list were Russian MiG-31 interceptors and MiG-AT jet trainers, rocket-firing T-72S tanks, "Msta" self-propelled howitzers, Smerch truck-mounted multi-launch rocket systems, Ka-52 "Alligator" helicopter gunships, Kilo-class attack submarines, and anti-submarine frigates. During the visit India agreed in principle to purchase six S-300V air defense systems, and agreement appeared to be close on the sale of the *Admiral Gorshkov,* an aircraft-carrying cruiser. However, Yeltsin was unable to deliver on his promise to Gowda to block the sale to Ukraine of key components for the Soviet-designed T-80UD tanks, 320 of which Pakistan had agreed to purchase from Ukraine.[61] Beyond the commercial attraction, the continued Russian ties to India represented a long-term hedge against a possible downturn in the Sino-Russian relationship. As the Russian ambassador to India put it—perhaps too optimistically—"If we are able to maintain close, friendly ties with India, that will be the best guarantee that China will make no territorial claims on our Far East."[62]

While Pakistan's importance to Russia has remained relatively high because of Moscow's concerns about the stability of the states of Central Asia, an exchange of visits by the two countries' foreign ministers in 1993 and 1994, aimed at normalizing relations and increasing trade, bore little fruit. Reports that Pakistan's prime minister would visit Moscow in 1994 proved premature, as the visit fell victim to Russia's renewed "tilt" toward India. Pakistan was not without alternatives, however, and it went shopping for arms in Ukraine while seeking to build its relations with the Muslim states of Central Asia. An October 1996 visit by the Pakistani president to Kazakhstan gained an endorsement from President Nursultan Nazarbaev for the idea of holding a referendum on the status of Kashmir. And, to Moscow's evident displeasure, the Pakistani official was also reported to be discussing with the Central Asian states the proposed Afghan-Pakistan pipeline as an alternative to the existing Russian pipeline.

Elections in Pakistan early in 1997 produced a new government, which adopted a less confrontational policy toward Russia. The country's foreign minister visited Moscow in July 1997 for wide-ranging talks, which produced press reports of closer relations. Pakistan invited Russia's assistance in bringing about a resolution of the Kashmir dispute, while Primakov advised his Pakistani counterpart that his country should avoid the Soviet Union's mistake of getting too deeply involved in the Afghan quagmire.[63]

Upon his appointment as foreign minister in January 1996, Primakov had listed nonproliferation of weapons of mass destruction among Russia's priority interests. Nevertheless, Moscow has not been in the forefront of international efforts to this end, and Washington has publicly accused it of assisting both Indian and Iranian nuclear programs. Thus, it was not especially surprising when the Russians failed to heed the U.S. call for G-8 sanctions against India and Pakistan when those countries tested nuclear weapons in May 1998. The Russians expressed regret, and Yeltsin promised to "make every effort to somehow overcome the problem" during his scheduled visit to "our very good friend" India, later in 1998. Although it must have shared the global concern about the heightened risk of nuclear war, Moscow evidently saw no benefit in alienating India in the face of an irreversible reality.

Beyond the Borders of the CIS: Southeast Asia, Africa, and Latin America

The post–Cold War period witnessed a considerable decline in the level of Moscow's interest and activity in the substantial regions of the "non-West" that are distant from the borders of the former Soviet Union. Facing a much reduced threat from the United States and China, and increasingly burdened with the financial costs of trying to maintain its global reach, the USSR under Gorbachev had participated in settling regional conflicts in Southeast Asia, Africa, and Latin America. This had allowed it to cut substantially the level of its involvement in these three regions.

As we have noted in chapter 3, Moscow's pressure on Vietnam to withdraw its troops from Cambodia helped to bring about the Sino-Soviet rapprochement, but it also allowed the Soviets to cut back the cost of their presence in Vietnam. Whereas the number of Soviet-Vietnamese summits in the Gorbachev period had averaged two per year prior to his visit to Beijing, there were none in 1990, and only one—described in the Russian press as "difficult and complicated"—in 1991. Trade between the two states was moved to a hard currency basis in January 1991, precipitating a fall in Moscow's share of Vietnam's trade from 60 percent in 1990 to 2 percent in 1996. In May 1992 the last Russian military advisors were withdrawn from Vietnam. Vietnam's premier Vo Van Kiet visited Moscow in June 1994 to sign new economic agreements, but the talks did not produce a new "cornerstone" document to replace the 1978 security treaty. Kozyrev journeyed to Hanoi in July 1995 to announce a Russian-Vietnamese agreement to keep the former Soviet naval base at Cam Ranh Bay open through 2004, and Chernomyrdin followed in November 1997 on a mission to boost still-sagging trade levels. But little progress was made in settling the issue of Vietnam's $10 billion debt to Russia.

There was much greater Russian interest in the enormous market potential of the noncommunist countries of Southeast Asia. Russia joined the Pacific Economic Cooperation Council in 1993, and Moscow's representatives attended the annual conferences of the foreign ministers of the Association of Southeast Asian Nations (ASEAN), first as observers and then as official "dialogue partners," as well as the ASEAN forums on regional security. At the 1996 foreign ministers' conference, Primakov described ASEAN as an "influential center of the developing multipolar world" and stated Russia's desire to have open access to the ASEAN free-trade zone scheduled for 2003. But a moratorium that had been placed on new membership in the Asian and Pacific Economic Council (APEC) kept Russia, as a relatively minor trading presence in the region, "on the outside looking in" with respect to the most ambitious of the new regional economic organizations. With Japan's assistance, the Russians finally were admitted to the APEC club late in 1997, though without expectations that their membership would produce "a shower of gold."[64]

When it came to Russia's most competitive product, there was relatively little interest among the ASEAN nations. Until 1997, only Malaysia had concluded a substantial arms deal with Moscow, and this was negotiated with considerable difficulty. A visit from Vice President Rutskoi to Malaysia in March 1993—the first to that country from a Russian leader—underscored Russia's interest in selling MiG-29M fighters. In the ensuing months, arms dealers from several Russian agencies were reported to be practically tripping over one another in Kuala Lumpur, each seeking to be the "lead agency" entitled to a sales commission. In the process, U.S. arms merchants entered the competition, substantially cutting their prices and ultimately dividing the Malaysian order. By the time Deputy Prime Minister Soskovets concluded the deal in June 1994, it was for only eighteen MiG-29s at a price of $775 million, part of which Russia accepted in palm oil. Nevertheless, the transaction was seen as a breakthrough for Moscow in the lucrative Southeast Asian arms market.

In August 1997 Indonesia—irritated by U.S. criticism of its human rights policies in East Timor—canceled an agreement to purchase F-16 fighters from the United States and signed an agreement with Russia for the purchase of twelve SU-30 warplanes. As talks developed, the deal expanded to include eight Mi-17 helicopters, infantry fighting vehicles, and armored personnel carriers. Originally valued at a half billion dollars, with payment primarily through barter of palm oil, coffee, and other products, the deal increased to $1 billion, with half to be paid in hard currency. But this agreement, together with prospects for further Russian arms sales in Asia, was jeopardized in November 1997 by the severe financial crisis that rocked the economies of Indonesia, Malaysia, South Korea, and other prospective customers.

The civil war in Angola was another conflict where Gorbachev's consent to a political settlement finally enabled the Soviet Union to extricate itself from a long and costly military involvement. The termination of this conflict, together with the de-escalation of violence in the Horn of Africa, provided an opportunity for Moscow to slash its expensive aid programs in sub-Saharan Africa, from a volume of 12.5 billion rubles in 1989 to 400 million rubles in 1991. To continue making soft loans to countries essentially peripheral to Moscow's interests would be to throw good money after bad, since by the end of 1991 these states already owed 14 billion rubles— 16 percent of the total debt outstanding to the USSR.

Angola alone owed the equivalent of $5 billion—an amount equal to that owed by all the other sub-Saharan African states combined; and like some of the other major debtors to the former Soviet Union, it simply refused to repay the debt to the new Russian government. So the Angolan government informed Foreign Minister Kozyrev, who was visiting the country as part of a five-day tour of Africa in February and March of 1992. There was little the Russians could do about the situation, and in fact they agreed to resume limited shipments of defensive weapons to Angola in 1993, when the civil war resumed.

Kozyrev's trip was intended to demonstrate that Russia was not giving up its global interests, but the facts argued otherwise. In light of the economic difficulties on both ends, there were few trade opportunities; indeed, Africa accounted for only 2 percent of Russia's foreign trade in 1992. Shortly after Kozyrev's trip, the foreign ministry announced that it was closing nine Russian embassies in Africa as an economizing measure. Toward the end of the year, four representatives of African ambassadors in Moscow met with acting Russian Prime Minister Gaidar to express their concern about Russia's apparent lack of interest in the continent, but there was little that Gaidar could do to reassure them.

South Africa was the one country of sub-Saharan Africa where the Russian government perceived significant trade and investment possibilities. The primary destination on Kozyrev's 1992 tour was Pretoria, where he participated in ceremonies to establish diplomatic relations with the De Klerk government. President De Klerk paid a state visit to Moscow in June of the same year, and announced that South Africa would extend a 100-million-rand credit to Russia. Yeltsin's communist predecessors in the Kremlin had long given support to the African National Congress (ANC), but the change of Moscow's ideological orientation was so dramatic that it was June 1993 before an ANC delegation was even received at the Russian foreign ministry. Thus when ANC leader Nelson Mandela became president of South Africa in May 1994, Moscow found itself in the awkward spot of having to rebuild its relationships with the former revolutionaries who now headed the government. Not surprisingly, the area in which progress was most notable was in the field of "military-technical cooperation." In July 1995, the two governments concluded a military cooperation agreement that called for joint exercises and training, and that provided for Russian aircraft engines to be sold to South Africa for use in its French-made Mirages. On the whole, however, with South Africa as with the rest of the continent, Russia's interests and involvement were at the lowest level of priority.

Latin America was the other region of low priority for Yeltsin's Russia, and there would have been relatively little activity at all had it not been for the need to look after the very sizable investments Moscow had made over a period of three decades in Cuba. Fidel Castro had enjoyed more success than most other Third World leaders in keeping the Soviet Union involved in his country during the Gorbachev period. Indeed, a friendship treaty between the two countries had been concluded during Gorbachev's April 1989 trip to Havana. Although the treaty made no reference to defense cooperation or to consultations in case of threat, Soviet weapons continued to flow to Cuba.

After August 1991, however, Gorbachev evidently felt that he needed the support of the United States badly enough that—without consulting Castro—he announced that the brigade of Soviet troops that had been stationed in Cuba since 1979 would be withdrawn. Relations between Moscow and Havana deteriorated rapidly on all fronts, especially after the ideological shift in Russia. The level of trade between the two fell in 1992 to 7 percent of the 1991 volume, and Cuba stopped making payments on its debt to Moscow (which was estimated by Russian officials to total $20 billion). Russia made it clear that Cuba would receive no more credits for the purchase of arms, and it demanded that Russian specialists remaining in Cuba be paid in hard currency. And finally, Russia voted in the United Nations Commission on Human Rights to condemn Cuba for mass violations of human rights. For his part, Castro announced in September 1992 that the nuclear power plant at Juragua, which was being constructed with Soviet assistance at a cost to date of $1.2 billion, would be mothballed. "And so the last beacon of 'fraternal cooperation' in Cuba is being extinguished," wrote a Russian journalist.[65]

However, the shift in Russian policy toward "pragmatic nationalism" soon produced a halt to the deterioration of relations. Moscow evidently decided that it needed to maintain some level of trade relations with Cuba in order to recoup any of its huge debt, and it also was reluctant to lose a key military asset in Cuba—an electronic tracking station and listening post at Lourdes that was capable, among other things, of tracking U.S. missile launches. In November 1992 the two countries concluded an important but limited trade agreement—essentially a bartering of two products—which contemplated the delivery of 1.5 million tons of sugar in return for 3.3

million metric tons of Russian oil and other petroleum products. They also agreed in principle to continue construction of the nuclear plant, contingent on finding a third country to provide financing. And although they failed to resolve the question of the Cuban debt, they did agree that Russia could continue to lease the Lourdes facility. This agreement was supplemented the following summer with a Russian promise of $380 million in credits to Cuba to allow continuation of the construction of a dozen vital projects. Included in this amount was $30 million to pay for the mothballing of the Juragua power plant.

In December 1993 a Cuban delegation led by Deputy Prime Minister Lionel Soto visited Moscow to renew the barter agreement, while seeking to expand trade by establishing direct relationships between Cuban and Russian firms. In principle, the Russians agreed to barter 4 million metric tons of petroleum for 1.5 million tons of sugar; they noted, however, that the numbers were soft, since Cuban sugar production had fallen and less than one million tons had actually been delivered to Russia in 1993. There were abundant signs of discord in the conversations. The Cubans reportedly demanded an annual lease payment of one billion dollars for the Lourdes station; the Russian Ministry of Defense agreed to pay one-sixth that amount. And Soto gave an interview in which he refused to speak of a Cuban debt, but rather referred to "mutual obligations"—a brazen concept according to which Moscow actually owed Cuba considerable sums: "We estimate your country's military presence and the losses Cuba has incurred as a result of the unilateral renunciation of economic obligations at approximately $40 billion."[66]

As domestic political winds in Russia continued to shift toward the hard-liners, the government demonstrated that its foreign policy was not subservient to the United States by making more concessions to Castro. In October 1994 Russia—which had previously abstained on the issue—voted in the United Nations General Assembly in favor of urging the United States to lift its embargo on Cuba. The following spring, Moscow shifted its vote from "yes" to "abstain" on the question of condemning Cuba for human rights violations. The Russian first deputy minister of defense visited Cuba in November 1994 to conclude an arrangement for paying an annual rent of $200 million on the Lourdes communications facility, to be paid in energy resources, lumber, and military spare parts.

Continuing the pressure on Yeltsin, the Duma held hearings on Russian-Cuban relations in January 1995, with the Cuban ambassador present as an honored guest. The Ministry of Finance reported that in just three years the volume of Russian-Cuban trade had declined 92 percent, from $9 billion to $710 million. Recent barter agreements had not been fulfilled by Cuba, whose sugar production had fallen sharply. The ministry estimated Cuba's debt at 17 billion transferable rubles, which Moscow deemed equivalent to the same number of dollars. Noting that Havana had made no payments since 1991, the official added that Cuba was insisting that the debt should be calculated at a ratio of $1 per 50 transferable rubles. Notwithstanding these adverse economic trends, nationalist legislators called for full restoration of political and economic ties, and for punishment of those (Russians?) responsible for the collapse of the Cuban economy.

As he had to several other key Third World countries with anti-American orientations, Oleg Soskovets, the hard-line deputy prime minister, led a large delegation to Cuba in October 1995. He sought to expand Moscow's once thriving ties with Castro, noting, "Russia regards Cuba as a strategic partner and intends to develop bilateral military-technical cooperation with it." Again, Cuba's unserviced debt was overlooked, and the eager Russian officials—discussing various additional projects, including the Juragua nuclear plant, for which Cuba could pay in sugar—were not deterred by the fact that Cuba had yet to meet its obligations under the sugar-for-oil barter arrangements.[67]

The following May, Evgenii Primakov paid an official visit to Cuba, where he declared that relations with Cuba were now a foreign-policy priority for Russia. The Russian foreign minister devoted most of his energies to denouncing the Helms-Burton Act, recently passed by the U.S. Congress, which sought to punish foreign companies that did business with Cuba. In an unusual gesture, Fidel Castro brought a large government entourage to the Russian embassy to meet with Primakov, and he expressed satisfaction with the visit as he saw Primakov off. Nevertheless, there appeared to be little that was achieved, beyond the political showiness; the concrete fruits seemed limited to one agreement on cultural and scientific cooperation. Both sides appeared to play down recent accusations that Cuban foreign trade officials had been lining their own pockets by delaying sugar deliveries to Moscow, while allowing French trading companies to sell Cuban sugar to Russia at inflated prices.

No progress was made during Primakov's visit on the difficult issue of debt repayment. However, a few months later a possible precedent for settlement was negotiated between Russia and Nicaragua on repayment of that country's $3.4 billion debt. After stubborn bargaining, Moscow agreed to write off 90 percent of the debt and schedule repayment of the remainder over a fifteen-year period, with interest at the prevailing market rates. In bitter tones, an *Izvestia* correspondent drew a parallel to Cuba's huge debt:

> This is a major factor, considering that Cuba, a habitual defaulter, would like to revise the whole system of settling debts owed to the former USSR. . . .

Now the wily Fidel is demanding that the entire debt be recalculated at the current dollar-ruble exchange rate. Were Moscow to accept such terms, the enormous debt owed it by developing countries—at least $140 billion—would be reduced by at least 5,500 times, to a ludicrous sum less than one-tenth what Nicaragua intends to pay us.[68]

Significantly, Primakov did not confine his Latin American journey to Cuba. His visit extended also to two important oil-producing countries—Mexico and Venezuela—whose economies, though currently depressed, had long-term growth prospects, and whose foreign policies had occasionally demonstrated irritation with Washington. In both countries, Primakov signed agreements on cooperation in economic, scientific-technical, and cultural fields, as well as on joint efforts to combat crime and trafficking in illegal drugs. The following year, the peripatetic foreign minister was back in Latin America, visiting Brazil, Argentina, and Colombia and spreading his message about the necessity of multipolarity in world politics. As he had elsewhere, Primakov won the plaudits of the Russian press for his efforts to demonstrate independence in Russia's foreign policy, and to further its continuing interests in the world beyond the former USSR. As the foreign minister expressed his objective, "As a great power, Russia naturally should have multilateral ties with all continents."[69]

For the most part, however, Moscow's interests in the "non-West" in the period since the ending of the Cold War have been distinctly more limited than in the prior period. The termination of the global ideological and geopolitical struggle with the United States, together with the significant limitations on Russia's ability to project economic influence, has caused a reorientation of Moscow's priorities to those areas that border the post-Soviet states. As we have noted above, however, the end of the Cold War has not brought peace to the countries of Asia, Africa, and Latin America. Thus, the inescapable fact that billions of dollars in advanced weaponry have been Moscow's dominant export to these regions is a sobering portent that future conflicts could pose even greater dangers to world peace.

8

Conclusion

Over the course of time, Russian foreign policy has exhibited many profound shifts in direction. Perhaps less obvious has been the continuity in behavior of governments headed by tsars, commissars, and presidents. In many respects, Russian foreign policy has been similar to that of other great powers, and in other respects it has been unique. We conclude this survey of Russian foreign policy with an analysis of the continuity and change we have observed in Russia's relations with the world, and of the degree to which that policy can be deemed distinctive.

Continuity and the International System

To begin with the continuities and similarities, we note that as a general rule of statecraft Russia has pursued *balance-of-power* policies. (Admittedly, it has not always fared well in these, as evidenced by the disaster of the 1939 Nazi-Soviet Pact,[1] but in that respect also, Russia has shared a characteristic with the other great powers in the world.) In principle, balance-of-power policies are the measures taken by governments whose interests or security are threatened, to enhance their power by whatever means are available.[2] The most common technique associated with the balance of power is forming or joining military alliances. But the balance of power may also entail, *inter alia,* military buildups, intervention in weaker countries, or resort to war. Essentially it involves the mobilization of power to countervail the power of an enemy or potential adversary. Thus, tsarist Russia was a member of the Triple Entente (with Great Britain and France) in the period leading up to World War I, as a counter to the Triple Alliance headed by Imperial Germany. In the Soviet period the Warsaw Pact served as a military counterpart to the North Atlantic Treaty Organization.

The Russian Federation differs from preceding regimes in not being a member of any military alliance. But that is because post-Soviet Russia, unlike preceding regimes, has no major enemies or threats to its national security. Nevertheless, it does have rivals and competitors—for example,

Iran and Turkey, to the south. And some aspects of Russia's foreign policy in Central Asia are strikingly reminiscent of the "great game" of power politics played by European powers in that region in the nineteenth century.[3] And in Europe, an example of Moscow's continuing pursuit of balance-of-power policies is Russia's opposition to NATO expansion.

The enduring goals pursued by Russia through its foreign policy have placed primary emphasis on ensuring national security, promoting the economic well-being of the country, and enhancing national prestige. In this respect, Russia's behavior is not markedly different from that of most great powers. But how these goals have been interpreted and achieved has changed with time and circumstances.

We can explain the similarities and continuities of Russian behavior in large part as a consequence of the *international system* which conditions the foreign policies of all states. As the primary units or actors in international politics, states—though in some respects interdependent—operate from the premise that they are sovereign and independent entities. Their independence stems from the lack of a global political authority to govern all states. Thus, the international system is decentralized; each nation is free in principle to determine the range of policies it will pursue for itself, including at times the use of force. Sometimes the term "anarchic" is used to describe this feature of the international system.[4]

In reality, foreign policy rarely expresses the principle of national sovereignty (or anarchy) in absolute terms. Just as states are not fully constrained by international norms, economic interdependence, or the power of other states, so they are never totally free of such constraints. But the larger and more powerful a state is, the greater is its freedom of action; small and weak states are more limited. Precisely because there is no world government or protective mechanism for nation-states, each must constantly be on guard to protect its security and interests from those states that periodically emerge on the world scene as a threat to others. In the words of Kenneth N. Waltz:

> Each state pursues its own interests, however defined, in ways that it judges best. Force is a means of achieving the external ends of states because there exists no consistent, reliable process of reconciling the conflicts of interest that inevitably arise among similar units in a condition of anarchy.[5]

Of the many interests pursued by states, none is more important than survival—maintaining territorial integrity and political independence. Unlike the individual in domestic society, the sovereign state is unprotected by legal institutions (police, courts, militias, and so on) and must look instead to the tools of statecraft—diplomacy, armaments, political and military alignments—for self-protection.

Explaining Variability in Foreign Policy Behavior

The international system defines the broad parameters of foreign policy behavior, but obviously it cannot explain the specific decisions which determine the behavior of states in the realm of international politics. While theory might have predicted that Moscow in 1939 would seek an alliance with some European power, it could not account for Stalin's choice of Germany over Great Britain and France. Exactly a half century later, theory also could not have predicted that the leaders of the Soviet Union would simply stand aside as the Warsaw Pact disintegrated before their eyes. Foreign policy cannot be predicted because it is the outcome of a large number of constantly changing variables.

Thus, for example, Soviet policy during the Cold War exhibited considerable variability, notwithstanding the fundamental antagonism between the communist world and the West. East-West relations were at times close to military confrontation, and at times they were cooperative. The arms race was interspersed with arms control agreements. Former friends became enemies, and intervention gave way to "new thinking." In a word, throughout the Soviet period there were multiple forces at play which constantly pushed Moscow in new directions.

In a study of Soviet foreign policy after World War II, the authors of this text identified seven general variables which we believe influenced the changing direction of Soviet foreign policy.[6] These were not the only factors influencing Moscow, but they were among the most important. These variables are:

(1) the change in the structure of the international system from bipolarity to multipolarity;

(2) the growth of polycentrism in the international communist movement, followed by the collapse of the movement altogether;

(3) the development of a military technology that makes possible the total destruction of an adversary;

(4) the achievement of military parity between the Soviet Union and the United States, followed by the collapse of the USSR as a superpower;

(5) the transition of the Soviet regime from a totalitarian system to an authoritarian oligarchy and then to a fragmented polity;

(6) the failure of the command economy;

(7) the differences reflected in the leadership of different personalities, from Stalin to Khrushchev to Brezhnev to Gorbachev.

Some of these variables were of an external nature reflecting changes in the international environment, and others were domestic or internal in nature. Together they reflect the fact that foreign policy has its roots in both domestic and foreign forces.

As we survey Russian foreign policy in the post-Soviet period, we can identify five broad underlying factors which collectively explain much of the change and variability in Russian foreign policy. These observations are necessarily preliminary; independent Russia has existed less than a decade, and it can be expected that over a longer period of time new determining forces will become evident. We consider the following particularly critical in explaining Russian foreign policy:

(1) the change in the structure of the international system from bipolarity to multipolarity;
(2) the decline in Russian military capability;
(3) Russia's transformation from a command economy to a market economy;
(4) Russia's integration into the global economy and its increasing reliance on the global market;
(5) Russia's domestic politics and the struggle between Yeltsin and Russian nationalists.

We have noted above the general impact of the international system on foreign policy. But clearly, the international system does not possess a fixed or unchanging structure; the number and hierarchy of great powers changes over time. The term *polarity* is commonly used to describe the structure of the international system. A universe dominated by one great power would be designated "unipolar"; one dominated by two powers (or blocs) is "bipolar"; and one characterized by several powers (usually five or more) is "multipolar." What impact does the structure of the international system have upon foreign policy and international politics? While political scientists are in disagreement about the precise impact of polarity on international politics, most would agree that there is a connection.[7]

A bipolar system is characterized as one in which the two dominating powers are juxtaposed against each other in an unceasing struggle for power. Each side sees the other as a deadly adversary and both view international politics as a "zero-sum game." That is, each adversary views any gain for the other as a loss for itself. International politics in a bipolar system is characterized by continuous tension and frequent crisis. There are occasional military clashes, but more commonly (because of the power of the adversary) the struggle is fought by means of economic competition, propaganda, and subversion.

By contrast a multipolar system is more benign. There is a competitive feature to international politics, but that competition is moderated by the fact that each state views the others as potential allies as well as adversaries. Relations between states in a multipolar system are thus more fluid and less antagonistic.[8] Most political scientists consider multipolarity to be more stable than bipolarity.[9]

The bipolar world comes closer to describing the cold war between the Soviet bloc and the Western bloc (1945–90). There was no cold war between the Soviet Union and the West before 1945 for the basic reason that international politics was multipolar and not bipolar. Indeed, bipolarity on a global scale had never existed until the end of World War II. The only examples of bipolarity prior to the twentieth century were within geographic regions.[10]

With the collapse of the Warsaw Pact and the disintegration of the Soviet Union, the international system was transformed from a bipolar to a multipolar one. (Though the United States became the most powerful state in the world, it did not dominate world politics in a way that would create a "unipolar" world.) Relations between post-Soviet Russia and the West quickly began to resemble those normally engaged in between states in a multipolar world.

We already have noted the improvement in 1992 in Moscow's most important relationship in the West—that with the United States—with negotiation of START II and American support for Russia's domestic reform. But Russia no longer treated the West as a monolith. Yeltsin moved to develop a differentiated relationship with the countries of Europe. Annual summits were planned between the presidents of Russia and Germany and Russia and France, independent of those between Yeltsin and Clinton. Annual summits were also agreed upon between Yeltsin and China's Jiang Zemin. At one of these summits in the spring of 1997, Yeltsin and Jiang signed a Joint Declaration on a Multipolar World and the Formation of a New International Order, in which the two presidents explicitly declared:

> The cold war has ended. The bipolar system has disappeared. Positive trends toward the formation of a multipolar world are developing at an accelerated pace, and relations are changing among the major states, including former cold war adversaries. Regional organizations for economic cooperation are showing significant vitality. Diversity in the political, economic, and cultural

development of all countries is becoming firmly established, and the role of forces that favor peace and broad international cooperation is growing.[11]

In the new multipolar world of the 1990s, Russia could and did pursue a more flexible policy toward its friends and enemies.

Whatever the international structure, the ability of a state to play an active role in world politics is linked to its *military capability*. Military power is traditionally assumed to be a prime shaper of foreign policy because it is the most immediately employable power asset for protecting populations, controlling territory, and coercing others. To a degree, economic power can compensate for military weakness—Japan is a case in point—but traditionally a state's capacity to project force abroad has been a vital element in defining its status as a great power. There would have been no cold war without the power of the Red Army backed by a nuclear capability. That explains why the Soviet Union between 1917 and 1945 was not a superpower and why there was no cold war until the USSR emerged following the defeat of Nazi Germany as the strongest military power in Europe.

Eventually the Soviet Union achieved an overall relative military parity with the West. With combat forces numbering in excess of four million, the Red Army was twice the size of the U.S. army. By most quantitative measures, the Warsaw Pact had more weapons than NATO, though qualitatively the West was superior. Since exact comparisons of capability are difficult to measure, it was assumed on both sides that a rough parity existed. Soviet military strength—both conventional and nuclear—continued to grow well into the Gorbachev era.

Militarily, the Russian Federation is another story. Following the collapse of the Warsaw Pact in 1991, Soviet and then Russian military capability has steadily declined. The Russian army is a hollow shell of its Soviet counterpart. At the heart of the problem is Russia's inability to finance a powerful fighting machine. Soldiers brought home from Eastern Europe were inadequately housed. The government's severe cash shortage led to the nonpayment of soldiers' wages. Equipment has not been maintained adequately. Russia's pilots have not been able to train adequately. Research and development of weapons have been sacrificed. As a consequence, morale has plummeted. Among Russian conscripts life has been so bleak that many have resorted to desertion or even suicide. If there were any doubt about the military collapse, the performance of Russian forces in Chechnia removed it. A ragtag army of Chechen guerrillas and combat forces defeated the armed forces of a country enormously larger and richer. Even when Chechen guerrillas invaded Russia twice in 1995, Russian forces were unable to prevent the escape of their leaders.

Yeltsin was bitterly condemned for the decline of the armed forces—of which he was constantly reminded. In the spring of 1997, when he fired Igor Rodionov as minister of defense, he exclaimed: "I am not merely dissatisfied. I am outraged . . . over the condition of the armed forces."[12] Yeltsin's proposed military reform contemplated substantial reductions in troop strength and ultimately the creation of a professional army without conscription. But at its root, the problem of military reform was economic. The president had been convinced of the need to reduce spending on defense, while many of his officers wanted an increase in military spending.

Russia's size, skilled population, resources, and nuclear weapons guarantee its ongoing status as a great power, but its military weakness, so long as it persists, will limit Russia's influence in world affairs. In relations with states of the near abroad, Russian influence will be paramount, because these states are even weaker. But in Europe, Russia will have to concede when the West is united on political or security issues (as it was on NATO expansion and ultimately was on Bosnia). From the perspective of its neighbors, Russia's military weakness can even create special problems. Russia's borders have become so porous that smuggling is widespread, and there is even a concern that nuclear materials may be illegally dispersed from military stockpiles. There is in addition the danger that dissatisfaction with the regime by the military may lead to efforts to topple or destabilize the constitutionally elected government.

Another variable is the transformation of Russia *from a command economy to a market economy*. Although that transformation has been mired in controversy in both Russia and the West, there is a general consensus that the old system has now been replaced by the new, though Russians disagree regarding the pace and scope of change. But economic production is now in private hands, the ruble is fully convertible, and prices are free to fluctuate with supply and demand.[13]

From the beginning Yeltsin has recognized that Russia needs both Western assistance and investment. And his government has solicited the advice of Western economists such as Jeffrey Sachs of Harvard University and Anders Aslund of Sweden. Indeed, reformist members of the Russian government, such as Egor Gaidar, Anatolii Chubais, and Boris Nemtsov, have maintained close relations with Western advisors, to the great suspicion of their critics in the Russian parliament.

United States economic aid for Russian reform began in 1992 with the passage of the Freedom Support Act. It has continued throughout the 1990s. This aid is defended in the U.S. Congress on the following grounds: "The primary U.S. interest in Russia and the NIS [newly independent states] is to prevent their reemergence as a security threat to the West. This can be best achieved if these states make a transition to market economies and democratic systems of government."[14] Total assistance to Russia from all sources in 1992–93 was around $60 billion. In direct foreign investment, Russia received $1.554 billion in 1992, $2.956 billion in 1993, and $3.558 billion in the first half of 1994.[15]

If Russia's economic reform succeeds in raising productivity and the country's standard of living, it seems clear that the economic linkages to the developed countries of the West will tend to promote cooperative relations with these countries. Increasingly, the resort to war for whatever reasons will be counterproductive to the larger goals of the regime.

Related to Russia's transformation from a command to a market economy is the growing linkage of Russia's economy to the *global economy*. The extent of that linkage should not be exaggerated, because Russia continues to impose significant barriers to the free flow of goods and capital between itself and the world. However, compared to the autarchic policies of the Soviet period, democratizing Russia has gone a long way toward joining the global economy. The ruble is now a convertible currency and is thus subject to the influence of capital flows throughout the world. Russia now sells stocks on the international market as well as domestically. Legislation has been enacted to encourage foreign investment. And Russia has joined international institutions like the International Monetary Fund (IMF) and World Bank as a means for promoting macroeconomic stabilization.

Economists differ on the full significance for national economies of the growing integration of the world economy; but at the least, that integration limits governments in their freedom of action in the pursuit of domestic economic policies. Boris Yeltsin has conveyed his desire for Russia to coordinate its macroeconomic policies with those of the major industrial states by joining the G-7 group of developed states. Russia is also trying to gain admission to the World Trade Organization.

The clearest evidence of international influence over the economic transformation of Russia is the reliance of the Yeltsin administration on the IMF and World Bank for assistance in macroeconomic stabilization. In July 1993 the IMF's executive board approved a credit to Russia of $1.5 billion, and in April 1994 a second credit was authorized. In February 1996 a three-year credit of $10.2 billion was extended to Russia by the IMF. The objective of these loans has been to stabilize the country's currency, stop inflation, and strengthen the conditions for fiscal stability with economic growth. IMF credits are always given conditionally and involve intrusive measures, many of which are politically controversial. Among the conditions imposed on the Russian government were the termination of export duties, improvement in tax collection, reduction of state subsidies, reduction of budget deficits, and reduction of credit through the banking system.[16]

The foreign policy implications of economic globalization are clear. War becomes more costly, particularly if it involves states on whose assistance Russia relies. So long as membership in international institutions is important to Russia, Moscow can be expected to make every effort to resolve its difference with the members of those institutions by peaceful means.

Political Leadership and the Future of Russian Foreign Policy

Finally, there is the role of *political leadership* in guiding Russian relations with the world. Democratizing Russia has had only the leadership of Boris Yeltsin. His political career has been a shifting one marked by many contradictions. From a communist *apparatchik,* he transformed himself into a democratic leader. The record of his two administrations as president reveals on balance a committed "Atlanticist" who sought cooperation with the West in the rebuilding of his country from the ravages of communism. If at times Yeltsin detoured from the Atlanticist path, one might find a partial explanation in his autobiographical self-description:

> Where is this Yeltsin taking us?
> I think the answer will intrigue many people. I am not presenting people with a global strategic goal. I am not setting my sights on some shining peak that must be scaled. Nor am I trying to wipe out the entire path traversed until now.
> No. The chief goal of this restless president is Russia's tranquillity.[17]

Yeltsin's Atlanticist orientation was personified in his choice of Andrei Kozyrev as foreign minister. Though from time to time Kozyrev gave utterance to nationalist sentiments, his influence was overwhelmingly pro-Western. And for that he incurred the wrath of communists and nationalists in the legislative branch of government (both the Supreme Soviet and State Duma). Eventually Yeltsin was induced to replace Kozyrev with Evgenii Primakov. Primakov was not anti-Western, but neither was he pro-West. He turned out to be a bridge between both orientations. The term most frequently used to describe Primakov was "pragmatist."

In post-Soviet Russia a new influential force emerged in politics—public opinion. The shift to the right reflected the growth of a nationalist sentiment far less accommodating to the West. The elections in 1993 brought Vladimir Zhirinovskii's Liberal Democratic Party to the forefront in the legislature. Two years later Gennadii Ziuganov's Communist Party of the Russian Federation emerged as the largest party in the Duma. Though their views were opposed to Yeltsin's, Yeltsin recognized the political forces that brought these groups to power. From 1993 on, he sought limited accommodation with his rivals. He won election to a second term by moving to the right, even to the point of bringing Aleksandr Lebed, a nationalist rival, into his administration. Clearly, domestic politics is now a significant factor in Russian foreign policy, even if we cannot predict the direction Russian politics will take in the future.

Thus, as Russia and the world move toward the millennium, there is a great deal of uncertainty regarding the future. Most of the factors we have examined point toward a period of peace and cooperation with the other great powers. Yet there are contradictions: NATO expansion eastward is premised on a potential Russian threat; the United States is even encouraging consideration of Baltic membership in NATO.[18] Russians are opposed. Russia is assisting Iran in the construction of nuclear power facilities; the United States is opposed. Russia and France have sought to bring an end to sanctions against Iraq; the United States and Great Britain support sanctions. Russia, Europe, and the United States are determined competitors for arms sales throughout the world. Nevertheless, these contradictions were relatively small compared to the larger forces at work, which produced more cooperation between Russia and its neighbors than at any previous time in the century just ending.

Notes

Chapter 1: Tsarist Roots

1. Paul Kennedy, *The Rise and Fall of the Great Powers: Economic Change and Military Conflict from 1500 to 2000* (New York: Random House, 1987), pp. 94–95.

2. Ibid., pp. 170–74.

3. Hugh Seton-Watson, *The Decline of Imperial Russia, 1855–1914* (New York: Frederick A. Praeger, 1952), pp. 22–24.

4. Ibid., pp. 90–93.

5. Ibid., p. 102.

6. Quoted in ibid., p. 213.

7. Kennedy, *Rise and Fall of the Great Powers,* p. 233. Much of the following paragraph is drawn from pp. 232–41 of this book.

8. Ibid., p. 240.

9. Henry Kissinger, *Diplomacy* (New York: Simon & Schuster, 1994), p. 140.

10. Ibid., p. 141.

11. Martin Malia, "Tradition, Ideology, and Pragmatism in the Formation of Russian Foreign Policy," in *The Emergence of Russian Foreign Policy,* eds. Leon Aron and Kenneth M. Jensen (Washington, DC: United States Institute of Peace Press, 1994), p. 41.

12. Quoted in John P. LeDonne, *The Russian Empire and the World, 1700–1917: The Geopolitics of Expansion and Containment* (New York: Oxford University Press, 1997), p. 368.

13. Kissinger, *Diplomacy,* p. 175.

14. Ibid., pp. 172–73.

15. Malia, "Tradition, Ideology, and Pragmatism," pp. 41, 45.

16. Kissinger, *Diplomacy,* p. 25.

17. Ibid., p. 143.

18. Bruce D. Porter, "Russia and Europe after the Cold War: The Interaction of Domestic and Foreign Policies," in *The Sources of Russian Foreign Policy after the Cold War,* ed. Celeste A. Wallander (Boulder, CO: Westview, 1996), p. 126.

19. Seton-Watson, *Decline of Imperial Russia,* pp. 317–18.

20. Malia, "Tradition, Ideology, and Pragmatism," pp. 40–41, 43.

Chapter 2: From Revolution to Cold War

1. Karl Marx and Friedrich Engels, *The Communist Manifesto,* in *Essential Works of Marxism,* ed. Arthur P. Mendel (New York: Bantam, 1961), p. 44.

2. V.I. Lenin, *Imperialism: The Highest Stage of Capitalism,* in *The Lenin Anthology,* ed. Robert C. Tucker (New York: W.W. Norton, 1975), pp. 204–74.

3. See Alexander L. George, "The 'Operational Code': A Neglected Approach to the Study of Political Leaders and Decision-Making," in *The Conduct of Soviet Foreign Policy,* eds. Erik P. Hoffmann and Frederic J. Fleron, Jr. (Chicago: Aldine-Atherton, 1971), pp. 165–90.

4. Nathan Leites, *A Study of Bolshevism* (Glencoe, IL: Free Press, 1953).

5. Quoted in Alfred G. Meyer, *Leninism* (New York: Frederick A. Praeger, 1962), p. 87.

6. Quoted in ibid., p. 87.

7. Leites, *A Study of Bolshevism,* p. 28.

8. An early and classic version of this debate, with contributions by R.N. Carew Hunt, Samuel Sharp, and Richard Lowenthal, appeared as "Ideology and Power Politics: A Symposium," in *Problems of Communism* 7, no. 2 (March-April 1958).

9. See, for example, Adam B. Ulam, "Soviet Ideology and Soviet Foreign Policy," *World Politics* 11, no. 2 (January 1959), pp. 153–72.

10. Vernon Aspaturian, "Soviet Foreign Policy," in *Foreign Policy in World Politics,* 4th ed., ed. Roy C. Macridis (New York: Prentice Hall, 1972), pp. 182–83.

11. Results of a content analysis of speeches of Soviet leaders may be found in Jan Triska and David Finley, *Soviet Foreign Policy* (New York: Macmillan, 1968), chap. 4.

12. The best account of the negotiations at Brest-Litovsk, on which the following paragraphs draw, is John Wheeler-Bennett, *The Forgotten Peace, Brest-Litovsk* (New York: Morrow, 1939).

13. Quoted in *The International Situation and Soviet Foreign Policy,* ed. Myron Rush (Columbus, OH: Charles E. Merrill, 1970), pp. 6–7.

14. Quoted in ibid., p. 12 (emphasis in original).

15. Quoted in *Soviet Russia and the West, 1920–1927,* eds. X.J. Eudin and H.H. Fisher (Stanford, CA: Stanford University Press, 1957), p. 94.

16. Quoted in Rush, *The International Situation,* p. 50.

17. Quoted in *Soviet Foreign Policy, 1928–1934: Documents and Materials,* vol. 1, eds. X.J. Eudin and R.M. Slusser (University Park, PA: Penn State University Press, 1966), p. 21.

18. For a more detailed account of the Lenin-Roy debate, see Robert H. Donaldson, *Soviet Policy toward India: Ideology and Strategy* (Cambridge, MA: Harvard University Press, 1974), pp. 8–13.

19. Quoted in Robert C. North, *Moscow and the Chinese Communists* (Stanford, CA: Stanford University Press, 1953), p. 96.

20. Quoted in *Soviet Documents on Foreign Policy, III: 1933–41,* ed. Jane Degras (London: Oxford University Press, 1953), p. 56.

21. Quoted in Rush, *The International Situation,* p. 82.

22. Quoted in ibid., pp. 93, 96.

23. Quoted in William L. Shirer, *The Rise and Fall of the Third Reich* (New York: Simon and Schuster, 1960), p. 531.

24. Quoted in Alan Bullock, *Hitler and Stalin: Parallel Lives* (New York: Alfred A. Knopf, 1991), p. 614.

25. The text of the treaty is found in *Nazi-Soviet Relations, 1939–1941,* eds. R.J. Sontag and J.S. Beddie (New York: Didier, 1948), pp. 76–78.

26. Ibid., p. 100.

27. Ibid., pp. 235–58.

28. Quoted in Shirer, *Rise and Fall,* p. 810.

29. Quoted in Gustav Hilger and Alfred Meyer, *The Incompatible Allies* (New York: Macmillan, 1953), p. 336.

30. The text of Khrushchev's secret speech to the Twentieth Party Congress may be

found in *Khrushchev Remembers,* trans. and ed. Strobe Talbott (Boston: Little, Brown, 1970), app. 4. The quotations are on pp. 587 and 589.

31. For the text of Stalin's radio address, see Joseph Stalin, *The Great Patriotic War of the Soviet Union* (New York: Greenwood, 1969), pp. 9–17.

32. For a full discussion of the circumstances and the evidence relating to the massacre, see Louis Fischer, *The Road to Yalta: Soviet Foreign Relations, 1941–1945* (New York: Harper and Row, 1972), pp. 75–90. When Poland's President Jaruzelski visited Moscow in April 1990, Mikhail Gorbachev presented him with "recently discovered documents" pertaining to the Katyn Forest incident that laid responsibility for the massacre on Lavrentii Beria and his henchmen in the Soviet secret police. A TASS statement was issued expressing "deep regret" over the tragedy and labeling it "one of the grave crimes of Stalinism" (*Pravda,* April 14, 1990).

33. Winston S. Churchill, *The Second World War: Closing the Ring* (Boston: Houghton Mifflin, 1951), pp. 359–62.

34. U.S. Department of State, *Foreign Relations of the United States: Diplomatic Papers: The Conferences at Cairo and Teheran 1943* (Washington, DC: U.S. Government Printing Office, 1961), pp. 567–68.

35. Quoted in Fischer, *The Road to Yalta,* p. 186.

36. Harry S. Truman, *Memoirs,* vol. 1 (Garden City, NY: Doubleday, 1955), p. 416.

37. Milovan Djilas, *Conversations with Stalin* (New York: Harcourt Brace and World, 1962), p. 114.

38. Excerpts from Stalin's speech may be found in Rush, *The International Situation,* pp. 117–23.

39. Djilas, *Conversations with Stalin,* p. 115.

40. Quoted in Talbott, *Khrushchev Remembers,* pp. 585, 600.

41. *The Eloquence of Winston Churchill,* ed. F.B. Czarnomski (New York: New American Library, 1957), p. 80.

Chapter 3: The Cold War

1. See Joseph L. Nogee and Robert H. Donaldson, *Soviet Foreign Policy since World War II,* 4th ed. (New York: Macmillan, 1992), pp. 91–92. Much of the material in this chapter is explicated more fully in our earlier book.

2. Quoted in Joseph M. Jones, *The Fifteen Weeks* (New York: Viking, 1955), p. 22.

3. George Kennan, "The Sources of Soviet Conduct," *American Diplomacy, 1900–1950* (New York: Mentor, 1952), p. 99.

4. Excerpts in Rush, *The International Situation,* pp. 125–39.

5. The tactical changes are discussed in Marshall D. Shulman, *Stalin's Foreign Policy Reappraised* (New York: Atheneum, 1965).

6. Quoted in Rush, *The International Situation,* pp. 160, 162.

7. Talbott, *Khrushchev Remembers,* p. 358.

8. Rush, *The International Situation,* pp. 166–85.

9. Talbott, *Khrushchev Remembers,* app. 4.

10. For a persuasive statement of the "missile deception" thesis, see Arnold L. Horelick and Myron Rush, *Strategic Power and Soviet Foreign Policy* (Chicago: University of Chicago Press, 1966).

11. Talbott, *Khrushchev Remembers,* pp. 493–94.

12. For a detailed analysis of the Cuban Missile Crisis, the most famous confrontation of the Cold War, see Graham T. Allison, *Essence of Decision: Explaining the Cuban Missile Crisis* (Boston: Little, Brown, 1971). For an updating based on more

recent exchanges with the Soviets, see Bruce J. Allyn, James G. Blight, and David A. Welch, "Essence of Revision: Moscow, Havana, and the Cuban Missile Crisis," *International Security* 14, no. 3 (Winter 1989/90), pp. 136–72, and Raymond L. Garthoff, "Cuban Missile Crisis: The Soviet Story," *Foreign Policy* 72 (Fall 1988), pp. 61–80.

13. E.M. Zhukov, "Contemporary Pace of Development of National-Liberation Revolution," *International Affairs* (Moscow), no. 5 (1967) pp. 52–54.

14. A detailed discussion is found in *Soviet Naval Diplomacy,* eds. Bradford Dismukes and James McConnell (New York: Pergamon Press, 1979).

15. For a comprehensive survey, see *The Soviet Union in the Third World: Successes and Failures,* ed. Robert H. Donaldson (Boulder, CO: Westview Press, 1981).

16. See David Floyd, *Mao Against Khrushchev* (New York: Frederick A. Praeger, 1963), p. 66, and William E. Griffith, *The Sino-Soviet Rift* (Cambridge, MA: MIT Press, 1964), p. 18.

17. For the text, see *Essential Works of Marxism,* ed. Arthur P. Mendel (New York: Bantam, 1965), pp. 517–62.

18. Henry A. Kissinger, *White House Years* (Boston: Little, Brown, 1979), pp. 183–86.

19. *Pravda,* July 22, 1973.

20. A first-hand account of these negotiations may be found in James S. Sutterlin and David Klein, *Berlin: From Symbol of Confrontation to Keystone of Stability* (New York: Praeger, 1989).

21. *The Washington Summit: General Secretary Brezhnev's Visit to the United States, June 18–25, 1973* (Washington, DC: U.S. Department of State, 1973), p. 49.

22. Ibid., p. 30.

23. *New York Times,* January 8, 1976.

24. *Documents and Resolutions, 25th Congress of the CPSU* (Moscow, 1976), p. 40.

25. *New York Times,* January 6, 1980.

26. *New York Times,* January 24, 1980.

27. Aleksandr Bovin in *Izvestia,* June 16, 1988.

28. Viacheslav Dashichev in *Literaturnaia gazeta,* May 18, 1988.

29. *Pravda,* February 25, 1986.

30. *Pravda,* July 26, 1988.

31. Quoted in Jack F. Matlock, Jr., *Autopsy on an Empire* (New York: Random House, 1995), p. 147. Matlock's analysis of the significance of this issue is particularly enlightening.

32. *Pravda,* July 11, 1990.

33. Quoted in Andrei Grachev, *Final Days: The Inside Story of the Collapse of the Soviet Union* (Boulder, CO: Westview Press, 1995), pp. 204–6.

34. Matlock, *Autopsy on an Empire,* pp. 650–77.

Chapter 4: Domestic Factors

1. For an elaboration of this point, see Margot Light, "Foreign Policy Thinking," in Neil Malcolm, Alex Pravda, Roy Allison, and Margot Light, *Internal Factors in Russian Foreign Policy* (Oxford: Oxford University Press, 1996), pp. 35–38, and Karen Dawisha and Bruce Parrott, *Russia and the New States of Eurasia: The Politics of Upheaval* (Cambridge: Cambridge University Press, 1994), pp. 26–29.

2. Sergei Stankevich, "Derzhava v poiskakh sebia," *Nezavisimaia gazeta,* March 28, 1992, quoted in James Richter, "Russian Foreign Policy and the Politics of National Identity," in *The Sources of Russian Foreign Policy after the Cold War,* ed. Celeste A. Wallander (Boulder, CO: Westview, 1996), p. 69.

3. See the description of Kozyrev's views in Jeffrey T. Checkel, *Ideas and International Political Change: Soviet/Russian Behavior and the End of the Cold War* (New Haven: Yale University Press, 1997), pp. 107–15.

4. Vladimir Abarinov and Vitalii Tretiakov, "The Union Left Russia with a Poor Foreign-Policy Legacy," *Nezavisimaia gazeta,* April 1, 1992, in *The Current Digest of the Post-Soviet Press (CDPSP)* 44, no. 13 (1992), pp. 4–6.

5. The terms "liberal westernizers," "pragmatic nationalists," and "fundamentalist nationalists" are from Malcolm et al., *Internal Factors.* See especially the chapter by Margot Light, pp. 33–100.

6. Sergei Parkhomenko, *Nezavisimaia gazeta,* July 31, 1992, in *CDPSP* 44, no. 31 (1992), pp. 22–23.

7. Stankevich, "Derzhava," translated in *CDPSP* 44, no. 13 (1992), pp. 1–4. Stankevich's essay bore some resemblance to Stalin's famous article, "Don't Forget the East," published almost three-quarters of a century before. Although it notably lacked the Marxist-Leninist terminology, it was similar to the earlier article in seeking to restore balance to Russia's policy. See Robert H. Donaldson, *Soviet Policy toward India: Ideology and Strategy* (Cambridge: Harvard University Press, 1974), p. 19.

8. Andranik Migranian, "Real and Illusory Guidelines in Foreign Policy," *Rossiiskaia gazeta,* August 4, 1992, in *CDPSP* 44, no. 32 (1992), p. 1.

9. Konstantin Eggert, "Russia in the Role of 'Eurasian Gendarme'?" *Izvestia,* August 7, 1992, in *CDPSP* 44, no. 32 (1992), pp. 4–5. Eggert's article attributes the quotations to Ambartsumov, who subsequently wrote to the newspaper, naming Migranian as their author. (*Izvestia,* August 25, 1992, in *CDPSP* 44, no. 34 [1992], p. 14). Margot Light, in Malcolm et al., *Internal Factors,* pp. 53–55, repeated this misattribution, apparently having failed to notice the letter and the newspaper's retraction.

10. "A Strategy for Russia," *Nezavisimaia gazeta,* August 19, 1992, quoted in Richard Sakwa, *Russian Politics and Society,* 2nd ed. (New York: Routledge, 1996), p. 289.

11. Vladimir Lukin, "America and Our Reforms," *Nezavisimaia gazeta,* September 10, 1992, in *CDPSP* 44, no. 36 (1992), pp. 16–17, 32.

12. Maksim Iusin, "Andrei Kozyrev's 'Shock Therapy,'" *Izvestia,* December 15, 1992, in *CDPSP* 44, no. 50 (1992), pp. 12–13.

13. Quoted in Checkel, *Ideas and International Political Change,* p. 117.

14. Vladislav Chernov, "Russia's National Interests and Threats to Its Security," *Nezavisimaia gazeta,* April 29, 1993, in *CDPSP* 45, no. 17 (1993), pp. 13–15. The quotations that follow are from this account. The final version of the "foreign policy concept" was classified and never published, but this summary, written by a member of the Security Council staff, is widely believed to be authoritative. See Malcolm et al., *Internal Factors,* pp. 69–70, and Leon Aron, "The Emergent Priorities of Russian Foreign Policy," in *The Emergence of Russian Foreign Policy,* eds. Leon Aron and Kenneth M. Jensen (Washington, DC: United States Institute of Peace Press, 1994), pp. 17–34.

15. "Primakov Starts with the CIS," *Moskovskie novosti,* 2, January 14–21, 1996, in *CDPSP* 48, no. 2 (1996), pp. 11–12.

16. "A Minister the Opposition Doesn't Curse," *Obshchaia gazeta,* 37, September 19–25, 1996, in *CDPSP* 48, no. 39 (1996), pp. 22–23.

17. Leonid Mlechin, "The Dark Glasses Keep One from Seeing the Man's True Face," *Izvestia,* May 15, 1996, in *CDPSP* 48, no. 20 (1996), pp. 11–12; Aleksei Pushkov, "Evgenii Primakov Goes Solo," *Moskovskie novosti,* 36, September 8–15, 1996, in *CDPSP* 48, no. 36 (1996), pp. 25–26.

18. *Moskovskie novosti,* 47, November 23–30, 1997, in *CDPSP* 49, no. 47 (1997), pp. 4–5.

19. Checkel, *Ideas and Foreign Policy,* especially pp. 123–32.

20. The text of the constitution can be found in Sakwa, *Russian Politics and Society,* pp. 395–429.

21. Malcolm et al., *Internal Factors,* p. 112. Although the council began to function earlier, a decree forming it was issued by Yeltsin on June 3 (*Rossiiskaia gazeta,* June 11, 1992, in *CDPSP* 44, no. 28 [1992], pp. 4–5), and a second decree on procedures for implementing its decisions was signed on July 7 (Stepan Kiseliov, "Boris Yeltsin's Quiet Coup," *Moskovskie novosti,* July 19, 1992, in *CDPSP* 44, no. 28 [1992], pp. 2–4).

22. V. Prokhvatilov, "In the Corridors of Power: It's Already Noon, but the Shadows Aren't Disappearing," *Komsomol'skaia Pravda,* April 29, 1992, in *CDPSP* 44, no. 17 (1992), pp. 22–23; Kiseliov, ibid.; Pëtr Lassavio, "Iurii Skokov—Man of the Year?" *Rossiiskie vesti,* December 19, 1992, in *CDPSP* 44, no. 51 (1992), p. 7; Vladimir Orlov, "The Real State of Affairs: Iurii Skokov's Farewell Bow," *Moskovskie novosti,* May 16, 1993 in *CDPSP* 45, no. 19 (1993), pp. 11–12.

23. Pavel Felgengauer, "Evgenii Shaposhnikov—Marshal-Destroyer?" *Segodnia,* June 18, 1993, in *CDPSP* 45, no. 24 (1993), p. 17; Vitalii Marsov, "The Secret Game in the Kremlin Continues," *Nezavisimaia gazeta,* August 12, 1993, in *CDPSP* 45, no. 32 (1993), pp. 12–13.

24. Mikhail Berger, "Idea of 'Economic Security' Resurrects Specter of Old State Planning Committee," *Izvestia,* April 2, 1994, in *CDPSP* 46, no. 13 (1994), p. 17.

25. Mikhail Sokolov, "All Power to the Security Council," *Segodnia,* January 12, 1995, in *CDPSP* 47, no. 3 (1995), pp. 19–20.

26. Soskovets' title of first deputy prime minister was taken by the departing Security Council secretary, Oleg Lobov, but Chernomyrdin clearly was not eager to assign Lobov major duties, and he was left out of the new government formed in March 1997.

27. In August 1997, Baturin was replaced as secretary of the Defense Council by Andrei Kokoshin. He was simultaneously appointed head of the new State Military Inspectorate in the president's office, created to coordinate measures connected with the implementation of military reform.

28. Mikhail Lantsman, "The Range of Powers of the New Security Council Secretary Is Outlined," *Segodnia,* October 22, 1996; Mikhail Karpov, "The Fifth Secretary of the Security Council Gets Down to Work," *Nezavisimaia gazeta,* October 22, 1996, in *CDPSP* 48, no. 42 (1996), p. 7.

29. Igor Korotchenko, "Reorganization of the Russian Security Council Is Completed," *Nezavisimaia gazeta,* January 21, 1997, in *CDPSP* 49, no. 3 (1997), pp. 15–16.

30. "Russian National Security: The Concept," *Prism: A Bi-weekly on the Post-Soviet States* 4, no. 1, in *Johnson's Russia List,* January 10, 1998.

31. "Yeltsin Decree Streamlines Security Council," *Jamestown Foundation Monitor,* March 30, 1998, in *Johnson's Russia List,* March 31, 1998. See also Pavel Felgengauer, " 'A Hero of Our Time' Becomes Secretary of the Security Council," *Segodnia,* March 4, 1998, in *CDPSP* 50, no. 9 (1998), pp. 5–6. Additional information on the operation of the Security Council may be found in F. Stephen Larrabee and Theodore W. Karasik, *Foreign and Security Policy Decisionmaking Under Yeltsin* (Santa Monica, CA: RAND, 1997), pp. 35–41.

32. Pavel Felgengauer, "The Defense Council as an Advisory Body," *Segodnia,* July 27, 1996, in *CDPSP* 48, no. 30 (1996), p. 5.

33. Evgenii Bai and Gennadii Charodeiev, "President Decides to Strengthen Foreign Policy with Another Council," *Izvestia,* December 28, 1995, in *CDPSP* 47, no. 32 (1995), p. 22; "Membership of Russian President's Foreign Policy Council Confirmed," *Segodnia,* January 25, 1997, in *CDPSP* 49, no. 4 (1997), p. 23.

34. Quoted in Malcolm et al., *Internal Factors,* pp. 117–18.

35. Ekaterina Akopova, "President Takes Ministry Under His Protection,"

Kommersant-Daily, March 16, 1995; Maksim Iusin, "Three Presidential Decrees that Will Transform the Foreign Ministry," *Izvestia*, March 17, 1995; Mikhail Karpov, "False Alarm," *Nezavisimaia gazeta*, March 17, 1995; Vladimir Abarinov, "Letter and Spirit of the Statute on the Ministry of Foreign Affairs," *Segodnia*, March 24, 1995, all in *CDPSP* 47, no. 11 (1995), pp. 7–9; *Rossiiskie vesti*, October 21, 1995, in *CDPSP* 47, no. 42 (1995), p. 2.

36. *Kommersant-Daily*, March 14, 1996; Leonid Velikhov, "Russian Foreign Ministry Named Coordinator of All Russian Foreign Policy for Second Time," *Segodnia*, March 14, 1996, in *CDPSP* 48, no. 11 (1996), pp. 20–21.

37. "A Minister the Opposition Doesn't Curse," p. 23.

38. Denis Babichenko, "The President's Staff Is No CPSU Central Committee Apparat," *Segodnia*, October 17, 1997, in *CDPSP* 49, no. 42 (1997), pp. 22–23.

39. Sakwa, *Russian Politics and Society*, pp. 281–82.

40. Malcolm et al., *Internal Factors*, pp. 122–23.

41. Abarinov, "Letter and Spirit of the Statute," p. 9.

42. For a discussion of military influence on Soviet foreign policy, especially during the Brezhnev years, see Edward L. Warner III, *The Military in Contemporary Soviet Politics: An Institutional Analysis* (New York: Praeger, 1977), and Dimitri K. Simes, "The Military and Militarism in Soviet Society," *International Security* 6, no. 3 (Winter 1981/82), pp. 123–43.

43. Pavel Felgengauer, "President Continues Purge in Defense Ministry," *Segodnia*, February 14, 1995, in *CDPSP* 47, no. 7 (1995), p. 20.

44. Pavel Felgengauer, "Igor Rodionov Becomes Minister of Defense," *Segodnia*, July 18, 1996, in *CDPSP* 47, no. 29 (1996), pp. 1–2.

45. Vasili Kononenko, "Russian Military Doctrine Lacks No-First-Use Pledge," *Izvestia*, November 4, 1993; Pavel Felgengauer, "Russia Shifts to Doctrine of Nuclear Deterrence," *Segodnia*, November 4, 1993; Roman Zadunaiski, "Military Doctrine Adopted," *Rossiiskie vesti*, November 5, 1993, in *CDPSP* 45, no. 44 (1993), pp. 11–12.

46. Roy Allison, "Military Factors in Foreign Policy," in Malcolm et al., *Internal Factors*, p. 255.

47. Pavel Felgengauer, "A Manilov-Style Reorganization of the Army," *Segodnia*, July 21, 1997, in *CDPSP* 49, no. 29 (1997), pp. 4–5. The theoretical underpinnings for the proposed military reform were provided in December 1997, with Yeltsin's approval of the National Security Concept.

48. Amy Knight, *Spies without Cloaks: The KGB's Successors* (Princeton: Princeton University Press, 1996). The following paragraphs draw on Knight's excellent study.

49. Ibid., p. 87.

50. Ibid., pp. 128–129.

51. "Text of President Yeltsin's Speech at the CIS Summit Session, Moscow, March 29, 1997," *RIA Novosti*, in *Johnson's Russia List*, March 31, 1997.

52. On this point see Alex Pravda, "The Public Politics of Foreign Policy," in Malcolm et al., *Internal Factors*, pp. 169–229.

53. Ibid., pp. 188–203, and Jack Snyder, "Democratization, War, and Nationalism in the Post-Communist States," in Wallander, *The Sources of Russian Foreign Policy*, p. 36.

54. See Wallander, ed., *The Sources of Russian Foreign Policy*, especially the chapters by Kimberly Marten Zisk, "The Foreign Policy Preferences of Russian Defense Industrialists: Integration or Isolation?" pp. 95–120, and Matthew Evangelista, "From Each According to Its Abilities: Competing Theoretical Approaches to the Post-Soviet Energy Sector," pp. 173–205.

55. The interlocking interests of the major financial-industrial groups are described in "The Tycoons Behind the Politicians," *The Economist*, April 4, 1998, pp. 56–57.

56. Andranik Migranian, "Russia, Bulgaria, and Gazprom," *Nezavisimaia gazeta* December 30, 1997, in *CDPSP* 50, no. 1 (1998), p. 19. The foreign policy influence of these business lobbies is discussed in Michael McFaul, "A Precarious Peace: Domestic Politics in the Making of Russian Foreign Policy," *International Security* 22, no. 3 (1997–98), pp. 5–35.

57. Malcolm et al., *Internal Factors,* p. 288.

Chapter 5: Russia and the Near Abroad

1. Gorbachev's differences with Yeltsin are described in Mikhail Gorbachev, *Memoirs* (New York: Doubleday, 1995), pp. 651–55.

2. John B. Dunlop, *The Rise of Russia and the Fall of the Soviet Empire* (Princeton: Princeton University Press, 1993), pp. 266–67.

3. For the origins of the Russian state, see George Vernadsky, *A History of Russia,* 3rd ed. (New Haven: Yale University Press, 1961), pp. 14–30.

4. *RFE/RL Research Report* 1, no. 1, March 13, 1992, p. 8.

5. The text of the CIS agreement is in *Current Digest of the Post-Soviet Press (CDPSP)* 43, no. 49 (1992), pp. 10–11.

6. *RFE/RL Research Report* 1, no. 4, January 4, 1992, p. 52. On the military issues see Stephen Foye, "The CIS Armed Forces," *RFE/RL Research Report* 2, no. 1, January 1, 1993, pp. 41–45, and "End of the CIS Command Heralds New Russian Defense Policy?" *RFE/RL Research Report* 2, no. 27, July 2, 1993, pp. 45–49.

7. For the text of the Lisbon Protocol see *Arms Control Today,* June 1992, pp. 34–37.

8. *New York Times,* October 20, 1993.

9. In exchange for its warheads Ukraine was promised money and nuclear fuel. *CDPSP* 46, no. 2 (1994), pp. 6–7.

10. A summary of the agreements between 1992 and 1994 is provided in Mark Webber, *The International Politics of Russia and the Successor States* (New York: Manchester University Press, 1996), pp. 186–87.

11. *Nezavisimaia gazeta,* July 13, 1993, p. 1.

12. Roman Solchanyk, "Ukrainian-Russian Confrontation Over the Crimea," *RFE/RL Research Report* 1, no. 8, February 21, 1992, p. 28.

13. *CDPSP* 44, no. 21 (1992), p. 4.

14. Ibid., p. 5.

15. *New York Times,* June 1, 1997.

16. *CDPSP* 50, no. 9 (1998), p. 6.

17. *Segodnia,* January 18, 1997.

18. See Ustina Markus, "Business as Usual with Lukashenka," *Transition* 1, no. 8, May 26, 1995, pp. 57–61, and "Missed Opportunities in Foreign Policy," *Transition* 1, no. 15, August 25, 1995, pp. 62–66.

19. Texts of these treaties are in *CDPSP* 48, no. 14 (1992), pp. 1–8.

20. A. Hyman, "Moving Out of Moscow's Orbit: The Outlook for Central Asia," *International Affairs* 69, no. 2 (1993), p. 295.

21. A good introduction to the relations between post-Soviet Russia and the Central Asian states in Martha Brill Olcott, *Central Asia's New States, Independence: Foreign Policy and Regional Security* (Washington, DC: United States Institute of Peace Press, 1996).

22. "Migranian: Near Abroad Is Vital to Russia—I," *CDPSP* 46, no. 7 (1994), p. 4.

23. Bess A. Brown, "Overriding Economics," *Transition* 1, no. 2, February 15, 1995, p. 53.

24. Quoted in John Lough, "Defining Russia's Relations with Neighboring States," *RFE/RL Research Report* 2, no. 20, May 14, 1993, p. 58.

25. See "Tashkent Summit Signals CIS Realignment," *CDPSP* 44, no. 9 (1992), pp. 1–5.

26. The literature on peacekeeping is extensive. Useful analyses are *The Evolution of UN Peacekeeping: Case Studies and Comparative Analysis,* William J. Durch, ed. (New York: St. Martin's Press, 1993); *The Blue Helmets: A Review of United Nations Peacekeeping* (New York: United Nations, 1990); *Peacekeeping, American Policy and the Uncivil Wars of the 1990s,* ed. William J. Durch (New York: St. Martin's Press, 1996); Steven R. Rather, *The New UN Peacekeeping: Building Peace in Lands of Conflict after the Cold War* (New York: St. Martin's Press, 1996).

27. This last contention is controversial and is argued in Suzanne Crow, "Russian Peacekeeping: Defense, Diplomacy or Imperialism?" *RFE/RL Research Report* 1, no. 17, September 18, 1992, pp. 37–40; Bruce D. Porter and Carol R. Saivetz, "The Once and Future Empire: Russia and the 'Near Abroad,' " *The Washington Quarterly,* Summer 1994, pp. 75–90; and Susan L. Clark, "Russia in a Peacekeeping Role," in *The Emergence of Russian Foreign Policy,* eds. Leon Aron and Kenneth M. Jensen (Washington, DC: The United States Institute of Peace Press, 1994), p. 120.

28. *CDPSP* 46, no. 12 (1992), p. 11.

29. In November 1992 an earlier and smaller peacekeeping force was formed with Russian and Uzbek troops. A detailed account of Russian peacekeeping in Tajikistan is Iver B. Neumann and Sergei Solodovnik, "The Case of Tajikistan," in *Peacekeeping and the Role of Russia in Eurasia,* eds. Lena Jonson and Clive Archer (Boulder, CO: Westview Press, 1996), pp. 83–101. See also Kevin P. O'Prey, "Keeping the Peace in the Borderlands of Russia," in Durch, *UN Peacekeeping,* pp. 429–36.

30. *New York Times,* June 28, 1997, p. 2.

31. Olcott, *Central Asia's New States,* pp. 140–44.

32. Carolyn McGiffert Ekedahl and Melvin A. Goodman, *The Wars of Eduard Shevardnadze* (University Park: Pennsylvania State University Press, 1997), pp. 245–48.

33. Thomas Goltz, "Letter from Eurasia: The Hidden Russian Hand," *Foreign Policy,* no. 92 (Fall 1993), p. 97.

34. See O'Prey, "Keeping the Peace," pp. 420–23. Also Karen Dawisha and Bruce Parrott, *Russia and the New States of Eurasia: The Politics of Upheaval* (Cambridge: Cambridge University Press, 1994), pp. 153–54.

35. Ekedahl and Goodman, *The Wars,* p. 265.

36. Goltz, "Letter," pp. 105–7.

37. *New York Times,* September 28, 1993. See also "Eduard Shevardnadze," *New York Times Magazine,* December 26, 1993, p. 19.

38. Catherine Dale, "The Case of Abkhazia (Georgia)," in Jonson and Archer, *Peacekeeping,* p. 127.

39. Security Council Resolution 937, July 21, 1994.

40. For a description of Armenian-Azeri animosity see Dimitry Furman and Carl Johan Asenius, "The Case of Nagorno-Karabakh (Azerbaijan)," in Jonson and Archer, *Peacekeeping,* pp. 139–46.

41. See Elizabeth Fuller, "Between Anarchy and Despotism," *Transition* 1, no. 2 (1994), pp. 60–65.

42. See Anthony Richter, "The Perils of 'Sustainable Empire,' " *Transition* 1, no. 3, March 15, 1995, pp. 14–15, 52; and Elizabeth Fuller, "The 'Near Abroad': Influence and Oil in Russian Diplomacy," *Transition* 2, no. 6, April 28, 1995, pp. 32–34.

43. Jeff Chinn, "The Case of Transdniester (Moldova)," in Jonson and Archer, *Peacekeeping,* p. 109.

44. O'Prey, "Keeping the Peace," p. 439.

45. Pal Kolsto and Andrei Edemsky with Natalia Kalashnikova, "The Dniester Conflict: Between Irredentism and Separatism," *Europe-Asia Studies* 45, no. 6 (1993), p. 994.

46. Porter and Saivetz, "The Once and Future Empire," p. 84.

47. *CDPSP* 46, no. 32, p. 16.

48. These figures are taken from Martin Klatt, "Russians in the 'Near Abroad,' " *RFE/RL Research Report* 3, no. 32, August 19, 1994, p. 35. The number of 1,725,000 Russians in the three states is from the 1989 census.

49. See Dzintra Bungs, Saulius Girnius, and Riina Kionka, "Citizenship Legislation in the Baltic States," *RFE/RL Research Report* 1, no. 50, December 18, 1992, pp. 38–40.

50. *Segodnia,* February 1, 1994, p. 3.

51. The highest degree of cooperation between the Baltic states has been in the formation of a Baltic Peacekeeping Battalion (BALTBAT) to serve in UN peacekeeping missions. Saulius Girnius, "Tiny Armed Forces Need Allies," *Transition* 1, no. 2, December 1, 1995, p. 61.

52. Saulius Girnius, "Relations between the Baltic States and Russia," *RFE/RL Research Report* 3, no. 33, August 26, 1994, pp. 30–31.

53. See "Russian Language Continues to Suffer Discrimination," *CDPSP* 50, no. 6 (1998), p. 17.

54. *CDPSP* 50, no. 4 (1998), p. 19.

55. Steven Erlanger, "U.S. Tries to Defuse Russia-Latvia Dispute," *New York Times,* April 16, 1998.

56. Ibid., p. 32.

57. Full membership is normally granted upon entry to the European Union. The Western European Union is the military arm of the European Union.

58. *Segodnia,* February 14, 1997, p. 7. The full text of the policy document was published in *Rossiiskaia gazeta,* February 13, 1997, p. 7.

59. *CDPSP* 49, no. 9 (1997), p. 19.

Chapter 6: Russia and the West

1. For some of the theoretical literature on bipolarity, see Kenneth N. Waltz, "The Stability of a Bipolar World," *Daedalus,* Summer 1964; Morton A. Kaplan, "Balance of Power, Bipolarity and Other Models of International Systems," *American Political Science Review,* September 1957; Wolfram F. Hanrieder, "The International System: Bipolar or Multibloc?" *Journal of Conflict Resolution,* September 1965; Karl W. Deutsch and J. David Singer, "Multipolar Power Systems and International Stability," *World Politics,* April 1964; Richard N. Rosecrance, "Bipolarity, Multipolarity and the Future," *Journal of Conflict Resolution,* September 1966. A critique of this literature is in Joseph L. Nogee, "Polarity—An Ambiguous Concept," *Orbis* 18, no. 4, Winter 1975.

2. For discussion of the post–Cold War international structure see Kenneth N. Waltz, "The Emerging Structure of International Politics," *International Security* 18, no. 2 (1993); Michael Mastanduno, "Preserving the Unipolar Moment: Realist Theories and U.S. Grand Strategy after the Cold War," *International Security* 21, no. 4 (1997); Christopher Layne, "The Unipolar Illusion: Why New Great Powers Will Arise," *International Security* 17, no. 4 (1993).

3. Mikhail Gorbachev, *Perestroika: New Thinking for Our Country and the World* (New York: Harper and Row, 1988), p. 134.

4. *Rossiiskaia gazeta,* February 3, 1992, *in Current Digest of the Post-Soviet Press (CDPSP)* 45, no. 5 (1993), p. 11.

5. *New York Times,* June 18, 1992.

6. Anders Aslund, *How Russia Became a Market Economy* (Washington, DC: The Brookings Institution, 1995), p. 41.

7. "B.N. Yeltsin's Speech," *Sovetskaia Rossiia,* October 29, 1991.

8. Andrei Kozyrev claimed that during the crisis "the Western embassies in effect began to work for us: through them, we received and passed on information." John Dunlop, *The Rise of Russia and the Fall of the Soviet Empire* (Princeton: Princeton University Press, 1993), p. 216.

9. In his autobiography Yeltsin acknowledges the support of the west. "[The] unequivocal position from the world community was a heavy blow to the White House occupier." Boris Yeltsin, *The Struggle for Russia* (New York: Times Books, 1994), p. 262.

10. See Michael MccGuire, *Perestroika and Soviet National Security* (Washington, DC: The Brookings Institution, 1991), pp. 264–72, 371–79.

11. In *CDPSP* 44, no. 5 (1992), p. 7.

12. *RFE/RL Research Report* 1, no. 33 (1992), p. 51. See also *New York Times,* June 8, 1992.

13. In criticizing the antimissile defense system, Aleksei Arbatov, director of the Foreign Policy Association's Center for Disarmament and Strategic Stability, said: "The U.S. government's policy toward our country of late deserves the highest marks. But strengthening relations with America hardly means agreeing with the present administration in.everything." *CDPSP* 44, no. 10 (1992), p. 13.

14. See Yeltsin's speech of January 29, 1992, in *CDPSP* 44, no. 4 (1992), p. 7, and *New York Times,* January 30, 1992.

15. Thomas L. Friedman, "Reducing the Russian Arms Threat," *New York Times,* June 17, 1992.

16. *Pravda,* June 18, 1992.

17. John W.R. Leppingwell, "The Trilateral Agreement on Nuclear Weapons," *RFE/RL Research Report* 3, no. 4 (1994), p. 14.

18. A good, brief account of the origins of the war in Bosnia is Warren Zimmerman, "Origins of a Catastrophe," *Foreign Affairs* 74, no. 2 (1995), pp. 2–20. A contrasting account of the responsibilities of the parties to the conflict is in Charles G. Boyd, "Making Peace with the Guilty," *Foreign Affairs* 74, no. 5 (1995), pp. 22–38.

19. The difficult choices confronting Gorbachev as a consequence of the Iraqi invasion of Kuwait in 1990 are described in Joseph L. Nogee and Robert H. Donaldson, *Soviet Foreign Policy since World War II,* 4th ed. (New York: Macmillan, 1992), pp. 392–96. See also Graham E. Fuller, "Moscow and the Gulf War," *Foreign Affairs* 70, no. 3 (1991), pp. 55–76.

20. Suzanne Crow, "Russia's Response to the Yugoslav Crisis," *RFE/RL Research Report* 1, no. 30, July 24, 1992, p. 32. See also *CDPSP,* 44, no. 21 (1992), pp. 19–21, and, *CDPSP* 44, no. 22 (1992), pp. 1–6.

21. "Russia's Vote to Punish Belgrade Draws Fire," *CDPSP* 44, no. 22 (1992), pp. 3,5.

22. *CDPSP* 44, no. 38 (1992), pp. 20–21. See also *CDPSP* 44, no. 35 (1992), pp. 16–17.

23. *Nezavisimaia gazeta,* January 11, 1993, p. 2.

24. For a thorough analysis of the political and military issues involved in the CFE issue, see Richard A. Falkenrath, "The CFE Flank Dispute: Waiting in the Wings," *International Security* 19, no. 4 (1995), pp. 118–44.

25. *Rossiiskaia gazeta,* July 6, 1993, p. 5.

26. *Rossiiskaia gazeta,* June 19, 1992, pp. 1–2.

27. *Pravda,* January 27, 1993, p. 1.

28. *Pravda,* April 6, 1993, p. 3.

29. Jerry F. Hough, *Democratization and Revolution in the USSR, 1985–1991* (Washington, DC: The Brookings Institution, 1997), p. 519.

30. Boris Yeltsin, *The Struggle for Russia,* p. 288.

31. Zhirinovskii's views are irreverently described by Graham Frazer and George Lancelle in *Absolute Zhirinovskii* (New York: Penguin Books, 1994).

32. Russia's "cohabitation" is described in Joseph L. Nogee and R. Judson Mitchell, *Russian Politics: The Struggle for a New Order* (Boston: Allyn and Bacon, 1997), pp. 121–24.

33. "Is Chechnia on the Verge of War?" *CDPSP* 46, no. 31 (1994), pp. 1–4.

34. For Yeltsin's policy toward the other republics see Edward W. Walker, "Federalism—Russia Style: The Federation Provisions in Russia's New Constitution," *Problems of Post-Communism* 42, no. 4 (1995), p. 4. See also Robert Sharlet, "The New Russian Constitution and Its Political Impact," *Problems of Post-Communism* 42, no. 1 (1995), pp. 6–7.

35. "At CSCE Summit, Yeltsin Warns of Cold Peace," *CDPSP* 46, no. 49 (1994), p. 8.

36. The poll was conducted by the Open Media Research Institute (OMRI) and reported by Michael Haney, "Russia's First Televised War: Public Opinion on the Crisis," *Transition,* April 14, 1995, p. 7.

37. "Duma Majority Votes Support of War," *CDPSP* 47, no. 4 (1995), p. 12.

38. This was the first successful vote of no confidence under the new constitution. Michael Specter, "Angry Russian Parliament Votes to Rebuke Yeltsin Government," *New York Times,* January 22, 1995. This action did not bring down the government because it was not followed by a second vote of no confidence within a three-month period, as required by the constitution.

39. "Yeltsin Names Primakov New Foreign Minister," *CDPSP* 48, no. 2 (1996), p. 10.

40. *CDPSP* 48, no. 19 (1996), p. 5.

41. *CDPSP* 48, no. 13 (1996), p. 1.

42. The text of the agreement is in *Izvestia,* September 3, 1996, p. 1.

43. *CDPSP* 49, no. 19 (1997), p. 10.

44. See Andreas Andrianopoulos, "The Long Arm of Oil Interests," *Transition* 4, no. 1 (1997), pp. 36–37.

45. *Nezavisimaia gazeta,* February 19, 1994, p. 3.

46. *CDPSP* 46, no. 15 (1994), pp. 5–6.

47. *Izvestia,* April 20, 1994, p. 1.

48. Steven Greenhouse, "Year's Effort by 5–Nation Group Accomplishes Little in Bosnia," *New York Times,* March 22, 1995, p. A4.

49. *CDPSP* 47, no. 21 (1995), p. 6.

50. *CDPSP* 47, no. 32 (1995), p. 8.

51. *CDPSP* 47, no. 43 (1995), p. 6.

52. A year after the Dayton Accords, the parties still were unwilling to comply with the agreement. See James A. Schear, "Bosnia's Post-Dayton Traumas," *Foreign Policy,* no. 104 (Fall 1996), pp. 87–101.

53. "Russia Issues a Warning on NATO Expansion," *CDPSP* 45, no. 47 (1993), pp. 11–13.

54. See Allen Lynch, "After Empire: Russia and Its Western Neighbors," Alfred E. Reisach, "Central Europe's Disappointments and Hopes," and Kjell Engelbrekt, "Southeast European States Seek Equal Treatment," in *RFE/RL Research Report,* 3, no. 33 (1994).

55. Michael Mihalka, "European-Russian Security and NATO's Partnership for Peace," *RFE/RL Research Report* 3, no. 33 (1994), p. 44.

56. Hall Gardner, *Dangerous Crossroads: Europe, Russia, and the Future of NATO* (Westport, CT: Praeger, 1997), p. 21.

57. *CDPSP* 46, no. 49 (1994), pp. 8–10.

58. *CDPSP* 46, no. 8 (1994), p. 13.

59. Gardner, *Dangerous Crossroads*, p. 22.

60. Ibid., p. 23.

61. See Almar Latour, "Lebed Warns NATO: Stall Plans to Expand Eastward," *Wall Street Journal*, October 8, 1996. Also, Vladimir Peresada, "Lebed in the Wolves' Den," *Pravda*, October 9, 1996, p. 3.

62. *New York Times*, May 15, 1997, p. A8.

63. *CDPSP* 49, no. 28 (1997), p. 2.

64. See, for example, the views of Viktor Kalashnikov, director of the Russian Federation Public Policy Center, "Should Russia Be in a Hurry to Join Europe?" *Segodnia*, November 18, 1993, in *CDPSP* 45, no. 46 (1993), pp. 29–30.

65. Boris Yeltsin, *The Struggle for Russia*, pp. 138–39.

66. Maksim Iusin, "Paying for Fraternalism," *Izvestia*, February 10, 1995, in *CDPSP* 47, no. 7 (1995), p. 24.

67. Stanislav Kondrashov, "Eastern Europe and Russia's Policy," *Izvestia*, November 6, 1993, in *CDPSP* 45, no. 44 (1993), p. 28.

68. Aleksei Pushkov, "Eastern Europe—A Time for Gathering Stones," *Moskovskie novosti*, no. 51, July 30–August 6, 1995, in *CDPSP* 47, no. 30 (1995), pp. 23–24.

69. Mikhail Tretiakov, "How Do We Answer Warsaw's Trybuna?" *Pravda*, June 23, 1993, in *CDPSP* 45, no. 25 (1993), pp. 20–21.

70. *Izvestia*, December 14, 1995, in *CDPSP* 47, no. 50 (1995), p. 24.

71. *Nezavisimaia gazeta*, April 10, 1996, in *CDPSP* 48, no. 15 (1996), p. 22.

72. Iana Mirontseva, "Gazprom as Lodestar of Slovak Foreign Policy," *Segodnia*, October 11, 1997, in *CDPSP* 49, no. 41 (1997), pp. 22–23.

73. Georgi Bovt and Natalia Kalashnikova, "Sides Hold to Their Own Opinions," *Kommersant-Daily*, March 10, 1995, in *CDPSP* 47, no. 10 (1995), pp. 18–19.

74. Aleksei Portanski, "Partnership with EU Becomes Reality," *Finansovie izvestia*, no. 51, July 20, 1995, in *CDPSP* 47, no. 29 (1995), p. 23.

75. *Rossiiskaia gazeta*, December 7, 1994, in *CDPSP* 46, no. 49 (1994), pp. 8–9.

76. Boris Vinogradov, "3,000 Peacekeepers Are Supposed to Create Conditions for a Settlement in Karabakh," *Izvestia*, December 9, 1994, in ibid., pp. 10–11.

77. Mikhail Karpov, "Sunrise for NATO, Sunset for the CSCE?" *Nezavisimaia gazeta*, December 7, 1994, in ibid., pp. 11–12.

78. *Rossiiskie vesti*, August 31, 1994, in *CDPSP* 46, no. 35 (1994), p. 3.

79. Nikolai Pavlov, "Forgotten Germany," *Izvestia*, March 18, 1992, in *CDPSP* 44, no. 11 (1992), pp. 8–9.

80. Leonid Velekhov, "Kohl Comes to Yeltsin's Rescue," *Nezavisimaia gazeta*, December 18, 1992, in *CDPSP* 44, no. 50 (1992), pp. 19–20.

81. The following year, the Russian press, relying on a report in *Der Spiegel*, described the whole incident as a German intelligence operation, designed to trace channels by which dangerous contraband entered Germany, and using agents provocateurs to test monitoring systems at Russian airports. Igor Korotchenko, "Nuclear Smuggling Case," *Nezavisimaia gazeta*, April 13, 1995, in *CDPSP* 47, no. 15 (1995), p. 23.

82. *Segodnia*, September 1, 1994, in *CDPSP* 46, no. 35 (1994), p. 2; Aleksandr Batygin, "Grab Your Greatcoat and Let's Go Home," *Rossiiskaia gazeta*, August 30, 1994, in ibid., p. 5.

83. *Izvestia*, August 31, 1994, in ibid., p. 1.

84. Natalia Kalashnikova, "German Defense Minister Is Not Eager to Meet with Russian Counterpart," *Kommersant-Daily*, January 24, 1995, in *CDPSP* 47, no. 4 (1995), p. 28.

85. *Segodnia,* February 21, 1996, in *CDPSP* 48, no. 8 (1996), p. 26.

86. Aleksandr Krausulin, "He Came, He Saw, He Persuaded," *Rossiiskaia gazeta,* November 22, 1994, in *CDPSP* 46, no. 47 (1994), pp. 23–24.

87. Natalia Kalashnikova and Vitali Dymarskii, " 'Go-for-Broke Diplomacy, But There's Nothing to Ante Up," *Kommersant-Daily,* October 24, 1995, in *CDPSP* 47, no. 43 (1995), pp. 23–24.

88. Gennadii Sisoev, "Russia Likes French Dissidence," *Kommersant-Daily,* September 25, 1997, in *CDPSP* 49, no. 39 (1997), pp. 21–22; Maksim Iusin, "Yeltsin's Friendship with Chirac Developing into a Russian-French Alliance," *Izvestia,* September 27, 1997, in ibid., p. 22.

89. Maksim Iusin, "Yeltsin's Visit to London Was a Complete Success," *Izvestia,* February 11, 1992, in *CDPSP* 44, no. 5 (1992), pp. 10–11.

90. "Kremlin Adopting a New Anti-American Line?" *Jamestown Foundation Monitor,* October 20, 1997, in *Johnson's Russia List,* October 21, 1997.

Chapter 7: Russia and the "Non-West"

1. Figures from the U.S. Congressional Research Service, cited in Philip Shenon, "Russia Outstrips U.S. in Sales of Arms to Developing Nations," *New York Times,* August 20, 1996.

2. Congressional Research Service, cited in Eric Schmitt, "Arms Sales to the Third World, Especially by Russia, Drop," *New York Times,* July 19, 1993.

3. Iuri Golotiuk, "Russia Is 'Aggressively' Entering World Arms Market," *Segodnia,* March 29, 1996, in *CDPSP* 48, no. 13 (1996), p. 22; Pavel Felgengauer, "Arms Trade Is Not as Lucrative for Russia as Russia Claims," *Segodnia,* March 10, 1995, in *CDPSP* 47, no. 10 (1995), pp. 16–17.

4. Andrei Ivanov and Judith Perera, "Unscrupulous Russia May Soon Surpass U.S. in Arms Sales," Interpress Service, *Johnson's Russia List,* no. 1180, September 7, 1997.

5. Pavel Felgengauer, "Arms Exports Aren't as Lucrative as They're Said to Be," *Segodnia,* December 26, 1997, in *CDPSP* 49, no. 52 (1997), p. 18; Konstantin Makienko,"There are Fewer Russian Weapons in the World," *Kommersant-Daily,* February 13, 1998, in *CDPSP* 50, no. 8 (1998), pp. 12–13; Interfax report, quoting Evgenii Ananev, general director, Rosvooruzhenie, in *Johnson's Russia List,* no. 2158, April 21, 1998.

6. Felgengauer "Arms Exports"; Makienko, "There Are Fewer Russian Weapons in the World."

7. Felgengauer, "Arms Trade Is Not as Lucrative," pp. 16–17.

8. Igor Korotchenko, "Russia Is Striving to Be Among the World Leaders in the Arms Trade: In the Words of Assistant to RF President for Military-Technical Cooperation with Foreign Countries Boris Kuzyk, This May Occur as Early as 1998," *Nezavisimoe voennoe obozrenie,* no. 11, March 22–28, 1997, *Johnson's Russia List,* March 29, 1997.

9. *Argumenty i fakty,* no. 16, April 1997, *Johnson's Russia List,* April 17, 1997.

10. Matthew Brzezinski, "Rival Arms-Makers Lure Buyers Away from Russia," *Wall Street Journal,* April 1, 1997.

11. Makienko, "There Are Fewer Russian Weapons in the World."

12. Wilson John, "Quality Decides: Russia Is No Longer the Cheapest and Most Quality-Conscious Arms Supplier," *The Pioneer* (Delhi), May 28, 1997, *Johnson's Russia List,* June 1, 1997.

13. Reports of Sino-Russian presidential visits may be found in Vasily Kononenko and Vladimir Skosyrev, "Russian-Chinese Declaration Is Essentially Tantamount to a

Nonaggression Pact," *Izvestia*, December 21, 1992, in *CDPSP* 44, no. 51 (1992), pp. 13–14; Aleksandr Chudodeev, "Partners, but not Allies," *Segodnia*, September 2, 1994, in *CDPSP* 46, no. 36 (1994), p. 13; Tatiana Malkina, "Boris Yeltsin Sees No One Who Could Stand Against Such a Pair as 'Great Russia' and 'Great China'," *Segodnia*, April 27, 1996, in *CDPSP* 48, no. 17 (1996), pp. 7–8; "A Breakthrough for Russian Policy on the Asian Front," *Rossiiskie vesti*, April 24, 1997, in *CDPSP* 49, no. 17 (1997), pp. 1–2; Aleksandr Chudodeev, "Boris Yeltsin and Jiang Zemin Find Harmony," *Segodnia*, November 12, 1997, in *CDPSP* 49, no. 45 (1997), p. 6.

14. Ilia Bulavinov, "Russia's Boundless Friendship with China," *Kommersant-Daily*, April 25, 1997, in *CDPSP* 49, 17 (1997), p. 5.

15. See James Clay Moltz, "Regional Tensions in the Russo-Chinese Rapprochement," *Asian Survey* 35, no. 6 (June 1995).

16. Emil Pain, " 'Illegals' on the Banks of the Amur," *Rossiiskie vesti*, May 6, 1997, in *CDPSP* 49, no. 19 (1997), pp. 1–3.

17. "Russia and China: Can a Bear Love a Dragon?" *The Economist*, April 26, 1997, pp. 19–21.

18. Andrei Bagrov, "In Every Propeller Breathes a Scandal," *Kommersant-Daily*, July 18, 1996, in *CDPSP* 48, no. 30 (1996), pp. 20–21.

19. Boris Barakhta, "Is China's Experience Outdated?" *Pravda*, December 22, 1992, in *CDPSP* 44, no. 51 (1992), pp. 14–15.

20. Pavel Felgengauer, "Russia Too Busy Arming China to Care about Consequences," *St. Petersburg Times*, July 14–20, 1997, *Johnson's Russia List*, July 17, 1997.

21. The juxtaposition of views is found in Pavel Felgengauer, "Russia and the Conflict in the Taiwan Strait," and Vladimir Abarinov, "Benefits of Alliance with China Are Dubious," *Segodnia*, March 13, 1996, in *CDPSP* 48, no. 11 (1996), pp. 10–12. See also Pavel Ivanov, "Fears that China Will Bite the Hand that Arms It," *Asia Times*, August 1, 1997, *Johnson's Russia List*, no. 1108, August 1, 1997.

22. Quoted in Euikon Kim, "The Territorial Dispute between Moscow and Tokyo: A Historical Perspective," *Asian Perspective* 16, no. 2 (Fall–Winter 1992), p. 145.

23. Robert F. Miller, "Russian Policy toward Japan," in *Russian Foreign Policy since 1990*, ed. Peter Shearman (Boulder, CO: Westview Press, 1995), p. 143.

24. Stanislav Kondrashov, "Trials and Tribulations of Making Peace with Japan," *Izvestia*, August 14, 1992, in *CDPSP* 44, no. 33 (1992), pp. 15–17.

25. Major-General Georgi Mekhov, "Military Aspects of 'Territorial Problem,'" *Krasnaia zvezda*, July 22, 1992, in *CDPSP* 44, no. 29 (1992), p. 18.

26. Maksim Iusin, "Visit's Cancellation Indicates a Change in the Alignment of Forces in the Russian Leadership," *Izvestia*, September 11, 1992, in *CDPSP* 44, no. 36 (1992), p. 7; Kozyrev interview in *Moskovskie novosti*, no. 38, September 20, 1992, in *CDPSP* 44, no. 37 (1992), pp. 18–19.

27. Kozyrev made this claim in his memoirs. See Robert Orttung, "Kozyrev Publishes New Book," *OMRI Daily Digest*, February 28, 1995.

28. Vasili Golovnin, "Evgenii Primakov Invites Japanese to the Southern Kuriles," *Segodnia*, November 19, 1996, in *CDPSP* 48, no. 46 (1996), p. 25.

29. "Argued for 52 Years, Settled in Two Days," *Rossiiskie vesti*, November 4, 1997, in *CDPSP* 49, no. 44 (1997), pp. 1–2.

30. *Izvestia*, June 18, 1994, in *CDPSP* 46, no. 24 (1994), pp. 14–15.

31. Natalia Kalashnikova, "In Expectation of Meat Soup and Silk Clothing," *Kommersant-Daily*, April 18, 1996, in *CDPSP* 48, no. 16 (1996), p. 24.

32. Ivan Shomov, " 'Patriot' Games: What's Good for American Manufacturers Is Good for Seoul," *Segodnia*, April 8, 1997, in *CDPSP* 49, no. 14 (1997), pp. 21–22.

33. Col.-Gen. Leonid Ivashov, "Old Friends Still Talking," *Asia Times*, May 21,

1997, *Johnson's Russia List,* May 21, 1997; "North Korea's Final Warning to Moscow," *Kommersant-Daily,* October 1, 1996, in *CDPSP* 48, no. 39 (1996), p. 26.

34. Vitali Naumkin, "Tajikistan: The USSR's Last War or the New Russia's First War? Moscow Still Has No Unified Policy," *Nezavisimaia gazeta,* July 29, 1993, in *CDPSP* 45, no. 30 (1993), pp. 12–13.

35. Aidyn Mekhtiiev, "Central Asian Commonwealth Could Become Alternative to CIS," *Nezavisimaia gazeta,* October 21, 1994, in *CDPSP* 46, no. 42 (1994), p. 23; Georgi Bovt, "Turkic Summit: 'I'm Telling You in Plain Russian,'" *Kommersant-Daily,* August 30, 1995, in *CDPSP* 47, no. 35 (1995), p. 28.

36. Vladimir Skosyrev, "Iran, Superpower of Persian Gulf, Builds Up Its Military Might with Moscow's Help," *Izvestia,* February 5, 1992, in *CDPSP* 44, no. 5 (1992), pp. 19–20.

37. Vladimir Abarinov, "Moscow and Washington Stick to Their Own Interests," *Segodnia,* May 12, 1995, in *CDPSP* 47, no. 19 (1995), pp. 1–2.

38. *Moskovskie novosti,* no. 1, January 1–14, 1996, in *CDPSP* 48, no. 1, pp. 23–24; *Kommersant-Daily,* November 29, 1996, in *CDPSP* 48, no. 48, p. 22.

39. Georgi Bovt, "Synchronizing Watches: With Accuracy Up to a Century," *Kommersant-Daily,* December 25, 1996, in *CDPSP* 48, no. 52 (1996), pp. 19–20.

40. "Moscow Makes Headway in Iran," *Asia Times,* June 27, 1997, *Johnson's Russia List,* June 30, 1997.

41. Leonid Gankin, "Primakov Persuades Netanyahu," *Kommersant-Daily,* October 28, 1997, in *CDPSP* 49, no. 43 (1997), p. 21.

42. Sergei Filatov, "Politics Is a Subtle Business, but One Would Like Clarity," *Pravda,* November 11, 1992, in *CDPSP* 44, no. 46 (1992), p. 18.

43. Vladimir Lukin, "Bengal Light in the Arabian Sands," *Moskovskie novosti,* no. 50, October 23–30, 1994, in *CDPSP* 46, no. 41 (1994), p. 13.

44. *Nezavisimaia gazeta,* September 5, 1996, in *CDPSP* 48, no. 36 (1996), p. 8.

45. See, for example, Kirill Dybski, "Oil and Money Will Flow to Russia through 'Iraqi Pipeline,'" *Segodnia,* December 11, 1996, in *CDPSP* 48, no. 50 (1996), p. 25.

46. *Moskovskie novosti,* no. 47, November 23–30, 1997, in *CDPSP* 49, no. 47 (1997), pp. 3–4.

47. Sergei Markov, "Iraq Intensifies Anti-Americanism the World Over," *Izvestia,* February 26, 1998, in *CDPSP* 50, no. 8 (1998), pp. 8–9.

48. Karen Brutents, "Time to Return," *Nezavisimaia gazeta,* October 5, 1994, in *CDPSP* 46, no. 41 (1994), pp. 13–14.

49. Konstantin Eggert, "Russia Wants to Be the Equal of the U.S. in the Middle East," *Izvestia,* April 26, 1996, in *CDPSP* 48, no. 17 (1996), p. 10.

50. Maksim Iusin, "Washington No Longer Wants to Share the Laurels of Peacemaker with Moscow—Evgenii Primakov's First Defeat," *Izvestia,* April 30, 1996, in *CDPSP* 48, no. 17 (1996), p. 11.

51. Leonid Gankin, "We Have Become Mature Partners," *Moskovskie novosti,* no. 23, June 9–16, 1996, in *CDPSP* 48, no. 23 (1996), pp. 13, 20.

52. Piotr Fedin, "Russians' Friend Arafat Goes Home Satisfied," *Kommersant-Daily,* February 20, 1997, in *CDPSP* 49, no. 8 (1997), pp. 20–21.

53. Aleksei Bausin, "Well, Friends, No Matter How You Sit, For Partnership You're Just Not Fit," *Obshchaia gazeta,* no. 10, March 13–19, 1996, in *CDPSP* 49, no. 11 (1996), p. 26.

54. Boris Vinogradov, "Conflict Brewing on Afghanistan-Tajikistan Border," *Izvestia,* February 19, 1993, in *CDPSP* 45, no. 7 (1993), pp. 19–20.

55. Evgenii Primakov, "Russia Doesn't Oppose Islam," *Nezavisimaia gazeta,* September 18, 1996, in *CDPSP* 48, no. 40 (1996), p. 32.

56. *Kommersant-Daily,* May 27, 1997, in *CDPSP* 49, no. 21 (1997), p. 26.

57. John F. Burns, "Would-Be Afghan Rulers Find Their Islamic Steamroller Halted," *New York Times,* July 27, 1997.

58. Vladimir Naumov, "Fate of 'Space Deal,'" *Rossiiskie vesti,* January 4, 1994, in *CDPSP* 46, no. 1 (1994), p. 18.

59. Michael Gordon, "Russia Selling Atomic Plants to India; U.S. Protests Deal," *New York Times,* February 6, 1997.

60. "India and Russia: Brothers in Arms," *The Economist,* November 23, 1996, pp. 38–40; Aleksandr Sychov, "India to Rely on SU-30," *Izvestia,* December 3, 1996, in *CDPSP* 48, no. 48 (1996), pp. 21–22.

61. Fred Weir for the *Hindustan Times,* March 26, 1997, *Johnson's Russia List,* March 27, 1997.

62. "Pakistan Will Go without Russian Weapons," *Kommersant-Daily,* March 30, 1996, in *CDPSP* 48, no. 13, p. 23; Maksim Iusin, "The Pakistani Titmouse and the Indian Crane," *Izvestia,* December 22, 1995, in *CDPSP* 48, no. 1 (1995), pp. 12–13.

63. Leonid Gankin, "Russia Is Losing Its Enemies," *Kommersant-Daily,* July 9, 1997, in *CDPSP* 49, no. 28 (1997), p. 23.

64. "No 'Shower of Gold' Expected," *Moskovskie novosti,* no. 48, November 30–December 30, 1997, in *CDPSP* 49, no. 48 (1997), p. 24.

65. Evgenii Bai, "Russia Concerned by Castro's Unilateral Decision to Stop Construction of Nuclear Power Plant in Cuba," *Izvestia,* September 9, 1992, in *CDPSP* 44, no. 36 (1992), p. 23.

66. *Nezavisimaia gazeta,* December 29, 1993, in *CDPSP* 45, no. 52 (1993), p. 28.

67. Leonid Velekhov, "Russia and Cuba: A Dialogue between a Poor Man and a Beggar," *Segodnia,* October 13, 1995; Pavel Felgengauer, "Russia Needs the Island of Freedom Again," *Segodnia,* October 17, 1995; Aleksei Basin, "Russia and Cuba: Back to the Future?" *Moskovskie novosti,* no. 71, October 15–22, 1995, in *CDPSP* 47, no. 42 (1995), pp. 6–7, 24.

68. Evgenii Bai, "Half a Loaf Is Better than None," *Izvestia,* October 10, 1996, in *CDPSP* 48, no. 41 (1996), p. 28.

69. Karen Khachaturov, "Russian Breakthrough in Latin America," *Nezavisimaia gazeta,* May 29, 1996; Anatoli Sosnovski, "On the Benefit of Routine Professionalism," *Moskovskie novosti,* no. 21, May 26–June 2, 1996, in *CDPSP* 48, no. 21 (1996), p. 27.

Chapter 8: Conclusion

1. While communist apologists praised the Nazi-Soviet Pact as a brilliant defensive maneuver, the case that it was a disaster is much stronger. See George Kennan, *Russia and the West under Lenin and Stalin* (New York: New American Library, 1961), pp. 295–327.

2. For a description of the balance of power, see Hans J. Morgenthau, *Politics Among Nations,* 6th ed. (New York: Alfred Knopf, 1985).

3. For a description of the nineteenth-century "great game," see Peter Hopkirk, *The Great Game: The Struggle for Power in Central Asia* (New York: Kodansha International, 1990).

4. See Kenneth N. Waltz, *Theory of International Politics* (Reading, PA: Addison-Wesley, 1979).

5. Kenneth N. Waltz, *Man, the State and War* (New York: Columbia University Press, 1959), p. 238.

6. Joseph L. Nogee and Robert H. Donaldson, *Soviet Foreign Policy since World War II,* 4th ed. (New York: Macmillan, 1992), p. 3.

7. The classic analysis of the behavior of states under different conditions of polarity is Morton Kaplan, *System and Process in International Politics* (New York: John Wiley, 1957). A summary of Kaplan's argument is in his "Balance of Power, Polarity and Other Models of International Systems," *American Political Science Review,* September 1957.

8. Analyses of bipolar and multipolar systems can be found in Kenneth N. Waltz, "The Stability of a Bipolar World," *Daedalus,* Summer 1964; Karl W. Deutsch and J. David Singer, "Multipolar Power Systems and International Stability," *World Politics,* April 1964; Joseph L. Nogee, "Polarity: An Ambiguous Concept," *Orbis,* Winter 1975.

9. A notable exception is Kenneth N. Waltz.

10. An original analysis of bipolarity at the regional level is Peter J. Fliess, *Thucydides and the Politics of Bipolarity* (Baton Rouge: Louisiana State University Press, 1966).

11. *Current Digest of the Post-Soviet Press (CDPSP)* 49, no. 17 (1997), p. 2.

12. *CDPSP* 49, no. 21 (1997), p. 1.

13. Anders Aslund, *How Russia Became a Market Economy* (Washington, DC: Brookings Institution Press, 1995).

14. Lee H. Hamilton, "The Debate on Aid to Russia," *Problems of Post-Communism,* May–June 1995, p. 37.

15. Anne Henderson, "The Politics of Foreign Investment in Eastern Europe," in ibid., p. 53.

16. Ernesto Hernandez-Cata, "Russia and the IMF: The Political Economy of Macro-Stabilization," in ibid., pp. 19–26.

17. Boris Yeltsin, *The Struggle for Russia* (New York: Random House, 1994), p. 293.

18. Steven Erlanger, "U.S. to Back Baltic Membership in NATO, but Not Anytime Soon," *New York Times,* January 12, 1998, p. 1.

Index

A

ABM. *See* Anti-ballistic Missile
Adenauer, Konrad, 69
Afghanistan, 12, 16, 42–43, 76–77,
  79, 87–88, 93–94, 96, 107, 128,
  140, 174, 189, 234, 256, 259,
  269–72, 276
Agrarian Party, 129
Akhromeev, Sergei, 140
Albania, 56, 80, 214
Albright, Madeleine, 218, 269
Alexander I, 8, 19, 21
Alexander II, 10–12, 14, 20, 24
Alexander III, 14, 24
Algeria, 77, 199
Aliev, Gaidar, 180–81
Alksnis, Viktor, 115
Allende, Salvador, 78
Ambartsumov, Evgenii, 114–15,
  150, 246
Amin, Hafizullah, 97
Andropov, Iurii, 89–92, 139, 146
Angola, 79, 86, 96, 277–78
  MPLA, 86
Annan, Kofi, 264
Anti-ballistic Missile (ABM), 84,
  92–93
APEC. *See* Asian and Pacific
  Economic Council
Arafat, Yasir, 266, 268
Arbatov, Georgii, 82, 95
Ardzinba, Vladislav, 177
Argentina, 250, 282

Armenia, 156–57, 159, 172–73,
  179–81, 196, 255
ASEAN. *See* Association of
  Southeast Asian Nations
Asian and Pacific Economic Council
  (APEC), 277
Aslund, Anders, 190, 289
Aspaturian, Vernon, 32–33
Association of Southeast Asian
  Nations (ASEAN), 276–77
Atlanticists, 114, 190, 197, 213, 234,
  291
Atlee, Clement, 56
Australia, 118
Austria, 7, 13–16, 37, 47, 97, 216
  Austrian State Treaty (1955),
  68–69
Avturkhanov, Umar, 200
Azerbaijan, 141, 149, 156–57,
  159–60, 173–74, 179–81, 196,
  206, 255–56, 258–59
  Treaty of Friendship and
  Cooperation (1994), 181
Aziz, Tariq, 261–63

B

Baburin, Sergei, 205
Bakatin, Vladimir, 147
Baker, James, 161, 193
Bakunin, Mikhail, 24, 45
Balance-of-Power, 19–21, 59–60,
  75, 90, 120, 283
Bangladesh, 85

Barsukov, Aleksandr, 128, 148
Basaev, Shamil, 201–202
Baturin, Iurii, 129, 131
Belarus (Belorussia), 8, 39, 50–51,
    103, 105, 149, 155–57, 159–61,
    167–69, 173, 180, 188, 193–94,
    224, 238
  Russo-Belarus Treaty, 125
Ben Bella, Ahmed, 77
Berezovskii, Boris, 152–53
Bessarabia, 8, 10, 13, 49, 181, 223
Bessmertnykh, Aleksandr, 135
Bismarck, Otto, 13–14
Blair, Tony, 231
Bonaparte, Napoleon (I), 18, 21
Bosnia-Herzegovina, 12–14, 16,
    116, 215, 219, 229–30, 268, 289
  Balkan war, 194–95, 206–12
  Dayton Accords, 208, 210–12
Boutros-Ghali, Boutros, 178
Brandt, Willy, 82
Brazil, 114, 237, 282
Brest-Litovsk Treaty (1918), 37–38,
    40, 59–60
Brezhnev, Leonid, 78, 81–89, 91–92,
    94–95, 101, 105, 108, 110, 124,
    139, 146, 233–66, 269, 272, 286
Brezhnev Doctrine, 104
Brutents, Karen, 266
Bukharin, Nikolai, 36, 45
Bulganin, Nikolai, 69, 76
Bulgaria, 12–14, 51, 54–56, 70, 99,
    103, 153, 214, 223–24, 236, 238
  Bulgarian Socialist Party, 89
Burbulis, Gennadii, 117, 249, 273
Burma, 65, 76
Bush, George, 95–96, 100, 102–103,
    191–92, 195, 197
Buzek, Jerzy, 221

C

Cambodia, 68, 79, 87, 93, 96, 276
Canada, 3, 197, 209, 218

Carter, Jimmy, 87–88
Castro, Fidel, 74, 279–82
Catherine II (The Great), 7–8, 19,
    50, 109
Ceausescu, Nicolae, 99, 223
CFE Treaty. See Conventional
    Forces in Europe Treaty
Chamberlain, Neville, 48
Charles XII, 21
Chechnia, 125, 127–30, 142, 144,
    147–49, 152, 175–77, 198,
    200–206, 210, 212, 219,
    224–28, 238, 256, 268, 288
Checkel, Jeffrey, 121
Chernenko, Konstantin, 91, 139
Chernobyl, 93
Chernomyrdin, Viktor, 117, 126–27,
    129, 139, 145, 153, 186, 202,
    205, 221–23, 237, 249, 253,
    256, 261, 273, 276
Chiang Kai-Shek, 44, 54–55, 65–66
Chicherin, Georgii, 40–41, 60, 134–35
Chile, 78
China, 11, 15–16, 20, 29, 43–47, 55,
    65
  People's Republic of, 66, 68, 72,
    74–76, 84, 87, 90, 93, 96, 108,
    114, 117, 209, 233, 236–37,
    239–46, 251–52, 269, 272–74,
    276
  Sino-Soviet conflict, 79–81, 239
  Sino-Soviet Treaty (1950), 65, 68
  Treaty of Alliance and Friendship
    (1945), 55
  Treaty of Khakhta, 7
  Treaty of Nerchinsk, 7, 11
  Treaty of Peking, 11
Chinese Communist Party, 43
Chirac, Jacques, 229–30
Christopher, Warren, 217, 267
Chubais, Anatolii, 143, 152–53, 235,
    289
Churchill, Winston, 53–56, 59, 63
Churkin, Vitaly, 207

Ciller, Tansu, 256
CIS. *See* Commonwealth of
    Independent States
Civic Union, 172
Clinton, Bill, 161, 186, 193, 197,
    204, 210–11, 213–14, 216–17,
    258, 264, 273, 287
CMEA. *See* Council for Mutual
    Economic Assistance
Cold War, 57–109, 120–21, 173,
    189, 191, 212, 215, 217, 231,
    233–35, 239, 251, 269, 272,
    282, 285, 287–88
Colombia, 237, 282
Commonwealth of Independent
    States (CIS), 103, 113–15, 118,
    120, 127, 130–31, 136, 138,
    140–43, 148–49, 151, 156–62,
    164–72, 176–78, 183, 188, 216,
    224, 226–27, 239, 255, 271
  Belovezhskaia Agreement (1991),
    103, 105
  Collective Security Treaty (1992),
    144, 168, 172–73, 271
  Peacekeeping, 173–83
Communist Information Bureau
    (Cominform), 64, 71, 233
Communist International (Comintern),
    27, 40–47, 52, 65, 135
Communist Party of the Soviet
    Union (CPSU), 26, 32, 35, 37,
    40, 67, 70, 72, 93, 101, 106,
    112, 122–23, 134–35, 140, 273
  General-Secretary of, 123
  Party congresses, 38, 41, 44, 46, 48,
    51, 58, 69–70, 73, 79–80, 86–87
  Politburo, 40, 101, 122, 131,
    138–39, 146, 180, 220
Conference on Security and
    Cooperation in Europe (CSCE),
    83, 100, 116, 118, 180, 195,
    218. Renamed in 1994; *see*
    Organization for Security and
    Cooperation in Europe (OSCE)

Conference on Security and
    Cooperation in Europe
    (continued)
  Helsinki Declaration, 83, 104
  Minsk Group, 180
Congress of Russian Communities,
    128, 184
Constituent Assembly, 35–36
Containment, 63–64, 104, 215
Conventional Forces in Europe
    (CFE) Treaty (1990), 100, 142,
    191, 196, 216, 218
Cooperative Threat Reduction
    Program (Nunn-Lugar), 193–94
Council of Europe, 185, 218–19,
    225–26, 232
Council for Mutual Economic
    Assistance (CMEA), 71, 219
CPSU. *See* Communist Party of the
    Soviet Union
Croatia, 194, 209
CSCE. *See* Conference on Security
    and Cooperation in Europe
Cuba, 74–75, 86, 96, 106, 189, 235,
    279–82
Cuban missile crisis, 75, 81
Cyprus, 237, 256
Czechoslovakia, 47, 55–56, 64, 76,
    100, 103–104, 219, 221
  Soviet invasion (1968), 88, 221–22
  Uprising (1989), 97–99
Czech Republic, 187, 213–14, 217,
    222
  Russo-Czech Treaty (1993), 221

D

Davydov, Oleg, 238, 258–59
De Gaulle, Charles, 199, 229
De Klerk, Frederic, 278
Demirel, Suleyman, 181, 255
Denmark, 18, 231
Detente, 78, 81–89
Djilas, Milovan, 57–58

Dole, Robert, 213
Dostum, Abdul Rashid, 271
Dubcek, Alexander, 103, 105
Dudaev, Dzhokar, 200, 203–204

E

Ecuador, 236
Eden, Anthony, 53
Egorov, Nikolai, 200
Egypt, 9, 71, 76, 78, 269
　Suez crisis (1956), 71–72
　Yom Kippur War, 85
Eisenhower, Dwight D., 69, 73
Elchibey, Abulfez, 181, 255
Elizabeth II (Queen), 231
Engels, Friedrich, 25, 27
Erbakan, Necmettin, 256
Erin, Viktor, 200
Estonia, 6, 37, 46, 56, 155, 183–87,
　214, 218, 225, 231
　Treaty of Tartu (1920), 186
Eurasianists, 114, 119, 190, 234
European Union (EU), 185, 187,
　208, 218–19, 224–25
Ethiopia, 47, 78–79, 87

F

Felgengauer, Pavel, 131, 143, 244
Finland, 3, 7–8, 37, 46, 50–51, 53,
　184, 198, 216, 231–32
Ford, Gerald, 86
France, 5, 9, 14–15, 20, 29, 36,
　46–48, 50, 53, 63, 65, 68, 71,
　73, 75, 99, 112, 124, 180, 199,
　208, 216, 229–30, 252, 254,
　259, 283, 285, 287, 292
　Franco-Russian Entente, 47
　Franco-Russian Treaty (1893), 14,
　229
　Paris Summit (1960), 73–74
Franz Ferdinand, 16
Frederick the Great, 21

G

G-7. *See* Group of Seven
Gaidar, Egor, 113, 116–17, 127,
　141, 227, 278, 289
Gamsakhurdia, Zviad, 176–77
Gandhi, Mohandas, 43
Geneva Agreement (1954), 68
Geneva Summit (1985), 92
Genghis Khan, 5
Genoa Economic Conference
　(1922), 41, 60
George, Alexander, 30
Georgia, 8, 143, 149, 156–57,
　173–79, 196, 206
　Abkhazia, 174, 176–78
　South Ossetia, 134, 176–77
　Treaty of Friendship and
　　Cooperation (1994), 178
Gerasimov, Gennadiy, 105
Germany, 3, 5, 13–15, 17, 35–38,
　41–42, 45–47, 52–54, 56, 62,
　68, 72–74, 82, 99, 105–106,
　246, 283, 285, 288
　Berlin blockade, 64–65
　Communist Party, 45–46
　Christian Democratic Union,
　　82
　Federal Republic of Germany,
　　68–69, 72–75, 82–83, 87, 91,
　　97, 99, 168, 207–209, 217,
　　220, 227–32, 256, 271, 287
　German Democratic Republic, 65,
　　67, 69, 73, 83, 97, 99,
　　103–104, 168, 180, 228
　Nazi-Soviet cooperation, 47–52
　Social Democratic Party, 27–28,
　　46
　Treaty of Rapallo (1922), 227
　Unification, 99–100
Ghana, 77
Gierek, Edward, 88
Godunov, Boris, 6
Gomulka, Wladyslaw, 71

Gorbachev, Mikhail, 69, 79, 91–92, 96, 101–103, 105–106, 108–10, 112, 119–20, 122–24, 130, 134, 136, 138–41, 143–44, 146–47, 149, 156, 167, 170, 175–77, 179, 182, 189–90, 194, 197–98, 200, 218, 223, 227, 230, 233, 235–36, 239, 245, 247, 251, 256–57, 260, 265, 269, 273, 276–77, 279, 286
  Glasnost, 93–94, 96, 101
  New Thinking, 93–100, 110, 191, 247, 285
  Perestroika, 92–93, 96, 101, 189
Gore-Chernomyrdin Commission, 197, 230, 258
Gowda, Deve, 274–75
Grachev, Andrei, 120–21
Grachev, Pavel, 128, 133, 140–44, 196, 200, 104, 228, 244, 247, 250, 255
Greece, 9, 63, 67, 114, 224, 231
Great Britain, 9, 12, 15–17, 20–21, 29, 36, 41–42, 48, 50–51, 53, 56–57, 60, 63, 71, 73, 91, 99, 109, 112, 207–208, 230–31, 236, 250, 254, 263, 271, 283, 285, 292
  Anglo-Soviet Trade Agreement, 41–42
Gromov, Boris, 140, 142
Gromyko, Andrei, 89, 134–35, 246
Group of Seven (G-7), 102, 218, 273, 290
Gulf War, 100–101

H

Hashimoto, Ryutaro, 250
Havel, Vaclav, 99, 219, 221
Herzen, Alexander, 24
Hilferding, Rudolf, 28
Hitler, Adolph, 18, 45–49, 52, 58
Hobson, John, 28

Ho Chi Minh, 68
Holbrooke, Richard, 211
Hungary, 8, 38, 51, 55–56, 70, 100, 103–104, 180, 187, 213–14, 217, 219, 222, 226, 236
  Uprising (1956), 71–72, 88, 222
  Revolution (1849), 10
  Revolution (1989), 97
Husak, Gustav, 99
Hussein, Saddam, 100, 260–64

I

Ideology, 30–33, 38, 40–41, 58–60, 64, 94–95, 112, 190, 233, 279
  Marxism-Leninism, 31–33, 58, 69–71, 9405, 111, 118, 122, 140, 240
  See also Karl Marx; V.I. Lenin
Iliescu, Ion, 99
IMF. See International Monetary Fund
India, 12, 29, 42, 44, 65, 76–77, 80, 85, 87, 114, 197, 235–39, 272–75
  Indo-Soviet Treaty (1971), 273
Indonesia, 65, 68, 77, 86, 236, 277
INF. See Intermediate Nuclear Forces Treaty under the heading Nuclear Weapons
International Atomic Energy Agency, 258
International Bank for Reconstruction and Development, 290
International Monetary Fund (IMF), 218, 290
International system, 283–88
  Bipolar, 14, 62–64, 76–77, 79, 108, 189, 233
  Multipolar, 59, 108, 189, 241, 277, 282, 285–88
  Unipolar, 189, 241, 287

Iran, 21, 43, 62, 71, 87, 96, 107,
    206, 232, 237–38, 254, 256–60,
    267–68, 270, 272, 284, 292
  Persia, 7–8, 20, 254
  Teheran conference, 53
Iraq, 71, 77, 87, 96, 107, 194–97,
    229, 232, 238, 260–64, 267, 292
  Baghdad Pact, 71–72
  Persian Gulf crisis, 100, 238,
    260–61
Israel, 67, 71, 118, 259, 265–69,
  Oslo Accords, 265
  Yom Kippur War, 85
Italy, 14–15, 63, 65, 180, 231, 271
Ivan III, 5, 6, 19
Ivan IV, 6, 19
Izetbegovic, Alija, 209–10

J

Japan, 3, 15–16, 43, 46, 49, 51–52,
    54–56, 66, 108, 117, 232,
    244–52, 277, 288
  Kurile Islands, 198, 245–50
  Shimodo Treaty (1855), 247
  Treaty of Portsmouth (1905), 246
Jaruzelski, Wojciech, 89, 97, 220
Jiang Zemin, 240–42, 287
Joffe, Adolph, 44
Johnson, Lyndon, 204
Jordan, 267, 279

K

Kamenev, Lev, 40
Karadzic, Radovan, 195, 207–10
Karmal, Babrak, 87
Kazakhstan, 81, 149, 156–57,
    159–61, 169–74, 193–94, 198,
    224, 239, 241, 255, 258, 275
Kellogg-Briand Pact, 46
Kennan, George, 63, 104
Kennedy, John F., 74–75
Kennedy, Paul, 17

Kerensky, Alexander, 34
KGB (Committee for State
    Security), 89, 102, 106, 119,
    122, 135, 146–47, 149, 180, 222
Khasbulatov, Ruslan, 142, 150,
    177–78, 183, 261, 270
Khodorkovskii, Mikhail, 153
Khomeini (Ayatollah), 256–57
Khrushchev, Nikita, 51, 67–77,
    79–81, 83, 89, 92, 108, 110,
    138–39, 163, 233, 246, 286
  Destalinization, 70, 75
  Peaceful Coexistence, 70, 81–82
  Secret Speech, 58, 79
Kim Il Sung, 253
Kirienko, Sergei, 139
Kissinger, Henry, 18–21, 83, 85
Kohl, Helmut, 69, 99, 227, 229
Kokoshin, Andrei, 115, 131
Kolesnikov, Mikhail, 196
Kondrashov, Stanislav, 220
Korea, 15–16, 18, 56, 66–68, 70,
    118, 251, 253
  North Korea, 66, 251–54
  Korean War, 66, 106
  South Korea, 66, 237, 245,
    251–53, 277
  Soviet-North Korea Treaty (1961),
    251
Kornilov, Lavr, 34
Korzhakov, Aleksandr, 128, 148, 200
Kosygin, Aleksei, 81, 89, 92
Kotelkin, Aleksandr, 237
Kozyrev, Andrei, 112–13, 115–17,
    119–20, 126, 131–33, 136–37,
    141, 150, 172, 178, 190,
    194–95, 197, 201–203,
    207–208, 210, 213, 215–16,
    218, 220, 225, 227, 229–30,
    234, 239–40, 248–49, 251–52,
    255, 257, 260–62, 265–66,
    268–70, 276, 278, 291
Kravchuk, Leonid, 105, 157, 159,
    161–64, 193

Kriuchkov, Vladimir, 102, 106, 146
Kuchma, Leonid, 162–63, 165, 193
Kulikov, Anatolii, 129
Kunadze, Georgii, 252
Kuomintang, 43–44, 47
Kuwait, 100, 194, 238, 260–62
Kuzyk, Boris, 237
Kwasniewski, Aleksei, 221
Kyrgyzstan, 81, 156–57, 159, 167,
    169–70, 173–74, 224, 239, 255,
    258

L

Laos, 68, 79
Latvia, 6, 37, 46, 56, 102, 105, 155,
    183–87, 214, 218, 231
Lavrov, Peter, 24
League of Nations, 42, 47, 50, 60
Lebanon, 267, 269
Lebed, Aleksandr, 128–29, 131,
    133, 142–44, 182–84, 204–205,
    217, 292
Leites, Nathan, 30–32
Lenin, Vladimir I., 23–26, 28–29,
    31–40, 42, 45, 59–60, 65, 69,
    76, 89, 95, 138, 254
Leninism, 25–26, 27–33, 38, 43, 52,
    57, 233
Li Peng, 96
Libya, 196, 260, 264–65, 267
Ligachev, Egor, 95
Lithuania, 8, 36–37, 49, 56, 102,
    105, 109, 156, 167, 183–85,
    187, 214, 218, 231
Litvinov, Maksim, 46–47, 49, 60,
    134–35
  Protocol, 46
Lobov, Oleg, 127–28, 131, 143, 200,
    240
Locarno Treaty, 42, 46
Lukashenko, Aleksandr, 168–69
Lukin, Vladimir, 115, 150, 225, 262
Luzhkov, Iuri, 163

M

Macedonia, 13
Major, John, 230
Malaya, 65
Malaysia, 197, 236, 259, 277
Malenkov, Georgii, 67, 68, 73
Malia, Martin, 21–22
Mandela, Nelson, 278
Mao Zedong, 44, 65, 72, 79–80
Marshall, George, 63
Marshall Plan, 63
Martov, Julius, 25
Marx, Karl, 23–25, 27–29, 32–33
Marxism, 24–31, 43, 52, 57, 76, 95
Maskhadov, Aslan, 204–205
Matlock, Jack F. Jr., 105–106
Mengistu, Mariam Haile, 78
Meri, Lennart, 186
Mexico, 12, 114, 282
Migranian, Andranik, 114–15,
    170
Mikolajczyk, Stanislas, 54
Milosevic, Slobodan, 195, 206–208,
    210, 212
Missiles, 87, 90, 95, 108, 145,
    191–93, 243, 259–60, 262, 268,
    273, 279
  Cruise, 91
  ICBMs, 81, 90, 94, 192
  INF, 90–92, 95
Mitterand, Francois, 199, 229
Moldova, 128, 141, 156–57,
    159–60, 173–74, 181–83, 214,
    223
  Trans-Dniester region, 128, 174,
    181–83, 198, 204
Molotov, V.M., 49, 51, 53, 134–35
Mongolia, 7, 16, 43, 55, 235
Moscow, 3, 5–6, 10, 13, 15, 40, 52,
    140–41
Moscow summit (1972), 84
Mubarak, Hosni, 269
Munich conference, 47–48

N

Nabiev, Rakhmon, 174
Nagorno-Karabakh, 173–74,
    179–81, 226, 255, 258
Nagy, Imre, 71, 222
Najibullah, 269, 271
Nasser, Gamal, 71
NATO. *See* North Atlantic Treaty
    Organization
Nazarbaev, Nursaltan, 159, 169–70,
    173, 275
Nazi-Soviet Pact (1939), 49–53,
    59–60, 181, 183, 223, 283
Near Abroad, 114, 117, 154–88,
    226, 233–34, 269
Nehru, Jawaharlal, 76
Nemtsov, Boris, 103, 250, 289
Netanyahu, Benjamin, 259, 268–69
New Economic Policy, 39
Nicaragua, 79, 95–96, 281
Nicholas I, 8–10, 19–20
Nicholas II, 15, 17, 20, 34
Nixon, Richard, 83–86, 204
Nkrumah, Kwame, 77
North Atlantic Treaty Organization
    (NATO), 65, 68–69, 72–73, 83,
    90–91, 99–100, 116, 165, 184,
    187–88, 196, 204, 207–12, 219,
    254, 268, 283, 288
    Expansion, 131, 142, 148, 185,
        187–88, 193, 201, 212–18,
        220, 222–23, 226, 229–30,
        232, 234, 241, 284, 289, 292
    Partnership for Peace, 187, 201,
        214–16
Norway, 222, 231–32
Nuclear weapons, 130–31, 144,
    160–61, 191, 252, 258, 274, 288
    Arms control, 191–94
    Atomic bombs, 56, 62, 66, 75, 81
    GPALS, 191
    Intermediate Nuclear Forces
        Treaty (INF), 191

Nuclear weapons *(continued)*
    Nonproliferation Treaty (1968),
        161–62, 193, 252, 258
    Nuclear Test Ban Treaty (1963),
        75
    See also Missiles

O

Oman, 260
Organization for Security and
    Cooperation in Europe
    (OSCE), 131, 180, 182,
    185–86, 201, 212–13,
    215–16, 226–27, 231. *See also*
    Conference on Security and
    Cooperation in Europe
    (CSCE)
Ortega, Daniel, 95
Our Home Is Russia, 129, 202
Owen, David, 206

P

Pacific Economic Cooperation
    Council, 276
Pain, Emil, 242
Pakistan, 72, 85, 87–88, 238,
    271–72, 274–76
Palestine, 9
Palestine Liberation Organization
    (PLO), 96, 266
Palestinians, 265–69
Palmerston, Henry (Lord), 19
Pankin, Boris, 135
Pavlov, Valentin, 102
Peacekeeping, 131, 173–83
Perry, William, 187
Peres, Shimon, 265, 267
Peter the Great, 6–7, 10–11, 18–20,
    109
Philippines, 65
Plekhanov, G.V., 24–25
Pleve, V.K., 15

PLO. *See* Palestine Liberation
  Organization
Pobedonostev, Konstantin, 24
Poland, 3, 6, 8, 13, 20, 36–37, 39,
  46–50, 53–56, 70, 82, 103–104,
  167, 184, 187, 213–14, 217,
  219–22, 231, 238
  Solidarity, 97
  Treaty of Riga, 39
  Uprising (1956), 71, 79
  Uprising (1980), 88–89
Poltoranin, Mikhail, 248
Porter, Bruce, 21
Portugal, 86, 161
  Lisbon Protocol, 161, 193
Posuvaliuk, Viktor, 262, 264,
267–68
Potsdam Conference, 56, 69
Prikhodko, Sergei, 125, 134
Primakov, Evgenii, 100, 119–21,
  133, 148, 188, 203, 214,
  216–17, 222, 234, 245, 250,
  259–60, 263–72, 275–77,
  281–82, 291
Prokhanov, Aleksandr, 115
Prussia, 7
Pugo, Boris, 102

R

Rabin, Yitzhak, 266
Raduev, Salman, 203
Rafsanjani, Hashemi, 257–58
Rakhmonov, Imomali, 174
Rapallo, 46, 60
  Treaty of (1922), 41
Reagan, Ronald, 88, 90, 92–93, 96
Reykjavik Summit (1986), 92–93
Ribbentrop, Joachim von, 49
Riurikov, Dimitrii, 125
Rodionov, Igor, 143–44, 244, 251,
  253, 289
Roh Tae Woo, 251
Rokhlin, Lev, 144

Romania, 13, 47, 51, 53–54, 99,
  181–82, 214, 219, 223
  National Salvation Front, 99
Romanov, Michael, 6
Roosevelt, Franklin, 53–57
Roosevelt, Theodore, 16
Roy, M.N., 42–43
Rumiantsev, Oleg, 248
Russia, 23–24, 29, 31, 36–37, 39–40,
  43, 60, 102, 105, 108–54, 156,
  167, 176, 202, 212, 214, 265,
  283–84, 286–88, 290–92
  Allied intervention, 38–39
  and arms control, 191–94
  and arms sales, 235–239, 243–44,
    253, 255–57, 261, 267,
    274–75, 277, 279
  and Balkan conflict, 13, 16, 20, 22
  and Baltics, 183–88, 206–12
  and Belarus, 167–69
  and Central Asia, 170–71
  Chechen War, 200–206
  Communist Party, 105, 111, 115,
    140, 152, 202–203, 291
  Congress of People's Deputies,
    115–16, 124, 150, 198, 227
  Constitution (1993), 124–25, 147,
    150, 199
  Crimean War, 10–12, 18, 20
  and Europe, 218–32
  Federation Council, 126, 129–33,
    148, 204–205
  Geography, 3–5, 17–17
  Intelligence agencies, 147–48
  Military, 139–49, 160–61, 288
  Ministry of Defense, 139, 141–42
  Ministry of Foreign Affairs, 132,
    135–39, 142
  and Near Abroad, 155–88
  and non-west, 189–232
  parliamentary crisis (1993),
    141–42, 147, 190, 261
  peacekeeping, 130, 143, 173–83,
    196, 226

Russia *(continued)*
  presidency, 124–34
  Presidential Election, 1996, 152,
    199, 201–205, 212, 215
  Russian Social Democratic Labor
    Party, 25–27
  Russo-Japanese war, 15–16, 22
  Security Council, 126, 129–33,
    148, 204–205
  Shock therapy, 198
  Siberia, 6
  State Duma, 125–26, 129–30, 142,
    145, 150–51, 183, 202, 210,
    229, 262, 291
  Tsarist legacy, 5–22
  and Ukraine, 162–165
  and west, 189–232
  Westerners and slavophiles, 10–11,
    21, 23–24
Russia's Choice, 201
Rust, Matthias, 140
Rutskoi, Aleksandr, 141–42, 150,
  162, 164, 177–78, 183, 265, 277
Rybkin, Ivan, 129–31

S

Sachs, Jeffrey, 289
Sadat, Anwar, 85, 87
SALT I. *See* Strategic Arms
  Limitation Talks
Samper, Ernesto, 237
Samsonov, Viktor, 143
SDI. *See* Strategic Defense Initiative
Serbia, 12–13, 16, 116, 194, 223, 261
Sergeev, Igor, 143–46
Seton-Watson, Hugh, 22
Shakhrai, Sergei, 207
Shaposhnikov, Evgenii, 126–27,
  140–41, 160
Shelov-Kovediaev, Fedor, 116, 172
Shepilov, Dimitrii, 134–35
Shevardnardze, Eduard, 94, 97, 101,
  134–36, 138, 175–78, 247
Shushkevich, Stanislau, 157, 168

Skokov, Iurii, 117, 126–27, 131–32
Slovakia, 125, 214, 221–23, 236, 238
Snegur, Mircea, 182
Sobchak, Anatolii, 164
Socialism, 29, 40–41, 43, 61, 69, 76,
  78, 101, 103, 233
  See also Ideology; Karl Marx; V.I.
    Lenin
Socialist International, 28
Socialist Revolutionary Party, 37
Sokolev, Sergei, 140
Solana, Javier, 188, 217
Somalia, 78, 87
Soskovets, Oleg, 128, 266, 281
Soto, Lionel, 280
South Africa, 114, 278–79
  African National Congress, 278
Spain, 12, 231
Stalin, Joseph, 35, 40–41, 43–45,
  47–49, 51–72, 77, 79, 83, 89,
  91, 94, 101, 104, 108–10,
  122–23, 138, 183, 200, 227,
  246, 249, 254, 285–86
Stankevich, Sergei, 112, 114–15
START I. *See* Strategic Arms
  Reduction Talks
Stepashin, Sergei, 200
Stolypin, Piotr, 16
Strategic Arms Limitation Talks
  (SALT I), 84
  SALT II, 84–87
Strategic Arms Reduction Talks
  (START I), 90–91, 102, 142,
  161, 191, 193
  START II, 150, 192–93, 196, 202,
    225, 287
Strategic Defense Initiative (SDI),
  90–93, 191
Sudan, 87, 267
Sukarno, Ahmed, 77
Sun Yat-Sen, 43–44
Sweden, 6–8, 18, 180, 216, 231–32
  Nystad Treaty, 7
Syria, 85, 238, 266–69

T

Taiwan, 80, 240–41, 244
Tajikistan, 81, 156–57, 159, 170,
 172–75, 239, 258–59, 270–71
Ter-Petrosian, Lev, 180
Thatcher, Margaret, 230
Third World, 86–88, 106–108
 and cold war, 75–79, 233–36, 266,
  272, 279, 281
Tibet, 16, 80
Tito, Josip Broz, 55, 64–65, 70, 72, 79
Tkachev, P.N., 24, 26
Triple Alliance, 16
Triple Entente, 16, 283
Trotsky, Leon, 25–26, 31, 35–36,
 40, 44–45, 60, 134–35
Trubnikov, Viacheslav, 148
Truman, Harry, 56–57, 63, 66
 Doctrine, 63, 233
Tudjman, Franjo, 209
Tuleev, Aman, 167
Turkey, 6–10, 12–14, 20, 37, 43, 54,
 56, 63, 67, 71, 77, 114, 180–81,
 196, 206, 236, 254–56, 284
 Dardanelles and Bosporus, 9, 16, 18
 Ottoman Empire, 9, 254
 Peace of Adrianople, 9
 Treaty of Belgrade, 7
 Treaty of Jassy, 8
 Treaty of Kuchuk Kainardji, 8
 Treaty of Paris, 12
 Treaty of San Stefano, 13
 Treaty of Unkiar Skelessi, 9, 13
Turkmenistan, 156–57, 159, 170–72,
 198, 155, 258–59, 271

U

Ukraine, 4, 6, 8, 37, 39, 50, 58, 101,
 103, 105, 141, 149–50, 156–57,
 159–61, 166–67, 173, 181,
 193–94, 199, 220, 238, 275
 Black Sea Fleet, 150, 159, 162–63,
  165, 193

Ukraine *(continued)*
 Crimea, 6, 8, 10, 17, 150, 159,
  162–64, 193, 198, 214
 and Russia, 162–65
 Trilateral Agreement (1994), 161
Ulbricht, Walter, 82
Ulmanis, Guntis, 186
Union of Soviet Socialist Republics
 (Soviet Union), 3, 5, 23–61,
 103–10, 112, 115, 120–21, 127,
 141, 156, 167, 175, 179, 182,
 189, 192, 194, 196, 225, 231,
 233–34, 236, 246, 257, 260,
 265, 266, 269, 272, 277–79,
 285, 287–88
 August coup (1991), 102, 119,
  123, 126–28, 140–41, 146–47,
  149, 156, 170, 190, 247
 Civil war, 38–39
 Cold war, 57–107
 Detente, 81–89
 Government, 35, 40–41, 67,
  123–24, 138–40, 147, 149
 Ministry of Foreign Affairs,
  134–35, 138
 Sino-Soviet conflict, 79–81
 Space program, 72
 State Committee for the State of
  Emergency, 102, 126
 Union Treaty, 102–103, 106
United Nations, 62, 66, 74–75, 83, 85,
 88, 96, 100, 106, 118, 130, 143,
 173, 178–79, 190, 195, 206–11,
 226, 230, 237, 260–64, 279–80
United States, 10, 12, 36, 53, 56–57,
 62–64, 66, 69, 72–73, 75–78,
 80–81, 83–88, 90–91, 94,
 99–102, 104, 106–108, 117,
 161, 186, 189–92, 194–95, 197,
 201, 107–108, 210, 215–16,
 218–19, 229–30, 232–37,
 244–46, 252, 257–59, 262–64,
 266–67, 269–74, 276–77, 279,
 281–82, 285, 287–89, 292

Urinson, Iakov, 237
Uzbekistan, 156–57, 159, 170, 172–74, 255, 258, 271

V

Vance, Cyrus, 206
Vietnam, 68, 83–87, 93, 96, 106, 204, 235, 244, 276
Venezuela, 282
Vo Van Kiet, 276
Vyshinksy, Andrei, 134–35

W

Walesa, Lech, 88, 97, 219–21
Waltz, Kenneth, 284
Warsaw Pact, 68–69, 71, 97, 99–100, 107, 177, 196, 212–13, 219, 221, 236, 283, 285, 287–88
Washington Summit (1987), 95
Wilhelm II (Kaiser), 14, 21
Wilson, Woodrow, 55
Witte, Sergei (Count), 15
Women of Russia, 201
World Trade Organization (WTO), 218, 290
World War I, 5, 16–17, 20, 22, 27, 34–35, 59, 283
World War II, 3, 5, 52–57, 59, 61–62, 84, 135, 200, 224, 228, 233, 246
WTO. *See* World Trade Organization

Y

Yabloko, 201–202
Yakovlev, Aleksandr, 95, 119–21, 247

Yalta Conference (1945), 55–56, 246
Yastrzhembskii, Sergei, 125
Yavlinskii, Grigorii, 115, 202
Yazov, Dimitrii, 102, 140
Yeltsin, Boris, 101–103, 105, 109–10, 112, 116–17, 119, 123–34, 137–43, 145–50, 152–54, 156–57, 159–60, 162–66, 168–72, 175–78, 180, 182–86, 188, 190–200, 202–204, 206–11, 213–14, 217–32, 234, 237, 239–42, 245, 247–52, 257–58, 260–62, 264–66, 268–70, 273, 275, 278–79, 286–87, 289–92
Yugoslavia, 51, 55–57, 64, 70, 72, 79, 107, 116, 120, 150, 195–97, 226
Balkan War, 194–95, 209–10, 212

Z

Zhdanov, Andrei, 64, 233
Zhelev, Zhelyu, 223
Zhirinovskii, Vladimir, 115, 152, 199, 202, 214, 220, 261, 265, 291
Liberal Democratic Party, 115, 152, 199, 202, 291
Zhou Enlai, 68
Zhukov, Georgii, 72
Zinoviev, Grigorii, 40–42
Ziuganov, Gennadii, 115, 128, 169, 202–205, 291

Robert H. Donaldson, educated at Harvard University, is Trustees Professor of Political Science at the University of Tulsa. A past president of both the University of Tulsa and Fairleigh Dickinson University, he also has taught and held administrative positions at Lehman College of the City University of New York and at Vanderbilt University. He has served at the U.S. Department of State as International Affairs Fellow of the Council on Foreign Relations, and at the Strategic Studies Institute of the U.S. Army War College as visiting research professor. Professor Donaldson has written extensively on Soviet policy in the Third World and has authored or co-authored five other books.

Joseph L. Nogee, professor of political science at the University of Houston, was educated at the Georgetown School of Foreign Service, the University of Chicago, and Yale University. Professor Nogee also has taught at Vanderbilt University, New York University, the University of Virginia, Rice University, and the U.S. Army War College. His teaching and research areas are international politics and Soviet and Russian politics. He is the author, co-author, or editor of eight books, including most recently *Russian Politics: The Struggle for a New Order* (1996).